Equality Beyond Debate

While many current analyses of democracy focus on creating a more civil, respectful debate among competing political viewpoints, this study argues that the existence of structural social inequality requires us to go beyond the realm of political debate. Challenging prominent contemporary theories of democracy, the author draws on John Dewey to bring the work of combating social inequality into the forefront of democratic thought. Dewey's "pragmatic" principles are deployed to present democracy as a developing concept constantly confronting unique conditions obstructing its growth. Under structurally unequal social conditions, democracy is thereby seen as demanding the overcoming of this inequality; this inequality corrupts even well-organized forums of political debate, and prevents individuals from governing their everyday lives. Dewey's approach shows that the process of fighting social inequality is uniquely democratic, and he avoids current democratic theory's tendency to abstract from this inequality.

Jeff Jackson is Harper-Schmidt Fellow and Collegiate Assistant Professor at the University of Chicago Society of Fellows in the Liberal Arts. His work has appeared in such journals as *Political Theory*, *Polity*, *Democratic Theory*, *The Pluralist*, and *Education and Culture*. He has published on a wide range of topics, including contemporary democratic theory, American pragmatist philosophy, Platonic and Hegelian philosophy, the possibilities for a universal basic income, and philosophy of education.

Equality Beyond Debate

John Dewey's Pragmatic Idea of Democracy

JEFF JACKSON
University of Chicago

CAMBRIDGE
UNIVERSITY PRESS

CAMBRIDGE
UNIVERSITY PRESS

University Printing House, Cambridge CB2 8BS, United Kingdom

One Liberty Plaza, 20th Floor, New York, NY 10006, USA

477 Williamstown Road, Port Melbourne, VIC 3207, Australia

314–321, 3rd Floor, Plot 3, Splendor Forum, Jasola District Centre, New Delhi – 110025, India

79 Anson Road, #06-04/06, Singapore 079906

Cambridge University Press is part of the University of Cambridge.

It furthers the University's mission by disseminating knowledge in the pursuit of education, learning, and research at the highest international levels of excellence.

www.cambridge.org
Information on this title: www.cambridge.org/9781108428576
DOI: 10.1017/9781108553049

First published 2018

Printed in the United States of America by Sheridan Books, Inc.

A catalogue record for this publication is available from the British Library.

ISBN 978-1-108-42857-6 Hardback

For Victor, my late friend and mentor

Contents

Acknowledgments

This book has its roots in research done during my time as a doctoral student in political science at University of California, Los Angeles (UCLA). I must first thank Joshua Dienstag, who guided me through the majority of my graduate student career. Joshua provided wonderful mentorship on the dissertation project that ultimately grew into this book and was always available with guidance even though he and I differ much in our intellectual interests. The challenge involved with trying to convince Joshua of the value of Dewey's principles, and of the benefits that can be gained from Dewey for our thinking on democracy, gave me a tough, smart audience for my ideas and forced me to clarify and bolster my arguments in ways that have significantly strengthened the project.

I must also thank Carole Pateman, one of the most important voices in democratic theory through the past five decades. Carole announced her retirement at UCLA around the time I began to think seriously about democratic theory, but as a professor emeritus she was no less willing to offer her invaluable commentary and her thought-provoking views on how to understand democracy. Giulia Sissa and Douglas Kellner also generously served on my dissertation committee at UCLA, and I am grateful to them for pushing me to reach beyond my own corner of the political theory field and to think carefully about how my work could speak to scholars of diverse intellectual backgrounds.

I want to give special thanks to Shane Ralston, who has been very generous to me with his expertise on Dewey, and his advice on various aspects of the project was crucial toward developing the project into a book. Much of the work involved in completing the book has been done while I have been a postdoctoral fellow at the University of Chicago Society of Fellows in the Liberal Arts, where I have had the privilege of participating in a highly interdisciplinary body and engaging in a give-and-take of ideas with other scholars from fields across the social sciences and humanities. While at the society I have benefited especially from the mentorship of John McCormick, who has pointed me in all the right directions in terms of getting across the finish line with this project. John's guidance helped shepherd the project into its final form and gave me precious clarity on navigating the final stages of the book process.

I have been fortunate to work with Robert Dreesen and Meera Seth from Cambridge University Press. They have stewarded the manuscript through the editorial process, and I am grateful for their professionalism and their openness during the different stages of that process. I am also grateful for the work of three anonymous reviewers, whose comments on the manuscript have helped immeasurably to improve the final product. The book has furthermore benefited from any number of formal and informal conversations with scholars at conferences, workshops, and symposia. Versions of Chapters 2 through 5 were presented at annual meetings of the Western Political Science Association, and a version of Chapter 6 was presented at a 100th anniversary celebration of Dewey's *Democracy and Education* at the University of Cambridge. I wish I could name all the individuals at these various events who provided insights that helped clarify and augment my thinking.

I wish to thank my brothers, Randall and David, for always serving as tremendous role models, and my parents, Peter and Sally, for teaching me to show discipline in the face of obstacles. My deep thanks also to my wife, Emily, who has helped me grow as an academic and as a person in ways I cannot begin to enumerate, and to our infant daughter, Penelope, whose smile can make anything worthwhile. Finally my thanks to Victor Wolfenstein, to whom I have dedicated this book. Victor passed away in 2010, a couple of years into my graduate school career when I had not yet fully figured out what I wanted to work on or even if I was suited for academic work. But the impact of his teaching and research on me in those early years of graduate school, as well as in my undergraduate career, and the belief he showed in my potential as a scholar have sustained me over the course of many difficult years.

Introduction

Contemporary analyses of democracy have a great deal of difficulty coping with social inequality. The predominant democratic thinking has focused on instituting proper forms of political debate and has held that democracy comes when different political viewpoints interact in a way that allows genuinely fair policy outcomes to be achieved. Deliberative democracy, the current preeminent model in democratic thought, associates democracy with a debate in which the different sides exchange reasons for their views that their opponents can accept. Through this reason-giving process, deliberative democrats argue that policy debates can be decided according to who gives the strongest reasons for their position and that policy outcomes can be based on reasons that everyone involved can endorse. Agonistic democracy, the most prominent challenger to deliberative democracy, disputes the idea that policy decisions can be based on reasons that are acceptable to all. The agonistic theory associates democracy instead with a vigorous contest in which nobody is seeking a policy decision that is somehow universally acceptable, but the different sides still uphold their opponents' right to take part in the contest now and in the future. Multiple deliberative and agonistic thinkers have recognized, though, that the political debates they describe could not be unaffected by the structural inequality that characterizes our broader society. The impact brought by such social qualities as poverty or systemic racism and sexism cannot be bracketed within political debate. Even the most proper deliberative or agonistic interaction of competing political viewpoints, then, cannot be assumed to be genuinely fair and democratic.

The deliberative and agonistic thinkers who have acknowledged this have thus had to shoe-horn into their arguments a demand that society must also be far more equal than it is now. The problem, though, is that the type of political debate that each theory equates with democracy is understood to be basically undemocratic under the unequal social conditions we actually confront. And because structural social inequality diminishes the democratic character of political debate, deliberative or agonistic practices are not likely by themselves to effect a reduction in this inequality. This inequality evidently represents a major democratic problem in its own right, and its reduction demands primary attention within democratic theory, but the deliberative and agonistic thinkers' focus on political debate leaves them able to only perfunctorily note that this inequality should not exist. Indeed, to address this inequality, it appears we must specifically *depart* from deliberative and agonistic practices.

In this book, I will use John Dewey's democratic thought to show how the process of overcoming social inequality can be made into an integral trait of democracy. When deliberative and agonistic thinkers attempt to simply say that society should be equal and keep their focus on proper political debate, they are failing to theorize the most essential work involved in achieving democracy. By conceding that structural inequality will corrupt the forms of political debate they describe, they must acknowledge that this inequality is a far more pressing obstacle in the way of democracy than is the issue of whether policy debate is meeting ideal standards. A democratic theory should not just make it a precondition of the theory that the most pressing obstacle in the way of democracy be already eliminated. Democratic theorists must theorize the process of overcoming social inequality and must show why this process is itself integral to democracy. Dewey's theory, as I will show, makes the overcoming of current social inequalities into a centerpiece of democratization. Spaces of political debate are not ignored in Dewey's thinking, but he does move the spotlight away from such spaces, and he helps us see how the pursuit of democracy must extend well beyond the realm of political debate.

A focus on Dewey is noteworthy, since he is frequently classified as being one of the primary forefathers of deliberative democracy. My analysis will thus not only challenge the prevailing democratic thought, but the common portrayal of Dewey as a political thinker. Fundamentally, I argue that when contemporary democratic theorists grant that their preferred forms of political debate will be corrupted by social inequality, these theorists must also grant that *both* political and social elements are involved in achieving democracy. I also argue that these theorists must not only acknowledge these multiple elements within democracy, but must present these elements as in a process of interlocking development, in which the current imperfections of one element can affect the democratic quality of the other element. This must be our conclusion once it is acknowledged that imperfections in the social realm directly obstruct the democratic quality of the political realm. Dewey, indeed, straightforwardly states that democracy is not only a *political* concept, but also, and perhaps even more so, a *social* concept. He presents democracy as a multifaceted concept, constituted by interrelated political and social elements that each develop and affect the development of the other element. This unique way of thinking about democracy, I will argue, is well suited for showing how the overcoming of social inequality is essential to democracy. Democracy is here seen as in a process of unending development, and the effort to overcome social inequality is integral to that development.

It is well known that Dewey associates democracy with "development," though it is also frequently complained that this association (and, thus, his democratic theory as a whole) is overly vague and abstract. My argument will clarify this apparently vague conception of development in Dewey's democratic thought, while also showing the unique value of this conception to contemporary democratic theory. I will illustrate the development that Dewey requires in each element – political, social, and, as I will address later, *individual* – of his democratic theory. I will show how the development of each element affects and is affected by the development of the other elements. This inevitably makes the analysis rather complex, but I will attempt to construct it as straightforwardly as possible. I will also not only identify the shortcomings within prominent models of democratic thought, but argue that other, currently less prominent models are justified by the Deweyan insights that I describe. Participatory democracy and cosmopolitan democracy, in particular, put significant emphasis on the need to reduce social inequality and are not fixated on instituting a certain kind of political debate. This, I argue, should lead democratic theorists closer to participatory and cosmopolitan democracy and away from models like deliberative and agonistic democracy that do focus primarily on a form of political debate.

I should clarify at the same time, though, that concerns regarding the quality of political debate are not absent from Dewey's thinking and that my argument does not imply that forums of political debate are unimportant. Deliberation, in fact, can be seen as an ideal for the political element of Deweyan democracy, an ideal that could be achieved alongside thoroughly democratic social conditions. Even under unequal social conditions, a Deweyan can say that deliberation is the right method of making decisions for groups (e.g., labor unions, social movements) in which members are actually substantively equal. But when it comes to dealing with the structural inequalities themselves, I argue that we should see deliberation as rather beside the point, and thus as largely inessential to the further development of democracy from within an unequal society. It should not be considered democratic when we call on individuals from structurally unequal positions in society to deliberate with each other, to exchange reasons for their views that the other side can endorse, and to find a mutually acceptable decision. This might even be distinctly undemocratic under unequal social conditions, because it can give off the appearance of substantive equality having been achieved when it really has not. Under such social conditions, democracy should be associated less with what is decided upon in a "fair" debate and more with the actions and policies that directly aim at overcoming the structural inequality. This structural inequality is our most pressing obstacle to democracy, and Dewey's theory shows us how it is democratically necessary to overcome that inequality and how an overemphasis on political debate can distract us from this urgent democratic work.

In essence, this book aims to answer the question: What if democratic theorists gave proper attention to the demand that social inequality be largely overcome in order for democratic political debate to be possible? This demand has been an addendum which certain deliberative and agonistic thinkers have affixed to their theory, but I argue that this issue of social inequality is far too monumental to be treated as merely supplementary in our thinking on democracy. I also argue that, simply by making this demand, democratic theorists are granting a number of concessions that work against the deliberative and agonistic approaches to democracy and that need to be fully explored. Among these concessions are (1) that democracy is again not simply a political concept and that there is a social element of democracy which shows why democratic theory must be about much more than a proper form of political debate; (2) that when we have a fundamentally unequal society, an "equal" debate among different political viewpoints is more undemocratic than democratic because of the greater material resources available to the socially advantaged, as well as the greater impact the advantaged can have on the ordinary discourse surrounding policy issues; (3) that we must often consider only certain sides in a political debate to represent "democracy" (i.e., those seeking to overcome structural social inequality) and consider other sides (i.e., those seeking to protect the advantaged) to represent "oligarchy," perhaps, but not democracy; (4) that we must associate democracy more with actual outcomes that benefit the socially disadvantaged and less with an indeterminate process in which competing viewpoints reach policy compromises; and (5) that practices in which the disadvantaged take direct action toward overcoming inequality – perhaps in the form of a workers' strike or a protest that disrupts the comfortable existence of the advantaged – are deserving of "democratic" classification, even though such practices seek to coerce the advantaged in a way that ideal forms of debate would not allow. These points will all be addressed in the course of this book, and I will argue that Dewey can help democratic theory account for these points far more effectively than it does at present.

While certain deliberative and agonistic thinkers have granted that democracy requires the overcoming of social inequality, the message of their theories is still that greater deliberation, or greater agonism, is itself the essential task in creating a more democratic world than we have at present. These thinkers intend to say that more deliberation, or more agonism, *right now* is the most important project we can undertake for further achieving democracy. But if we doubt that such forms of political debate could be democratic without assuming away exactly the major ills (i.e., social inequalities) that most need to be addressed, and if we take that requirement of overcoming social inequality seriously, then we cannot place our focus on the achievement of more deliberation or more agonism. The centrality that these concepts receive in their respective theories, and that political debate receives in democratic theory generally, is not tenable. Structural social inequality is the most pressing current obstacle in the way of democracy, and we should not assume that this obstacle will just go away on its own. Deliberative and agonistic principles do provide interesting accounts of what political debate should look like once genuine social equality has been achieved, but as far as creating a more democratic world from where we are at present, these principles have little to tell us. The challenge for democratic theory, then, is to go beyond political debate and to come to grips with the idea that the process of overcoming social inequality is more central to democracy's development.

SOCIAL INEQUALITY, DEMOCRATIC THEORY, AND DEWEY

There are many available contemporary examples of the inequality I am talking about and of how that inequality can make democracy, as both a social and political concept, ultimately hollow. To help focus the analysis here at the outset, I will briefly describe a particularly important and controversial example: the 2011 fight in Wisconsin over collective bargaining rights. Shortly after beginning his first term as governor of Wisconsin, Republican Scott Walker took aim at the collective bargaining rights of public-sector workers. Walker presented this action as necessary in order to address the state's budget deficit – though this deficit was worsened by Walker himself with his decision immediately after his inauguration to cut taxes in a way that significantly benefited the wealthy. Public-sector workers were willing to accept cuts in their pensions and welfare benefits, but this was not enough to satisfy Walker. He insisted on the significant curtailment of these workers' right to collectively bargain, such that they could bargain only on the subject of basic wages. To properly analyze this contentious debate over unions and collective bargaining rights, we must identify the exceptionally powerful interests that were in Walker's corner. Particularly important was Americans for Prosperity (AFP), a Virginia-based political advocacy group with chapters in many states, including Wisconsin, and which is funded by the wealthy businessmen, Charles and David Koch. Since its founding in 2004, the AFP has fought battles against unions, environmental regulations, and Barack Obama's health care law. Before Walker even began his term as governor of Wisconsin, the president of AFP, Tim Phillips, started pressing for a fight in Wisconsin against unions, saying that teachers, police officers, firefighters, and other state and local employees were getting too much in the way of pay and benefits. Despite the Koch brothers' connection to AFP, and the fact that Koch Industries PAC was one of the largest contributors to Walker's 2010 election campaign, the Kochs still did maintain that they had no stake in this union debate and were not seeking to influence it. Their spokespeople stated that because Koch Industries was involved in the private sector, it had nothing in particular to gain from the curtailment of public-sector unions' bargaining rights. As one spokesman put it, "This is a dispute between public-sector unions and democratically elected officials over how best to serve the public interest."[1]

It is, of course, not terribly difficult to see through this kind of claim. The Koch brothers' own production facilities in Wisconsin have laid off workers multiple times in order to increase profits. The Kochs would then have a general interest in weakening unions, and there is also clear benefit to be gained from sowing seeds of division between public-sector

---

[1] Eric Lipton, "Billionaire Brothers' Money Plays Role in Wisconsin Dispute," *New York Times*, February 21, 2011.

and private-sector workers. The AFP's actions in this Wisconsin debate cannot thus be separated from the interests of its wealthy backers. The AFP set up a website and rallies in support of Walker and paid for buses to transport counter-protestors to the state capitol in Madison to try to rally against the large numbers of pro-union protestors. Further, as the debate raged on, the AFP began airing campaign-style TV ads in support of Walker's plan.[2] Along with the Wisconsin Club for Growth, another group with deep ties to the Koch brothers' political network, the AFP was one of the largest spenders on TV ads during the fight over collective bargaining rights.[3] This was a clear attempt by exceptionally powerful business interests to influence the discourse around a controversial issue so that public opinion might be swayed in their direction and they could more likely get the policy outcome they desired.

It would be hard to argue that these efforts to influence public discourse in an anti-union direction did not work. Walker's presence as governor alone can speak to the Kochs' influence, and public opinion on the debate over collective bargaining rights trended far enough in the anti-union direction to help push Walker's plan forward. In polls taken in the latter stages of the debate (after the TV ads would be able to have some impact), more people were typically found to oppose, rather than favor, the weakening of collective bargaining rights; but at the same time, more people were found to favor than oppose cutting state workers' pay, and more people were found to believe state workers in Wisconsin were paid too much rather than paid too little.[4] Also, depending on the wording of the poll question, percentages could shift in the anti-union direction even on the issue of weakening collective bargaining rights. If the question of weakening bargaining rights was posed in the context of the issue of reducing the state budget deficit, then more of those polled would favor the curtailment of those rights.[5] Getting voters to draw a link between the budget deficit and collective bargaining rights was crucial for Walker and his powerful allies. The public-sector workers were again willing

---

[2] Greg Sargent, "Americans for Prosperity to Run Ads in Wisconsin," *Washington Post*, February 22, 2011.

[3] Craig Gilbert, "Budget Fight TV Ads Top $3 Million," *Milwaukee Journal Sentinel*, March 15, 2011.

[4] As we are talking about workers who made an average salary of $48,348, getting significant portions of the population to believe those workers are overpaid is a significant victory; see Monica Davey and Steven Greenhouse, "Angry Demonstrations in Wisconsin as Cuts Loom," *New York Times*, February 16, 2011.

[5] Scott Rasmussen, "What You Can Learn about Wisconsin Dispute from Differences in Poll Questions," *Rasmussen Reports*, March 7, 2011.

to give Walker exactly the cuts in pensions and welfare benefits that he wanted, and so they were already willing to do their part to help the state address its financial problems. The workers were not willing, though, to give up their entire right to bargain over issues like pensions and welfare benefits. Since Walker was seeking (it appears at the behest of powerful donors like the Kochs) to take away that right, it was important for Walker's side to promote the notion that the budget crisis required *both* that workers make the concessions on their pay and benefits and that their bargaining rights be severely restricted. It seems Walker's allies were able to effectively promote the idea of a link between the deficit and collective bargaining rights, and Walker was ultimately able to enact his plan with minimal political consequences. He pushed his law curtailing unions' bargaining rights through the Republican-controlled legislature, and an attempt later in 2011 to change the balance of power in the state Senate through recall elections failed.

If we were to view this situation through the lens of deliberative democratic theory, we would say that those who held opposing views on collective bargaining should have debated with one another more properly. Deliberative thinkers associate democracy with a policy debate in which debaters exchange reasons for their various policy positions. Within such a debate, the deliberators are to give reasons that could be endorsed by their opponents. To the extent that deliberators exchange these types of reasons, the theory goes, the resulting policy decisions will have democratic quality because everyone involved has been treated respectfully, has had the opportunity to articulate their views and to challenge others', and has had the policy decisions justified to them with reasons they can accept. According to deliberative theorists, this use of reason-giving can ensure that policy decisions are not affected by broader power relations prevailing outside the deliberative forum and that policy decisions are determined simply by who makes the most convincing argument. Reason-giving is also meant to ensure equality of opportunity to influence policy outcomes, in that all deliberators are equally required to give reasons for their policy proposals, and all proposals are equally subject to being challenged by others. And reason-giving is meant to lead deliberators to think more about the common good, because the requirement of giving reasons that can be accepted by others will force deliberators to consider more than what merely serves their own self-interest. Deliberative democracy would likely take both the anti-union and pro-union sides of the Wisconsin debate to task for not deliberating properly with their opponents. Walker and the Republican legislators, and also the

Democratic Party legislators, could both be said to have not taken the time to carefully consider the views of the opposing side. The actions of the pro-union protestors would also be troubling for deliberative theorists, since these protestors were specifically trying to make Walker and the Republican legislators uncomfortable by invading the capitol building and shouting and chanting slogans, rather than exchanging mutually acceptable reasons with the anti-union voices (I will say more on these protestors' actions in a moment). Ultimately, the deliberative solution to this situation would lie in the institution of better standards for debate within the state legislature, and also perhaps the establishment of additional forums outside the legislature, where ordinary citizens with competing views would have the chance to debate and exchange reasons with one another.

Agonistic democratic theory's approach to the Wisconsin situation would similarly focus on improving the quality of the debate between the opposing views on collective bargaining. Agonistic theory does differ from deliberative theory by challenging the idea that reason-giving can produce policies that are acceptable to all who are affected by those policies. The agonistic democrats instead argue that democracy comes through recognizing the exclusionary quality of all policy decisions and making sure that the political contest remains open so that previous decisions are always open to challenge. They further argue that democracy comes when those engaged in political contest treat each other as "adversaries" to debate rather than as "enemies" to be potentially fought with violence; when political contest proceeds this way, it is an "agonistic" contest rather than an "antagonistic" contest. Agonistic democracy thus would not restrict the participants in the Wisconsin debate to only exchanging reasons their opponents could endorse in order to somehow find a universally acceptable decision. The theory would also seem to tolerate actions like those of the pro-union protestors, since democracy on these terms does not require participants to seek out harmonious agreement between different viewpoints. Still, what agonistic democrats would find disconcerting about the situation in Wisconsin is the way that the participants saw views that opposed their own as "objectively" wrong. An agonistic thinker could say that each side of the debate was operating under philosophical foundations about what was good for the entire state. The belief of each side's participants that they knew such philosophical foundations gave them the idea that they had the truly "right" answer about whether collective bargaining rights were good for the state. The opposing side, therefore, was taken as being objectively

wrong. The debate would have proceeded more democratically, an agonistic democrat would say, if the participants from each side had accepted
that their own viewpoint was purely subjective and no more objectively
or universally valid than the opposing viewpoint. If a debate proceeds in
this vigorous yet respectful fashion, then democracy is present, regardless
of which viewpoint is ultimately victorious, as long as the side that loses
has the opportunity to contest that outcome in the future.

When we focus on the issue of structural social inequality, however,
there is much that we can find problematic in both the deliberative and
agonistic theories. We can look at a situation like that in Wisconsin and
question whether the undemocratic qualities of the situation are really
rooted in the nature of the debate that took place. Rather than calling
mainly for a more proper form of debate between the opposing views
on collective bargaining, we might say that the more pressing issues
that need to be addressed are (1) why it is possible for individuals like
the Koch brothers to have such a disproportionate influence over who
becomes the governor of Wisconsin; (2) why it is possible for those individuals to so heavily influence the policies that the governor proposes
and the general public discourse surrounding those policies; and (3) why
such individuals are even in a position in the first place where they can lay
off workers, cut them off from their livelihoods, and thus fundamentally
control the direction of their lives. The basic underlying root of these
issues, I think we can say, is structural inequality. In other words, there
is a firm, entrenched gap between the power and resources available to
the Koch brothers for affecting the world around them and that available
to many other individuals – which in turn leaves many individuals' lives
subject to the dictates of powerful individuals like the Kochs. Due to their
extreme wealth, the Kochs can wield excessive authority in the social
realm (e.g., by firing workers in order to increase their own profits) and
can exercise inordinate influence over political campaigns and debates.
Structural inequality effectively gives exclusive political power to these
advantaged individuals, which should render null any talk of a truly democratic political process. And beyond its impact on political institutions,
the inequality can leave the condition of most individuals' everyday lives
at the whims of the advantaged individuals. The quest to achieve democracy, it would seem, should focus far more on the need to overcome this
structural social inequality than it does on trying to change how political
debate takes place.

When we think this way, it should lead us to a different evaluation
of Wisconsin's pro-union protestors, in particular. These opponents of

Walker's plan were certainly not meeting what we might think of as ideal standards of debate. They entered the capitol building and shouted at Walker and Republican legislators; they filled the area around the capitol and chanted and waved signs; they camped out near the capitol's rotunda, and teachers canceled their normal classes and held "teach-outs" in the capitol; they even protested near Walker's home and the homes of Republican legislators.[6] None of this represents anything like deliberative reason-giving, since the protestors were not looking to give reasons for their views that Walker and his allies would find acceptable and were rather aiming to compel their opponents to make concessions (although it must also be noted that the protestors did not resort to violence, which is a topic I will come back to later in the book). To be sure, deliberative thinkers would not likely just condemn the protestors for their actions, but would point to a lack of adequate deliberative forums where the collective bargaining issue could be debated. If there were such forums, though, the deliberative theory implies that fair political debate would then be possible, despite the outsized influence that individuals like the Kochs can exert over the broader discourse on the issue (i.e., through TV ads). Conversely, agonistic theory might again be seen as accommodating the protestors' actions, because the theory has no expectation of a universally acceptable policy outcome. But agonistic democracy does not have any way to endorse the pro-union protests without also endorsing the counter-rallies organized by the AFP, even though the latter were seeking to reinforce, rather than fight, structural inequality. Agonistic principles only allow us to say that both sides of this dispute are operating out of purely subjective viewpoints and that they should each see the partiality of their views and treat their opponents as adversaries rather than enemies. If democracy depends more, though, on the overcoming of structural social inequality than on creating a certain form of political debate, then we need a way to understand the pro-union protestors' actions as democratic and their opponents' actions as oligarchic.

As already noted, some deliberative and agonistic thinkers have tried to address structural inequality by adding into their theories a demand that this inequality be largely overcome. But by simply issuing this demand, these thinkers are again making it a precondition of their theories that the most essential work involved in achieving democracy be already accomplished. Democratic theory must theorize the process of overcoming this inequality and not just insist that the inequality should not exist

---

[6] Davey and Greenhouse, "Angry Demonstrations in Wisconsin as Cuts Loom."

so that political debate can finally proceed properly. I will also show later in the book that there is no coherent way for deliberative or agonistic democracy to address that process of overcoming social inequality. In brief, these theories either have to maintain (1) that a deliberative or agonistic debate must produce exactly the kinds of policies we need to reduce inequality – in which case the theories would be predetermining the outcomes of these supposedly open-ended debates – or (2) that the broad-scale overcoming of inequality is a prerequisite to proper deliberation or agonism – in which case the theories would be admitting that these forms of political debate do not effectively redress the most pressing current obstacle to democracy and that such debates can be democratic only after that obstacle has somehow gone away. Relatedly, certain deliberative democrats have tried to fix their theory's inability to accommodate forms of direct action aimed at overcoming inequality (such as we saw in Wisconsin) by conceding that we can engage in certain types of coercive, "nondeliberative" practices (e.g., protests, marches, strikes) while dealing with unequal social conditions.[7] This only further indicates the lengths, though, that deliberative democrats must stray from their principles in order to account for the conditions we actually confront. By defending the use of *non*-deliberative practices for achieving democracy within our current reality, deliberative thinkers must uncomfortably hold that deliberation must be both central to our democratic thought and largely disregarded in the current effort to achieve democracy. I argue that we should more squarely face up to the fact that deliberation and democracy are not identical.

One Dewey scholar has stated that "[a] consensus appears to be forming among political theorists that John Dewey's political thought can be subsumed under the rubric of deliberative democracy."[8] This book will challenge that consensus, while also turning democratic theory away from the prevalent way of thinking about democracy that the deliberative model represents. For Dewey, democracy is principally defined by individuals participating in the governance of their lives, or, exercising control over their lives. This control does include the opportunity to

---

[7] Archon Fung, "Deliberation before the Revolution: Toward an Ethics of Deliberative Democracy in an Unjust World," *Political Theory* 33, no. 2 (2005): 397–419; Jane Mansbridge et al., "A Systemic Approach to Deliberative Democracy," in *Deliberative Systems: Deliberative Democracy at the Large Scale*, eds. John Parkinson and Jane Mansbridge (Cambridge: Cambridge University Press, 2012), 18–19.

[8] Jason Kosnoski, "Artful Discussion: John Dewey's Classroom as a Model of Deliberative Association," *Political Theory* 33, no. 5 (2005): 654.

influence political institutions (i.e., the typical institutions of government) and that could potentially include taking part in policy deliberation. But at least as important to Dewey is the opportunity to control one's life within everyday social spheres, or, to direct one's own development in the course of interactions with others. He points out

> the distinction between democracy as a social idea and political democracy as a system of government. The two are, of course, connected ... Yet in discussion they must be distinguished. The idea of democracy is a wider and fuller idea than can be exemplified in the state even at its best. To be realized it must affect all modes of human association, the family, the school, industry, religion.[9]

When individuals are excluded from self-government in the work-place – for example, when they are forced by poverty into occupations they have not genuinely chosen and must spend their work lives experiencing subordination to others – democracy is directly obstructed. Those individuals are prevented from exercising control over their lives in their everyday social experience. Further, Dewey holds that such undemocratic qualities in society will unavoidably obstruct the possibilities for democratic politics. Those who experience subordination within the work-place, family, religion, school, etc., cannot be said to be able to influence the typical institutions of government simply because they are not formally barred from having that influence. Their undemocratic social experience cannot be merely bracketed for the purpose of creating a truly democratic political experience. On Dewey's terms, structural social inequalities are undemocratic in themselves due to the way they prevent individuals from controlling their lives, and they concurrently interfere with any possibility of a democratic political system.

We can see here how democracy for Dewey exists in a process of development and is defined by multiple interrelated elements. Deweyan democracy depends not only on genuinely equal access to political institutions, but on the equal opportunity to govern oneself within everyday social life, and Dewey shows us how the undemocratic quality of society can directly interfere with the democratic quality of political institutions. Hence, those who suffer from poverty and must spend their lives in alienating workplaces are prevented from exercising control over their lives, and they are concurrently blocked from effective political influence. If certain individuals have to work two jobs to survive, while others have the resources to influence broader political discourse (as well as having

---

[9] John Dewey, *The Public and Its Problems* (Chicago, IL: Swallow Press, [1927] 1954), 143.

greater access to positions of power and authority throughout society), then it follows for Dewey that political power lies far more with the latter group than the former. With a situation like we saw in Wisconsin, then, where there was a vast disparity in social status and resources between the two sides of the debate, setting up a more dignified political debate, in Dewey's view, would not actually contain the impact of social inequality on the debate. As Dewey puts it, "The smoothest road to control of political conduct is by control of opinion. As long as interests of pecuniary profit are powerful ... those who have this interest will have an unresisted motive for tampering with the springs of political action in all that affects them."[10] The further development of democracy, in its social as well as its political meaning, thus depends in this context on the enactment of measures that reduce poverty and democratize the typical work experience for many individuals. At the same time, Dewey recognizes that because poverty, undemocratic workplaces, and other instances of social inequality are affected by policy outputs from political forums, political democracy is not merely derivative of social democracy. If political institutions do not in any way resist the influence of wealth, then we are even less likely to see policies that benefit the poor. It is also essential, then, that we close down the institutional openings for unequal political influence. We must have measures (e.g., campaign finance reform) that counteract the wealthy's ability to inordinately affect election and policy outcomes with their fortunes. Democracy is both a social and political concept for Dewey, and democracy's development requires that we take action to progressively, and concurrently, overcome both the social and political obstacles to self-government. Neither set of obstacles can be addressed in isolation from the other.

I argue that this shows Dewey's divergence from democratic theories that focus on improving political debate. Dewey places greater importance on the overcoming of social inequality, since this is essential to individuals' capacity to govern their lives, and political debate itself will be corrupted as long as that inequality exists. Also, while I will grant that Dewey would eventually like to see something like deliberation in political forums, deliberation is not central to even the *political* side of his plans for achieving democracy within our unequal conditions. He focuses more on making specific changes to our important decision-making institutions (Congress, regulatory agencies, etc.) in order to directly alter

---

[10] Ibid., 182.

political power in favor of the socially disadvantaged. This is not primarily a search for more deliberation, but an attempt to change political institutions to specifically combat the excessive influence of the advantaged. I will further show in the course of this book that Dewey provides a compelling defense of nondeliberative practices, the practices that seek to coerce and compel concessions from the powerful. This is an aspect of Dewey's thinking that is often overlooked, but I will argue that it is an integral part of his democratic thinking. He commits to these practices because they are appropriate for unequal social conditions, in that they can be used to directly overcome inequality and create a more democratic society. The development of Deweyan democracy is intimately intertwined with practices that treat social inequality as requiring direct remedy.

Overall, I portray Dewey as providing a *pragmatic* idea of democracy. Dewey is indeed considered one of the founders of American pragmatist philosophy from the late nineteenth and early twentieth centuries. His pragmatism, in brief, signifies that there are no eternally true ideas and principles, but that ideas and principles gain provisional truth to the extent that they can be put into practice in the situations that individuals experience and that they produce the effects on those situations that the individuals intend. On this view, whether institutions and practices qualify as *democratic* depends on their suitability to the situation; and further, institutions and practices that perhaps have been democratic at a past time, or would be democratic at some point in the future, may not be democratic now. Dewey does not treat democracy as ever reaching a fixed, final state, and so democracy is defined by an unending process of actualization in the face of the obstacles that inevitably arise from our changing concrete circumstances. By associating democracy with actions and policies that aim at overcoming structural social inequality, Dewey is "pragmatically" identifying the most pressing obstacle in the way of democracy's further development and making the overcoming of that obstacle into a defining quality of democracy. This way of thinking about democracy, I argue, can help current democratic theory solve its quandary regarding structural inequality.

DEMOCRACY AS A PERSONAL WAY OF INDIVIDUAL LIFE

There is one more crucial element of Dewey's democratic thought that needs to be introduced here before we begin. I have established that democracy for Dewey is fundamentally defined by individuals' self-government (i.e., their exercise of control over their lives). This capacity to exercise some self-conscious control over our lives, in Dewey's view, is the distinctly human capacity, the quality that separates human beings from animals that act merely on instinct. There are both social and political elements of Deweyan democracy, since opportunities to govern oneself within everyday social spheres, as well as in political institutions, must be present. But because, as Dewey says, "the ideal of democracy ... roots itself ultimately in the principle of moral, self-directing individuality,"[11] there is also an *individual* element of Dewey's theory. In this book, I will illustrate the meaning of this individual element of democracy, and I will show how it coheres with the social and political elements of democracy.

The individual element of Deweyan democracy is reflected in Dewey's famous statement that "democracy is a *personal* way of individual life ... it signifies the possession and continual use of certain attitudes, forming personal character and determining desire and purpose in all the relations of life."[12] I will explain what this democratic individual way of life entails and how it both requires, and is required by, the social and political elements of democracy. The democratic individual way of life signifies, on my reading, the essence of individual self-government for Dewey. My reading of democratic individualism will draw heavily on the influence of G.W.F. Hegel on Dewey, an influence that has received increasing attention from Dewey scholars. I will explore how Dewey draws on Hegel to convey how individuals' lives are in a process of constant development and how, under modern conditions in particular, individuals confront constantly changing conditions that lack stable, eternal truths. Under these conditions, Dewey also emphasizes how individuals find themselves increasingly interconnected with others beyond their immediate circle of acquaintances. Dewey reasons that, under such conditions, individuals can no longer rely on supposedly eternally wise principles, or eternally wise individuals, to direct their lives in the way that will be most fulfilling to them personally and most valuable to their society. To approach the standard of democratic individualism, and to thus more genuinely govern

---

[11] MW3: 235. In line with the common practice in Dewey scholarship, many references in this book will cite the volume number and page number of either the *Early Works* (EW), the *Middle Works* (MW), or the *Later Works* (LW) of *The Collected Works of John Dewey*.

[12] John Dewey, "Creative Democracy – The Task before Us," in *John Dewey: The Political Writings*, eds. Debra Morris and Ian Shapiro (Indianapolis, IN: Hackett Publishing Company, [1939] 1993), 241.

their lives, Dewey holds that individuals must engage in the often-painful process of reconstructing their past habits and beliefs, when those habits and beliefs have been "negated" (i.e., rendered irrelevant) by unique situations of experience. By intelligently reconstructing past principles in the face of the ever-changing, never-finished situations of experience, individuals may increase their capacity to exercise control over their future uncertain experience, rather than becoming paralyzed when past principles no longer pertain to new circumstances. In essence, democratic individualism is defined by precisely the kind of *pragmatic* development through changing circumstances that is also required of democracy in its social and political meanings.

Democratic individualism, for Dewey, is certainly aided by a society that does not force many individuals to live under the command and control of others. Individuals who are forced by poverty into alienating workplaces, for example, and who must merely follow commands when working, are obstructed from exercising any unique, self-chosen effect on the situations they experience while working and are prevented from using their experience to develop new principles for carrying out that work. Dewey holds that there is no such thing as a nonsocial individual. While individuals are distinguishable and unique entities within society, there is no individual who exists in complete separation from social relations and social institutions, or who is not largely constituted by the type of society in which she interacts. If society is thus characterized by poverty, systemic racism, or other forms of structural inequality, it will hinder the self-government of many individuals, who will not be able to simply isolate themselves from the effects of such social qualities. Democratic individualism, then, is interrelated with the development of social democracy and, by extension, of political democracy, because, as I will discuss later on, measures and policies coming from the political realm are crucial for creating the conditions for individuals' self-government, but undemocratic traits in society make it more likely that political institutions will serve only the powerful. At the same time, social democratization for Dewey does depend itself on individuals' own conduct, since the everyday social interactions of individuals represent essential space for the achievement of democracy. For example, if individuals cling to ideas of natural inequality along racial or gender lines, and if they hold that poverty and wealth are just, then they are obstructing the social element of democracy. Once we recognize a social element of democracy, we cannot avoid giving individuals' own conduct a fundamental role in the achievement of democracy.

On Dewey's terms, the Hegelian qualities of democratic individualism should lead individuals to put uncritically held beliefs about other groups of individuals up for potential revision. Any discriminatory beliefs are not only harmful to those other individuals, but under increasingly interconnected modern conditions, one will have to maintain such beliefs while likely confronting individuals against whom one discriminates. Indeed, a major factor Dewey sees in the rapidly changing conditions brought by modernity is that we are inevitably confronted with diverse others who differ greatly from us in their ideas and behaviors. As with Hegel's famous lord-bondsman narrative, the concept of democratic individualism conveys that there are limitations on one's own freedom when one subordinates and suppresses others. The freedom available to such an individual is less than to one who can uphold others' equality and does not need to rely on their subservience. An individual who can interact with diverse others without requiring their subordination is able to live more freely within a world where one is constantly confronted with such diversity. An individual who cannot tolerate the equality of those who are alien to her will be often discomfited by the inevitability of interacting with those others. This shows how the individual element of democracy itself promotes the social and political elements of democracy. To the degree an individual is developing further in her possibilities for governing her own life (in the Deweyan sense), she is also buttressing the possibilities for the diverse others she confronts to govern their own lives.

The self-government signified by democratic individualism is certainly never fully and perfectly achieved. Because Dewey leads us to see democracy as in a process of development, democracy can never be seen as completed. As he puts it, "Since things do not attain such fulfillment but are in actuality distracted and interfered with, democracy in this sense is not a fact and never will be."[13] Individuals never achieve perfect control over their lives, any more than we can likely expect a society with no forms of inequality or governing institutions that allow perfectly equal access to all individuals across society. But democracy for Dewey can be further actualized – that is, we can progressively develop the individual, social, and political elements of democracy. To do this, we must be aware of democracy's multiple, mutually influencing elements and of how democracy's development depends largely on individuals' own actions and interactions. If individuals recognize their interdependency with others under modern conditions, and if they actualize democratic

---

[13] Dewey, *Public and Its Problems*, 148.

social relations in their everyday interactions, they can contribute to the realization of democracy's social and political elements. In doing so, they can also directly aid their own self-government. On Dewey's terms, upholding the subordination of others and clinging rigidly to past habits and principles in a general sense will not grant individuals control over their own lives under constantly changing, increasingly interconnected circumstances. For individuals to participate in the governing of their lives, there, of course, have to be opportunities for participation within social spheres such as the workplace, as well as within the typical governing institutions. But Dewey also gives us a cogent case for how individuals contribute to their own self-government by challenging limits on others' self-government – that is, by promoting social and political democracy in their everyday interactions.

There is particular benefit to thinking of democracy as being in a process of unending development, constituted by multiple elements (individual, social, and political) that are themselves never finished developing. Specifically, we see democracy as only having been imperfectly achieved up to this point in history, and those modern polities that have been commonly called "democracies" can be seen as in fact imperfect manifestations of democracy's development. The United States, for instance, is normally considered a democracy because of this nation's widespread suffrage, frequent elections, and establishment of individual rights against the government. But at the same time, something should feel askew when we consider how this nation has, throughout its history (and among other atrocities), enslaved, exploited, and allowed for the murder of black individuals. The American commitment to elections, voting rights, etc., can be seen as an important aspect of democracy's development up to this point and can be preserved as we seek to develop democracy further. But the experience of African Americans alone must lead us away from simply characterizing the United States as a "democracy." Dewey's approach allows us to more properly define the United States as an imperfect manifestation of democracy, containing a mix of both democratic and undemocratic elements. For Dewey, democracy is fundamentally about individuals' self-government, and as this self-government inevitably meets unique obstacles in the way of its development, there will likely never be (and has not been up to this point) perfectly achieved democracy. We can thus comprehend how elections and voting rights have brought individuals' self-government further into existence and how something like the structural inequality experienced by African Americans remains an obstacle to be overcome.

OUTLINE OF THE ARGUMENT

This book consists of six chapters. The first three chapters will address important scholarly debates surrounding Dewey's democratic theory, while also elucidating the individual, social, and political elements of that theory. The last three chapters will draw on the analysis in the first three to show where Dewey stands in relation to contemporary models of democratic theory and to show how Dewey can help democratic theory account for the essentiality of overcoming social inequality to democracy.

Chapter 1 will begin the analysis of Dewey's democratic individual way of life. The chapter will mainly focus on Dewey's apparently puzzling statements of admiration for Plato[14] (an evident anti-democrat) and will show that this admiration relates to Dewey's appreciation of the way Plato emphasizes an ideal individual character type over and above the creation of an ideal state. While Dewey has a far more positive evaluation of the "democratic individual" than Plato does, he finds Plato's focus on individual character type, and recognition of the role of that character type in the construction of a good state, to be hugely important insights. The chapter will also begin clarifying the qualities of democratic individualism by drawing both on Platonic principles and on Dewey's connection to the German *Bildung* tradition. I will start elucidating here how democratic individualism entails continuous individual development, widespread interaction with diverse others, and a willingness to combat forms of social inequality.

In Chapter 2, I will continue the analysis of democratic individualism by exploring Dewey's relationship to Hegel. The first chapter will have already addressed the *Bildung* tradition, which is centered on the unending development of individuals, and Hegel is the figure in that tradition with whom Dewey has the strongest connection. My discussion of Hegel will expand on how democratic individualism involves the continuous reconstruction of one's habits in response to the obstacles to one's self-development brought by changing circumstances. Also, this chapter will use Hegel to analyze the social and political elements of Deweyan democracy. Individuals, for both Dewey and Hegel, are inevitably social beings, and they both see individual self-development as dependent upon social qualities (e.g., nonalienating workplace relations) that truly allow individuals to control their lives. Hegel will relatedly be used to show

---

[14] John Dewey, "From Absolutism to Experimentalism," in *Contemporary American Philosophy*, Vol. II, eds. George P. Adams and Wm. Pepperell Montague (New York, NY: The Macmillan Company, 1930), 21.

the continuous effort required from political institutions toward creating these more equal social conditions. For Dewey, a government's democratic quality depends heavily on its efforts to help overcome the undemocratic features (e.g., extreme poverty) that arise within society. This chapter will culminate in a discussion of the differences between Dewey's view on democracy and that of the famous neo-pragmatist, Richard Rorty. While Rorty claims to be closely following Dewey, I will show that because Rorty diverges from Hegelian principles, he does not require the same level of development in democracy as Dewey does, and he is more satisfied that the traditional liberal institutions found in the United States are sufficient to produce democracy.

Chapter 3 will provide a thorough analysis of the political element of Deweyan democracy. Chapter 2 will have established that political democracy entails continuous action from governments in order to help remedy social problems such as extreme poverty and alienating workplaces, and Chapter 3 will show how Dewey would ensure that political institutions themselves are open to the voices of individuals and groups throughout society. I will explain how Dewey conceives of an unending process of democratizing political institutions, a process which requires that we – in pragmatic fashion – continuously overcome the evolving forms of exclusive control of those institutions by powerful interests. This development is parallel to, and interrelated with, the development of the individual and social elements of democracy. Furthermore, in response to Sheldon Wolin's claim that Dewey's theory is blind to the effects of power inequities on politics, I will argue that radical democratic thought would be well served by turning in a Deweyan direction, as opposed to the thoroughly anti-institutional approach of thinkers such as Wolin and Jacques Ranciere. I will show that Dewey's theory accounts for the temporary uprisings against established institutions valued by Wolin and Ranciere, while also conceiving (unlike Wolin and Ranciere) of how institutions can be meaningfully democratized as a result of these uprisings.

In Chapter 4, I will argue that Dewey's focus on overcoming social inequality leads to a compelling critique of deliberative democracy and gives strong support to participatory democracy. Dewey responds "pragmatically" to our unequal social conditions, recognizing how social inequality can be undemocratic in itself and can nullify any possibility of a democratic political debate. He associates democracy's development, under these conditions, with the enactment of plans for overcoming social inequality, plans that may require nondeliberative practices that compel concessions from advantaged social interests. Deliberative democrats equate democracy with a deliberative political debate, and either must assume that social inequality will be neutralized through this practice or must concede that they are avoiding the most essential work involved in democracy's further achievement. Participatory democracy, by contrast, puts its attention on broad-scale changes to society. I will show that the participatory theory gains support from Dewey's conception of social and political elements in democracy and from his reasoning for the use of nondeliberative practices to attack social inequality.

Chapter 5 will extend this Deweyan analysis into a discussion of agonistic democracy, communitarianism, and cosmopolitan democracy. I will show that agonistic democracy (in a similar fashion to deliberative democracy) abstracts from the problem of social inequality with its equation of democracy with agonistic contest and that agonistic thinkers cannot insist on the reduction of social inequality without compromising the central features of their theory. Communitarianism is not distinctly a model of democracy, but it still merits attention because Dewey's theory has been linked with this tradition of thought by several scholars (though by fewer than have linked him with deliberative democracy). I will demonstrate that the communitarians' focus on maintaining traditional communal identities is at odds with the type of individual self-government signified by Dewey's democratic individual way of life. I will argue that cosmopolitan democracy, though, has similar virtues as participatory democracy. The cosmopolitan model can be seen as extending the interrelated political and social democratization that Dewey emphasizes to a global scale and can be elevated over deliberative and agonistic democracy as a model that can cope with social inequality.

Walter Lippmann, one of Dewey's own intellectual rivals in democratic thought, remarks that "education has furnished the thesis of the last chapter of every optimistic book on democracy written for one hundred and fifty years."[15] I would not describe this book as "optimistic,"[16] but

---

[15] Walter Lippmann, *The Phantom Public* (New York, NY: Harcourt, Brace and Company, 1925), 22.

[16] Dewey in fact criticizes both "optimistic" and "pessimistic" philosophies and explains that his own arguments are *melioristic*, which means that present conditions can be improved through intelligent action, but that this improvement is never guaranteed; see John Dewey, *Reconstruction in Philosophy*, Enl. ed. (Boston, MA: Beacon Press, [1948] 1957), 178.

my final chapter will indeed focus on education, Dewey's favorite topic. The issue of education will emerge in each of the first four chapters, and in Chapter 6, I will analyze the role of education in Deweyan democracy. In particular, I will show how Dewey challenges prevalent educational practices like grading and standardized testing and how his views on these practices connect with his conception of democratic individualism. Dewey sees these practices as leading students to seek to end their growth as quickly as possible and to view themselves as isolated consumers in a market – qualities that are antithetical to democratic individualism. Additionally, I will argue that Dewey's view helps diagnose shortcomings in the deliberative democrats' analysis of schooling. Deliberative theorists have identified education as the most important institution, outside of government, for enacting deliberative democracy.[17] These thinkers have associated democratic education with improved deliberations over educational policy and with teaching students to deliberate with each other. I will argue that their view does not account for how prevalent educational policies and practices are already reflective of social inequality and of the dominance of certain social interests (e.g., the wealthy's) over others. Dewey's position highlights how typical schooling practices, like grading and standardized testing, can reflect this inequality and can transmit undemocratic social norms to students.

I want to note a couple final points before we begin. First, I do not mean to imply that Dewey's social and political context is identical to our own, nor that Dewey's specific ideas can be simply applied to our own situation without any alteration. For instance, Dewey was writing in a time when issues related to industrialization and urbanization were really just emerging, and he could not have addressed a world transformed by computers and the Internet like our own. But I do maintain that Dewey's way of thinking about democracy is extremely valuable for our own time. K. Sabeel Rahman, in an important recent book that draws on a variety of thinkers from the Progressive era, including Dewey, to describe how to democratize economic regulatory agencies, makes a similar point: "Though the specific proposals of these turn-of-the-century reformers may not be directly applicable today, this ethic of seeking a specifically democratic response to the moral challenges of the market

---

[17] Amy Gutmann and Dennis Thompson, *Why Deliberative Democracy?* (Princeton, NJ: Princeton University Press, 2004), 61.

economy is instructive."[18] In my book, Dewey is likewise not to be seen as responding to conditions identical to our own, but more as providing inspiration for how to cope with our unique social and political problems. I would also say, though, that Dewey's specific concerns often show great similarity to (what should be) our main concerns regarding the achievement of democracy. When he addresses issues such as extreme poverty, alienating workplaces, a government controlled by wealth, or a world that is becoming increasingly interconnected by new technology and forms of communication, he is discussing issues that are very much with us today. We might even say that these issues are more pressing today than in Dewey's time – for example, the interconnection brought by the Internet is even more extraordinary than that brought by late nineteenth- and early twentieth-century industrialization.

Also, my critique of democratic theory's focus on political debate may lead one to wonder how social inequalities are to be identified and named if not through forums of debate. As I have already indicated, though, my argument does not forbid debate from taking place, and something like deliberative debate would be appropriate within groups whose members are actually substantively equal. If members of a labor union, social movement, etc., are genuinely equal, it would be appropriate for those individuals to debate over the nature of the oppressions they face and over what actions they should take. Also, Dewey's democratic individualism does carry a responsibility to interact with diverse others, particularly those who are outside of one's normal circle of acquaintances. This can allow an individual to hear the stories of people she may not otherwise know and to become aware of social ills that she would otherwise never encounter. Democratic individualism can thus make possible an intelligent social analysis in which an individual can comprehend social problems that go beyond her own immediate experience. But while discussion and debate are not absent from my thinking, I still hold that the presence of structural social inequality, and the concurrent corruption of forms of political debate that this inequality brings, require us to move beyond spaces of debate in our pursuit of democracy. If we put a pressing issue of inequality up for debate within our current circumstances, democracy must be associated with certain positions within that debate, and not just with the

---

[18] K. Sabeel Rahman, *Democracy Against Domination* (New York, NY: Oxford University Press, 2016), 4.

debate itself, regardless of its outcome. In other words, the sides of the debate that are pursuing policies like basic income, affirmative action, and pay equity for women need to be understood as democratic, and those that oppose such policies need to be seen as opposing democracy. In my view, deliberative and agonistic thinkers cannot avoid this kind of thinking once they begin insisting (as they commonly do) on policies like these being in place and on social inequality being largely overcome. We must face up to the way that even the most ideal forums for political debate are, at best, contingently democratic under our unequal conditions and place more of our focus on the process of directly overcoming social inequality.

I

The Democratic Individual

For John Dewey, the effort to achieve democracy cannot be overly cen-tered on our typical institutions of government.[1] The political bodies that exercise legislative, executive, administrative, and judicial power are not the only institutions that significantly affect how individuals live their lives. In Dewey's view, if norms, practices, and relationships at the *social* level (e.g., in the spheres of the workplace, family, or religion) are deny-ing individuals the opportunity to exercise control over their lives, then political institutions, no matter how apparently democratic, will likely do little to allow those individuals to become more genuinely self-governing. Dewey's vision of democratic possibilities ultimately comes down to the individual level, and the course of an individual's life is determined at least as much by her social relations as by her political institutions.[2] As he puts it, "democracy cannot now depend upon or be expressed in political institutions alone ... for democracy is expressed in the attitudes of human beings and is measured by consequences produced in their lives."[3]

On Dewey's terms, then, we must take the behavior and conduct of individuals as essential for determining if we have democracy – thus, Dewey's famous remark that "democracy is a *personal* way of individual life ... it signifies the possession and continual use of certain attitudes, forming personal character and determining desire and purpose in all the

---

[1] Parts of this chapter are modified from an article originally published as "The Democratic Individual: Dewey's Back to Plato Movement," *The Pluralist* 9, no. 1 (2014): 14–38.
[2] Dewey often objects to any kind of dualism between "individual" and "society"; I will discuss this in more detail later in the chapter.
[3] John Dewey, *Freedom and Culture* (New York, NY: G. P. Putnam's Sons, 1939), 125.

relations of life."[4] Dewey's democratic thought is largely founded on this conception of a democratic individual way of life, because the exhibition of this particular type of behavior by individuals is his primary measure for the existence of democracy.

In this chapter, I will begin elucidating the meaning of Dewey's democratic individual way of life. The chapter will focus mainly on Dewey's philosophical relationship to Plato, for whom Dewey expresses surprising admiration (given Plato's evident antidemocratic views). Dewey conveys his admiration by declaring that "[n]othing could be more helpful to present philosophizing than a 'Back to Plato' movement."[5] I argue that Dewey's view on Plato is rooted in his appreciation for Plato's emphasis on an ideal individual character type and for Plato's analysis of how that character type is essential to the achievement of a truly good polity. Dewey sees great insight in Plato's goal (sought most famously in *The Republic*) of "such a development of man's nature as brings him into complete harmony with the universe of spiritual relations, or, in Platonic language, the state."[6] In *The Republic*, Plato depicts five different states and the corresponding five types of individuals; his aim is to demonstrate why his ideal "aristocratic individual," and aristocratic state, are crucial for the realization of humans' unique capacities and for the best governance of a community. For Dewey, we can no longer reasonably hold to the assumptions underlying Plato's "universe of spiritual relations"[7] – we can no longer cling to an idea of a static, eternal truth that only a select few are capable of grasping, nor to the idea that human relations are so ordered that individuals may be placed in strictly defined classes and narrow functional roles. In Dewey's view, human (especially scientific) advancements have progressively knocked down claims to any type of unchanging truth, making the pursuit of truth a continuous, never-ending task that can only be tackled through engagement with

---

4 John Dewey, "Creative Democracy – The Task before Us," in *John Dewey: The Political Writings*, eds. Debra Morris and Ian Shapiro (Indianapolis, IN: Hackett Publishing Company, [1939] 1993), 241.

5 John Dewey, "From Absolutism to Experimentalism," in *Contemporary American Philosophy*, Vol. II, eds. George P. Adams and Wm. Pepperell Montague (New York, NY: The Macmillan Company, 1930), 21.

6 EW1: 241.

7 Dewey does not make it entirely clear what this phrase means, though he does associate it with the Platonic "state." Because I emphasize the Hegelian qualities of Dewey's thought (I will provide a thorough analysis of Dewey's relationship to Hegel in Chapter 2), I interpret "*spiritual* relations" as signifying for Dewey the human relations which are aimed at the greatest possible development of human potential, both at an individual and a collective level, as opposed to human relations which serve merely the aim of natural survival.

the transient qualities of ordinary human experience. And "a new age of human relations" has emerged that is primarily characterized by disorder, with scientific and economic changes so thoroughly intertwining the peoples of the world such that all individuals' lives are affected by "indirect consequences" caused by remote forces beyond their immediate control.[8] Dewey thus cannot endorse Plato's aristocratic individual and state. But despite this, Dewey still sees great value in the unique role Plato gives to individual conduct within political thought. Dewey aims to push modern democratic thinking to similarly focus on the individual level of analysis.

I will show that Plato can help us to begin illuminating the precise meaning of Dewey's democratic individual way of life. In *The Republic*, Plato describes the democratic state as one where virtually nothing is held to be unchanging and sacred, and where diverse individuals from different corners of society interact with each other and neglect to stay within their limits. He similarly condemns the "democratic individual" for failing to stick with a single function and instead leading a life characterized by variety, diversity, and multiplicity. For Dewey, as for Plato, democratic individualism is chiefly defined by diversified experience that overcomes limits and engages with plural forms of life. Under modern conditions, Dewey reasons, this continuous, active interaction with changing, often-unforeseen forces is crucial for the fullest realization of individuals' potential. Dewey holds that our "universe of spiritual relations" has shown itself to be fundamentally democratic – there is no form of life that can be said (to the exclusion of others) to attain "truth," we are stuck in a fundamentally uncertain world where there is no eternal knowledge, and we are all inextricably connected with others by the indirect consequences of remote forces beyond anyone's immediate control. Democratic individualism allows individuals some measure of control over their lives and the opportunity to fulfill their unique potential in the face of such a world. It leads individuals away from futilely trying to isolate themselves from these constantly changing, increasingly interconnected conditions and spurs individuals to continuously develop themselves in interaction with these conditions. Ultimately, going back to Plato sheds important light on the meaning of Dewey's democratic way of life and helps us conceive of a democracy that is defined by individuals' control over their everyday lives.

---

[8] John Dewey, *The Public and Its Problems* (Chicago, IL: Swallow Press, [1927] 1954), 96–109.

As we can already see, though, it is undoubtedly true that Dewey is not fully a Platonist, and so the analysis of democratic individualism cannot be completely derived from Plato. Certain essential qualities of democratic individualism will be discussed more fully in Chapter 2, where I will explore Dewey's relationship to Hegel. Toward the end of this chapter, though, I will show how my Plato-inspired portrait of democratic individualism coheres with useful recent scholarship on Dewey's connection to the German *Bildung* tradition. This discussion will particularly highlight the way *Bildung* emphasizes a capacity for social critique, and commitment to social reform, that a self-governing, developing individual must exhibit. As a philosophical concept, *Bildung* conveys the idea of individuals' continuous, self-determined development, and underscores the importance of diversity of interaction, since this diverse interaction is essential for an individual's own self-determined growth. But further, *Bildung* draws out how it is integral to an individual's self-government to engage in an effort to fight the oppressive aspects of society that interfere with the possibilities for self-government and for a diversity of ways of life. It specifically connects individuals' self-government with the act of immanently critiquing social norms and institutions, such that an individual can help combat obstacles brought by society to both her own growth and that of others. The portrait of the democratic individual that comes from this chapter will be of an individual who exercises control over her unending growth, who actively engages with diverse individuals who unsettle her own fixed habits and beliefs, and who specifically seeks to alter society to help overcome structural disadvantage.

EXPLAINING THE DEWEY–PLATO RELATIONSHIP

Dewey's democratic way of life has received much commentary, with scholars often interpreting the concept with a reference to Dewey's interest in individuals' growth and connectedness with other individuals. Some analyses have been more specific[9] than others[10] on what this growth and

---

[9] John Stuhr, *Pragmatism, Postmodernism, and the Future of Philosophy* (New York, NY: Routledge, 2003), 57–8; Gregory Pappas, *John Dewey's Ethics: Democracy as Experience* (Bloomington, IN: Indiana University Press, 2008), 191, 290.

[10] Robert Westbrook, *John Dewey and American Democracy* (Ithaca, NY: Cornell University Press, 1991), 534; Steven Rockefeller, *John Dewey: Religious Faith and Democratic Humanism* (New York, NY: Columbia University Press, 1991), 245–6; Alan Ryan, *John Dewey and the High Tide of American Liberalism* (New York, NY: W. W. Norton & Company, 1995), 314; James Campbell, *Understanding John Dewey: Nature*

connectedness might require of individuals. Certain scholars have connected democratic life with qualities that evoke the principles of deliberative democracy, associating democratic life with "public deliberation,"[11] with an "open[ness] to the perspectives, concerns, and purposes of others,"[12] and with engagement in "free, informed exchange ... situated in mutual regard for one another."[13] The democratic way of life is indeed characterized by growth, connectedness with others, and openness to others' views – though I will argue later in the book that this should not lead Dewey to be classified as a deliberative democrat. With my analysis in these first two chapters, I will shed new light on these qualities of democratic individualism, and will thereby illuminate the individual element of Deweyan democracy.

Dewey's relationship to Plato has not been widely addressed in Dewey literature, and among the scholars who have discussed it, some have focused on the clear differences between the two. H. S. Thayer explains how Dewey objects to Plato's devaluation of the constant change that defines human experience, pointing out Dewey's disapproval of the idea that "there must be some ultimate end, or aim, to all action and desire, something intrinsically good, the Good. Without such a Good, the activities of life seem aimless, and ethically meaningless; experience is then conceived as the labors of Sisyphus in the absence of a focal Good to deliver and consummate all action."[14] Similarly, Larry Hickman states that, for Dewey, "*The Republic* richly documents the consequences for social thought in general, and for democracy in particular, of this turn against experience in its full-bodied sense."[15] On this view, the Dewey–Plato relationship is defined by contrast between Plato's emphasis on a transcendental realm of unchanging Forms (the comprehension of which is necessary for true knowledge) and Dewey's focus on the never-ending pursuit of knowledge through engagement with the transience of ordinary

and Cooperative Intelligence (Chicago, IL: Open Court, 1995), 180; Peter Manicas, *Rescuing Dewey: Essays in Pragmatic Naturalism* (Lanham, MD: Lexington Books, 2008), 178.

[11] William Caspary, *Dewey on Democracy* (Ithaca, NY: Cornell University Press, 2000), 153.

[12] Noelle McAfee, *Democracy and the Political Unconscious* (New York, NY: Columbia University Press, 2008), 156.

[13] Michael Eldridge, *Transforming Experience: John Dewey's Cultural Instrumentalism* (Nashville, TN: Vanderbilt University Press, 1998), 99.

[14] H. S. Thayer, *Meaning and Action: A Critical History of Pragmatism*, 2nd edn. (Indianapolis, IN: Hackett Publishing Company, 1981), 399.

[15] Larry Hickman, *Pragmatism as Post-Postmodernism: Lessons from John Dewey* (New York, NY: Fordham University Press, 2007), 113.

experience. Thayer, in fact, contends that it is mainly in response to Plato that Dewey builds his *pragmatic* conception of "ends" as existing only in a process of continuous actualization, rather than as a static achievement separate from the hazards of experience.[16]

Dewey does display this disagreement with Plato in *Logic: The Theory of Inquiry*, where he states that "in Plato change, altering or othering, has a direct ontological status. It is a sign of the defective ontological character of that which changes, its lack of full Being."[17] He also describes in *The Quest for Certainty* how both Plato and Aristotle "brought with them the idea of a higher realm of fixed reality of which alone true science is possible and of an inferior world of changing things with which experience and practical matters are concerned. They glorified the invariant at the expense of change, it being evident that all practical activity falls within the realm of change."[18] Dewey's concern is with how the Platonic view "translated into a rational form the doctrine of escape from the vicissitudes of existence by means of measures which do not demand an active coping with conditions."[19] Dewey, unlike Plato, conceives nothing outside the changeful realm of experience, and thus he reasons that "[s]ince changes are going on anyway, the great thing is to learn enough about them so that we be able to lay hold of them and turn them in the direction of our desires."[20] The importance of scientific advancements, in Dewey's view, lies largely in how they have progressively broken down old, fixed beliefs arrived at through abstraction from concrete experience. As such, ideas of rigid intellectual hierarchy, and of static, completed knowledge available only to an exclusive few, have been shown to be untenable. Dewey argues that philosophy must leave behind the search for immutable truth and accept the quest for necessarily imperfect knowledge, which can aid individuals in their everyday experience.

If philosophy clings to its search for immutable principles that are safe from the transience of ordinary experience, Dewey warns "this subject-matter [of philosophy] becomes arbitrary, aloof – what is called 'abstract'

---

[16] Thayer, *Meaning and Action*, 399.

[17] John Dewey, *Logic: The Theory of Inquiry* (New York, NY: Henry Holt and Company, 1938), 188.

[18] John Dewey, *The Quest for Certainty* (New York, NY: Minton, Balch & Company, 1929), 16–17. Dewey is aware how some may argue that Aristotle gave "change" an ontological status more in line with modern thinkers than with Plato; he rejects this view explicitly in *Reconstruction in Philosophy*, Enl. ed. (Boston, MA: Beacon Press, [1948] 1957), 57–60, 107.

[19] Dewey, *Quest for Certainty*, 17.

[20] Dewey, *Reconstruction in Philosophy*, 116.

when that word is used in a bad sense to designate something which exclusively occupies a realm of its own without contact with the things of ordinary experience."[21] Useful philosophic knowledge comes instead through fully inquiring into the transitory qualities of experience, and discovering how individuals may direct the changes that are going on: "that is, a method of purposefully introducing changes which will alter the direction of the course of events ... The quest for certainty by means of exact possession in mind of immutable reality is exchanged for search for security by means of active control of the changing course of events."[22] Undoubtedly, this exhibits a substantial divide between the ontological and epistemological principles of Dewey and Plato.

Richard Posner highlights the political significance of this divide between Dewey and Plato. Noting the difference between Deweyan and Platonic epistemology, he asserts that "Dewey's philosophical project of overturning Platonic epistemology provides support for making democracy the default rule of political governance in the same way that Platonic epistemology provides support for the authoritarian political system described in the *Republic*."[23] He thus concludes that "Dewey turned Plato on his head by accepting the linkage between knowledge and politics but arguing that knowledge is democratic and so should politics be."[24] Indeed, when referring to "the Platonic notion that philosophers should be kings," Dewey writes that "[i]t is impossible for high-brows to secure a monopoly of such knowledge as must be used for the regulation of common affairs. In the degree in which they become a specialized class, they are shut off from knowledge of the needs which they are supposed to serve."[25] Clearly separating himself from any political scheme like that in *The Republic* (where only the exclusively wise philosophers have political rule), Dewey's democratic view is that "the practical consequence of giving the few wise and good power is that they cease to remain wise and good."[26] Since we cannot trust that philosophers actually have epistemic access to any eternal Good, we cannot trust that they would exercise power wisely when unchecked by the public. It is thus true that

---

[21] John Dewey, *Experience and Nature* (New York, NY: Dover Publications, [1925] 1958), 6.

[22] Dewey, *Quest for Certainty*, 100, 204.

[23] Richard Posner, *Law, Pragmatism, and Democracy* (Cambridge: Harvard University Press, 2003), 103, 104.

[24] Ibid., 104.

[25] Dewey, *Public and Its Problems*, 205–6.

[26] EW1: 242.

Dewey diverges from Plato by turning philosophy toward a quest for necessarily imperfect knowledge that can aid individuals in their everyday experience – a quest that cannot be limited to only a few "wise" individuals.

The argument has also been made, though, that Dewey actually views Plato as an exemplar of the continuous, never-ending inquiry he advocates. When Dewey makes his call for a "Back to Plato" movement, he specifies that "it would have to be back to the dramatic, restless, cooperatively inquiring Plato of the Dialogues, trying one mode of attack after another to see what it might yield; back to the Plato whose highest flight of metaphysics always terminated with a social and practical turn."[27] Thomas Alexander suggests Plato's work is, in fact, an example of Deweyan cooperative inquiry: "A Platonic dialogue can be just an exhibition of 'mutual coordination' in which each party genuinely participates with the other in trying to define the object of the quest, such as the definition of courage, justice, or friendship."[28] Along similar lines, David Fott maintains that "Socratic dialectic ... aims to challenge all fixed tenets, so that any tenet advanced in an argument or used to justify one's action would be fortified, not merely asserted."[29]

To support this view, we might think of Platonic dialogues in which the figure of Socrates does not reach any comprehensive answer to the questions under discussion, but rather simply engages with others in an exhaustive, open-ended inquiry. In the *Protagoras*, the dialogue begins with Socrates believing that virtue cannot be taught and Protagoras believing virtue can be taught; by the end, the two have reversed their positions, and Socrates finishes by imploring, "I should like to carry on the discussion until we ascertain what virtue is, and whether capable of being taught or not."[30] In the *Euthyphro*, the discussion of piety similarly does not lead to any clear conclusion, but rather ends with Socrates stating "we must begin again and ask, What is piety? That is an enquiry which I shall never be weary of pursuing."[31] And in the *Apology*, Plato famously

---

[27] Dewey, "From Absolutism to Experimentalism," 21.

[28] Thomas Alexander, *John Dewey's Theory of Art, Experience, and Nature: The Horizons of Feeling* (Albany, NY: State University of New York Press, 1987), 163.

[29] David Fott, *John Dewey: America's Philosopher of Democracy* (Lanham, MD: Rowman & Littlefield, 1998), 143.

[30] Plato, "Protagoras," in *The Dialogues of Plato*, 3rd edn., Vol. I, translated into English, with analyses and introductions, by B. Jowett (London: Oxford University Press, 1924), 186–7.

[31] Plato, "Euthyphro," in *The Dialogues of Plato*, 3rd edn., Vol. II , translated into English, with analyses and introductions, by B. Jowett (London: Oxford University Press, 1924), 92.

presents Socrates, not as illuminating any fixed truth, but as a "gadfly" who constantly pesters those who claim to be wise in order to see whether their claims hold up under scrutiny.[32] This depiction of the Dewey–Plato connection in fact coheres with Gregory Vlastos's distinction between the "Socrates" of the early Platonic dialogues – including each of the dialogues just mentioned – in which Plato presents (according to Vlastos) the actual historical figure of Socrates and the "Socrates" we find once we reach the middle dialogues, where Plato apparently begins to use Socrates as a mouthpiece for his own viewpoints. Vlastos claims that the Socrates of the early dialogues, as opposed to his later counterpart, is not so hostile to democracy, has no conception of unchanging Forms, and focuses on an unending pursuit of moral truth.[33] When Plato's works are read this way, it is justifiable to say that Dewey would admire their quality of continuous, never-ending inquiry.

Dewey does indeed praise Plato by claiming that "the Platonic system is the most splendid fruit" of a revolution against unreflective reliance on custom for "directing action and belief"; he also contends that Plato recognized how "[while] it may be held that institutions and social regulations determine rightfully enough the beliefs of the great mass of men ... the rightfulness of this approximate control depends upon the institutions themselves having already undergone criticism."[34] Elsewhere, Dewey describes the primary contribution that philosophy can make to our lives as being that of "criticism," which creates "a heightened consciousness of deficiencies and corruptions in the scheme and distribution of values that obtains at any period."[35] One could argue that no one more effectively than Plato has exposed the conflicting qualities of a dominant (in Plato's case, Athenian) value system; and Dewey, in an apparent reference to the famous remark in the *Apology*, declares that "[c]onflict is the gadfly of thought. It stirs us to observation and memory. It instigates to invention. It shocks us out of sheep-like passivity, and sets us at noting and contriving."[36] This would suggest that Plato, in Dewey's view, was

[32] Plato, "Apology," in *The Dialogues of Plato*, 3rd edn., Vol. II , translated into English, with analyses and introductions, by B. Jowett (London: Oxford University Press, 1924), 123–4.

[33] Gregory Vlastos, *Socrates, Ironist and Moral Philosopher* (Ithaca, NY: Cornell University Press, 1991), 46–50.

[34] MW6: 24–5.

[35] Dewey, *Experience and Nature*, 412.

[36] John Dewey, *Human Nature and Conduct* (New York, NY: Henry Holt and Company, 1922), 300.

perhaps the most successful practitioner of philosophy there has been. Although he worked within a very different intellectual context from Dewey's (and ours), his commitment to exposing conflicting tendencies within any and all fixed, dogmatic beliefs fulfilled philosophy's function of unsettling his readers and forcing them to think.

It is reasonable to say that Dewey would esteem the rigorous inquiry displayed in the early Platonic dialogues. However, the admiration that Dewey expresses for Plato, on my reading, carries implications that are not accounted for by this depiction of the Dewey–Plato relationship. In fact, Dewey's praise for Plato indicates the importance of *The Republic* (not an early dialogue) to Dewey, and in particular, the importance of Plato's ethical thought to Dewey's principle that democracy is "an ethical conception, and upon its ethical significance is based its significance as governmental."[37] While Dewey certainly may have also had a fondness for those early dialogues, I see his admiration for Plato as connecting directly to the value he places on the democratic individual way of life.

THE DEMOCRATIC INDIVIDUAL IN PLATO AND DEWEY

As noted earlier, Dewey describes Plato's *Republic* as seeking "such a development of man's nature as brings him into complete harmony with the universe of spiritual relations, or, in Platonic language, the state." He conveys the value he sees in Plato's task when he states that "[i]f [the Platonic Republic] had no value for philosophical reasons, if its theory of morals, of reality and of knowledge had disappeared as utterly as the breezes which swept the grasses under the plane tree by which Plato and his disciples sat and talked, the Republic would be immortal as the summary of all that was best and most permanent in Greek life."[38] Even if Plato's ontological and epistemological principles can no longer be reasonably upheld under modern circumstances, Dewey insists that *The Republic* remains "immortal" because "it seizes upon the heart of the ethical problem, the relation of the individual to the universal, and states a solution."[39] He thus argues that "[n]othing could be more aside from the mark than to say that the Platonic ideal subordinates and sacrifices the individual to the state."[40] Dewey does differ from Plato on how the ideal

---

[37] EW1: 240.
[38] EW1: 241.
[39] Ibid.
[40] Ibid.

"relation of the individual to the universal" should specifically look and on how exactly individuals are to both realize their unique potential and contribute their talents to their society. But his description of democracy as being fundamentally an individual, ethical conception is rooted, in my view, in his call for a "Back to Plato" movement. Indeed, going back to Plato ourselves can help us begin to figure out what Deweyan democratic individualism represents.

In *The Republic*, Plato declares that "[c]onstitutions cannot come out of stocks and stones; they must result from the preponderance of certain characters which draw the rest of the community in their wake. So if there are five forms of government, there must be five kinds of mental constitution among individuals."[41] For Plato, any discussion of an ideal political structure must directly connect to an inquiry into the ideal individual disposition – thus his famous analysis of different types of states and the corresponding dominant character types in each of those states. There is a sense in Plato that neither the ideal individual nor the ideal state can exist without the other; although, if there is one that we could say is primary for Plato and that could exist separately from the other, it is the ideal individual.

Plato's ideal aristocratic state requires that philosophers become rulers,[42] for only philosophers have knowledge of the eternal Forms, which are truly real because they are not subject to the transitory experiential world.[43] The philosophers can comprehend what makes truly good statesmanship, rather than getting stuck in mere opinion or belief about wise management of public affairs. The mass of the people, on the other hand, are for Plato simply incapable of such unchanging knowledge: "the philosophers are those who can apprehend the eternal and unchanging, while those who cannot do so ... are lost in the mazes of multiplicity and change."[44] The best the majority can do, therefore, both for themselves and for the good of the state, is stick with the practical function they are suited for and refrain from overstepping their limits into matters of political rule.[45] When this happens, a just state can emerge where the wise philosophers rule, the courageous warriors assist the philosophers in maintaining the health of the state, and the productive masses stay

[41] Plato, *The Republic of Plato*, translated with introduction and notes by Francis Cornford (London: Oxford University Press, 1941), 267.
[42] Ibid., 207–8.
[43] Ibid., 183–90.
[44] Ibid., 190.
[45] Ibid., 128–9.

under control – a state with perfect order and no conflict across class boundaries.

For the aristocratic individual character type corresponding to this state, Plato describes a strictly ordered individual "soul" in which the rational part of the soul (which is capable of true knowledge) is in charge, the spirited part of the soul assists the rational part in maintaining the health of the soul, and the appetites (the largest part of the soul) are kept under control.[46] However, because "the multitude can never be philosophical,"[47] most individuals are not capable of such an ordered soul. The ideal aristocratic disposition will inevitably be found only in the few wise philosophers, thus making the ideal aristocratic state dependent on a small minority retaining a politically dominant status. This is in large part the reason Plato has Socrates remark that such a state could only likely exist "in the heavens."[48]

A democratic state, by contrast, is for Plato one in which the masses (those dominated by appetite) exercise political power. As opposed to the strict order and hierarchy of the aristocratic state, where all individuals perform the one function they are naturally suited for, the democratic state allows interaction of diverse elements of society, which should be kept separate – thus creating a "mixture of colours" which appeals to immature minds – and dictates equality "for equals and unequals alike."[49] Political victory, therefore, belongs to "anyone who merely calls himself the people's friend."[50] Furthermore, in the *Gorgias*, Plato has Socrates contend that democratic politics is when "an ignorant person is more convincing than the expert before an equally ignorant audience,"[51] and in the *Crito*, Socrates repeatedly dismisses "the opinion of the many" as without validity.[52] This condemnation of democracy extends to the analysis of the democratic individual character type. Such individuals, in Plato's view, lead lives of varied experience rather than sticking to a single function, assume equality between necessary and unnecessary appetites,

[46] Ibid., 130–41.
[47] Ibid., 201.
[48] Ibid., 319.
[49] Ibid., 282–3.
[50] Ibid., 283.
[51] Plato, *Gorgias*, rev. ed., translated by Walter Hamilton and Chris Emlyn-Jones (London: Penguin Classics, 2004), 23.
[52] Plato, "Crito," in *The Dialogues of Plato*, 3rd edn., Vol. II, translated into English, with analyses and introductions, by B. Jowett (London: Oxford University Press, 1924), 145, 149.

and are "subject to no order or restraint."[53] With no strict, hierarchical order, and with constant change elevated over the eternal and unchanging, democracy fails at producing true goodness in either the individual or the state.[54]

Although Plato does suggest that the creation of his ideal state is far-fetched in the face of his Athenian democratic context, he holds out greater hope that an individual may still "found [the ideal state] in himself."[55] The commonwealth as a whole may be beyond saving, unable to comprehend the wisdom of his aristocratic government, but wise philosophers such as himself (and his teacher, Socrates) can nonetheless establish the ideal, ordered, harmonious state in their souls. Surely, Plato does see the cultivation of aristocratic individuals as being aided greatly by the presence of his aristocratic state, which can provide the proper kind of education for the unique young individuals who are capable of being philosophers.[56] But still, while a proper aristocratic state for Plato absolutely cannot exist if there are not individual philosophers with properly ordered souls, it is possible to see aristocratic individuals even in a deeply nonideal state. What's more, the individual soul is, in Plato's view, eternal and unchanging, living beyond the death of the earthly body. The state, on the other hand, is earth-bound and thus, in a way, inevitably corrupted, subject to the inescapable changes of earthly experience. Earlier, we saw that Dewey praises "the Plato whose highest flight of metaphysics always terminated with a social and practical turn." We can interpret the ideal aristocratic state depicted in *The Republic* as merely an impractical flight of metaphysics, i.e., an account of something that Plato himself thinks

---

53 Plato, *Republic*, 284–6.

54 The argument has been made that Plato is not in fact as hostile to democracy as commonly believed. Such an argument can be found in S. Sara Monoson, *Plato's Democratic Entanglements: Athenian Politics and the Practice of Philosophy* (Princeton, NJ: Princeton University Press, 2000). Monoson claims that Plato is not actually presenting a "decline" of regimes in Book 8 of *The Republic*, but rather a "typology"; she thus argues that Plato does not see democracy as the second-worst regime after despotism, that he prefers the "pleasures and attractions" of democracy over the "misery and division" of oligarchy, that he does not elevate the wealthy over the poor, and that he approves of democratic life as "colorful, beautiful, attractive, easy, gentle" (pp. 115–16). Monoson's argument overlooks how Plato elevates necessary over unnecessary appetites (which forms the basis of his elevation of oligarchy over democracy); how oligarchy maintains a kind of temperance lacking in democracy because oligarchy privileges those who are thrifty with their money over the pleasure-seeking; and how Plato dismisses the diverse, varied, "colorful" democratic existence as antithetical to both a good state and a good individual.

55 Plato, *Republic*, 319–20.

56 Ibid., 63–111, 235–63.

cannot be brought into reality. His ideal, reason-driven individuality, though, is a matter for practical inquiry, a goal that can manifest itself in the here and now.

For Dewey, the individual level holds similar priority. Of course, this does not mean that Dewey considers *political* democracy to be unimportant; I will discuss the political element of his democratic thought more fully later on (particularly in Chapter 3), but we can note here, for one, that the "earthly" quality of political institutions would certainly not bother Dewey. Still, Dewey insists that we can no longer "entertain the hope that given political freedom as the one thing necessary all other things will in time be added to it."[57] He explains that "the ideal of democracy ... roots itself ultimately in the principle of moral, self-directing individuality,"[58] and thus "the supreme test of all political institutions ... shall be the contribution they make to the all-around growth of every member of society."[59] Dewey's focus is at the individual level, and so his main concern regarding political institutions is their actual impact on individuals' capacity to govern their lives. Relatedly, he emphasizes that individuals' ability to control their lives is affected not only by the quality of their political system, but the quality of their broader society. It is possible, in Dewey's view, for a political system to meet apparently democratic standards, while many individuals still lack meaningful opportunity to govern themselves, due to social relations, norms, and practices that simply take away that opportunity. It does not make sense to say democracy is fully achieved, Dewey argues, when individual traits that are characteristic of genuine self-government are so lacking. A certain kind of individual conduct, and the necessary conditions for individuals to display that conduct, must then be the central components of our democratic thinking: "powerful present enemies of democracy can be successfully met only by the creation of personal attitudes in individual human beings ... we must get over our tendency to think that its defense can be found in any external means ... if they are separated from individual attitudes so deep-seated as to constitute personal character."[60]

On my reading, we can better understand what Dewey means by a democratic individual way of life by studying both his overall admiration for Plato, and his specific differences from Plato. Dewey differs from Plato by objecting to Plato's notion that any individuals are so perfectly

---

[57] Dewey, *Freedom and Culture*, 6.
[58] MW3: 235.
[59] Dewey, *Reconstruction in Philosophy*, 186.
[60] Dewey, "Creative Democracy," 242.

wise that they must place other individuals in their correct functional roles, rather than allowing those others to determine their own paths.[61] He also contends that individual diversity is far more expansive than Plato presents, since individuals may develop in unique, unforeseen ways that do not neatly fit into any established class; this in turn shows how we cannot cling to fixed ideas of classes and how they rank in superiority.[62] Nonetheless, Dewey remains committed to what he praises as the "immortal" task of *The Republic*, arguing that "[t]he problem of constructing a new individuality consonant with the objective conditions under which we live is the deepest problem of our times."[63] He notes how, under modern conditions, no individual can act free of impact from remote, unforeseen forces beyond immediate control: "Recent inventions have so multiplied and cheapened the means of transportation, and of the circulation of ideas and news through books, magazines, and papers, that it is no longer physically possible for one nationality, race, class, or sect to be kept apart from others, impervious to their wishes and beliefs."[64] Hence, Plato's requirement that individuals remain in their own spheres and avoid diverse interaction (if they are to achieve harmony with an aristocratic universe of spiritual relations) will, under modern conditions, leave individuals futilely seeking to remain still in the midst of rapidly changing circumstances. The universe of spiritual relations brought about by modern advancements lacks strict order; has done away with any notions of exclusive, eternal truth; and is constantly changing because the component individuals unavoidably affect and are affected by diverse others in unforeseen ways. In other words, the modern universe of spiritual relations has demonstrated itself as democratic. Dewey, like Plato, seeks a harmony of individual disposition with the universe of spiritual relations facing the individual: "Individuals will refind themselves only as their ideas and ideals are brought into harmony with the realities of the age in which they act."[65] But because the assumptions underlying Plato's universe of spiritual relations have been undone by modern conditions, it is the democratic, not the aristocratic, individual who may achieve such harmony. Dewey admires Plato's approach to the problem of harmonizing individuals with the conditions under which

---

[61] EW1: 242–3.
[62] MW7: 317.
[63] John Dewey, *Individualism Old and New* (New York, NY: Capricorn Books, [1930] 1962), 32.
[64] MW2: 84.
[65] Dewey, *Individualism Old and New*, 70.

they live, but he endorses the continuous individual development and diverse interaction that Plato rejects.

With his conception of an aristocratic individual, Plato is seeking the realization of all individuals' unique capacities. The few who can reach the aristocratic individual standard will be truly self-governing, and they will also place the many, who cannot attain this ideal, into their proper functional roles so that they each engage in the activity they are uniquely suited for. Dewey also seeks the development of all individuals' unique potential, but sees democratic individualism instead as the proper standard for bringing about this development. For both Plato and Dewey, the democratic life is stuck in the world of constant change and is defined by varied experience and interaction of diverse sectors of society. Within modern circumstances, Dewey insists this life is exactly what is necessary for effective fulfillment of individuals' potential. He explains how "[i]t is because ... autocracy means uniformity as surely as democracy means diversification that the great hope lies with the latter. The former strains human nature to the breaking point; the latter releases and relieves it."[66] No group of individuals can any longer be assumed either to possess perfect knowledge of reality or to be incapable of knowledge, which means "diverse interests [must] have a chance to articulate themselves."[67] Individuals may increase their wisdom, then, through varying their experience and interacting with diverse others: "Each contributes something distinctive from his own store of knowledge, ability, taste, while receiving at the same time elements of value contributed by others ... in the degree in which there is genuine mutual give and take [ideas] are seen in a new light, deepened and extended in meaning, and there is the enjoyment of enlargement of experience, of growth of capacity."[68] In Dewey's view, this active interaction with otherness and willingness to unsettle one's own fixed habits and beliefs can allow individuals some measure of control over their lives, which are inevitably affected by remote, unforeseen forces. Democratic individuals can more intelligently interact with the diverse ways of life they are confronted with because of their varied experience, as opposed to those who cannot "walk the earth freely" because they are "obsessed by the need of protecting some private possession of

---

[66] MW11: 105–6. Dewey's reference to "human nature" can seem a bit odd because he frequently objects to ahistorical notions of human nature separate from social/historical circumstances; "human nature" should perhaps be interpreted as "human development."

[67] Dewey, *Freedom and Culture*, 128.

[68] John Dewey and James Tufts, *Ethics*, rev. edn. (New York, NY: Henry Holt and Company, 1932), 383–4.

belief and taste."[69] Thus, "[v]ariability, initiative, innovation, departure from routine, experimentation," which signify slavery to appetite for Plato, are what distinguish freedom from slavery for Dewey[70] – he even brings to mind Plato's depiction of the "colorful" quality of democratic life with his call for "a free, flexible and many-colored life."[71]

In Plato's philosophy, the ideal individual is required not only for individual flourishing, but for the wise regulation of collective affairs. When those who are capable of living their life by the rational part of their soul are cultivated and given political power, political rule will serve the true good of the entire community. Dewey's democratic way of life aims at similar twin purposes: "The key-note of democracy as a way of life may be expressed ... as the necessity for the participation of every mature human being in formation of the values that regulate the living of men together: which is necessary from the standpoint of both the general social welfare and the full development of human beings as individuals."[72] On the Deweyan view, what is required for the "general social welfare" could never be completely determined, since the social realm is composed of constantly developing, changing individuals. This social welfare would have to be constantly discovered through the interaction of diverse individuals, none of whom possesses a monopoly on truth. Dewey advocates "the idea of a plurality of interconnected meanings and purposes [replacing] that of *the* meaning and purpose. Search for a single, inclusive good is doomed to failure."[73] As there is no group with access to eternal truth, the wisdom necessary to intelligently regulate collective affairs depends on all individuals interacting with plural forms of life, thereby both contributing to, and benefiting from, the knowledge of others. A collectivity composed of fully developing individuals who are "learning from all the contacts of life"[74] will thus display greater wisdom regarding how to best serve the general social welfare. These individuals will also then be better able to move governing institutions to serve that welfare: "The foundation of democracy is ... the power of pooled and cooperative experience ... to generate progressively the knowledge and

[69] Dewey, *Individualism Old and New*, 162.
[70] Dewey, *Human Nature and Conduct*, 310–11.
[71] Dewey, *Public and Its Problems*, 217.
[72] LW11: 217–18.
[73] LW5: 272.
[74] John Dewey, *Democracy and Education* (New York, NY: The Free Press, [1916] 1966), 360.

wisdom needed to guide collective action."[75] And when certain individuals lack equal status and are effectively excluded from contributing to this wisdom, "the whole social body is deprived of the potential resources that should be at its service."[76]

It should be noted here that Dewey distinguishes between *individuality* and *individualism*. This helps separate his conception of individuals' self-government from other, prevalent modern conceptions that are further from Platonic principles than Dewey's. Individuality, for Dewey, signifies precisely the kind of individual self-government that underlies Deweyan democracy. It represents the quality of realizing one's unique self through self-conscious, self-governed activity. As Dewey explains in *Individualism Old and New*, though, individualism may or may not be conducive to individuality. He describes individualism as a philosophy that focuses primarily on individuals' conduct, and it is a philosophy that can take different forms. In the modern age, it has mainly taken the form of seeing individuals as supposedly having responsibility only for themselves and their own actions, since they are believed to be able to govern their lives without impact from the actions of others. Individuals, according to this philosophy, are to pursue their self-interest (which typically relates to the pursuit of money) and are not seen as dependent on, or responsible to, other individuals in any meaningful way. As I will discuss more fully in Chapter 2, this "old" individualism has particularly served the interests of economic elites by justifying the kind of society that gives them tremendous power over the lives of others. Dewey points out "the irony of the gospel of 'individualism' in business conjoined with suppression of individuality in thought and speech."[77] The "individualism" that takes individuals as isolated beings does not correspond with genuine individuality. Such a philosophy takes individuals out of step with the interconnected conditions they face, especially given the technological and economic interconnections brought by modernity. It also allows blame to be placed on individuals who find themselves in subordinate social relations with others, since they are held to be in total control of their own fate. Plato, on a Deweyan view, has the virtue of presenting individuals' conduct as an inherently *social* matter and as carrying significant direct responsibility for the health of their collectivity. When Dewey calls for a "new individualism,"[78] a new philosophy of individual conduct in

[75] LW11: 219.
[76] LW11: 218–19.
[77] Dewey, *Individualism Old and New*, 91.
[78] Ibid., 33–4, 83, 93, 98–9.

contrast to the "old" individualism, he aims to show how individuals can genuinely govern their lives and manifest their unique individuality, while accounting for the inevitably social quality of their actions. This "new" individualism is democratic individualism. Indeed, the reason I refer to "democratic individualism," rather than "democratic individuality," is because individuality itself is basically equivalent to democratic individualism. Individuality is the fundamental aim of Dewey's democratic thinking, and it is obstructed by the old individualism that treats individuals as isolated beings, but it can be realized through a new, democratic individualism.

For a final point regarding the Platonic qualities of Dewey's democratic individualism, we can look to Dewey's educational theory.[79] While disagreeing with the specific content of Plato's educational theory, Dewey still sees Plato as making the crucial point that a model social and political order requires educational practices that prepare children to fulfill their potential in harmony with that order: "Plato ... realized that the foundation in any established political organized life was the child and the shaping and directing of the life of the child through educational instruments from his birth up to his full emergence into civic life."[80] He explains that Plato's work has been critical to understanding "that social life was capable of intelligent direction. The first step in getting at this direction was to begin with the child and prepare him from the first for the type of social life held in view."[81] To be sure, the theory of education laid out in *The Republic* is based on rigid class boundaries, with the children who show the capacity for true knowledge being given a philosophic education separate from the masses. Deweyan education rejects such separation and seeks to develop the diverse intellectual capacities of all children, in large part through educating them to accept and affirm that they live in a constantly changing world and must adapt to unforeseen circumstances: "[The school] must provide at least part of that training which is necessary to keep the individual properly adjusted to a rapidly changing environment ... It must make up to him in part for the decay of dogmatic and fixed methods of social discipline ... it must provide means for bringing people and their ideas and beliefs together, in such ways as will lessen friction and instability."[82]

---

[79] I will provide a thorough analysis of Dewey's educational theory in Chapter 6.
[80] EW5: 213.
[81] EW5: 214.
[82] MW2: 90.

But despite the divergent prescriptions, Dewey appreciates Plato's recognition of education as the tool for "harmonizing" the individual with the "universe of spiritual relations." Dewey praises Plato's view that "[t]he education that discovers and trains the peculiar powers of an individual is at the same time the method by which intrinsic, instead of coerced, harmony is achieved in the state."[83] While noting that "progress in knowledge has made us aware of the superficiality of Plato's lumping of individuals and their original powers into a few sharply marked-off classes," he insists that "[w]e cannot better Plato's conviction that an individual is happy and society well organized when each individual engages in those activities for which he has a natural equipment, nor his conviction that it is the primary office of education to discover this equipment to its possessor and train him for its effective use."[84] Dewey also contends that, in contrast with Aristotle's mere description of existing regimes, "[Plato's] *Republic* is an attempt at least to sketch ideally the conditions under which politics and morals might become truly rational"[85] and that the importance of *The Republic* is shown in how Plato's educational scheme "regards the period of immaturity ... as an opportunity of progress to be taken advantage of in the process of creating a new and better society."[86] As we will see more fully in Chapter 6, education is for Dewey, as it is for Plato, most essential for cultivating qualities that allow individuals to realize their capacities in harmony with the conditions they face. It is largely through education that the self-governed development of democratic individualism is to emerge.

DEMOCRATIC INDIVIDUALISM AND THE GERMAN
BILDUNG TRADITION

I have so far used Dewey's admiration for Plato as a jumping-off point for understanding Dewey's democratic individual way of life. Dewey's view is that "[i]f democracy is possible it is because every individual has a degree of power to govern himself,"[87] and Platonic principles give us insight into the qualities that define this kind of individual self-government. But nevertheless, since Dewey is clearly not a wholesale Platonist, we cannot

---

[83] MW7: 317.
[84] Dewey, *Democracy and Education*, 90.
[85] LW11: 72.
[86] MW13: 400.
[87] LW6: 431.

get a complete picture of democratic individualism by studying Plato. My analysis of democratic individualism will continue in Chapter 2, where I will explore Dewey's relation to Hegel. To finish this chapter and form a bridge to the next chapter, I will expand on Dewey's case for why individuals' self-governed development is bound up with the presence of social equality and why, under structurally unequal social conditions, this self-governed development requires one to help combat the forms of structural inequality. To do this, I will address Dewey's relation to the German philosophical tradition known as *Bildung* (which includes such thinkers as Johann Herder, Friedrich Schiller, Wilhelm von Humboldt, Friedrich Schleiermacher, and Hegel). The particular value of *Bildung*, we will see, is that it emphasizes how an individual's self-government is linked with her effort to combat aspects of society that obstruct the self-government of others. This discussion will further clarify Dewey's Platonic point that realizing one's own individuality involves achieving a harmony with the individuality of others and understanding the inevitably social quality of one's actions.

Among Dewey scholars, James Good and Jim Garrison have led the way in terms of illuminating the link between Dewey and the *Bildung* tradition. On their account, *Bildung* reflects precisely the kind of continuous individual development that Dewey is interested in, a development that not only actualizes an individual's own unique identity but simultaneously contributes to the self-development of others. Good and Garrison explain how thinkers in the *Bildung* tradition "envisioned an endlessly actualizing self that is both willing and able to make unique cultural contributions through immanent critique and creative reconstruction of cultural norms, beliefs, and values, positively affecting their subsequent self-development and the education of future generations."[88] Referring to Herder in particular, they state that "[f]or Herder, philosophy is the theory of *Bildung*, the theory of how individuals develop into the sort of organic unity that unceasingly works toward the full development of their talents and abilities."[89] This simultaneous individual and social development speaks to the need of an individual to interact with diverse others and to not assume she can realize her potential in isolation and without any reliance on others: "Herder and [Johann] Goethe had launched a neo-humanist tradition that stressed the individual's unique talents as

[88] James Good and Jim Garrison, "Traces of Hegelian *Bildung* in Dewey's Philosophy," in *John Dewey and Continental Philosophy*, ed. Paul Fairfield (Carbondale, IL: Southern Illinois University Press, 2010), 44.
[89] Ibid., 45.

well as the need to live in a society in which the talents of others comple-
ment their own. Hence, a well-developed society is one that allows wide
scope for the unique development of individuals. Individual diversity is
the very engine of social development."⁹⁰ The concept of *Bildung* thus
carries the ethical principle that "we must seek ... the widest variety of
experience," but this is a principle that itself depends on the existence of
"a society in which there is scope for all kinds of complementary individuals and activities. Exposure to different kinds of people and experimentation with different types of lives is crucial to moral development."⁹¹
There is a concurrence of developments here, in which an individual is
to look inward in order to develop her own unique capacities, while also
looking outward in order to promote the development of those around
her – and her ability to do this is itself aided by the degree to which society is already characterized by diverse, self-governing individuality. W. H.
Bruford, in his oft-cited study of the *Bildung* tradition, refers to the significant "tension" involved in reconciling "inward-looking and outward-
looking thought" and to the difficulty thus involved with achieving the
"harmony of developed capacities" that defines the "kind of individual
perfection aimed at by the theory of classical 'Bildung.'"⁹² The task of
overcoming this tension is the distinctive challenge posed to individuals
by the idea of *Bildung*.

Good describes Dewey as a member of the "American *Bildung* tradition" and remarks that Dewey, like the German *Bildung* thinkers,
believes "the purpose of personal growth is to seek harmony within the
self and within the world."⁹³ We can see the affinity between this reading of Dewey through the lens of *Bildung* and my reading through a
Platonic lens. In both ways, we see how Dewey conceives individuality
as a process of development intertwined with the development of other
individuals. In other words, there is an indissoluble link between an individual's growth and the quality of her broader society; it is essential to
an individual's self-determined growth that she engage with diverse perspectives and ways of life (especially under the changing, highly interconnected conditions of modernity), and her possibilities for growth are
intertwined with the existence of a society that provides conditions for

⁹⁰ Ibid., 47.
⁹¹ Ibid., 51–3.
⁹² W. H. Bruford, *The German Tradition of Self-Cultivation: "Bildung" from Humboldt to
Thomas Mann* (Cambridge: Cambridge University Press, 1975), 264.
⁹³ James Good, *A Search for Unity in Diversity: The "Permanent Hegelian Deposit" in the
Philosophy of John Dewey* (Lanham, MD: Lexington Books, 2006), 198.

the development of such a diversity of individuals. With the concept of *Bildung*, we get particular attention on the type of social reform that is required in the midst of social conditions that obstruct genuine self-government for many individuals. More specifically, we get emphasis on the responsibility individuals have to identify and challenge aspects of society that hinder not only their own self-government, but that of others. Good and Garrison explain how *Bildung* entails such a commitment: "people of *Bildung* do not accept social norms unreflectively; they accept norms only for which they can see rational justification. To the extent that the actual practices of their society are inconsistent with the rational basis of its social norms, they seek to reform their society."[94] Therefore, "[r]ather than acceptance of the sociopolitical status quo, *Bildung* requires the ability to engage in immanent critique of one's society, challenging it to actualize its own highest ideals."[95] An individual is not only to engage with diverse others, but to specifically engage the perspectives of those who are disadvantaged by society and to contribute to efforts that would alter society in order to overcome that disadvantage. In this way, *Bildung* requires an individual to accept the unsettling of beliefs she may have previously had about the nature of her society so that she can aid the development of others, and simultaneously her own development: "Harmonization of the self is achieved through a wide variety of experiences that challenge the individual's accepted beliefs."[96] Relatedly, *Bildung* brings a responsibility to challenge the practices of the state, since "[t]he modern state must permit individuals to seek their own self-satisfaction by determining their own identities ... The state has a responsibility toward its members to provide social environments that facilitate *Bildung*."[97] These topics, particularly regarding the state's responsibility to facilitate individual self-government, will be addressed again in Chapter 2. Right here, though, these points help connect democratic individualism with the effort to specifically overcome aspects of society that suppress individuals' self-development.

We have seen that Dewey's concept of democratic individualism involves widespread interaction with diverse others and "learning from all the contacts of life." But as the *Bildung*-focused reading of Dewey underscores, democratic individualism within a structurally unequal society does not mean we simply treat all perspectives encountered as

---

[94] Good and Garrison, "Traces of Hegelian *Bildung* in Dewey's Philosophy," 49.
[95] Ibid., 54.
[96] Ibid., 53.
[97] Ibid., 52–3.

equally valid. As a structurally unequal society does not often allow for any unity of interest or viewpoint between the advantaged and the disadvantaged, democratic individualism entails siding with the disadvantaged in situations where inequality has led to conflict with the advantaged. For instance, if we think again of the debate over collective bargaining rights in Wisconsin in 2011, a democratic individual would avoid assuming that the Koch brothers' perspective, and that of the workers, are equally situated and thus should be given equal consideration. It would be highly problematic to make such an assumption, given that the Kochs enjoy a structurally advantaged social position and can exercise tremendous influence over the general discourse on an issue like collective bargaining. If an individual ends up siding with the advantaged Kochs or tries to remain neutral on the entire debate, she obstructs the development of the democratic social relations that are intertwined with the possibilities for her own self-development.

Democratic individualism, read in relation to Plato and to the *Bildung* tradition, brings a conception of (what political theorists often call) *positive freedom*. Dewey focuses on an individual's effective capacity to actively govern herself in the face of the conditions she confronts and to help build the kind of society that buttresses both her own self-government and that of others, and these are defining traits of positive freedom. We have seen Plato deride democratic freedom as leaving individuals "subject to no order or restraint"; Dewey describes how "Plato gives a vivid illustration of what he means by democratic freedom. It is doing as one likes ... Its result is loss of reverence and of order. It is the denial of moderation, of the principle of limit."[98] But for Dewey, democratic freedom need not represent "mere self-assertion, nor unregulated desire."[99] The freedom that characterizes Deweyan democracy refers to an individual actualizing her unique development – i.e., responding to changing, interconnected conditions by actively interacting with the forces affecting her life and realizing her unique individuality through that interaction: "In the degree in which we become aware of possibilities of development and actively concerned to keep the avenues of growth open, in the degree in which we fight against induration and fixity, and thereby realize the possibilities of recreation of our selves, we are actually free."[100] Dewey

---

[98] EW1: 244.

[99] Ibid.

[100] Dewey and Tufts, *Ethics*, 340. Those familiar with Hegel will notice a strong resemblance between Dewey's and Hegel's conceptions of freedom. This will be explored in Chapter 2.

does see *negative freedom* – the possession of rights to protect from extreme intrusion into one's life by others or by government – as a "necessary transition," but he sees it as insufficient for allowing individuals to effectively exercise control over their lives.[101] The premise of negative freedom is that individuals are free when they are "being left alone"[102] and can act "unregulated," but Dewey holds that this does not account for whether social conditions genuinely allow individuals to direct their own development within a changing, increasingly interconnected world.

When Dewey insists that individual freedom is bound up with social equality, he is not giving us a rigid conception of equality or trying to erase all differences between individuals and unduly limit how free individuals may develop. He explains, "We do not mean that people are physiologically or psychologically equal, but we do mean that every human being who is normal has something so distinctive that no other individual can be substituted for him."[103] While Plato fears democracy imposes equality on "equals and unequals alike," Dewey mainly argues that there is no tenable foundation on which we could, a priori, subordinate one individual's potential for another's. Dewey thus espouses "[t]he democratic faith in human equality ... that every human being ... has the right to equal opportunity with every other person for development of whatever gifts he has."[104] Dewey draws a link between freedom and equality by pointing out how, if we accept structural inequality – and that some individuals are gifted far greater opportunity than others to actualize their unique development – then we are snuffing out the potential of many individuals' free development right from the outset.[105] If freedom is a primary concept for us, then we must commit to a principle of there being equal meaningful opportunity for all to manifest their unique individuality and to exercise control over their development.

To the extent we have a society characterized by structural inequality, those directly disadvantaged by that inequality are obstructed from becoming democratic individuals – i.e., from directing their own development in the face of constantly changing conditions. And those who

---

[101] Dewey, *Freedom and Culture*, 7.
[102] Dewey, *Public and Its Problems*, 168. Negative freedom will also be addressed in Chapter 2.
[103] MW15: 170–1. The use of the word "normal" may be striking, but Dewey simply means that "barring complete imbecility," we cannot assume any individual is completely without potential; see MW13: 294.
[104] Dewey, "Creative Democracy," 242.
[105] MW13: 296.

apparently benefit from the inequality are also obstructed. When interactions are marred by social inequality and by the inability of a disadvantaged individual to actualize her unique development, that individual's potential to contribute to the development of others is curtailed. Those who seem to benefit from this inequality, in order to reap the apparent advantages, must (either consciously or not) uphold the subordination of the disadvantaged, and thus deny themselves the expansion of experience that may come from the unique development of others. For example, white individuals who are moved to discomfort in the presence of racial minorities (because of prejudiced ideas about the latter) limit their own potential expansion of experience – and thus hinder their own freedom – in interactions with these other individuals. Commenting at the onset of World War II, Dewey deems it insincere for Americans to "denounce Naziism ... if, in our personal relations to other persons ... we are moved by racial, color or other class prejudice."[106] He explains how "[o]ur anti-democratic heritage of Negro slavery has left us with habits of intolerance toward the colored race – habits which belie profession of democratic loyalty."[107] The concept of democratic individualism thus highlights how advantaged individuals themselves suffer from restricting the distinctive growth of others, due to the limits on one's own growth that come when one believes others deserve subordinate social status. It follows that a democratic individual, for Dewey, would challenge forms of subordination – such as racial discrimination – even if the individual is not subject to that subordination herself. As is emphasized by the concept of *Bildung*, one's own freedom is not advanced through the subjection of others, and the possibilities for self-government grow when one can interact with others who are themselves self-governing.

Since we live under changing, interconnected conditions, Dewey reasons that individuals who try to simply shut unfamiliar others out from their lives are not likely to gain the control over their surroundings that they seek. Dewey points out that "[r]apid transportation and communication have compelled men to live as members of an extensive and mainly unseen society ... they have to have some notions about [that society] upon which to base their actions."[108] And if one wishes to not only shut certain others out, but rely on the idea that those others deserve subordinate social status, that individual is unlikely to be able to maintain this

---

[106] Dewey, "Creative Democracy," 242.
[107] LW14: 277.
[108] MW13: 329–30.

worldview without some discomfort: "Bigotry, intolerance, or even an unswerving faith in the superiority of one's own religious and political creed, are much shaken when individuals are brought face-to-face with each other, or have the ideas of others continuously and forcibly placed before them."[109] The democratic individual, though, accepts the unsettlement of her beliefs and rejects the suppression of difference. She expands her experience and increases her wisdom through active interaction with the unique, unfamiliar forces affecting her life. The unease that comes from confronting diverse individuals and ideas cannot be avoided, and the standard of democratic individualism leads one toward accepting that insecurity and building a "higher" security through effective interaction with a wider range of individuals and ideas. This democratic individual can realize her unique self through a broader range of experiences, rather than becoming lost in modern conditions because she cannot cope with novel situations. This is a challenging standard, for "[m]ost persons object to having their habits unsettled, their habits of belief no less than habits of overt action."[110] But this standard must be met, Dewey claims, if an individual is to truly govern her life in the midst of our current conditions. An individual must allow for her present habits and beliefs to be unsettled, and in particular, she must be willing to challenge accepted social norms and practices if they are having the effect of obstructing self-governed development, whether her own or that of others. To the extent that self-developing individuals interact without subordinating the development of any of the individuals involved, we approach a condition in which "all individuals may share in the discoveries and thoughts of others, to the liberation and enrichment of their own experience."[111] When unequal social conditions make this impossible, it serves the development of all (even the advantaged) to challenge those conditions and overthrow the pernicious forms of inequality.

We must also recall how Dewey sees the "collective wisdom" on public policy as suffering from the subjection of certain individuals. The ordinary discourse on issues of public concern, when we have a structurally unequal society, is constituted by far less (as Dewey puts it) "pooled and cooperative experience" that can generate "the knowledge and wisdom needed to guide collective action." On the subject of gender, for instance, Dewey highlights how male-established social norms can deny women

[109] MW2: 84.
[110] Dewey, *Public and Its Problems*, 59.
[111] Dewey, *Individualism Old and New*, 154.

the opportunity to supply the wisdom of their unique experiences: "Present ideas of love, marriage, and the family are almost exclusively masculine constructions. Like all idealizations of human interests that express a dominantly one-sided experience, they are romantic in theory and prosaic in operation ... The growing freedom of women can hardly have any other outcome than the production of more realistic and more human morals."[112] Because women's development is often obstructed by social norms regarding their proper role in marriage and the family, men themselves are denied the expansion of experience that would result from interacting with freely growing women – which impedes men (as well as women) from becoming democratic individuals. And because it has long been socially acceptable for men to essentially speak for women, we cannot currently know what women living with freedom and equality would contribute to a society's collective wisdom. On many issues of public concern, then, we lose "the possibility of a public opinion intelligent enough to meet present social problems."[113] When Dewey thus addresses a specific issue such as contraception, he exposes how the debate over the issue is itself "undemocratic,"[114] since unequal social status can silence women's distinct perspectives on the matter. A society's ability to wisely regulate the issue is thereby impeded. We can look in a similar way at an issue like affirmative action (which is under particular attack by the Trump administration), for when the perspectives of racial minorities are effectively denied equal standing with that of whites, the entire discourse surrounding the issue is deficient because crucial perspectives on the subject are erased from view.[115] Democratic individuals, whether they are men or women, white or black, are to engage in immanent critique of these social inequalities and help reform society in order to shore up the collective wisdom that determines responses to issues of public concern.

Having explored these traits of the democratic individual way of life, it is worthwhile to consider a provocative recent critique of Dewey made by Robert Talisse. Talisse claims that Dewey's ideal of the democratic way of life is inevitably oppressive. His primary concern is that "if pluralism is correct, any conception of what a democratic citizen should be, or what

---

[112] LW5: 276.

[113] Dewey, *Freedom and Culture*, 149.

[114] LW6: 389. Dewey also addresses birth control in LW6: 146–8.

[115] Elizabeth Anderson has indeed drawn on Dewey to make the point that whites' opinions on affirmative action are more sensitive to blacks' economic circumstances when we have more truly integrated social conditions; see Elizabeth Anderson, *The Imperative of Integration* (Princeton, NJ: Princeton University Press, 2010), 132–3.

values and virtues are most important to cultivate among a democratic citizenry, will be reasonably rejectable."[116] Given how pluralism reflects a diversity of approaches to human existence, any notion of *the* democratic way of life must, for Talisse, represent an arbitrary imposition on reasonable individuals: "the recognition that there are reasonable persons who hold non-Deweyan and anti-Deweyan views exposes the incoherence of the Deweyan social ideal of democracy as a way of life: It is a democratic ideal that prescribes the oppression of reasonable persons."[117] Talisse therefore concludes that "Deweyan democracy is antipluralist."[118]

With the qualities of democratic individualism that I have described, though, we are able to effectively respond to Talisse's charges. The qualities of the democratic way of life, as derived from Dewey's connection to Plato and to the *Bildung* tradition, absolutely support the preservation of pluralism and the existence of a wide diversity of worldviews. In their analysis of Dewey and *Bildung*, Good and Garrison specifically note how "[p]luralistic diversity, interaction, unique potentiality, and change are ... critical to Dewey," since Dewey's "ideal of pluralistic democracy is that everyone interacts to advance reciprocal self-development."[119] While it may be understandable for someone like Talisse to worry that positing an ethical standard could potentially threaten pluralism, Dewey's own statements should allay concerns that he is dismissive of the existence of a plurality of forms of life. His democratic way of life in fact requires recognizing that "[t]here are many meanings and many purposes in the situations with which we are confronted ... Each offers its own challenge to thought and endeavor, and presents its own potential value."[120] Democratic individuals willingly and actively unsettle their habits and beliefs and increase their wisdom in a world lacking eternal truth by interacting with a wide variety of ideas and perspectives. Dewey places particular importance on preserving cultural pluralism, stating that when any of the "many sorts of independent vigorous life" in a diverse society are prevented from maintaining their way of life (provided they are not "dangerous to the welfare of other peoples or groups"), that society loses

---

[116] Robert Talisse, *A Pragmatist Philosophy of Democracy* (New York, NY: Routledge, 2007), 37.

[117] Ibid., 51.

[118] Robert Talisse, "Can Democracy Be a Way of Life? Deweyan Democracy and the Problem of Pluralism," *Transactions of the Charles S. Peirce Society* 39, no. 1 (2003): 13.

[119] Good and Garrison, "Traces of Hegelian *Bildung* in Dewey's Philosophy," 57, 63.

[120] LW5: 272.

out on potential sources of wisdom that should be at its service.[121] Far from dismissing the existence of an inevitable plurality of worldviews, Dewey "welcomes a clash of 'incompatible opinions'"[122] as integral to his democratic way of life: "giving differences a chance to show themselves because of the belief that the expression of difference is not only a right of the other persons but is a means of enriching one's own life-experience, is inherent in the democratic personal way of life."[123] And as we have seen, when structural social inequality obscures the presence of a plurality of worldviews, it is incumbent upon individuals to combat that inequality in order to allow pluralism to more genuinely manifest itself.

All the same, it is undoubtedly true that certain values and beliefs are not consistent with democratic individualism. For instance, if a particular community holds that its members are not to be exposed to diverse ways of life and are to fulfill a predetermined function within that community's customary social structure, then that community's values clearly do not cohere with Dewey's standards. In other words, values and beliefs that are (on the terms I have laid out here) simply *undemocratic* cannot be neatly reconciled with Dewey's democratic individualism. It seems unlikely, however, that these values and beliefs are specifically what Talisse hopes to defend, since they are reflective of a particularly *communitarian* mind-set, and it is precisely communitarianism that Talisse links to Dewey, by charging that Dewey's democratic way of life requires communities to form individuals according to a predetermined path of development.[124] My analysis in this chapter has shown why that charge is not justified. I will address communitarianism in detail in Chapter 5 (since the connections made between Dewey and communitarian thought have gone beyond Talisse alone), but it is surely ironic that it would be these quite-communitarian values and beliefs that are buttressed by Talisse's argument.[125] Still, it is a serious question how a democratic society should react to communal practices and forms of life that are inconsistent with democratic principles. My depiction of Dewey's theory indicates that

---

[121] MW10: 286–91. Shane Ralston, also responding to Talisse, has provided a Deweyan account of attempts to accommodate Muslim women wearing the niqab (veil) within Canadian law requiring voters to show their face when voting; see Shane Ralston, "In Defense of Democracy as a Way of Life: A Reply to Talisse's Pluralist Objection," *Transactions of the Charles S. Peirce Society* 44, no. 4 (2008): 645–6.

[122] Dewey, *Freedom and Culture*, 98.

[123] Dewey, "Creative Democracy," 244.

[124] Talisse, "Can Democracy Be a Way of Life?," 1–21.

[125] Certain communitarians have claimed that communitarian principles are, in fact, truly *democratic*; I will address these arguments in Chapter 5.

a society is, in fact, not democratic to the degree that individuals are caught in situations that rob them of the opportunity to control their own development. The idea that it is democratic to affirm undemocratic communal practices actually goes hand-in-hand with the assumption that democracy is simply a set of political procedures and that the *social* realm should not be held to democratic standards, which is an assumption I am disputing in this book. Deweyan democracy requires that we pursue the social conditions that allow individuals to govern their own lives. However, because Dewey's theory carries such a significant ethical component, individuals themselves also carry heavy responsibility for dealing with the difficulties of governing their lives. If an individual, for instance, has genuine opportunity to govern her life but refuses to do so, preferring instead to uncritically abide by inherited values and beliefs, Dewey's principles do not suggest that there can be any attempt to force that individual to think and act differently. If an individual simply refuses any possibility of separating from her inherited beliefs and denies the possible validity of any alternative worldview, there is nothing in Dewey's work that calls for her to be somehow forced to take on new beliefs. By acting the way she does, she can be said to be acting within the *negative freedom* that Dewey, again, absolutely sees as necessary and wants to preserve. Genuine freedom, though, is for Dewey defined by *positive freedom*. This freedom is often obstructed by iniquitous social conditions, but even with the proper conditions, an individual may still avoid the ethical requirements for actively realizing her unique self in the face of a changing, interconnected reality. If we follow Dewey, we do not have to in some way force her into a different life, but we also do not have to say her behavior is *democratic*. So while democratic individualism may not be compatible with all values and principles, I do maintain that it is absolutely conducive (and certainly not antithetical) to a plurality of worldviews. Dewey indeed associates individual self-government in large part with an active interaction with that plurality of worldviews.

Before we finish, let us briefly remark on the role of political institutions in creating the social conditions for democratic individualism. I will address this topic more fully in Chapter 2, but can note here how the political realm is itself crucial to democracy at the individual and social levels. As noted earlier, Good and Garrison describe how the state must allow individuals to "[determine] their own identities" and must "provide social environments that facilitate *Bildung*." Dewey indeed argues that "[t]he political and governmental phase of democracy is a means, the best means so far found, for realizing ends that lie in the wide

domain of human relationships and the development of human personality. [Democracy] is ... a way of life, social and individual."[126] As democratic individualism carries a responsibility to combat aspects of society
that obstruct the possibilities for individuals' self-government, there is
specifically a need to pressure the state to act in favor of the disadvantaged rather than the advantaged. The state must be pressed into helping
to develop social conditions that in turn make democratic individualism
more possible. As Dewey says, "A certain amount of specific change in
legislation and administration is required in order to supply the conditions under which other changes may take place in nonpolitical ways."[127]
If governing institutions are to be pressured in this way, it, of course,
also helps greatly if those institutions allow more than the voices of the
powerful to be heard on policy matters. The process of democratizing
these political institutions will be addressed in Chapter 3. A political system is thus not merely derivative of the individual and social levels for
Dewey, since democratic individualism, and a democratized society, can
be aided greatly by action from the political realm. But still, such political action cannot be expected to take place in a vacuum either, without
democratic changes taking place at the individual and social levels. Civil
rights legislation in the 1960s, for example, involved government action
that extended into social spheres, such as housing and private business,
in order to help remove barriers to African Americans' access to housing,
jobs, and commercial goods, and thus to fight barriers to their opportunity to realize their individuality and control their lives. This legislation
would not have come, though, without democratic changes that were
also underway as a result of individuals' actions to combat racial inequality. Society's "collective wisdom" on racial matters was itself evolving – in
large part due to protests and other forms of direct action that sought to
combat structural racism – and political institutions were influenced by
this evolution. In Dewey's view, it is both true that the state should help
provide the conditions for democratic individualism and that the state
cannot do this without democratic individualism already expressing itself
to some degree: "It is only by the choice and the active endeavor of many
individuals that this result can be effected."[128] The willingness of individuals themselves to critique and challenge iniquitous aspects of our society
remains essential to democracy's development.

---

[126] LW11: 217.
[127] Dewey, *Individualism Old and New*, 113–14.
[128] Dewey, *Freedom and Culture*, 151.

We must remember throughout this book how democracy for Dewey is never completely achieved: "Since things do not attain such fulfillment but are in actuality distracted and interfered with, democracy in this sense is not a fact and never will be."[129] When we speak of democratic individualism depending on the presence of a democratic society, and vice versa, and of the state being required to both democratize society and to draw upon democratic qualities in society, it may seem we are describing a multilayered vicious circle, where each element in democracy (individual, social, political) is depending on the other elements, but none of the elements is in existence. But if we keep in mind Dewey's conception of democracy as being in a process of unending development, in which the various elements of democracy are never fully achieved but can move in a democratic direction, this apparent problem dissipates. Democratic qualities that do exist in current society give room for democratic individualism, and democratic behavior from individuals helps create democratic qualities in society. Concurrently, the state can function democratically by helping create conditions for democratic social relations that are composed of democratic individuals, and it can be moved to function this way by the actions of democratic individuals who form democratic social relations. None of the individual, social, or political elements of this overall development comes *first*. There is not one that we can say is primary and foundational while the others are merely secondary and derivative. Each element is essential, and on Dewey's terms, each one is already present to a certain degree, but each is also very far from fully achieved. Dewey does not expect us to ever see the complete achievement of democracy, but he does hold that each element of democracy can be further developed and can thereby aid the development of the other elements.

DEMOCRACY AT THE INDIVIDUAL LEVEL

This chapter has examined Dewey's idea of a democratic individual way of life and has shown the vital qualities that a democratic individual must exhibit. I have so far characterized democratic individualism as a Platonic attempt to harmonize the individual with a democratic "universe of spiritual relations." Given the changing circumstances, impacts from remote forces, and lack of stable truths facing modern individuals,

---

[129] Dewey, *Public and Its Problems*, 148.

Dewey calls on individuals to live democratically by continuously growing through varied experience and active engagement with diverse others. This allows individuals to direct their own development, as opposed to futilely attempting to isolate themselves from novel conditions and unfamiliar others. By becoming democratic individuals, Dewey argues they can fulfill their unique potential and contribute to the wise functioning of society, two goals Plato aims to achieve through ideas of fixed truth and of an exclusive few capable of accessing this truth. Additionally, I have connected Dewey's democratic individualism with the German *Bildung* tradition, which helps illustrate how a democratic individual must be committed to social reform in the midst of deeply unequal social conditions. Individuals are to critique, and make effort to help remedy, structural inequalities that leave many unable to govern their lives or contribute their distinct experiences to society's collective wisdom. This is integral to the development of social conditions that are crucial for an individual's own self-determined growth, and for that of others. Through this analysis, we can thus illuminate the individual element of Deweyan democracy and understand the intrinsic connection between individuals' self-government and a genuinely equal society.

The fact that Dewey promotes such an ethical standard may concern some readers. It may appear that he is unnecessarily limiting and regulating individuals' behavior, which is the essence of Talisse's critique of Dewey. I would say first, though, that any theory that conceives of a social element of democracy cannot avoid addressing the ethical requirements of the individuals who compose that society. If we are not satisfied with simply seeing democracy as a set of political procedures and/ or a type of political debate and instead require the presence of certain kinds of social relations, we cannot avoid discussing the conduct of the individuals who comprise those social relations. Further, there is hardly a democratic theory that allows individuals to simply act however they want with no substantial restrictions. (This will become clearer as we engage with various democratic theories in Chapters 4 and 5.) I maintain that Dewey is not at all imposing onerous limitations on how individuals can act. I also hold that he provides an effective case for how an individual's own self-government can be buttressed by her efforts to promote the equality of other individuals.

On the topic of *political* democracy, Dewey writes that "[w]herever it has fallen it was too exclusively political in nature. It had not become part of the bone and blood of the people in daily conduct of its life. Democratic forms were limited to Parliament, elections and combats between parties ... unless democratic habits of thought and action are part of the fiber of a people, political democracy is insecure. It can not stand in isolation. It must be buttressed by the presence of democratic methods in all social relationships."[130] By bringing democracy down to the individual level, Dewey leads democratic thinkers toward focusing on whether individuals are genuinely exercising control over their lives, rather than on the presence of a particular political machinery alone. Forms of structural social inequality obstruct individuals' self-government even when political institutions do not authorize those inequalities. When women and racial minorities, for example, have thoroughly less opportunity to realize their individuality and to control their lives than do men and whites, respectively, and when the lives of women and racial minorities are thereby often left essentially under the control of men and whites, then we would say that our society is characterized by structural inequalities. These inequalities, according to Dewey's thinking, limit the possibilities for self-government for all involved, even the advantaged. For Dewey, government should help overcome obstacles to individuals' freedom and equality, but democracy still depends largely on individuals exhibiting democratic behavior – expanding their experience through diverse interaction and inviting the unique development of others. There is more to be said about the democratic individual way of life, and the next chapter will expand this discussion by exploring Dewey's relationship to the other philosopher he holds in similar esteem as Plato: Hegel.

[130] LW11: 225.

2

The Hegelian Development of
Deweyan Democracy

While expressing his admiration for Plato, Dewey also declares, "Were it possible for me to be a devotee of any system, I still should believe that there is greater richness and greater variety of insight in Hegel than in any other single systematic philosopher."[1] He attests to the enduring influence Hegel has had on him, stating that "acquaintance with Hegel has left a permanent deposit" on his thinking.[2] Dewey's relationship to Hegel, in my view, is pivotal to understanding the entirety of his democratic thought. And, particularly for my purposes, it is crucial for seeing how Dewey takes the process of overcoming structural social inequality as integral to democracy. In this chapter, I will draw on Hegel to analyze each of the individual, social, and political elements of Deweyan democracy. We have established that democratic individualism is defined mainly by continuous development. It is a standard that calls for individuals to govern their lives by continuously expanding their experience, which requires an active interaction with diverse others and a willingness to unsettle one's own current habits and beliefs. We have seen how this individual self-development is bound up with the presence of a society that is free of rigid, structural inequality and how political institutions play a necessary role in helping to overcome that inequality. None of the individual, social, or political elements of Dewey's theory are (or are expected to ever be) fully achieved, but rather each is itself in a process of development that

[1] John Dewey, "From Absolutism to Experimentalism," in *Contemporary American Philosophy*, Vol. II, eds. George P. Adams and Wm. Pepperell Montague (New York, NY: The Macmillan Company, 1930), 21.
[2] Ibid.

is interrelated with the development of the other elements. The nature of the development in each of these elements is greatly illuminated by engaging with Hegel. Hegel, quite famously, seeks to present all entities that constitute our human experience as existing in a process of development. Dewey's depiction of democracy as itself in a process of unending development is, I argue, a fundamentally Hegelian move.

At the individual level, Hegel is excited by what he sees as the possibility of a genuinely "scientific" approach to human experience. In essence, this approach requires individuals to "see themselves" in what "negates" them in the course of their experience. In other words, individuals see the novel, alien objects of experience that they, as subjects of experience, inevitably confront as essential to their own development. They see such objects (e.g., new ideas, unexpected situations, unfamiliar other individuals) as part of their own selves, even though these objects take away the stability and comfort individuals feel before they confront such an object. To think and act scientifically – to see themselves in the objects that negate their prior "stable" selves – is surely a challenging standard, and Hegel concedes that it works against more comforting and familiar ways of thinking. He remarks that "[t]he standpoint of consciousness which knows objects in their antithesis to itself, and itself in antithesis to them, is for Science the antithesis of its own standpoint."[3] To become scientific, it appears that the "natural consciousness" has to try to "walk on its head"[4] by taking what seems to obstruct the individual as actually essential to the individual's development. If an individual can meet this challenge, though, and intelligently reconstruct herself through active interaction with the alien objects of experience that negate her, this individual can further determine and realize her own unique identity. Dewey, for his part, holds that "the future of democracy is allied with spread of the scientific attitude."[5] He says that it is by thinking and acting scientifically that individuals – who must cope with changing, increasingly interconnected circumstances – can effectively govern their lives. By reconstructing their habits and principles (and, indeed, reconstructing themselves) in interaction with the ever-changing, never-finished situations of experience, individuals can intelligently develop themselves and exercise (albeit provisional) control over their lives. Neither Hegel nor Dewey, though, sees individuals exhibiting the scientific mind-set to

[3] G.W.F. Hegel, *The Phenomenology of Spirit*, translated by A.V. Miller (New York, NY: Oxford University Press, [1807] 1977), 15.
[4] Ibid.
[5] John Dewey, *Freedom and Culture* (New York, NY: G. P. Putnam's Sons, 1939), 148.

nearly the degree he would like. For both of them, this is partly due to the sheer difficulty involved with approaching experience in the scientific way, but it is also due to oppressive qualities of society that prevent individuals from governing their lives.

Hegel and Dewey each see how such a scientific mind-set, and the self-government it entails, depends on social conditions that actually provide meaningful opportunity for individuals to direct their own paths of development. Both thinkers understand that society can bring significant threats to individuals' self-government and that the specific threats we must deal with can evolve over time. For instance, the extreme poverty and alienating work experiences that are characteristic of modern capitalism are unique historical problems, not identical to threats to self-government that were pressing prior to capitalism's emergence, and these newer threats surely hinder the possibilities for individuals to exhibit the scientific mind-set and realize their unique identities in the way Hegel and Dewey describe. The achievement of social conditions that are conducive to self-government is thus a matter of continuous development. Further, the political realm has a necessary role, for Dewey as well as for Hegel, in working to achieve these social conditions, and so political institutions must continuously develop in their efforts to remedy the evolving social threats to individuals' self-government. As I will show, Hegel sees a state as "actual" – rather than merely "existing" – to the degree that this state overcomes the evolving obstacles to freedom (extreme poverty, for example) generated by an unregulated "civil society." The state's actuality, then, is in a process of continuous, indeterminate development. For Dewey, when social conditions are preventing many individuals from exercising control over their lives, it is similarly incumbent upon government to act to help overcome these conditions. The democratic character of a political system, as with Hegelian "actuality," depends on its efforts to fight pernicious forms of inequality within society. This democratic character is always uncertain and never perfectly achieved, because that character is heavily determined by the government's responses to constantly changing social conditions. For instance, Dewey sees that if a government only acts to preserve individuals' rights against intrusion into their lives by the government and by other individuals (i.e., negative freedom), then that government is not adequately developing in response to new circumstances and problems that make negative freedom insufficient for allowing individuals to effectively govern themselves. A government, on Dewey's terms, cannot be seen as a neutral entity in the face of structural social inequality. If a government does not (or perhaps cannot, due to constitutional restrictions) act to overcome this inequality, it is indirectly reinforcing the inequality by denying those who suffer from it an effective means for redress. Surely, the democratic character of political institutions also depends for Dewey on whether their decisions can be influenced by more than just the socially powerful, and that topic will be the focus of Chapter 3. But given the fact of severe social inequality, Dewey's principles hold that political institutions must contribute to individuals' self-government (the essence of democracy) by helping to overcome that inequality.

This analysis of the Hegelian qualities of Deweyan democracy will culminate in a comparison of Dewey's democratic theory with that of Richard Rorty. Rorty claimed to be closely following Dewey while he reinvigorated the American pragmatist tradition in the late 1970s and early 1980s, but I will show that because Rorty diverges significantly from Hegelian principles, he winds up with a conception of democracy that misses the most valuable features of Dewey's democratic thinking. Rorty specifically distances himself from any philosophy that commits to "scientific" thinking, and he maintains that when philosophers attempt to be scientific, they are guilty of searching for fixed, unchanging truth. Dewey, whose pragmatism is deeply influenced by Hegel, would deny that he is searching for fixed truth, but he does hold that scientific thinking can give us at least provisional truth about the world and about how society and politics can develop from here in order to be said to be "progressing." Conversely, Rorty defines pragmatism as having a mainly "negative" purpose: he sees pragmatism as *not* systematic, *not* constructive, *not* rigorous, and *not* "scientific," and he finds pragmatism's value to lie in its use of "satires, parodies, aphorisms" to tear down philosophies that seek to be systematic, constructive, and scientific.[6] I cannot claim in this book to fully dispel Rorty's doubt as to whether there is any kind of provisional truth that comes from Hegel's and Dewey's scientific principles. But I will show that Rorty, who sees himself as going even further than Hegel and Dewey in rejecting a reliance on fixed concepts, ends up giving us a basically fixed conception of democracy. Because he does not want to philosophically justify any specific idea about how the world should develop further, he mainly seeks to buttress the negative freedom that has characterized already-existing "democracies." He says pragmatism's obliteration of truth claims is simply useful for someone

---

[6] Richard Rorty, *Philosophy and the Mirror of Nature* (Princeton, NJ: Princeton University Press, 1979), 369.

who is personally committed, as he is, to a democratic political system and its negative liberties (liberties which, relatedly, he thinks have been effective at protecting individuals from having truth claims imposed on them). Democracy, therefore, exists where negative freedom is present and does not require further development in response to changing conditions. Rorty at times seems aware of how there might be something insufficient about a commitment to negative freedom – particularly in the face of such problems as extreme economic inequality, alienating workplaces, etc. – and he does make some reference to the need to achieve social conditions that allow for *positive freedom*. In order to do that, though, he cannot avoid committing to some kind of philosophical justification for how the world should develop from here. Dewey's Hegelian-"scientific" principles, I would say, provide the (suitably modest) philosophical justification for why negative freedom is necessary and should be preserved, but is insufficient in the face of our new conditions, and why democracy must develop toward a commitment to positive freedom.

DEWEY'S PERMANENT HEGELIAN DEPOSIT

Until recently, the common belief regarding Dewey and Hegel was that Dewey abandoned Hegelian principles at an early point in his career during the 1890s. This belief goes at least as far back as Morton White's 1943 statement that Dewey decided to "throw Hegel overboard"[7] and remained the dominant view through the 1990s. David Fott makes the claim that "[i]n the two decades surrounding the turn of the [20th] century Dewey's thought made a gradual yet obvious shift away from Hegelian idealism and toward pragmatism."[8] And, in fact, the idea that Dewey must have abandoned Hegel in order to become a pragmatist is the dominant theme underlying the depictions of Dewey's break from Hegel. George Dykhuizen, D. C. Phillips, and Andrew Reck each declare that Dewey had to turn away from Hegel and toward William James to develop the idea of an empirical self actively adjusting to a precarious environment.[9] H. S. Thayer points more toward Charles Sanders Peirce as

[7] Morton White, *The Origin of Dewey's Instrumentalism* (New York, NY: Columbia University Press, 1943), 151.

[8] David Fott, *John Dewey: America's Philosopher of Democracy* (Lanham, MD: Rowman & Littlefield, 1998), 21–2.

[9] George Dykhuizen, *The Life and Mind of John Dewey* (Carbondale, IL: Southern Illinois University Press, 1973), 68; D. C. Phillips, "James, Dewey, and the Reflex Arc," *Journal of the History of Ideas* 32, no. 4 (1971): 565, 567; Andrew Reck, "The Influence of William

the thinker who led Dewey to "free himself from Hegelianism."[10] James and Peirce, along with Dewey, are seen as the founders of American pragmatism, and it was believed for many years that Dewey could not have aligned with them without discarding Hegel.

Since the turn of the century, though, scholars have increasingly come to the conclusion that Dewey remained indebted to Hegel throughout his career. James Good, in rejecting the idea that Dewey abandoned Hegel in the 1890s, explains that what Dewey actually rejected was the reading of Hegel by the British neo-Hegelians (e.g., T. H. Green) which emphasized the (impossible) attainment of a "transcendent absolute"; he further argues that Dewey's conception of individual experience is an adaptation of Hegel's dialectical interaction of subject and object in which both terms "are always changed in and by the process."[11] Good also reveals why some of Dewey's critical language toward Hegel in his later works, particularly during World War I, should not be taken as a rejection of Hegel's fundamental principles.[12] John Shook, quite similarly to Good, provides an account of Dewey's break from the neo-Hegelians, rather than Hegel himself[13]; Larry Hickman describes how "Dewey's Hegel was historicist, instrumentalist, and functionalist"[14]; and Richard Bernstein states that, for both Hegel and Dewey, "Subject and object are … *functional* distinctions within the dynamics of a unified developing experience."[15] Jim Garrison focuses on their shared emphasis on continuously expanding experience,[16] and he and Good together stress Dewey and Hegel's common principle that diversity of individual development is

---

James on John Dewey in Psychology," *Transactions of the Charles S. Peirce Society* 20, no. 2 (1984): 87–8, 94, 102.

[10] H. S. Thayer, *Meaning and Action: A Critical History of Pragmatism*, 2nd ed. (Indianapolis, IN: Hackett Publishing Company, 1981), 166–7.

[11] James Good, *A Search for Unity in Diversity: The "Permanent Hegelian Deposit" in the Philosophy of John Dewey* (Lanham, MD: Lexington Books, 2006), 130, 144. See also, James Good, "Dewey's 'Permanent Hegelian Deposit': A Reply to Hickman and Alexander," *Transactions of the Charles S. Peirce Society* 44, no. 4 (2008): 577–602; and John Shook and James Good, *John Dewey's Philosophy of Spirit, with the 1897 Lecture on Hegel* (New York, NY: Fordham University Press, 2010).

[12] James Good, "John Dewey's 'Permanent Hegelian Deposit' and the Exigencies of War," *Journal of the History of Philosophy* 44, no. 2 (2006): 310.

[13] John Shook, *Dewey's Empirical Theory of Knowledge and Reality* (Nashville: Vanderbilt University Press, 2000), 154.

[14] Larry Hickman, "Dewey's Hegel: A Search for Unity in Diversity, or Diversity as the Growth of Unity?," *Transactions of the Charles S. Peirce Society* 44, no. 4 (2008): 571.

[15] Richard Bernstein, *The Pragmatic Turn* (Cambridge: Polity Press, 2010), 92.

[16] Jim Garrison, "The 'Permanent Deposit' of Hegelian Thought in Dewey's Theory of Inquiry," *Educational Theory* 56, no. 1 (2006): 5.

the "engine of social development."[17] For Tom Rockmore, the important point is that both Hegel and Dewey "rejected Kant's a priori approach to knowledge in favor of an a posteriori epistemological strategy."[18] And for Torjus Midtgarden, we can use Dewey's Hegelian deposit to gain a more solid understanding of Dewey's process of social reform by viewing this process as moving through a stage of struggle/mediation and resulting in a wider resolution/unity.[19] Increasingly, the question for scholars is not whether Dewey remained a Hegelian, but in what ways precisely his Hegelianism can illuminate his mature philosophy.[20]

This recent scholarship on Dewey and Hegel has clarified important aspects of Dewey's thought, particularly regarding his depiction of individual experience. I will expand this discussion by exploring the Hegelian qualities of Dewey's theory of democracy. I will use Hegel to illuminate the qualities of Dewey's democratic individual way of life and show how the social and political elements of democracy develop alongside, and are interrelated with, this individual element. Through the course of my discussion, it should also become clear why Peirce's claim that "the whole function of thought is to produce habits of action"[21] and James's claim that "[p]ragmatism unstiffens all our theories, limbers them up and sets each one at work"[22] are hardly incompatible with the core of Hegel's thought. There should then be no trouble in seeing how Dewey could have become a pragmatist without giving up Hegelianism.

HEGEL

In order to explore the principles of Hegel's philosophy, we will have to engage with Hegel's rather tortuous language. Nonetheless, I will

---

[17] James Good and Jim Garrison, "Traces of Hegelian *Bildung* in Dewey's Philosophy," in *John Dewey and Continental Philosophy*, ed. Paul Fairfield (Carbondale, IL: Southern Illinois University Press, 2010), 47.

[18] Tom Rockmore, "Dewey, Hegel, and Knowledge after Kant," in *John Dewey and Continental Philosophy*, ed. Paul Fairfield (Carbondale, IL: Southern Illinois University Press, 2010), 38.

[19] Torjus Midtgarden, "The Hegelian Legacy in Dewey's Social and Political Philosophy, 1915–1920," *Transactions of the Charles S. Peirce Society* 47, no. 4 (2011): 372–3.

[20] I have also sought to contribute to the understanding of Dewey's Hegelianism, specifically in regard to education; see Jeff Jackson, "Reconstructing Dewey: Dialectics and Democratic Education," *Education and Culture* 28, no. 1 (2012): 62–77.

[21] Charles S. Peirce, "How to Make Our Ideas Clear," *Popular Science Monthly* 12 (1878): 286–302.

[22] William James, *Pragmatism: A New Name for Some Old Ways of Thinking* (New York, NY: Longmans, Green, and Co., 1907), 53.

attempt to make Hegel's thinking as clear as possible before I show how Hegelian principles illuminate Dewey's pragmatism and democratic theory. I should also note that I am not attempting to give a comprehensive account of Hegel's thought here, but only to examine the elements of his thought that I see as crucial to the understanding of Dewey. As such, I do not aim to provide the *one* possible interpretation of Hegel (which would require a book of its own), but to show what it is in Hegel's philosophy that appears to inspire Dewey's thinking on democracy.

In *The Phenomenology of Spirit*, Hegel depicts experience as a dialectical process in which a subject grows and advances by encountering a novel object – an obstacle that initially seems to obstruct the development of that subject – and by turning that object into an entity that instead promotes the subject's development. The subject grows primarily because, by struggling with the object, it expands its own identity through the experience of that struggle. Hegel states that "experience is the name we give to just this movement, in which the immediate, the unexperienced, i.e., the abstract ... becomes alienated from itself and then returns to itself from this alienation, and is only then revealed for the first time in its actuality and truth."[23] If we focus on the human individual as a subject of experience, we would say that, on Hegel's terms, an individual cannot expect to go on interacting with the world without having her past, stable habits disrupted by alien circumstances. This confrontation with a novel object of experience "negates" the subject of experience, that is, takes the subject out of an initial "simplicity" and stimulates it to more expanded development. An object of experience facing a subject could be another individual, a task, an idea, or any situation that takes the subject out of simple, habitual interaction with its surroundings. The challenge for the subject, then, is to reconstruct itself by engaging with the alien object – or, the "other" that "contradicts" it – and making that object into a *positive* part of the subject's own development, thus further actualizing the subject's own developing identity. An individual who is negated by such an object must reflect on how her previous habits must change and act on that change in order to overcome the negation and "return into simplicity" in expanded form.[24] As Hegel puts it, "The living creature is always exposed to danger, always bears within itself an other, but can endure this

[23] Hegel, *Phenomenology of Spirit*, 21.
[24] Ibid., 12.

contradiction which the inorganic cannot. But life is also the resolving of this contradiction."[25]

In *The Science of Logic*, Hegel connects the possibility for intelligent action with instances "when the content that motivates a subject to action is drawn out of its immediate unity with the subject and is made to stand before it as an object."[26] This immediate unity between a subject and object, the breaking up of this unity in the course of experience, and the work then involved in reconstructing a substantial unity between subject and object are immensely important for Hegel. Individual subjects might be inclined to see alien objects as fully separate from themselves and might wish to just not encounter them. This, however, is a futile wish. But if an individual can see an underlying unity between herself and these objects and can see the possibility of bringing those objects back – through intelligent action – into a meaningful unity with her own development, she can rationally determine her own identity rather than seeking fruitlessly to avoid novel objects. What's more, an individual can in this way exercise her own unique effect on the objects she confronts; for Hegel, just as subjects are defined by continuous development through interaction with objects, objects are defined by continuous development through interaction with subjects, and so an object's own identity is expanded through the particular subject's unique interaction with it.[27] Individuals have the capacity to self-consciously transform the world even as it transforms them. To unlock this capacity, though, requires what Hegel calls the "scientific" approach to the world. Hegelian science is defined by the recognition of an underlying unity between entities that appear to radically oppose one another. An individual acts scientifically by seeing the objects that seem to be merely "other" as actually part of her (constantly developing) self and by taking on the difficulty and struggle involved with making that underlying unity between herself and the object into a genuine unity, that is, by actively interacting with the object and bringing it into harmony with her own development. Hegel says that "[p]ure self-recognition in absolute otherness, this Aether *as such*, is the ground and soil of Science or *knowledge in general*."[28] Put another way,

[25] G.W.F. Hegel, *Philosophy of Nature: Part Two of the Encyclopedia of the Philosophical Sciences*, translated by A.V. Miller (Oxford: Oxford University Press, [1830] 2004), 274.

[26] G.W.F. Hegel, *The Science of Logic*, translated and edited by George di Giovanni (Cambridge: Cambridge University Press, [1812] 2010), 17.

[27] Hegel, *Phenomenology of Spirit*, 54.

[28] Ibid., 14.

the 'I' already possesses *in itself*, or in principle, difference within itself, or, in other words, since it is *in itself* the unity of itself and its Other, it is necessarily related to the difference existent in the object and immediately reflected out of this its Other into itself. The 'I' overlaps or overarches, therefore, the actual difference from itself, is at home with itself in this its Other, and in every intuition remains self-certain.[29]

The scientific mind-set brings recognition of the underlying unity between an individual and the objects of experience she confronts and a willingness to take on the hard work of experiencing all that the object can add to her development. Hegel states that "[s]cientific cognition ... demands surrender to the life of the object"[30] – that is, allowing oneself to develop in unforeseen ways through interaction with the object – and continuous testing of one's habits and principles in the face of inevitably changing circumstances, rather than merely "assuming something as familiar, and accepting it on that account."[31] Because there is no way to keep oneself in a fixed, unchanging condition, Hegel is most impressed by individuals who see their own selves as in a process of unending actualization and who intelligently determine their developing identities.

This capacity to intelligently realize one's developing identity, and to self-consciously affect the objects one confronts, is in Hegel's view the uniquely human capacity. In fact, it signifies a genuinely human freedom. Hegel explains that "the 'I' sets itself over against itself, makes itself its own object and returns from this difference."[32] An individual, in other words, not only can see the objects she confronts as part of her own development, but she can take her own development as an object, that is, she can cognize herself as a developing being and self-consciously act with her development in mind. This relates to Hegel's famous distinction between a being *in-itself* and a being *for-itself*. An individual is a being in-itself simply on account of existing, and there is really nothing more an individual need do to have this status than be alive. An individual is a being for-itself, though, by cognizing how her own self develops through interaction with objects outside of her immediate being. She thereby sees her own development and can think about it and evaluate it, and so her own being exists "for herself." Hegel declares that "[w]e have the most obvious example of being-for-itself in the *I* ... Saying 'I' is the expression

---

[29] G.W.F. Hegel, *Philosophy of Mind: Part Three of the Encyclopedia of the Philosophical Sciences*, translated by A.V. Miller (Oxford: Oxford University Press, [1830] 1971), 154.

[30] Hegel, *Phenomenology of Spirit*, 32.

[31] Ibid., 18.

[32] Hegel, *Philosophy of Mind*, 11.

of an infinite and at the same time a negative relation to oneself. It can be said that human beings distinguish themselves from animals and hence from nature generally by knowing themselves [in each case] as an I."[33] Unlike animals, human beings can comprehend themselves as in a process of development and can self-consciously act so as to further their development. Individuals are free in a uniquely human way, then, to the extent that they cognize their development and self-consciously move their development in self-determined directions: "I am free ... when my existence depends upon myself. This self-contained existence of Spirit is none other than self-consciousness—consciousness of one's own being."[34] This freedom is what Hegel's philosophy and political thought are fundamentally pursuing.

To help make this rather abstract discussion more concrete, let us take the example of an individual in the teaching profession, an example frequently used by Dewey for showing the challenges involved with self-governed development, and the harmful consequences brought about when an individual is plainly prevented from controlling her development (I will come back to this example later). On Hegel's terms, even an individual with substantial prior experience in the activity of teaching may become lost and ineffective in her work if she assumes her work will bring no unique obstacles while she further engages in the activity (i.e., if she tries to avoid "surrender to the life of the object"). An experienced teacher will likely have developed many habits and principles from her interactions with the objects of experience brought by teaching. But although her principles can certainly help guide her future teaching activity, those principles must be kept open for further testing and development, because the experience of teaching will likely continue presenting novel objects – unique students, new classroom scenarios, etc. – that require her earlier principles to be revised and expanded. For Hegel, such a continuously expanding principle "contains all [prior] moments as superseded within itself,"[35] "not only not losing anything through its dialectical advance ... but, on the contrary, carrying with itself all that it has gained, inwardly enriched and compressed."[36] The teacher would not

---

[33] G.W.F. Hegel, *Encyclopedia of the Philosophical Sciences in Basic Outline, Part I: Science of Logic*, translated and edited by Klaus Brinkmann and Daniel Dahlstrom (Cambridge: Cambridge University Press, [1830] 2010), 152–3.

[34] G.W.F. Hegel, *The Philosophy of History*, translated by J. Sibree (Mineola, NY: Dover Publications, [1837] 2004), 17.

[35] Hegel, *Phenomenology of Spirit*, 108.

[36] Hegel, *Science of Logic*, 750.

then be seeking in futility to avoid novel objects of experience brought about by teaching. She would be continuing to exercise her own self-conscious effect on those objects and would thus be governing her life by transforming the objects as those objects also transform her.

We begin to see here, as we saw in Chapter 1, how individuals' self-government is bound up with the presence of particular social conditions. When individuals must work in conditions that do not allow them to exercise their own unique effect on the objects of experience they confront, then the possibilities for self-government are severely hindered. Also, it is essential for Hegel that an individual interact with genuinely equal other individuals if she herself is to become self-governing. As noted earlier, other individuals are, of course, among the novel objects of experience that an individual subject inevitably confronts. Hegel's conception of free self-development thus entails a willingness to interact with these others and to allow oneself to grow in unforeseen ways in the course of such interactions. And Hegel builds a famous case for why interacting with equal others is more conducive to an individual's self-governed development than is attempting to keep others in subordinate positions. In his lord-bondsman narrative, Hegel argues that "[s]*elf-consciousness achieves its satisfaction only in another self-consciousness.*"[37] His claim is that "[s]elf-consciousness exists in and for itself when, and by the fact that, it so exists for another; that is, it exists only in being acknowledged,"[38] which means that although an individual can cognize herself as a developing being and observe and evaluate her own development, the meaning of her development becomes more genuinely confirmed when it is acknowledged by other individuals. Hegel specifies, though, that this acknowledgment must come from equal, independent others, rather than from others who are unequal and who thus may not be free to provide genuinely independent confirmation of another's development. This leads Hegel to seek a "unity of the different independent self-consciousnesses which, in their opposition, enjoy perfect freedom and independence," and to explore what he calls "the process of Recognition."[39] A relation of mutual recognition is one in which equal individuals, neither of whom is forced to recognize the other due to being in a state of dependence, each freely recognize the other, and thus each contributes to the other's development while seeing their own development expanded through this

---

[37] Hegel, *Phenomenology of Spirit*, 110.
[38] Ibid., 111.
[39] Ibid., 110, 111.

interaction. The equal status of the other allows for the acknowledgment the other provides to be genuine; and further, by interacting with others who are themselves able to actualize their own unique development, an individual is promoting the expansion of her own development because the others she confronts are more likely to provide novel ideas and perspectives. Hegel's story of lord and bondsman, on the other hand, shows the consequences of a relation where individuals are deeply unequal, with "one being only *recognized*, the other only *recognizing*."[40] Both individuals are harmed by this inequality, in that both are denied the possibility of expanded self-development that comes with acting as an autonomous subject interacting with equal others. In a surprising twist, in fact, Hegel argues that the lord's development is hampered to a greater degree than the bondsman's, largely because the lord can only receive forced recognition from a subordinate, and because the fact that the bondsman does all of the lord's work means that the lord cannot even see his own individuality reflected in work he performs upon objects.[41]

While responding to the idea that individuals are most free when they are unrelated to others, Hegel grants that "[l]imitation is certainly produced by Society and the State, but it is a limitation of the mere brute emotions and rude instincts ... We should on the contrary look upon such limitation as the indispensable proviso of emancipation. Society and the State are the very conditions in which Freedom is realized."[42] Existing in social relations with others is essential to a genuinely human freedom. But Hegel certainly does not think that any type of social relation is conducive to freedom, and to the extent we have a society that obstructs freedom, he calls for direct alteration of that society, particularly through the actions of the state. In *The Philosophy of Right*, Hegel declares that there are three stages of "ethical life" – the family, civil society, and the state – that are each necessary for individuals' freedom. He remarks that "in a family, one's frame of mind is to have self-consciousness of one's individuality within this unity as the absolute essence of oneself, with the result that one is in it not as an independent person but as a member,"[43] meaning that in the family, an individual is connected with others by immediate bonds of love, but also does not yet have the opportunity for self-chosen individuality and widespread

[40] Ibid., 113.
[41] Ibid., 116–19.
[42] Hegel, *Philosophy of History*, 41.
[43] G.W.F. Hegel, *The Philosophy of Right*, translated with notes by T. M. Knox (Oxford: Clarendon Press, [1821] 1945), 110.

interaction among diverse others. This makes civil society necessary for Hegel, in which "the moments bound together in the unity of the family ... must be released from the concept to self-subsistent objective reality."[44] But whereas civil society does (more so than the family) provide room for individuals to manifest their unique selves, unregulated civil society hinders freedom by creating severe inequality and insecurity, and by leaving individuals with only a superficial connection to others based on the mere market value of one's activities. Hegel says that "[t]he state is the actuality of concrete freedom"[45] because it is meant to bring back the meaningful connection with others that was present in the family, but in a way that preserves the widespread interaction and self-sufficiency of civil society, while also ameliorating the defects generated by civil society. Hegel's state does not obliterate family and civil society, but rather preserves its earlier stages in an elevated form – the family's intimate connections remain but no longer serve to limit individuality, whereas civil society's opportunities for self-chosen individuality and diverse interaction remain but no longer serve to create insecurity and superficial connection between individuals.[46] With civil society specifically (which is the realm where most human relationships exist), the state is not to thoroughly take over society, but still must directly alter society when the society generates conditions that obstruct individuals' self-development: "[the state] maintains [individuals] as persons, thus making right a necessary actuality, then it promotes their welfare, which each originally takes care of for himself, but which has a thoroughly general side; it protects both family and civil society ... it interferes with those subordinate spheres and maintains them in substantial immanence."[47]

The example of poverty illustrates the severe inequality, insecurity, and superficial connection between individuals that concern Hegel about civil society.[48] Hegel notes that unregulated civil society generates "excessive poverty and the creation of a penurious rabble" and leaves impoverished individuals without the conditions necessary to actualize their own

---

44 Ibid., 122.
45 Ibid., 160.
46 Ibid., 281.
47 Hegel, *Philosophy of Mind*, 264.
48 Elsewhere, I have provided a detailed account of how Hegel's state may impose on civil society in order to fight poverty; see Jeff Jackson, "The Resolution of Poverty in Hegel's 'Actual' State," *Polity* 46, no. 3 (2014): 331–53.

unique development.[49] Poverty also brings social relations that resemble the lord-bondsman relation, because the poor can lack the opportunity to provide genuinely independent confirmation of others' development. Because poverty prevents individuals from becoming self-governing and corrupts healthy social relations, Hegel declares poverty to be "one of the most disturbing problems which agitate modern society."[50] Hegel gives the state the primary responsibility of combating this problem, and his reasoning for this becomes clear once we understand the meaning of two terms that are central to his philosophy: *actuality* and *sublation*. We have seen how a developing individual preserves and elevates her prior principles and habits as she develops further, and Hegel indeed holds that any entity is "actual" to the extent it so develops while preserving and elevating its earlier stages: "the actuality of this simple whole consists in those various shapes and forms which have become its moments, and which will now develop and take shape afresh, this time in their new element, in their newly acquired meaning."[51] The actual whole thus "sublates" its earlier stages, with *sublate* meaning "'*to keep*,' 'to preserve,' and 'to cause to cease,' '*to put an end to*.' Even 'to preserve' already includes a negative note, namely that something, in order to be retained, is removed from its immediacy."[52] Hegel repeatedly associates the state with actuality, asserting that

[t]he state is actual ... Actuality is always the unity of universal and particular, the universal dismembered in the particulars which seem to be self-subsistent, although they really are upheld and contained only in the whole. Where this unity is not present, a thing is not actual even though it may have acquired existence. A bad state is one which merely exists; a sick body exists too, but it has no genuine reality.[53]

For Hegel, then, the state becomes further "actual" to the extent that it sublates civil society by preserving the qualities of civil society that promote freedom (e.g., opportunity for self-directed individuality) and negating those that hinder freedom (e.g., poverty). When the state does not continuously develop in its effort to overcome the defects generated by civil society, then that state "merely exists."

---

[49] Hegel, *Philosophy of Right*, 150.
[50] Ibid., 278.
[51] Hegel, *Phenomenology of Spirit*, 7.
[52] Hegel, *Science of Logic*, 81–2.
[53] Hegel, *Philosophy of Right*, 283.

DEWEY'S HEGELIANISM

Although a number of recent scholars have explored Hegel's influence on Dewey's philosophy, there has not been a clear link drawn between Hegel and Dewey's thinking on democracy. On my reading, each of the individual, social, and political elements of Dewey's democratic thought bear a significant Hegelian quality. Regarding the individual element, we have seen that Dewey associates democracy with "spread of the scientific attitude." The importance he places on this scientific attitude is strikingly similar to what we have seen with Hegel. For Dewey, the effect of modern scientific advancements has been that past notions of eternal truth and fixed social hierarchy have been progressively overthrown.[54] Dewey also emphasizes that "[t]oday the influences that affect the actions performed by individuals are so remote as to be unknown ... The career of individuals, their lives and security as well as prosperity is now affected by events on the other side of the world."[55] Under circumstances that are constantly changing, increasingly interconnected, and lacking stable truths to rely upon, Dewey holds that a distinctly scientific mind-set can allow individuals to govern their lives and determine their unique identities. He explains that "the term 'science' is likely to suggest those bodies of knowledge which are most familiar to us in physical matters; and thus to give the impression that what is sought is reduction of matters of conduct to similarly physical or even quasi-mathematical form. It is, however, analogy with the method of inquiry ... which is intended."[56] This emphasis on a scientific approach to one's experience jumps out as a conspicuous example of Dewey's "permanent deposit" of Hegelian influence, and it shows Hegelian quality in the individual element of Deweyan democracy.

As with Hegel, though, Dewey sees individuals' capacity to think and act scientifically as largely unrealized. He remarks that "[b]ecause the free working of mind is one of the greatest joys open to man, the scientific attitude, incorporated in individual mind, is something which adds enormously to one's enjoyment of existence. The delights of thinking, of inquiry, are not widely enjoyed at the present time. But the few who experience them would hardly exchange them for other pleasures."[57]

---

[54] This point is central to the argument of *The Quest for Certainty* (New York, NY: Minton, Balch & Company, 1929); I have elaborated on this point in Chapter 1.

[55] Dewey, *Freedom and Culture*, 45, 165.

[56] MW3: 4–5.

[57] John Dewey, *Individualism Old and New* (New York, NY: Capricorn Books, [1930] 1962), 161.

As far as why the scientific attitude is not yet widely enjoyed, Dewey points to the difficulty involved with displaying that attitude and to how science is generally seen as applicable to specialized, technical matters but not to our everyday social experience:

as long as 'scientific' thinking confines itself to technical fields, it lacks full scope and varied material. Its subject-matter is technical in the degree in which application in human life is shut out. The mind that is hampered by fear lest something old and precious be destroyed is the mind that experiences fear of science. He who has this fear cannot find reward and peace in the discovery of new truths and the projection of new ideals.[58]

The belief that scientific thinking does not pertain to our everyday lives, as well as the discomfort that comes from confronting ideas and principles that challenge previously held "truths," are leading individuals away from exhibiting the scientific mind-set. In Hegelian fashion, Dewey describes science as identifying the underlying connection between entities that appear opposed to one another. It should thus lead individuals to see the novel, unfamiliar situations they experience as essential to their development, rather than as something to avoid: "It is a property of science to find its opportunities in problems, in questions. Since knowing is inquiring, perplexities and difficulties are the meat on which it thrives. The disparities and conflicts that give rise to problems are not something to be dreaded … they are things to be grappled with."[59] Dewey is excited that some individuals, though unfortunately "not very numerous," have developed a scientific "morale having its own distinctive features," with the most crucial feature being "enjoyment of new fields for inquiry and of new problems."[60] To see thorough engagement with "problems" as integral to one's own development is to show the capacity for governing one's own life in the midst of a constantly changing world. But "[u]ncertainty is disagreeable to most persons; suspense is so hard to endure that assured expectation of an unfortunate outcome is usually preferred to a long-continued state of doubt"; indeed, "[f]ear of the unknown, fear of change and novelty, tended, at all times before the rise of scientific attitude, to drive men into rigidity of beliefs and habits."[61]

[58] Ibid., 161–2.
[59] Ibid., 162.
[60] Dewey, *Freedom and Culture*, 145.
[61] Ibid., 146–7.

For Dewey, an individual who actively engages with the problems that disrupt her prior habits and beliefs, and keeps those habits and beliefs open for continuous revision, can intelligently direct her own development. By taking action toward "unifying" herself with (rather than futilely seeking to avoid) the alien situations and individuals she confronts, this individual can "profit by [the changing world] instead of being at its mercy" by effecting "processes of change so directed that they achieve an intended consummation."[62] This thorough inquiry into problems can help an individual develop effective methods for interacting with novel objects of experience, and for thus bringing those objects into harmony with the individual's development: "If the inquiry is adequately directed, the final issue is the unified situation that has been mentioned."[63] Dewey's portrait of a developing individual's experience is, indeed, extremely Hegelian. He sees experience as a subject-object interaction in which "things and events belonging to the world, physical and social, are transformed through the human context they enter, while the live creature is changed and developed through its intercourse with things previously external to it."[64] As with Hegel, individual subjects transform, and are transformed by, the objects they interact with, and so subjects are defined by continuous development through interaction with objects, while objects develop through continuous interaction with subjects. An individual who confronts a novel object of experience is (as Hegel would say) "negated" – that is, her prior stable self has been disrupted. In order to bring the object into harmony with her development, she will need to show, as Dewey says, "willingness to endure a condition of mental unrest and disturbance"[65] and go through the struggle required to reconstruct herself in a way that effectively accounts for the object. If an individual does overcome the disparity between herself and the object, she can (as Hegel would again say) "return into simplicity," meaning that she can interact simply again with the world because the object no longer disrupts her principles and habits. It is an *expanded* simplicity, though, because "in a growing life, the recovery is never mere return to a prior state, for it is enriched by the state of disparity and resistance through which

[62] John Dewey, *Experience and Nature* (New York, NY: Dover Publications, [1925] 1958), 70, 161.
[63] John Dewey, *Logic: The Theory of Inquiry* (New York, NY: Henry Holt and Company, 1938), 107.
[64] John Dewey, *Art as Experience* (New York, NY: Perigee Books, [1934] 1980), 246.
[65] John Dewey, *How We Think* (Boston, MA: D. C. Heath & Co., 1910), 13.

it has successfully passed."[66] This individual will have developed more expansive principles and habits for engaging with previously unforeseen circumstances. And at the same time, the individual is readier for the likelihood that even these newer principles and habits will have to expand further in the future: "things retained from past experience that would grow stale from routine or inert from lack of use, become coefficients in new adventures and put on a raiment of fresh meaning."[67]

In Chapter 1, we began exploring the meaning of Dewey's democratic individual way of life. Dewey claims that "democracy is a *personal* way of individual life ... it signifies the possession and continual use of certain attitudes, forming personal character and determining desire and purpose in all the relations of life."[68] Democracy for Dewey cannot be simply defined, as it often is, by a certain kind of political system. He maintains that "the ideal of democracy ... roots itself ultimately in the principle of moral, self-directing individuality"[69] and that "[i]f democracy is possible it is because every individual has a degree of power to govern himself."[70] The discussion of Hegel further illuminates qualities of democratic individualism that were established in Chapter 1. We saw in the last chapter that democratic individualism is defined by continuous development, and here we see how this development entails a "scientific" approach to the objects of experience that "negate" an individual, such that an individual can intelligently reconstruct herself so as to bring those objects into harmony with her development: "The growing, enlarging, liberated self ... goes forth to meet new demands and occasions, and readapts and remakes itself in the process. It welcomes untried situations."[71] We relatedly saw in Chapter 1 how democratic individualism is in touch with the lack of fixed truths in the world and the lack of perfectly wise individuals who can direct the growth of others. As Dewey says, "[M]en [have] the responsibility for ... subjecting to the test of consequences their most cherished prejudices. Such a change involves a great change in the seat of

---

[66] Dewey, *Art as Experience*, 14.

[67] Ibid., 60–1.

[68] John Dewey, "Creative Democracy – The Task before Us," in *John Dewey: The Political Writings*, eds. Debra Morris and Ian Shapiro (Indianapolis, IN: Hackett Publishing Company, [1939] 1993), 241.

[69] MW3: 235.

[70] LW6: 431.

[71] John Dewey and James Tufts, *Ethics*, rev. ed. (New York, NY: Henry Holt and Company, 1932), 341.

authority and the methods of decision in society."[72] Hegel helps elucidate how a "democratic individual" can generate provisional truth through active, continuous, and self-directed interaction with the changeful qualities of ordinary experience. An individual is to see the objects that negate her as integral to her own self and develop new, provisionally "true" principles through engagement with those objects, all while understanding that her development may take her in unforeseen directions such that she cannot be wholly guided by any other individual.

I also explained in Chapter 1 how a democratic individual's development is bound up with a willingness to actively interact with diverse others and to challenge aspects of society that prevent others from becoming self-governing. An individual can expand her experience through engaging with the diverse others she confronts, but this potential is squashed when those others are denied the opportunity to generate their own unique identities. This exemplifies the interrelation between the individual and social elements of Deweyan democracy, and our discussion of Hegel clarifies this as well. Hegel's philosophy conceives of how diverse other individuals are primary among the objects of experience that tend to negate an individual subject's prior stable existence. If an individual can reconstruct herself in interaction with these others and contribute to their development as they contribute to hers, she will intelligently expand her development and determine her identity. But as the lord-bondsman narrative indicates, relations that are severely unequal will harm not only those who are directly disadvantaged by the inequality, but those who appear to be advantaged by it as well. The bondsman in this story is, of course, prevented from directing his own development, while the lord's instinctual desire to be served by the bondsman stops the lord from creating his own development and having his own unique impact on objects. The lord remains undeveloped and dissatisfied, because he cannot view his own development in interaction with objects of experience (i.e., his own self does not exist "for himself"), and he also cannot receive genuine recognition of his development from an equal, independent other, due to the bondsman's having a subordinate status. Dewey's accounts of the harm brought by severe social inequality have a strikingly similar character. When referring to the inequality in a modern capitalist society between workers who labor and the owners who command the workers' labor, Dewey states that the workers are left in the alienating condition

---

[72] John Dewey, *Reconstruction in Philosophy*, enl. ed. (Boston, MA: Beacon Press, [1948] 1957), 160.

of having "no concern with their occupation beyond the money return it brings."[73] And with the owners, Dewey alludes to their lack of self-development and authentic recognition, suggesting that because of "the hardening effects of a one-sided control of the affairs of others,"[74] there can be a lack "of inner contentment on the part of those who form our pecuniary oligarchy."[75] The advantaged and the disadvantaged alike, then, would become freer in a society without such structural inequality, in which "all individuals may share in the discoveries and thoughts of others, to the liberation and enrichment of their own experience."[76] An individual's own self-government is promoted by a society of equal others, which is why it is an integral quality of democratic individualism to challenge forms of structural inequality.

Thus, the individual element of democracy depends on social conditions that are free of structural inequalities and that allow opportunities for individuals to direct their development and interact with diverse others. The social element of democracy, at the same time, depends on individuals exercising control over their lives, interacting with diverse others, and challenging forms of inequality. When I addressed this interrelationship of individual and social democracy in Chapter 1, I stated that Dewey also sees the political element of democracy as having itself a growing role in the development of individual and social democracy. The discussion in this chapter, specifically of Hegel's conception of an "actual" state, helps expand this point about Deweyan political democracy. It may seem odd to link Hegel with an account of political democracy, because the internal organization of the state that he appears to defend in *The Philosophy of Right* is rather undemocratic, an organization that Dewey in fact calls "the most artificial and the least satisfactory portion of [Hegel's] political philosophy."[77] I will address in Chapter 3 how Dewey seeks to develop political institutions that assure equal political influence to individuals throughout society. But still, Dewey parallels Hegel's description of an actual state by giving government the specific responsibility to help provide the social conditions for democratic individualism. He explains that "[d]emocracy is a way of personal life controlled ... by faith in the capac-

---

73 John Dewey, *Democracy and Education* (New York, NY: The Free Press, [1916] 1966), 317.
74 Ibid., 318.
75 Dewey, *Individualism Old and New*, 54.
76 Ibid., 154.
77 From Dewey's 1897 Lecture on Hegel, printed in Shook and Good, *John Dewey's Philosophy of Spirit*, 159.

ity of human beings for intelligent judgment and right action if proper conditions are furnished."[78] These "proper conditions" are far from fully present, in Dewey's view, and government can help bring these conditions further into existence: "factors of democratic government are means that have been found expedient for realizing democracy as the truly human way of living."[79] I noted earlier Dewey's concern with hierarchical work relations that leave many individuals with no opportunity to control their own work; such working conditions, along with material insecurity and the danger of poverty, lead individuals into onerous occupations in which they "have no share ... in directing the activities in which they physically participate."[80] (This topic of undemocratic workplaces will be discussed further in the next section.) He thus calls directly for "political action to bring about equalization of economic conditions in order that the equal right of all to free choice and free action be maintained,"[81] and he particularly hopes that "[t]he inequitable distribution of income will bring to the fore the use of taxing power to effect redistribution by means of larger taxation of swollen income and by heavier death duties on large fortunes."[82] On Dewey's terms, this kind of action from government is integral to the further development of democracy, because individuals' self-government depends on social conditions that political institutions can help provide.

The distinction Dewey draws between "state" and "society" is analogous to Hegel's. Dewey explains,

I mean by 'state' the organization of the resources of community life through governmental machinery of legislation and administration. I mean by 'society' the less definite and freer play of the forces of the community which goes on in the daily intercourse and contact of men in an endless variety of ways that have nothing to do with politics or government or the state in any institutional sense.[83]

As with Hegel, Dewey does not wish to erase this distinction by allowing the state to impose total control over social relations. But when society generates threats to individuals' self-government such as economic inequality and poverty, Dewey, like Hegel, requires a state to interfere with society in order to help create conditions where individuals can exercise

---

78 Dewey, "Creative Democracy," 242.
79 LW11: 218.
80 Dewey, *Individualism Old and New*, 131.
81 Dewey, *Freedom and Culture*, 162.
82 Dewey, *Individualism Old and New*, 112.
83 MW2: 81–2.

control over their lives. For Dewey, we must judge the presence of democracy primarily by whether individuals are actually exercising control over their lives. When social conditions deny individuals the opportunity to do this, for Dewey, political institutions become democratic not just when they are organized a particular way, but when they fulfill their capacity to help remedy the oppressive aspects of society. Thus Dewey declares that "the supreme test of all political institutions ... shall be the contribution they make to the all-around growth of every member of society"[84] and that "[t]he political and governmental phase of democracy is a means, the best means so far found, for realizing ends that lie in the wide domain of human relationships and the development of human personality. [Democracy] is ... a way of life, social and individual."[85] If a society is characterized by structural inequality, a government cannot try to take a neutral position with respect to this inequality and still be seen as a government that upholds individuals' control over their own lives. The Deweyan view is that a government is inevitably wrapped up in the effects of this inequality and that it can either act democratically by working to ameliorate the inequality, or it can act undemocratically by denying those who suffer from inequality a potentially effective means for redress. As with the "actuality" of Hegel's state, political democracy for Dewey requires continuous effort from a state toward overcoming the threats to freedom that are generated in the social realm.

THE PROBLEM OF UNDEMOCRATIC WORK

We have referred to Dewey's concern with severe inequality in work relations, but this topic deserves a more extensive discussion. This is not only because Dewey displays a long-term interest in the democratization of the workplace, but because this topic will help us more clearly illustrate (1) what it means for individuals to exercise control over their lives; (2) why this individual self-government can be affected even more so by the quality of *social* relations than by our typical *political* institutions; and (3) how political institutions are still crucial to the development of the conditions for individual self-government. Dewey's conception of democracy, as I am presenting it throughout this book, exists in a process of unending development and is composed of individual, social, and political elements that are themselves continuously developing. Democracy is

---

[84] Dewey, *Reconstruction in Philosophy*, 186.
[85] LW11: 217.

never fully achieved, but is further actualized to the degree that obstacles to its achievement are overcome. The typical organization of the workplace, in Dewey's time and in ours, represents a problem, or, in Hegelian language, a "negation" of democracy itself. It is an immense obstacle in the way of many individuals' ability to exercise control over their lives. As is distinctly Deweyan, each of the individual, social, and political elements of democracy are implicated in this obstacle, and further development is required in each if the obstacle is to be overcome.

The concept of *work* is indeed central to both Hegel's and Dewey's thought. For both, work represents (at least potentially) a uniquely human form of interacting with objects of experience in order to exercise a particular effect on the world. I noted earlier how Hegel's bondsman, despite being far from genuinely free because he cannot control his own development, still develops further than the lord, in part because he does at least work at all. This does not make Hegel complacent, though, about the problem of an individual's work being controlled by someone else, for he argues that "[b]y alienating the whole of my time, as crystallized in my work, and everything I produced, I would be making into another's property the substance of my being, my universal activity and actuality, my personality."[86] Such an individual is obstructed from seeing herself in the objects of experience brought by her work activity, because her interaction with objects is dictated by another individual. For Dewey, work encompasses any activity in which "continuous attention ... [and] intelligence must be shown in selecting and shaping means" to an end[87] and which aims at producing "an objective result."[88] Work, therefore, is what we do when we engage in extended interaction with objects of experience, with the conscious aim of producing an intended objective result. As such, work cannot be simply reduced to individuals' employment.[89]

---

[86] Hegel, *Philosophy of Right*, 54. Jeffrey Church has further shown how Hegel's political philosophy can be seen as requiring democracy in "economic associations" in order for individuals to become genuinely self-determining; see Jeffrey Church, "G.W.F. Hegel on Self-Determination and Democratic Theory," *American Journal of Political Science* 56, no. 4 (2012): 1029–33.

[87] Dewey, *Democracy and Education*, 204.

[88] Dewey, *Art as Experience*, 279.

[89] This point brings to mind the issue of housework, which does not have the status of a paid occupation. On Deweyan terms, housework would not qualify less as work than any occupation, but it is still clearly problematic when economic and/or customary circumstances move women disproportionately into housework and cut them off from opportunities to interact with other types of objects of experience. Dewey's support for gender equality in fact exhibits an important point of divergence between him and Hegel; see LW 5: 276, and *Philosophy of Right*, 114.

But nonetheless, employment merits attention due to the way that many individuals are forced by current social conditions to alienate their entire capacity to produce "objective results" to the control of others within this institution. Individuals largely cannot avoid this institution, and because there can be little opportunity for individuals to direct their own development while they are employed, their capacity to control their lives can be severely obstructed, thus hollowing out the value of any apparent opportunity to participate in political institutions: "political democracy is not the whole of democracy ... it can be effectively maintained only where democracy is social ... where there is a wide and varied distribution of opportunities."[90] The way many individuals experience their workplace is a pressing problem in the way of individuals' self-government, and the fact that it "proceed[s] from the social conditions"[91] illustrates how democracy is far more than a political concept.

When explaining the importance of the workplace, Dewey reasons that "the ways in which activities are carried on for the greater part of the waking hours of the day ... can only be a highly important factor in shaping personal dispositions."[92] Because the way individuals experience their workplace has such a strong impact on their character, it is an independently significant factor in the discussion of democracy, beyond any connection to the quality of political processes (although it is also important how an alienating everyday experience of work can negatively affect an individual's political efficacy, which is a topic that will get greater attention in Chapter 4). Deweyan democracy is rooted in individuals' exercise of control over their lives, and so a work experience that is characterized by uncritical execution of the plans of others is clearly antithetical to such democracy. As noted earlier, Dewey sees many individuals in his society who "have no share ... in directing the activities in which they physically participate." As a result, "many persons have callings which make no appeal to them, which are pursued simply for the money reward that accrues ... such callings constantly provoke one to aversion, ill will, and a desire to slight and evade."[93] The factor of poverty in particular displays the iniquity of this situation, because many individuals engaged in such work have not made any genuine, self-conscious (in the Hegelian sense) choice to do so, and rather they must do

---

[90] MW10: 138.
[91] John Dewey, *Human Nature and Conduct* (New York, NY: Henry Holt and Company, 1922), 123.
[92] LW11: 221.
[93] Dewey, *Democracy and Education*, 317.

the work mainly to achieve necessary means of survival. Under "unfree economic conditions,"[94] many individuals are forced to engage in work for no purpose besides the wage which comes at the end. This makes encounters with novel objects of experience in the course of working into merely needless difficulty in the way of finishing the activity and receiving that needed wage. Dewey concludes that, for those caught in such a situation, "minds are warped, frustrated, unnourished by their activities" and that a society discards significant potential wisdom "when multitudes are excluded from occasion for the use of thought and emotion in their daily occupations."[95] Dewey's democratic individualism involves an individual seeing herself in the objects of experience generated by her activity. But he recognizes how this is not very possible if the objects she encounters are generated by activity that she has not determined herself to engage in and if the way she interacts with those objects is dictated by superiors.

To illustrate the problem of undemocratic work, Dewey frequently uses the example of the teaching profession. Dewey's educational theory will be discussed in detail in Chapter 6, but we can note here how he sees effective teaching as depending on individual teachers exercising control over their work and intelligently developing themselves in interaction with unique objects of experience. In response to the idea that there should be uniform, inflexible plans for students' classroom activity, Dewey states that

there is incumbent upon the educator the duty of instituting a much more intelligent, and consequently much more difficult, kind of planning. He must survey the capacities and needs of the particular set of individuals with whom he is dealing and must at the same time arrange the conditions which provide the subject-matter or content for experiences that satisfy these needs and develop these capacities. The planning must be flexible enough to permit free play for individuality of experience and yet firm enough to give direction towards continuous development of power.[96]

Such teaching requires intelligent, self-directed individuals who can flexibly develop their methods and habits in response to the new situations and new individuals they confront in the classroom. This exemplifies democratic individualism, because the teacher is developing her identity as a teacher and is generating new principles for how to be a teacher in

[94] Ibid., 204.
[95] Dewey, *Individualism Old and New*, 132–3.
[96] John Dewey, *Experience and Education* (New York, NY: Macmillan Company, 1938), 65.

interaction with novel objects of experience. She is acting as a subject exercising a distinct, self-determined impact on those objects, and she is thus contributing to the further development of teaching itself (which we can also see as an object) by helping to expand the manner in which the profession is carried out. In one of his many statements on the nature of the teaching profession, Dewey affirms that it is a difficult profession full of many challenges, but he says he is "not interested in putting any obstacles in the way of those who think of becoming teachers by dwelling on the obstacles it presents. To an active and energetic character, these will prove only stimuli to greater effort."[97] In other words, democratic individuals who become teachers will see the obstacles generated by their activity as essential to their own selves.

Dewey points out, however, that teachers are frequently not given the opportunity to genuinely control their work. He describes how educational methods and aims are often dictated to teachers, and his description still rings true today: "The dictation ... of the subject-matter to be taught, to the teacher who is to engage in the actual work of instruction, and frequently, under the name of close supervision, the attempt to determine the methods which are to be used in teaching, mean nothing more or less than the deliberate restriction of intelligence, the imprisoning of the spirit."[98] When a teacher must merely execute the will of superintendents and politicians, she is then not a unique subject exercising a distinct, self-chosen effect on the objects of experience generated by teaching. As a result, the potential wisdom available from those who are actually engaged in the practical application of teaching methods is effectively suspended. As Dewey puts it, "since it is the teachers who make the final application, ought they not to play a large part in developing and making concrete and real the ideas which they are engaged in executing?"[99] If teachers cannot help determine the educational principles to be put into practice in the classroom, then their potential wisdom is lost to society. Accordingly, they are hindered from becoming democratic individuals because they are prevented from controlling their work, and from generating new principles and habits that are suited to the novel situations they encounter, and that help the teaching profession itself develop further.

---

[97] LW13: 346.
[98] MW3: 232.
[99] MW15: 185. This does not mean, though, that Dewey would want teachers to exercise tyrannical control over the classroom, since the students themselves must be able to exercise an effect on the classroom experience; I will address this point in Chapter 6.

Dewey was indeed a college professor, with a career that included positions at the University of Michigan, University of Minnesota, University of Chicago, and Columbia University. His commentary on the undemocratic work experience of teachers does address the problem of college faculty being obstructed from having an effective voice in the governance of their schools; although, he expresses even greater concern over the situation faced by teachers at lower levels of education. He remarks that "there is, I am confident, much more autocracy on the part of superintendents and principals in public schools than by presidents and deans in colleges. Our lower schools are ridden by 'administrators'; they are administration mad ... College teachers will most readily win their own emancipation when they recognize their solidarity with all other teachers." [100] Dewey's emphasis on democratizing all teachers' working conditions is, furthermore, connected with a broader goal of democratization across the spheres of industrial life. He describes

the need of securing greater industrial autonomy, that is to say, greater ability on the part of the workers in any particular trade or occupation to control that industry, instead of working under these conditions of external control where they have no interest, no insight into what they are doing, and no social outlook upon the consequences and meaning of what they are doing. [101]

Workers must then be directly involved in workplace decision making and must be able to do their work with a thorough understanding of the social meaning and significance of that work. Dewey makes reference to the famous Hawthorne studies that took place in the 1920s near Chicago, which helped illustrate the benefits for workers, and for the enterprises they work in, when they are given a voice in decision making and can see themselves as part of an undertaking with a distinct social purpose, rather than just as individuals attempting to gain a wage. He explains that "this was an angle of that investigation which appealed especially to me: the changed response, the changed attitude even toward technical problems of production, that came about when individuals found that their opinions were regarded as being worth asking for, that they were really worth consulting in the conduct and management of the affairs of the factory"; he also refers to how "the role of thought or understanding, a recognition of the meaning and the significance of the activities that constitute work and labor," brought workers to feel more personal

[100] LW3: 278–9.
[101] LW13: 313.

interest in the internal quality of their work activities.[102] When a worker can be a genuine decision maker and can interact with fellow workers on matters of evident social significance, she has meaningful opportunity to become a self-governing, democratic individual.

The problem of autocracy in the workplace, and of workers being plainly prevented from exercising control over their activity, is no less pressing today than in Dewey's time. The issue has in fact been getting increasing attention from scholars, who have explored the precise features of workplace relations that make autocracy so prevalent, and the possibilities for overcoming that autocracy. Gregory Dow, for instance, provides a measured account of the possibilities for workplaces to become democratically controlled by workers under current capitalist conditions, and he provides evidence that workers' control of an enterprise increases workers' commitment and productivity.[103] Tom Malleson argues for workplace democracy under our current conditions, while noting that "[F]or the average person in today's advanced capitalist societies, there is little free choice about the governance structure under which one will work. True, one may exit a particular workplace, but it's very difficult to escape hierarchical work altogether."[104] The arguments made by Elizabeth Anderson (a Dewey-influenced scholar) are particularly noteworthy, for she describes individuals as being subject to "private government" when they are employed, which is a concept that escapes us when we see only our typical institutions of government as threatening individuals' freedom.[105] This highlights the mistake involved when we suppose that the capacity to govern one's life relates only to the quality of political institutions. Anderson provides a thorough account of the ways that workplaces can strip individuals of their freedom, saying:

Imagine a government that assigns almost everyone a superior whom they must obey. Although superiors give most inferiors a routine to follow, there is no rule of law. Orders may be arbitrary and can change at any time, without prior notice or opportunity to appeal ... The most highly ranked individual takes no orders but issues many. The lowest-ranked may have their bodily movements and speech minutely regulated for most of the day ... Everyone lives under surveillance, to

---

[102] LW5: 239.

[103] Gregory Dow, *Governing the Firm: Workers' Control in Theory and Practice* (Cambridge: Cambridge University Press, 2003).

[104] Tom Malleson, "Making the Case for Workplace Democracy: Exit and Voice as Mechanisms of Freedom in Social Life," *Polity* 45, no. 4 (2013): 627.

[105] Elizabeth Anderson, *Private Government: How Employers Rule Our Lives (and Why We Don't Talk about It)* (Princeton, NJ: Princeton University Press, 2017), 6, 36.

ensure that they are complying with orders. Superiors may snoop into inferiors' e-mail and record their phone conversations.[106]

She asks, "Would people subject to such a government be free? I expect that most people in the United States would think not. Yet most work under just such a government: it is the modern workplace, as it exists for most establishments in the United States."[107] Anderson thus identifies how, in the United States in particular, it is largely taken for granted that employers have dictatorial power over workers, because "[i]n the United States, the default employment contract is employment at will," under which "workers, in effect, cede *all* of their rights to their employers."[108] This hierarchical relation is, oddly, not often seen as incompatible with individuals' freedom. Anderson notes how, in our common language, "*government* is often treated as synonymous with the state, which, by supposed definition, is part of the *public sphere*. The supposed counterpart *private sphere* is the place where, it is imagined, government ends, and hence where individual liberty begins."[109] In this book, I am treating terms like "government," "state," "political institutions," etc., as largely interchangeable, because Dewey for the most part treats those terms in that way. But Anderson's point about language is well taken, because it highlights the erroneous belief that only the state "governs" individuals, when in fact "private" spheres such as the workplace do at least as much governing.

In her arguments regarding how workplaces could be democratized, Anderson calls for a strong "workers' bill of rights" that would effectively protect workers' political rights and free speech, which employers can often curtail.[110] She recognizes, though, that such a bill of rights alone is insufficient to ensure workers' freedom if the workers are not allowed adequate "voice" in workplace decisions, explaining that "workers need *some* voice within the workplace to protect against employer abuses of power, and, more generally, to empower them to assert their standing, respectability, and autonomy interests in the workplace."[111] As she makes her case for workers' participation in decision making, she makes the particularly Deweyan point that

[106] Ibid., 37–8.
[107] Ibid., 39.
[108] Ibid., 53–4.
[109] Ibid., 41.
[110] Ibid., 68.
[111] Ibid., 133.

[e]xercising autonomy – directing oneself in tasks, no matter how exacting and relentless they are – is no ordinary good. It is a basic human need ... Having a genuine say in how one's work is directed, even when one must adjust to the claims of others, as in a collectively governed workplace, and even when one doesn't get one's way, still is an exercise of autonomy in the decision-making process, if not the outcome.[112]

As we have seen Dewey argue, if workers must engage in tasks that are dictated to them, and that do not allow them to exercise their own unique impact on the objects of experience they confront, then the workers are robbed of their distinctly human capacity to direct their own development. To ensure that workers have genuine voice in their workplaces, Anderson specifically calls for strengthening labor unions,[113] and she speaks positively about the German system of "codetermination,"[114] which gives workers the right to participate directly in the management of the companies that employ them.

The analysis of scholars like Anderson helps connect Dewey's views on the problem of undemocratic work to contemporary situations. It also illuminates what specific actions and efforts are needed if democracy is to develop further through this problem. I discussed in Chapter 1 how democratic individualism depends on social conditions that help make it possible for individuals to govern their lives. I also explained how a democratic individual must challenge the aspects of society that interfere with that self-government, not only for herself but for others. This was described through the lens of Dewey's relation to *Bildung* philosophy, which is defined in part by immanent critique of social norms and by critique of practices that are inconsistent with the rational basis of those norms. Thus, as American social norms hold that all individuals should be truly free, the fact that so many work under essentially tyrannical conditions surely represents a matter for major critique. Chapter 1 noted how Dewey distinguishes between *individuality* (the realization of one's unique identity) and *individualism* (an individual-focused philosophy that may or may not be conducive to individuality), and Dewey exhibits the gap between the dominant American idea of individualism – which treats individuals as isolated entities driven by desire for money – and the achievement of meaningful individual freedom: "One cannot imagine a bitterer comment on any professed individualism than that it subordinates

[112] Ibid., 128.
[113] Ibid., 69–70.
[114] Ibid., 70, 142–3.

the only creative individuality – that of mind – to the maintenance of a regime which gives the few an opportunity of being shrewd in the management of monetary business."[115] This is a critique of America's current individualistic norms and of a practice (the suppression of workers' individuality for the private pecuniary benefit of powerful owners) that is inconsistent with the rational basis of American norms (i.e., the freedom of all individuals). Democratic individualism, quite differently from the dominant individualism in America, entails a readiness to critique, and to make effort to combat, such qualities in American society that obstruct the possibilities for individual self-government. There are certainly many examples of these qualities in current workplaces, and individuals can act democratically by supporting efforts to improve workers' conditions. Anderson refers, for instance, to Amazon warehouses where workers are set to work at an outrageous pace in stifling heat and often suffer injuries on the job before ultimately being fired; and to Walmart, which notoriously subjects workers to unreliable schedules and horrible treatment from their managers, all while providing the workers with low wages and no benefits.[116] The 2011 elimination, led by the Koch brothers, of Wisconsin public-sector workers' right to bargain on more than just their wages provides another example. Dewey's principles do not require individuals to unreflectively side with workers in disputes with employers, with no study of the specific situations and issues that give rise to each dispute. But in cases where workers are flagrantly prevented from controlling their activities, democratic individualism does call for siding with workers against employers, and for thus contributing to social conditions that expand the possibilities for self-government for all.

These points further illustrate how the individual and social elements of Deweyan democracy are in a process of interlocking development. The political element of democracy is again also essential here, since it is political institutions that can act (if they are pressured to, at least) most effectively to alter working conditions in a democratic direction. Dewey looks forward to a time when "[t]he problem of social control of industry and the use of governmental agencies for constructive social ends will become the avowed centre of political struggle," so that we can introduce "social responsibility into our business system to such an extent that the doom of an exclusively pecuniary-profit industry would follow."[117] It is

---

[115] Dewey, *Individualism Old and New*, 91.
[116] Anderson, *Private Government*, 128–9, 136–7.
[117] Dewey, *Individualism Old and New*, 113–14, 117–18.

not acceptable for government to simply try to take a "neutral" position with respect to the internal organization of workplaces, because that serves to uphold the common authoritarian structure of work and denies workers an effective means for redress. Anderson indeed points out how the state is already deeply implicated in the issue of workplace organization, because "the state supplies the indispensable legal infrastructure" and "establishes the default constitution of workplace governance" by authorizing the "employment-at-will" system that gives employers just about complete control over workers' lives.[118] A state cannot be purely uninvolved in the "economic" relations of the workplace, and this lends support to the Deweyan position that political democracy requires political institutions to act to overcome, rather than uphold, qualities in the workplace that are antithetical to individuals' self-government.

Dewey does not provide clear blueprints of what a democratic workplace should look like. He passionately defends the general principle of workplace democracy and focuses on responding to pressing examples of how workplaces suppress individuals' self-development. His emphasis is on the process of democratizing workplaces, as well as on the process of fighting poverty, so that individuals may not be forced by lack of material security into work that carries no intrinsic interest for them. As Dewey puts it, we must recognize that "material security" as well as "socialized economy [are] the means of free individual development as ends."[119] But as far as what specific features a democratic workplace should have and how far democracy in the workplace should extend (i.e., whether enterprises should be wholly owned and governed by workers), Dewey does not give us precise guidance. This is consistent, though, with his overall conception of democracy, which focuses on democracy's unending development through overcoming the pressing obstacles in the way of individual self-government. The common organization of workplaces is clearly such an obstacle. It is true that "not much experience is available about the relation of economic factors, as they now operate, to democratic ends and methods."[120] Because there is not a great deal of experience with democracy in workplaces, we cannot immediately lay out

[118] Anderson, *Private Government*, 60. This point about the state being responsible for establishing the supposedly "free market" situation where owners dominate workers is also famously made in Karl Polanyi, *The Great Transformation: The Political and Economic Origins of Our Time* (Boston, MA: Beacon Press, [1944] 2001).

[119] John Dewey, *Liberalism and Social Action* (New York, NY: G. P. Putnam's Sons, 1935), 57, 90.

[120] Dewey, *Freedom and Culture*, 71–2.

the exact blueprint for workplace democracy. Dewey thus calls for us to understand that the process of democratizing workplaces will likely only "come slowly and painfully."[121] He is committed, ultimately, to the goal of achieving "a state of affairs in which the interest of each in his work is uncoerced and intelligent"[122] and, "a social-economic order in which all those capable of productive work will do the work for which they are fitted."[123] This broad goal is continuously filled with content through overcoming the evident obstacles to its achievement. Within many workplaces, there is a lack of subjects (in the Hegelian sense) who exercise their own unique effect on objects, since their interaction with objects is wholly determined by others.[124] The individual self-government that underlies democracy is thus under threat, and, as with the "actuality" of Hegel's state, the democratic quality of a political system for Dewey depends on its efforts to help directly overcome this problem.

DEWEY AND RORTY ON PRAGMATISM AND DEMOCRACY

Those who are familiar with pragmatism will have noticed how much of the preceding Hegelian analysis of Dewey is in line with pragmatic principles. Before proceeding further, I will just sum up here the key attributes of Dewey's pragmatic philosophy. The fact that this is Dewey's is noteworthy, because although Dewey's philosophy shares many similarities with Peirce's and James's, there is not (as many pragmatist scholars have pointed out) one identical version of pragmatism that all three hold to, and certainly there are significant points of difference between Dewey and some of the later twentieth-century thinkers who have called themselves pragmatists, as the forthcoming discussion of Rorty will illustrate. Because this book focuses on the value of Dewey's pragmatic philosophy for our thinking about democracy, his version of pragmatism will get the spotlight. His pragmatism denies assumptions that there are eternally true ideas and concepts, and instead holds that ideas and concepts can gain provisional truth through being put into practice in the situations

---

[121] LW17: 131.

[122] Dewey, *Democracy and Education*, 316.

[123] LW13: 317.

[124] Axel Honneth has similarly connected Deweyan democracy with individuals' contributions to society through their self-chosen activities (in a Hegelian sense); he goes wrong, however, in suggesting that this idea is exclusive to Dewey's early writings; see Axel Honneth, "Democracy as Reflexive Cooperation: John Dewey and the Theory of Democracy Today," *Political Theory* 26, no. 6 (1998): 763–83.

that individuals experience. This truth is attained by testing our concepts against the changing circumstances we inevitably confront and determining if the concepts produce the effect on our experience they are intended to have. Hence, Dewey's pragmatism involves the continuous development of concepts, in that individuals are to be ready to continuously reconstruct the concepts through which they understand the world, so that those concepts might be intelligently adapted and suited to novel conditions. In one of his most complete accounts of pragmatism, Dewey asserts that "[i]t is ... in submitting conceptions to the control of experience, in the process of verifying them, that one finds examples of what is called truth"; and further, that truths "are always subject to being corrected by unforeseen future consequences or by observed facts which had been disregarded."[125] Our concepts inevitably face problems, or, in Hegelian terms, they are "negated" by new situations brought by experience; but these concepts can develop further through these problems when they are intelligently reconstructed by individuals. Additionally, this pragmatism holds that when individuals transform their ideas and concepts, they produce change not only in their minds, but in the actual world, which is not a fixed entity: "If we form general ideas and if we put them in action, consequences are produced which could not be produced otherwise. Under these conditions the world will be different from what it would have been if thought had not intervened."[126] In other words, individuals can transform themselves, and exercise their own unique impact on their world, by acting in a "pragmatic" fashion.

Dewey's pragmatism is, indeed, a distinctly *democratic* philosophy. There is no fixed truth that individuals must uncritically adhere to, nor are there any individuals with a monopoly on truth who deserve the uncritical obedience of others. Dewey states that "[p]ragmatism and instrumental experimentalism bring into prominence the importance of the individual. It is he who is the carrier of creative thought, the author of action, and of its application ... The individual mind is important because only the individual mind is the organ of modifications in traditions and institutions, the vehicle of experimental creation."[127] Any individual can potentially generate truth in the course of her experience, and an individual can draw (though not uncritically) on the truths generated by other individuals – past and present – in building her own development, which exhibits how

[125] LW2: 11–12.
[126] LW2: 13.
[127] LW2: 20.

one individual's unique path of development can benefit from others who are pursuing their own unique paths. At this point, we should certainly see the connection between this philosophical standpoint and a commitment to democracy. Dewey's defense of pragmatism is in fact explicitly linked with the fundamental aim of his democratic thought, which is the cultivation of individuals' capacity to control their lives: "The function of intelligence is ... not that of copying the objects of the environment, but rather of taking account of the way in which more effective and more profitable relations with these objects may be established in the future."[128] As we have seen, Dewey is mainly interested in showing how individuals can exercise control over their lives in the face of constantly changing, increasingly interconnected circumstances. Individuals are to accept the dissolution of their prior habits and principles, and further develop themselves in response to the novel situations that bring about that dissolution. This not only helps individuals to respond intelligently to particular problems they face, but to gradually develop their overall capacity to respond to novelty in the future. We thus come back here to the "scientific" mind-set that we have seen Dewey say is intertwined with the future of democracy. Pragmatism, for Dewey, is essentially one and the same with a scientific approach to one's experience,[129] that is, an individual's recognition of a basic unity between herself and the objects of experience that "negate" her, and her reconstruction of herself through interaction with those objects, in order to bring those objects into harmony with her own development.

After falling out of intellectual fashion in the mid-twentieth century, pragmatism experienced a revival in the later twentieth century, in large part due to the work of Rorty. Rorty claims that his pragmatism closely follows Dewey's, and some have argued that Rorty does in fact capture, and effectively update, Dewey's philosophical position.[130] Quite a number of scholars, though, have claimed that Rorty diverges too widely from many of Dewey's most important ideas.[131] My own view on the Dewey-Rorty

---

[128] LW2: 17.

[129] LW2: 21.

[130] For example, see Colin Koopman, *Pragmatism as Transition: Historicity and Hope in James, Dewey, and Rorty* (New York, NY: Columbia University Press, 2009), 2–3, 50, 170; and William Curtis, *Defending Rorty: Pragmatism and Liberal Virtue* (New York, NY: Cambridge University Press, 2015), 7–9, 22–3.

[131] Richard Bernstein, "One Step Forward, Two Steps Backward: Richard Rorty on Liberal Democracy and Philosophy," *Political Theory* 15, no. 4 (1987): 538–63; Hilary Putnam, *Renewing Philosophy* (Cambridge: Harvard University Press, 1992), 180; Susan Haack, *Evidence and Inquiry: Towards Reconstruction in Epistemology* (Oxford:

relationship is more in line with this latter group. What I want to do here, though, is emphasize Rorty's specific rejection of the "scientific" qualities of Dewey's philosophy. I will draw out the implications of Rorty's opposition to Dewey's scientific principles, principles that we have seen are fundamentally Hegelian in nature. This chapter has shown how Dewey's Hegelian influence, and his commitment to the scientific thinking espoused by Hegel, illuminates his depiction of democracy as existing in a process of continuous development. Rorty similarly wants to avoid a reliance on fixed, unchanging entities in his philosophy, but I will show that his rejection of scientific thinking leaves him with a fixed conception of democracy itself. In particular, Rorty's version of democracy cannot tell us why we might have to go beyond the protection of already-existing "negative freedom" in order to have genuine democracy.

Although I have described Dewey's pragmatism as a distinctly democratic philosophy, Rorty argues that pragmatism is "compatible with both wholehearted enthusiasm and whole-hearted contempt for democracy."[132] He thinks that if we follow Dewey's principles, we are not necessarily led "either to democracy or antidemocracy."[133] Rorty claims this because of his belief that pragmatism is not meant to provide a philosophical foundation for anything in particular, but rather to destroy past attempts to provide stable philosophical foundations. The attempt to provide such foundations, in his view, is characteristic of philosophies that attempt to be "scientific," which for Rorty must inevitably involve an attempt to find eternal philosophical truth. He uses Dewey to support his view, portraying Dewey as someone who sought merely to obliterate past philosophical claims, rather than constructing any new proposals for philosophy: "[Dewey's work] is therapeutic rather than constructive,

---

Blackwell Publishers, 1993), 182–3, 189, 193–4; Richard Shusterman, "Pragmatism and Liberalism between Dewey and Rorty," *Political Theory* 22, no. 3 (1994): 391–413; Matthew Festenstein, *Pragmatism and Political Theory: From Dewey to Rorty* (Chicago, IL: University of Chicago Press, 1997), 140–3; Joseph Margolis, *Reinventing Pragmatism: American Philosophy at the End of the Twentieth Century* (Ithaca, NY: Cornell University Press, 2002); Joseph Margolis, *Pragmatism without Foundations: Reconciling Realism and Relativism*, 2nd ed. (London: Continuum International, 2007), 139, 153, 224, 267; David Hildebrand, *Beyond Realism and Antirealism: John Dewey and the Neopragmatists* (Nashville: Vanderbilt University Press, 2003); Robert Westbrook, *Democratic Hope: Pragmatism and the Politics of Truth* (Ithaca, NY: Cornell University Press, 2005), 1–17.

[132] Richard Rorty, "Pragmatism as Romantic Polytheism," in *The Revival of Pragmatism: New Essays on Social Thought, Law, and Culture*, ed. Morris Dickstein (Durham: Duke University Press, 1998), 25.

[133] Ibid., 27.

edifying rather than systematic, designed to make the reader question his own motives for philosophizing rather than to supply him with a new philosophical program ... Great systematic philosophers, like great scientists, build for eternity. Great edifying philosophers destroy for the sake of their own generation."[134] As such, the elements of Dewey's thought that clearly do aim at a constructive philosophical program – and in particular, at a "scientific" program – must be explained away. Rorty claims the "recurrent flaw in Dewey's work" is "his habit of announcing a bold new positive program when all he offers, and all he needs to offer, is criticism of the tradition."[135] The importance Dewey places on science, on rigorous construction – through interaction with objects of experience – of provisional principles for effectively guiding future experience, is a problem for Rorty. He responds with an assertion akin to those which have held that Dewey abandoned Hegel in the early years of his career: "[Dewey's] constant exaltation of something called 'the scientific method,' was an unfortunate legacy of Dewey's youth."[136] Rorty insists that Dewey's pragmatism ultimately does rid itself of the "spirit of *seriousness*"[137] characteristic of philosophies which aim to be scientifically constructive, and thus does not serve as a philosophical foundation for any social and political order, democratic or otherwise.

Rorty further argues that democracy is actually better served when we do not attempt to provide it with philosophical foundations. He believes the search for such foundations embroils democracy in unnecessary controversy, because the intrinsic desirability of democratic freedom is obscured by conflict over who possesses philosophical truth. Again drawing on Dewey, Rorty states that "[t]hose who share Dewey's pragmatism ... [deny] there is any sense in which liberal democracy 'needs' philosophical justification at all" and that such thinkers are "putting politics first and tailoring a philosophy to suit."[138] On this view, "liberal institutions would be all the better if freed from the need to defend themselves in terms of [philosophical] foundations – all the better for not having to answer the question 'In what does the privileged status of freedom

---

[134] Rorty, *Philosophy and the Mirror of Nature*, 5–6, 369.

[135] Richard Rorty, *Consequences of Pragmatism* (Minneapolis: University of Minnesota Press, 1982), 78.

[136] Richard Rorty, *Objectivity, Relativism, and Truth* (Cambridge: Cambridge University Press, 1991), 17.

[137] Rorty, *Consequences of Pragmatism*, 87.

[138] Richard Rorty, "The Priority of Democracy to Philosophy," in *The Virginia Statute for Religious Freedom: Its Evolution and Consequences in American History*, eds. Merrill Peterson and Robert Vaughan (Cambridge: Cambridge University Press, 1988), 260.

consist?'"[139] Instead, Rorty urges that the defining features of modern democracy – especially the liberal "negative" liberties that have emerged with this democracy – should be taken for what they are, without any need for philosophically justifying their existence. He declares that democracy demands no justification because "liberal political freedoms ... require no consensus on any topic more basic than their own desirability," and, more particularly, because without "the standard 'bourgeois freedoms' ... people will be less able to work out their private salvations, create their private self-images."[140] We can thus see how Rorty's conception of democracy is defined primarily by negative freedom – by the intrinsic desirability of giving all individuals the rights and protections against government characteristic of liberal thinking and leaving people alone to act as they wish. Referencing John Stuart Mill, Rorty insists "the only exception to democracy's commitment to honor the rights of individuals" is preventing harm to others' private self-images.[141] And again, negative freedom requires no justification beyond the fact that it emerged at modern democracy's onset and has been shown to be desirable to those who live with it: "democratic institutions are ... [not] to be measured by anything more specific than the moral intuitions of the particular historical community that has created those institutions."[142] For Rorty (and, according to Rorty, for Dewey as well), it is crucial that "democracy takes precedence over philosophy,"[143] so that we do not entangle our desirable democratic freedom in unnecessary philosophical conflict.

Rorty's pragmatist philosophy, then, is meant to reinforce his particular conception of democracy. On his terms, pragmatism does not justify democracy, but can still be useful for someone who is already committed to the type of liberal democracy he outlines. His democratic theory focuses on the idea that liberal political freedom allows individuals to create their own private self-images, and protects individuals from having conceptions of the good life imposed on them. Relatedly, his "characterization of pragmatism is that it is simply anti-essentialism applied to notions like 'truth,' 'knowledge,' 'language,' 'morality,' and similar objects of philosophical theorizing."[144] For Rorty, pragmatism simply uproots

---

[139] Richard Rorty, *Contingency, Irony, and Solidarity* (Cambridge: Cambridge University Press, 1989), 57.
[140] Ibid., 84–5.
[141] Rorty, "Pragmatism as Romantic Polytheism," 33.
[142] Rorty, "Priority of Democracy to Philosophy," 269.
[143] Ibid., 270.
[144] Rorty, *Consequences of Pragmatism*, 162.

past claims to philosophical truth and shows that all we really have are different languages and vocabularies for describing the world, none of which bring objective truth. Pragmatism does not justify democracy, then, because one could surely have such a stance against philosophical truth and commit to an undemocratic social and political order. Although Rorty does maintain that his pragmatism is useful for someone who is committed to democracy (as he defines it). The democratic idea of leaving people alone to create their private self-images, for Rorty, is buttressed by the pragmatic idea that no one has access to philosophical truth. He thus does not define pragmatism (as Dewey does) by a construction of provisional truth through intelligent interaction with objects of experience. A pragmatist simply recognizes that there is no truth independent of our linguistic descriptions of the world,[145] and he applauds how "edifying" thinkers use this recognition to "prevent [philosophy] from attaining the secure path of a science."[146]

I do not mean to argue here that there is something intrinsically wrong with Rorty's philosophical views or that he is definitely wrong about the possibilities for "scientifically" generating provisional truth. My aim is to highlight how the Hegelian-scientific quality of Dewey's pragmatism is absent from Rorty's and how this absence divides Rorty's democratic theory from Dewey's. I would first say, though, that Dewey's commitment to science surely need not be seen as an unfortunate detour he takes into seeking fixed truth. For Dewey, the scientific mind-set is such that "the existence of fixed kinds of things, has ... been destroyed,"[147] and that "knowledge is obtained ... through deliberate institution of a definite and specified course of change"[148] – that is, through putting principles developed from experience into practice in order to exercise a distinct, self-chosen effect on novel objects of experience. Interestingly, Rorty aligns himself with Hegel[149] as well as with Dewey, praising Hegel for uprooting past philosophical ideas and for moving philosophy away from the search for eternal truth. But Hegel might likely deem Rorty someone whose supposed scruples create "a mistrust of Science, which in the absence of such scruples gets on with the work itself, and actually cognizes something," and who thus seeks to be "exempt from the hard work

[145] Rorty, *Contingency, Irony, and Solidarity*, 4–5.
[146] Rorty, *Philosophy and the Mirror of Nature*, 372.
[147] Dewey, *Art as Experience*, 286.
[148] Dewey, *Quest for Certainty*, 84.
[149] Rorty, *Consequences of Pragmatism*, xli.

of Science."[150] Dewey would certainly seem to be more to Hegel's liking, since Dewey's pragmatism does not only deny that there are eternally true ideas, but puts ideas into action through interaction with objects of experience and determines the truth of those ideas by whether they "successfully modify conditions in the direction desired."[151] As Rorty recognizes, Dewey does reject "the quest for a certainty which shall be absolute and unshakeable" and the attempt to "grasp universal Being, and Being which is universal is fixed and immutable."[152] But although he renounces the search for perfect "certainty" that fixed truth could provide, Dewey explores how individuals may develop a more meaningful – though provisional – certainty through intelligently interacting with their changing conditions: "The quest for certainty by means of exact possession in mind of immutable reality is exchanged for search for security by means of active control of the changing course of events."[153] Through provisional, not fixed, principles derived from practical interaction with objects of experience, individuals may achieve "active control of objects" by "purposefully introducing changes which will alter the direction of the course of events," thus becoming "a participator in [the world's] changes."[154]

For Rorty, it is still too large of a metaphysical assumption to hold that individuals can scientifically generate greater control over their lives through intelligent resolution of the problems brought by experience. He insists that this scientific position represents yet another belief in a fixed truth about the nature of the world and how people should live in it. He thus seeks a more modest philosophical position that simply opposes all claims about truth, including the claim that provisional truth – and control over one's life – can be progressively generated in the course of experience. And because philosophy again provides no justification for anything, including democracy, Rorty mainly wants to uphold the "democracy" that already exists and that he, as well as many other Americans, personally favor. He commits to the liberal negative freedom that defines American democracy, not because this signifies a kind of objective truth, but because this is the subjective commitment that Americans happen to have. According to Rorty, negative freedom is indeed effective at protecting individuals from having universal truth

---

[150] Hegel, *Phenomenology of Spirit*, 47–8.
[151] MW4: 185.
[152] Dewey, *Quest for Certainty*, 6–7.
[153] Ibid., 204.
[154] Ibid., 37, 100, 213.

claims, and substantive ethical conceptions of the good life, imposed on them. His pragmatism's rejection of truth claims is just useful for upholding this democracy.

Rorty once again invokes Dewey to justify this basic commitment to liberal negative freedom. He claims that Dewey aimed to undermine the "philosophical foundations" of liberalism, because Dewey saw "this undermining as a way of strengthening liberal institutions,"[155] for if liberals were freed from having to posit such eternal foundations, it would be easier for a liberal society to "leave people alone, to let them try out their private visions of perfection in peace."[156] It is correct to say that Dewey's thought undermines the philosophical foundations of liberalism. But the reason Dewey does this is not simply for the sake of undercutting those foundations. He instead does this because he sees the foundations that gave rise to liberalism as having become undemocratic in practice and as requiring intelligent reconstruction. In particular, he worries that the "special interpretation of liberty" put forward by liberals has been largely "frozen ... into a doctrine to be applied at all times under all social circumstances."[157] Dewey appreciates how the negative, "bourgeois" freedoms achieved by liberalism have successfully worked in favor of "liberation from despotic dynastic rule" and "from inherited legal customs that hampered the rise of new forces of production."[158] However, the assumption that these struggles for freedom were *the* struggles for freedom can blind us to how new circumstances call for new means to address uniquely oppressive situations. We may then identify liberty simply as "ability to make money,"[159] and thus "ignore the immense regimentation to which workers are subjected, intellectual as well as manual workers."[160] This is precisely the problem we have discussed earlier, regarding how workers can be assumed to have freedom even as they are clearly hindered from exercising control over their lives, that is, from interacting with objects of experience in self-determined ways. As Dewey says, "Persons acutely aware of the dangers of regimentation when it is imposed by government remain oblivious to the millions of persons whose behavior is regimented by an economic system through whose intervention alone they obtain

---

[155] Rorty, *Contingency, Irony, and Solidarity*, 57.
[156] Rorty, "Priority of Democracy to Philosophy," 273.
[157] Dewey, *Liberalism and Social Action*, 34.
[158] Ibid., 48.
[159] LW11: 366.
[160] LW11: 294–5.

a livelihood."[161] Thus, "[w]e are now forced to see that positive conditions ... are required. Release from oppressions and repressions which
previously existed marked a necessary transition, but transitions are but
bridges to something different."[162] Negative freedom was necessary for
responding to certain problems, such as the problem of government being
dynastically ruled and having excessive room to intrude into individuals'
lives. But in response to the problem of the economic hierarchies generated by the modern world, negative freedom alone is an insufficient
remedy. If liberals wish to promote free individuality in these new circumstances, Dewey argues that they need not give up negative freedom,
but they must recognize (as noted earlier) that "material security" and
"socialized economy [are] the means of free individual development as
ends." Rorty, therefore, misses the point of Dewey's undermining of the
philosophical foundations of liberalism. Dewey does not merely assume
"liberal democracy" is achieved and then aim to save its defenders the
effort of justifying its existence. Rather, he emphasizes that liberalism
has to cope with an evolving world, and he exposes how liberalism may
become undemocratic if it does not itself evolve toward a commitment
to positive freedom. Rorty, by contrast, implies that the struggles for negative freedom were *the* struggles for freedom and that democracy needs
no further evolution.

Although it seems clear that Rorty misinterprets Dewey, this broader
discussion of negative freedom may strike us as simply representing a disagreement between the two over how far government must go to uphold
individuals' freedom, with no basis for determining which view should
be seen more favorably. However, for one, something should feel askew
when Rorty – a thinker who is so committed to avoiding a reliance on
fixed entities in his thinking – leaves us with a fixed conception of democracy that needs no further development beyond the protection of negative
freedom. But furthermore, Rorty, in responding to issues that are pressing
in the present-day United States, does advocate some "leftist" policies
that aim at achieving "economic and political change" and at combating
the advantages of "the rich and powerful" (although his policy positions
on these matters are a bit more moderate than Dewey's).[163] This shows
an understanding on his part of how existing negative liberties may be
inadequate for coping with current situations (e.g., in the workplace)

---

[161] Dewey, *Freedom and Culture*, 167–8.
[162] Ibid., 7.
[163] Richard Rorty, *Achieving Our Country: Leftist Thought in Twentieth-Century America* (Cambridge: Harvard University Press, 1998), 30–1, 48, 104.

where individuals are plainly not self-governing. The problem with this, though, is that Rorty cannot insist on policies pursuing "economic change" and positive freedom without committing to some kind of philosophical foundation for saying why already-existing democracy is inadequate and how democracy needs to develop from here in order to actualize the individual freedom that democracy signifies. In order to say that rightist policies that, for instance, redistribute wealth from the poor to the rich are less democratic than leftist policies, he must concede that the philosophically modest precept of "leave people alone" may actually interfere with individuals' freedom, and he must philosophically justify a more substantive notion of what freedom involves. Rorty's philosophical position, though, has locked him into the view that democracy has already been achieved in the United States, and so all he can really do is throw his lot in with a leftist rather than rightist picture of America's future. When Rorty states that democratic institutions are (as noted earlier) not "to be measured by anything more specific than the moral intuitions of the particular historical community that has created those institutions," he tells us that American institutions are to be judged only by the predominant moral intuitions which have characterized the American historical community as "democratic" – intuitions that have primarily sought the achievement of negative freedom. Hence, when he argues that America should go beyond negative freedom, he cannot say that America's democratic status might depend on the achievement of positive freedom, because democracy must be said to already exist. Again misinterpreting Dewey, Rorty asserts that "[Dewey's] pragmatism is an answer to the question 'What can philosophy do for the United States?' rather than to the question 'How can the United States be philosophically justified?'"[164] As I have shown, Dewey does not simply assume that America has achieved democracy, and he does not merely tailor a philosophy to suit this already-accomplished democracy. Dewey's philosophical position does not treat democracy as a fixed fact, and it allows him to account for the possibility that America might become more or less democratic in the face of changing circumstances. In our current circumstances, if the US government avoids creating the conditions for positive freedom and simply seeks to uphold negative freedom, then America does indeed become less democratic on Dewey's terms.

Dewey's scientific, and Hegelian, philosophy does effectively justify the pursuit of positive freedom. He sees individuals as capable of actively

[164] Ibid., 27.

exercising control over their lives through a scientific interaction with objects of experience, and he conceives of how this individual development is intertwined with the continuous pursuit of social conditions that are conducive to that development, since society can generate unique threats to individuals' capacity to control their lives. This does involve a commitment to philosophical foundations, regarding the idea that provisional control over one's life is possible, and that it can be achieved through an active, intelligent interaction with constantly changing circumstances. But the risk of not making such a commitment is that we can declare individuals to be free when they are formally given certain rights and liberties, but are in fact facing social conditions that deny them meaningful opportunity to direct the course of their lives. I maintain, further, that Dewey's philosophical commitment is in fact quite modest. He commits to the idea that individuals can actively govern their lives, but he does not at all arbitrarily curtail the directions in which individuals can take their lives, and his emphasis on the continuous development of ideas and concepts requires that we not hold fixed our principles regarding what democracy specifically entails. This is why I not only say that Dewey's pragmatism specifically justifies a commitment to democracy, but that he provides a *pragmatic* idea of democracy itself. He presents democracy as in a process of continuous development, such that what we consider to be "democratic" today may not be democratic in the future. He relatedly challenges the commonly held idea that democracy is mainly a political concept, and he instead shows that democracy must be seen as *individual* and *social*, as well as political, and that each of these elements must develop alongside the other elements. This is particularly important to realize under our current circumstances, where political democracy apparently exists but many individuals are still prevented from governing their lives: "democracy cannot now depend upon or be expressed in political institutions alone. We cannot even be certain that they and their legal accompaniments are actually democratic at the present time – for democracy is expressed in the attitudes of human beings and is measured by consequences produced in their lives."[165] Democracy is not exclusively political, and even its political element may not be democratic if it does not help build the social conditions for individuals' self-government. We surely cannot say democracy is fully present, even in its political element, when a government simply upholds negative freedom. Dewey, who

---

[165] Dewey, *Freedom and Culture*, 125.

declares that the democracy he seeks "is not a fact and never will be,"[166] avoids the Rortyan trap of presuming democracy has already been satisfactorily achieved.

DEMOCRACY IN DEVELOPMENT

This chapter has used Hegel to illuminate the development required in each of the individual, social, and political elements of Deweyan democracy. Dewey's commitment to the type of "scientific" principles advocated by Hegel elucidates how individuals can govern themselves by intelligently interacting with, and exercising control over, the novel objects of experience they inevitably confront. His commitment to these principles also helps us see how government must be alert to, and actively ameliorate, the unique threats brought by changing social conditions (e.g., the conditions of work) to the capacities of individuals to so govern themselves. The typical, hierarchical relations of the workplace present a clear example of structural social inequality, whereby many individuals are obstructed from governing their lives, and their lives are instead essentially under the control of powerful others.

I have also distinguished Dewey's pragmatic idea of democracy from the version of democracy offered by Rorty. I have shown how Rorty's divergence from Hegelian-scientific principles leads him to a fixed conception of democracy. Rorty's pragmatism aims to simply break down past claims to truth in a way that is useful for upholding the current features of modern democracy. These features primarily relate to the negative freedom achieved by liberalism, and so we are left assuming democracy has been achieved in nations such as the United States and needs no further development in the face of changing circumstances. Dewey's pragmatic idea of democracy does carry some philosophical foundations, but these foundations call for treating all concepts as in a process of development, and he conceives of democracy itself as continuously developing, rather than a fixed fact. When it comes to dealing with structurally unequal social conditions, I would say Dewey should be favored over Rorty.

Dewey contends that no one "was ever emancipated merely by being left alone. Removal of formal limitations is but a negative condition; positive freedom is not a state but an act which involves methods and

---

[166] Dewey, *Public and Its Problems*, 148.

instrumentalities for control of conditions."[167] By connecting democracy with individuals' never-finished exercise of control over their lives, Dewey avoids any fixed conception of democratic government and steers clear of becoming satisfied with what passes for democracy at the moment. The dominant political understanding of democracy abstracts from the threats to individual self-government that exist in the social realm, and Dewey shows why political institutions themselves must continuously work to alter social conditions in a democratic direction. As he says, instead of allowing democracy to "become so associated with a particular political order," we must associate democracy with "individuality ... [with] unique modes of activity that create new ends, with willing acceptance of the modifications of the established order entailed by the release of individualized capacities."[168] Dewey's theory leads us to see democracy as more than a form of government and to see that government itself must continuously develop to maintain democratic character.

[167] Ibid., 168.
[168] MW13: 297.

3

The Pursuit of Democratic
Political Institutions

We have seen how political democracy requires a political system to act to overcome *social* threats to individual self-government, such as forms of structural inequality. But for Dewey, political democracy also depends on the makeup and organization of political institutions themselves. He does not suggest that a government's actions toward democratizing society should be simply done for the people by an exclusive group of politicians. Dewey, for one, does not think that political actors, when unchecked by the public at large, can be expected to work for the benefit of individuals throughout the polity. He indeed argues that politicians cannot even truly know how to work for that benefit if individuals throughout the polity do not have an effective voice in political decision-making processes. Additionally, Dewey sees the opportunity to influence political institutions as a necessary aspect of individuals' self-government. I have described how Dewey's democratic individualism depends on actual opportunities for individuals to direct their lives in social spheres like the workplace, and the opportunity to influence the political institutions they live under is also indispensable. Dewey highlights how one's political efficacy does not exist in a vacuum and how it can be inhibited by, for instance, an alienating everyday experience in the workplace. But he still presents political influence as independently significant to the achievement of democracy.

In this chapter, I will provide a thorough analysis of the political element of Deweyan democracy, with a focus on the organization of political institutions. I will specifically portray Dewey as presenting a *radical* stance toward political institutions. In the essay, "Democracy Is Radical," Dewey states that *"the end of democracy is a radical end"* and that democracy "is radical because it requires great change" in established institutions.[1] He further claims in *The Public and Its Problems* that, for a populace to exercise control over its government, it often "has to break existing political forms."[2] In essence, Dewey holds that no set of institutions ensures the presence of political democracy in perpetuity and that democracy often requires radical change in its political institutions.

Dewey's status as a radical political thinker, though, would be disputed by some, particularly the prominent radical, Sheldon Wolin. Wolin characterizes Dewey's democratic theory as a platitude-filled theory that does not effectively respond to power inequities and does little to actually question the exclusive political power held by elite actors. In *Politics and Vision*, Wolin writes that "Dewey never squarely associated democracy, local or otherwise, with participation in the exercise of power or self-government. His definitions of democracy were surprisingly pallid."[3] In his own democratic thinking, Wolin calls on us to see democracy as gravely inhibited whenever modern political institutions are present. He rejects "[t]he common assumption ... that the extent and degree of democratization ... is a function of, the extent to which democracy has been embodied in the 'core' political institutions of that society."[4] For Wolin, modern political institutions inevitably separate an exclusive group of political actors from the vast majority of citizens and strictly regulate the opportunities for citizens to exercise power. Democracy, then, must not be associated with a set of institutions, but rather with transgressions of established institutions by those without political power. And because institutionalization is inevitable in modern politics, Wolin affirms that democracy can only be a temporary, momentary phenomenon.[5] It is true that Dewey does not reject modern political institutions to the degree that Wolin does, and for Wolin, this would mean that Dewey is inadequately prepared to combat undemocratic political power.

As I explore Dewey's approach to political institutions in this chapter, I will also defend him against Wolin's charge that he is not attuned to

[1] LW11: 298–99.
[2] John Dewey, *The Public and Its Problems* (Chicago, IL: Swallow Press, [1927] 1954), 31.
[3] Sheldon Wolin, *Politics and Vision*, exp. ed. (Princeton, NJ: Princeton University Press, 2004), 517.
[4] Sheldon Wolin, "Norm and Form: The Constitutionalizing of Democracy," in *Athenian Political Thought and the Reconstruction of American Democracy*, eds. J. Peter Euben, John R. Wallach, and Josiah Ober (Ithaca, NY: Cornell University Press, 1994), 40.
[5] Sheldon Wolin, "Fugitive Democracy," in *Democracy and Difference: Contesting the Boundaries of the Political*, ed. Seyla Benhabib (Princeton, NJ: Princeton University Press, 1996), 39.

problems of exclusive political power, and that he is thus insufficiently radical. Dewey, in fact, pays no less attention than Wolin to the ways that
modern political institutions tend to be captured by powerful interests.
Their divergence, I will show, relates to a difference in their fundamental principles that cannot easily be resolved in one direction or the other,
though there is certainly reason to favor Dewey's position over Wolin's. For
Wolin, the fact that political institutions cannot completely erase disparities in political influence – and that institutions by definition establish political roles for certain individuals to fulfill that others do not – should lead us
to deny that we can ever have democracy when institutions are present and
functioning normally. Dewey, for his part, is committed to a broad goal of
allowing all individuals across society to have equal influence over governing institutions. He recognizes that no set of institutions will likely ever
ensure this full equality of political influence, and that actually existing
institutions often serve to systematically privilege certain voices over others
in political decision making. Dewey does not say, though, that democracy
thus cannot exist when we have institutions, but rather he conceives of
democratic political institutions as a matter of continuous development.
He holds that political democracy is never perfectly achieved, but it can be
continuously actualized through intelligent reconstruction of institutions
in response to unique forms of undemocratic governance. Wolin, therefore, can be said to take the more "radical" position, in that he simply
rejects institutions and equates democracy only with momentary instances
where there is a kind of uprising against institutions. He demands that we
only look for a democracy that is pure and undiluted by any association
with institutions. By contrast, Dewey, who once again displays a *pragmatic*
philosophy, argues that we can progressively remedy the current undemocratic qualities in our institutions, and thus push those institutions in a
democratic direction. Dewey, in fact, calls (as Wolin does) for thorough
disruptions of existing institutions – and they both provide justification
for social movements that directly challenge the undemocratic qualities of
institutions – but for Dewey this is for the purpose of constructing institutions that move democracy's imperfect development forward rather than
being simply for the purpose of disruption itself. On Dewey's terms, the
construction of new institutions that effectively combat, for example, the
control of government by wealth represents the further development of
political democracy, even though these institutions would not be seen as perfectly, eternally democratic, either. Dewey grasps that political democracy
cannot be fully realized through any particular set of institutions, but he
does not abandon this goal simply because of its unavoidable incompletion.

The analysis in this chapter will further exhibit the "permanent deposit" left by Hegel on Dewey's thinking.[6] Specifically, I will show how Dewey's approach to political democracy accounts for, in Hegelian terms, the *negation* of institutions (as Wolin does), and also for the *negation of the negation*, that is, the construction of new institutions out of the rejection of old institutions so that political freedom and self-government can have *actual* content. Dewey does not assume any set of institutions will fully achieve political democracy, and in Hegelian and pragmatic (two terms I showed in Chapter 2 to be deeply intertwined) fashion, he conceives of how an institution that helps move democracy forward at one point in history may eventually begin to obstruct democracy if it is not altered in response to new conditions. He calls for radical action against – or, negation of – institutions that have become undemocratic, but also insists on the intelligent reconstruction of institutions to make *actual* the self-government signified by democracy. If we focus merely on destroying the currently oppressive institutions, we would not then be allowing the idea of political democracy to take on meaningful content. In the course of this chapter, I will show that Hegel makes precisely these kinds of points while critiquing the anti-institutional features of Jean-Jacques Rousseau's political thought. I will thus be using Hegel not only to illuminate Dewey's process of achieving democratic political institutions, but also to show how Dewey's "radical" approach to political democracy can be defended against the more thoroughly anti-institutional approach. The anti-institutional tradition can be seen as encompassing Wolin as well as Rousseau, and also contemporary thinkers such as Jacques Ranciere. This analysis of Dewey will thus provide a significant challenge to prevalent ways of thinking about a radical theory of democracy.

IS DEWEY "INSTITUTIONAL" OR "RADICAL"?

Dewey has often been accused of lacking a clear political strategy. William Caspary refers to "Dewey's failure to provide a concrete political strategy,"[7] and Peter Manicas notes how "[h]e is sometimes unclear, sometimes just where one wants a clear statement most of all."[8] Perhaps due to

---

[6] John Dewey, "From Absolutism to Experimentalism," in *Contemporary American Philosophy*, Vol. II, eds. George P. Adams and Wm. Pepperell Montague (New York, NY: The Macmillan Company, 1930), 21.

[7] William Caspary, *Dewey on Democracy* (Ithaca, NY: Cornell University Press, 2000), 2–3.

[8] Peter Manicas, *Rescuing Dewey: Essays in Pragmatic Naturalism* (Lanham, MD: Lexington Books, 2008), 187.

this apparent lack of clarity, scholars have differed on whether Dewey is interested in any significant change to the political institutions that are associated with democracy at present. Some have indeed depicted Dewey as largely comfortable with existing institutions. Melvin Rogers, who has also taken on the Dewey/Wolin comparison, agrees with Wolin that Dewey does not provide a radical stance toward institutions: "Dewey is sensitive to the fact that society's functioning will often require us to be habituated for its stability. This may include, in contrast to Wolin's view, reliance on hierarchical relationships such as we see, for example, in the management of schools and government agencies."[9] He thus presents Dewey as accepting the division of responsibility between "experts, political representatives, and the larger public," and as primarily seeking to prevent powerful experts and politicians from acting unchecked.[10] Similarly, David Fott asserts that Dewey's political theory does not require "the establishment of a new state or even a significant modification of the structure of the old one."[11] For Caspary, Dewey's theory embraces "representative institutions; participation is not identical with direct democracy,"[12] and Michael Eldridge argues that "[f]or Dewey democracy was specific forms, including open deliberation, representative assemblies, and frequent elections."[13] These analyses thus present Dewey as basically a defender of the rationality of current institutions; as Keith Snider sums up, "Dewey's politics ... would simply not allow merely experimental or casual treatment of constitutions or any other state institution."[14]

For other commentators, though, Dewey provides a radical challenge to current institutions. Manicas, for instance, labels Dewey an anarchist, arguing that "[e]xcept for explicit anarchist thought – and even then, not all of it – no one saw more clearly than Dewey that for the modern age, the State was not part of the solution, but was, instead, an essential part of the problem."[15] Roger Ames emphasizes Dewey's skepticism of present-day political routines: "On Dewey's understanding, the familiar

[9] Melvin Rogers, *The Undiscovered Dewey: Religion, Morality, and the Ethos of Democracy* (New York, NY: Columbia University Press, 2009), 216.

[10] Ibid., 22, 195.

[11] David Fott, *John Dewey: America's Philosopher of Democracy* (Lanham, MD: Rowman & Littlefield Publishers, 1998), 41.

[12] Caspary, *Dewey on Democracy*, 15.

[13] Michael Eldridge, *Transforming Experience: John Dewey's Cultural Instrumentalism* (Nashville: Vanderbilt University Press, 1998), 96.

[14] Keith Snider, "Response to Stever and Garrison," *Administration & Society* 32, no. 4 (2000): 488.

[15] Manicas, *Rescuing Dewey*, 193.

institutionalized forms of democracy – a constitution, the office of president, the polling station, the ballot box, and so on – far from being a guarantee of political order, can indeed become a source of just such coercion."[16] And James Stever claims that "Dewey made it quite clear that constitutions were merely historical artifacts to be cast aside when new circumstances, problems, and new political logic dictated."[17] On this view, present political institutions are a threat to Deweyan democracy and must be cast aside once they become irrelevant to changing circumstances.

On my reading, neither the "institutional" nor the "radical" interpretation of Dewey is wholly inaccurate. I will show that Dewey does call for significant change to institutions that obstruct the development of political democracy; however, he does not merely look to reject such institutions and cast them aside, but rather to preserve the aspects of those institutions that do promote democracy while reconstructing the aspects that do not. Dewey conceives a continuous process of political democratization which requires that no single political form be deemed sacrosanct in the face of evolving circumstances. His theory does not lead us to simply reject established institutions, though, and we are instead to preserve the democratic aspects of previous institutions while intelligently rectifying the undemocratic aspects.

DEWEY AND WOLIN ON POLITICAL INSTITUTIONS

In Wolin's view, genuine rule by citizens at large cannot be a consistent feature of modern politics. Unlike in ancient Athens (as he portrays it), modern politics for Wolin is defined by institutionalization, or settled rules for governing practices which limit the more spontaneous action of the masses: "Institutionalization marks the attenuation of democracy: leaders begin to appear; hierarchies develop; experts of one kind or another cluster around the centers of decision; order, procedure, and precedent displace a more spontaneous politics."[18] Wolin argues that the frequent rotation of office and selection of officials by lot in the Athenian city-state

---

[16] Roger Ames, "Tang Junyi and the Very 'Idea' of Confucian Democracy," in *Democracy as Culture: Deweyan Pragmatism in a Globalizing World*, eds. Sor-Hoon Tan and John Whalen-Bridge (Albany, NY: State University of New York Press, 2008), 179.

[17] James Stever, "The Parallel Universes: Pragmatism and Public Administration," *Administration & Society* 32, no. 4 (2000): 457.

[18] Wolin, "Fugitive Democracy," 39.

limited institutionalization,[19] but with such practices being hardly feasible in large-scale modern nation-states, it is inevitable that "distance is quickly established between knowledgeable professionals and ignorant citizens."[20] Rule by an exclusive group of professional politicians, rather than rule by the mass of ordinary citizens, is thus the inescapable, undemocratic norm for modern politics. Wolin further claims that a constitution, ostensibly set up to limit the power of governmental institutions over the people, severely restricts democracy. He holds that constitutions set rigid limits on democracy, using rules that restrict the "voice of the people" to be heard only during periodic elections held every few years.[21] Far from establishing democracy, a constitution confines citizens to narrow channels for the exercise of power, channels that are not significant enough to grant them genuine rule over their polity: "Constitutionalism and electoral democracy became complementary. Together they signified the destruction of the demos as actor, its marginalization as voter."[22] For Wolin, therefore, we can never deem *democratic* any situation where voting in elections is the main governing responsibility of the majority of citizens.

To find examples of genuine democracy, Wolin contends we must look for extra-institutional action by those excluded from political power, action that takes place outside the limits set on the people by the constitution. He proposes "accepting the familiar charges that democracy is inherently unstable, inclined toward anarchy, and identified with revolution and using these traits as the basis for a different, *a*constitutional conception of democracy."[23] Although institutionalization is the norm in modern politics, democracy may still seep through in "moments," certain instances where entrenched hierarchies and old political forms are brought down, and where those typically marginalized or excluded from politics temporarily gain access to political power.[24] Institutionalization inevitably follows the democratic moment, but that institutionalization is still not democratic; there was only democracy during the moment when entrenched political forms were brought down: "Democracy in the late modern world cannot be a complete political system ... Democracy

---

[19] Wolin, "Norm and Form," 43.
[20] Ibid.
[21] Wolin, "Fugitive Democracy," 34.
[22] Sheldon Wolin, "Democracy: Electoral and Athenian," *PS: Political Science and Politics* 26, no. 3 (1993): 476.
[23] Wolin, "Norm and Form," 37.
[24] Wolin, "Fugitive Democracy," 37–8.

needs to be reconceived as something other than a form of government ... doomed to succeed only temporarily."[25] On Wolin's terms, the Athenian city-state did in fact achieve democratic governance where barriers to participation had been effectively overcome and there was "the practice of collective action on a continuing basis."[26] In large-scale modern nation-states, though, new barriers to participation unavoidably arise, and democracy is only achieved in the moment of transgressing such a barrier.

Wolin sees Dewey, by contrast, as making only a feeble attempt at conceiving political democracy. He complains that, for Dewey, democracy "is communicated experience; or democracy consists of mutual interests; or democracy is the process of continuous adjustments to change. Had Dewey foreseen the future, his democracy might have found fulfillment in the Internet's paradox of intimate communication without face-to-face contact."[27] He sees Dewey as providing only vacuous phrases to define democracy, and he further charges that "Dewey's most crucial concepts – experimentation, method, and culture – were ways of evading questions about power. His society appears fixated on the findings of method, the conduct of experiments, and the communication of results. Questions of how problems become identified, who controls the communication of results, and who evaluates the consequences were all left indeterminate."[28] Wolin is correct that concepts such as experimentation and continuous adjustment to change are central to Dewey's democratic theory; however, his interpretation of these concepts is highly superficial, and this leads him to miss the radical quality of Deweyan political democracy.

Like Wolin, Dewey emphasizes how modern institutions have often bred severe inequalities in political power. He in fact draws a direct connection between fundamental challenges to those institutions and movements to expand human liberty: "the great movements for human liberation have always been movements to change institutions and not to preserve them intact."[29] In *The Public and Its Problems*, he also remarks that "[a]lmost as soon as [the state's] form is stabilized, it needs to be re-made," and that "since conditions of action and of inquiry and of

---

[25] Wolin, "Norm and Form," 54–5.
[26] Sheldon Wolin, "Transgression, Equality, and Voice," in *Demokratia: A Conversation on Democracies, Ancient and Modern*, eds. Josiah Ober and Charles Hedrick (Princeton, NJ: Princeton University Press, 1996), 85.
[27] Wolin, *Politics and Vision*, 517.
[28] Ibid.
[29] LW11: 362.

knowledge are always changing, the experiment must always be retried; the State must always be rediscovered."[30] Wolin's skepticism of an established set of "democratic" state institutions is thus mirrored in Dewey. Wolin should seemingly appreciate Dewey's approach, because it displays that Wolinian doubt that political democracy can be presumed to exist through a set of fixed institutions.

Furthermore, Dewey objects to the idea that democracy comes through rigidly adhering to a constitution. In *Freedom and Culture* he argues we must "get rid of the ideas that lead us to believe that democratic conditions automatically maintain themselves, or that they can be identified with fulfillment of prescriptions laid down in a constitution," and he ridicules the notion "that the observance of formulae that have become ritualistic are effective safeguards of our democratic heritage."[31] His reasoning is that if we uncritically abide by long-established constitutional forms, we can be wholly unprepared if changing conditions render those forms ineffective at generating democratic control of government. As such, the rights, liberties, and electoral processes established in the US Constitution cannot be considered eternal markers of democracy, because new circumstances call for new means to address new obstacles to political self-government. Dewey laments that "[i]t has even been regarded as unpatriotic to say or teach anything that would give pupils the idea that our Constitution and the system under which we live are not so perfect that any serious problems remain" and argues that students should be encouraged to question whether "a system adopted in the era of the stage-coach and candle light" is "perfectly adapted to the era of the railway, electricity, and airplane."[32] Without such critical thought, schools end up producing "a truly religious idealization of, and reverence for, established institutions."[33] As with Wolin, therefore, Dewey does not leave us merely abiding by customary institutions to achieve political democracy.

Most importantly, Wolin's claim that Dewey's focus on concepts such as "experimentation" and "continuous adjustment to change" serves to evade questions of power is simply incorrect. For instance, Dewey stresses in many different works the importance of recognizing and fighting against the exclusive control of political institutions by powerful economic interests. He asks, "Why have power and rule passed from the

---

[30] Dewey, *Public and Its Problems*, 31–2, 34.
[31] John Dewey, *Freedom and Culture* (New York, NY: G. P. Putnam's Sons, 1939), 34–5.
[32] LW9: 161.
[33] Dewey, *Public and Its Problems*, 169–70.

people to a few? Everybody knows who the few are, and the class-status of the few answers the question ... They are an oligarchy of wealth. They rule over us because they control banks, credit, the land, and big organized means of production."[34] He thus perceives how "[e]conomic privilege has taken possession of government,"[35] as well as the need for "a radical change in the forces which control our government – a change from reactionary standpattism in support of big business to support of the common people who are suffering."[36] This demand for radical change in fact drove Dewey's own efforts in the 1930s (in the midst of the Great Depression) to form a new leftist political party in the United States, as he considered both the Democrats and Republicans to be too deeply entwined with dominant pecuniary interests: "The existing parties are the servants of those economic interests which use the government and which debauch governmental agencies to do their will at the expense of society."[37] The political aim of this new party, Dewey explains, was to progressively wrest control of government away from dominant interests and to make government more genuinely accountable to the public as a whole:

> The dominant issue is whether the people of the United States are to control our government, federal, state, and municipal, and to use it in behalf of the peace and welfare of society or whether control is to go on passing into the hands of small powerful economic groups who use all the machinery of administration and legislation to serve their own ends.[38]

Dewey's "experimentation" and "continuous adjustment to change," which Wolin objects to, in fact highlight the need for continuous critical evaluation of political institutions and rectification of the evolving undemocratic qualities that emerge in those institutions over time.

This last statement exhibits the significant point of divergence between Dewey and Wolin. They agree that participation, self-government, public control of the polity, etc., are not made actual simply through a set of institutions; but whereas Wolin searches for temporary experiences of pure democracy that are removed from modern institutionalization, Dewey advocates continuous, critical evaluation of institutions so that

---

[34] LW9: 76.
[35] LW6: 174.
[36] LW6: 253.
[37] LW6: 151.
[38] LW6: 149. Dewey's efforts at forming this new party will be discussed further in Chapter 4.

their undemocratic qualities can be identified and progressively remedied: "Extensive critical examination of our own practices provides the
only way in which the adequacy of our claim to be genuinely democratic
may be tested in the concrete. It is also the only way in which measures
for correction of defects can be discovered and put into effect."[39] Both
thinkers understand that modern politics requires the establishment of
governing institutions and procedures. For Dewey, changing conditions
continuously generate new undemocratic qualities in those institutions,
which in turn necessitates the (never completely achieved) process of
democratizing institutions. For Wolin, the inevitable incompleteness of
democratic control of institutions renders that control necessarily illu-
sory, and thus only temporary anti-institutional actions are genuinely
"democratic." He claims "democracy is wayward, inchoate, unable to
rule yet unwilling to be ruled."[40] I do not mean to argue here that Dewey
is clearly right and Wolin clearly wrong. But I do hold that there is good
reason to favor Dewey's position. If democracy is indeed to signify some
meaningful idea of individuals exercising control over their lives, and if
Wolin's conception leaves (as he says) democratic "rule" as essentially
nonexistent, then it follows that we should seek instead to make that
"rule" into something of an actuality.

At the level of politics, Dewey is fundamentally interested in allowing individuals to affect the policies that affect them. Because we face
constantly changing circumstances, he points out how political institutions that once allowed individuals to do this may eventually cease to do
so. In its distinctly "political phase," democracy for Dewey means that
"government exists to serve its community, and that this purpose cannot
be achieved unless the community itself shares in selecting its governors
and determining their policies."[41] Therefore, institutions must be reconstructed when they exclude voices and hinder the capacity of certain individuals to become self-governing. This reconstruction aims at allowing
individuals to affect the policies of the political institutions under which
they live. Wolin, though, confines democracy to "[s]ignificant political
changes [that] are the product of transgressive actions. They disturb the
power relations, interests, expectations, and taboos that typically cluster
around all laws and institutions."[42] Again, with Wolin, we are forced to
consider any modern institutional setup to be undemocratic. With Dewey,

[39] LW16: 405.
[40] Wolin, "Norm and Form," 50.
[41] Dewey, *Public and Its Problems*, 146.
[42] Wolin, "Transgression, Equality, and Voice," 79.

we seek progressive improvements in institutions to resolve problems of individuals being subject to decisions they cannot influence.

We have seen in the prior chapters how for Dewey, political institutions must contribute to democracy's development by producing the kinds of policies that help remedy undemocratic aspects of society. He asserts that "[t]he political and governmental phase of democracy is a means ... for realizing ends that lie in the wide domain of human relationships and the development of human personality."[43] Political institutions can act to expand individuals' opportunity to govern their everyday lives, but Dewey recognizes that when institutional processes are exclusive and undemocratic, the outputs from those institutions will also likely be undemocratic, that is, they will work against individuals' capacity to control their lives. It is thus essential to democracy that institutions not simply reflect the voices of the socially powerful. Dewey explains that "[l]egislation ... can help unload the burdens that politicians subservient to great wealth have piled on the backs of the helpless consumer; it can assist the return of employment by taking away some of the favors that have been given to the privileged class."[44] Writing during the Great Depression, though, he points out "[w]hy does not President Hoover face the real issue? Is it because measures of relief would impose heavier surtaxes on the favored few and lessen contributions to campaign funds?"[45] When the wealthy – due to the excessive amount of money they can donate to political campaigns – have disproportionate influence over institutions, we are likely to have "policies that put the burden of debt and increased cost of living upon those least able to stand it, while refusing to use power to tax higher incomes and estates."[46] But if governmental institutions are composed of voices beyond the wealthy, we may "force the wealthy owners of the nation to surrender their control over the lives and destinies of the overwhelming majority of the American people."[47] Hence, if wealthy voices control the discussion of welfare policy, white voices control the discussion of school desegregation, or male voices control the discussion of women's health, institutional changes that address these exclusionary qualities represent an advance in democracy's development. Individuals who are often affected by policies without being able to influence them could thereby exercise some manner of control over their political institutions.

43 LW11: 217.
44 LW6: 345.
45 LW6: 345.
46 LW9: 278.
47 LW6: 386.

If only anti-institutional transgression is democratic, though, then there are no institutional changes that can give excluded individuals the opportunity to govern themselves.

While I again do not claim that Dewey has unquestionably the better argument than Wolin, Dewey's position should surely be appealing to us if we want democratic "rule" to have actual content, that is, if we want individuals at large to be able to influence the policies that affect them. Dewey presents similarly *radical* challenges to current political institutions as Wolin does, but the transgressions of institutions that Dewey seeks are meant to aim at pushing institutions in a more democratic direction. The democratic advancements sought during such transgressions are to be installed within new institutions so that excluded individuals can take advantage of them and influence the policies produced by government. Prior to the passage of the Nineteenth Amendment, Dewey argues that "woman's political enfranchisement is necessary ... to complete the democratic movement," and on the notion of a property qualification for voting, he says, "The propertied classes will protect themselves pretty well under any conditions ... Hence it is the masses – the poor – that most need the protection of the ballot."[48] These excluded groups of individuals are not only to challenge the institutions that exclude them, but to pursue reconstructed institutions that give them access to political decision making. Wolin's singular focus on anti-institutional moments, though, leaves typically excluded individuals "unable to rule." For Dewey, achieving suffrage for women and the poor is a meaningful democratic advance, and the institutionalization of this right to vote in a constitution should not be seen as undemocratic. This does not prevent Dewey from identifying how voting processes may still contain undemocratic qualities. He mocks "the blessed opportunity to vote for a ticket of men mostly unknown to [citizens], and which is made up for them by an under-cover machine in a caucus whose operations constitute a kind of political predestination."[49] He also contends, "There is no sanctity in universal suffrage, frequent elections, majority rule, congressional and cabinet government ... [their] purpose was rather that of meeting existing needs which had become too intense to be ignored."[50] Dewey would not have us get complacent, then, when universal suffrage is achieved, and he understands how

---

[48] MW6: 153.

[49] Dewey, *Public and Its Problems*, 119–20. Dewey is writing prior to 1970s reforms to the presidential nomination process, though the notion that nominations are now substantially more democratic is highly questionable, at best.

[50] Ibid., 144–45.

further significant change to institutions like elections will be necessary in response to changing circumstances. But he does allow us at least to preserve and make use of the advancements in suffrage, which Wolin cannot do. Thus, although both Dewey and Wolin value fundamental challenges to entrenched political institutions, Dewey leads us to reconstruct institutions so that they are not influenced exclusively by the powerful and to move political democracy further (even if imperfectly) into existence.

DEWEY'S HEGELIAN "NOTION" OF POLITICAL DEMOCRACY

Shane Ralston has recently argued that "[w]hile Dewey's Hegel-influenced pragmatism dispenses with the *Absolute*, it retains a concern for how ideas and ideals influence the growth and reconstruction of institutions."[51] I have discussed in Chapter 2 the extensive influence that Hegel appears to have had on Dewey's philosophy, and in particular on his thinking about democracy. The developmental quality in each element of Dewey's democratic theory bears striking Hegelian qualities. I will now show how Dewey's process of making political institutions more democratically inclusive (the focus of this chapter) is illuminated through an analysis of Hegel. It may seem odd to turn to Hegel in this regard, because he does appear to endorse an undemocratically organized political system in *The Philosophy of Right*. For one, though, some good recent scholarship has challenged the idea that Hegel is therefore an anti-democratic thinker[52]; but further, my aim here is to use Hegel to expand

---

[51] Shane Ralston, "Can Pragmatists be Institutionalists? John Dewey Joins the Non-ideal/Ideal Theory Debate," *Human Studies* 33, no. 1 (2010): 76.

[52] For example, Jeffrey Church effectively argues that Hegel is, in fact, a strong supporter of democracy in "economic associations" and that Hegel can support democracy in "political association" as long as it recognizes individuals as members of social groups, as opposed to Rousseau's political thought, which holds that individuals must come to the political assembly free of any prior social interest and unaffected by any prior social discussion; see Jeffrey Church, "G.W.F. Hegel on Self-Determination and Democratic Theory," *American Journal of Political Science* 56, no. 4 (2012): 1021–39. Also, Blake Emerson makes a compelling case that Hegel provided an institutional framework that American progressives, like Dewey, drew upon but also pushed in a more democratic direction. In particular, Emerson argues that Hegel built a state that effectively accounts for "conflicting demands" like for "predictable and responsive law," and for "negative and positive liberty," and that Dewey and other progressives were influenced by his ideas but also filled the gap in his thinking, i.e., the fact that his state did not allow for broad-scale participation by the people at large in political decision making; see Blake Emerson, "The Democratic Reconstruction of the Hegelian State in American Progressive Political Thought," *The Review of Politics* 77, no. 4 (2015): 545–74.

on not only the meaning of, but also the justification for, Dewey's *radical* approach to political democracy. I will explore Hegel's objection to the anti-institutional qualities in Rousseau's thought, and I will show how Hegel's reasoning can buttress Dewey's position on political democracy against Wolin. Hegelian principles help justify why a continuous process of democratization, rather than a focus on momentary transgressions of established power, can radically challenge current institutions *and* bring meaningful content to political democracy.

In Hegelian fashion, Dewey's conception of political democracy cannot be established in its final form once and for all. Rather, the conception only becomes "actual" through overcoming the inevitable negations it endures due to changing conditions. As we saw in Chapter 2, an entity becomes "actual" for Hegel by continuously developing through negation and by preserving and elevating its earlier stages of development as it grows further. Dewey's political element of democracy is indeed never fully completed, but is to be manifested in a process of unending development, and is to preserve and elevate its earlier forms as it further develops. Dewey describes how democracy "is an ideal in the only intelligible sense of an ideal: namely, the tendency and movement of some thing which exists carried to its final limit, viewed as completed, perfected. Since things do not attain such fulfillment but are in actuality distracted and interfered with, democracy in this sense is not a fact and never will be."[53] We may establish what political democracy signifies as a bare abstract notion, and Dewey does this by stating that "[p]olitically, democracy means a form of government which does not esteem the well-being of one individual or class above another."[54] But what that notion entails in practice must evolve to meet new circumstances, so that it maintains relevancy in the face of unique forms of exclusive political power. When past instantiations of political democracy meet novel conditions, our notion of political democracy is negated and requires further development to negate the negation, to overcome the "divisions, between attitudes emotionally and congenially attuned to the past and habits that are forced into existence because of the necessity of dealing with present conditions."[55] For instance, Dewey holds that, in response to dynastic control of government in past centuries, the emergence of free elections, formal rights and liberties, etc., represented a genuine advance in political

[53] Dewey, *Public and Its Problems*, 148.
[54] MW10: 137.
[55] Dewey, *Freedom and Culture*, 49.

democracy. But as governing institutions have fallen under the disproportionate influence of powerful economic interests, a free election by
itself – which does not counteract the effects of wealth – is not necessarily
democratic.[56] The further actualization of political democracy, therefore,
requires growth beyond the electoral processes we currently have in
the United States. This does not mean we abandon elections – because
prior stages of a development are not to be eliminated but preserved and
elevated – but rather we must intelligently reconstruct elections so that
they can overcome this unique problem.

Dewey recognizes that this process of reconstructing institutions when
they devolve in an undemocratic direction is formidable and bound to
suffer delays and regressions.[57] But without this process, he fears we
will be left with only the illusion of democratic freedom, while our institutions have become exclusive and undemocratic: "freedom is an eternal goal and has to be forever struggled for and won anew. It does not
automatically perpetuate itself and, unless it is continually rewon in new
effort against new foes, it is lost."[58] Political democracy must be continuously regenerated in the face of novel circumstances, and we could
say this requires what Hegel famously calls "the strenuous effort of the
Notion."[59] Hegel's "Notion" is an immediate abstract principle that can
only attain actuality by being worked out, by being continuously filled
with content from the ongoing process of negating the negations intrinsic
to the principle's growth. In other words, our Notion of political democracy serves as a broad, guiding ideal, but the process of overcoming forms
of exclusive political power in practice is itself the actualization of that
Notion. This Notion can likely never be fully, stably achieved, because
new obstacles to its realization will likely constantly emerge. Dewey holds
that "ideals take shape and gain a content as they operate in remaking
conditions,"[60] which conveys the essence of his thinking about political
institutions. Dewey's ideal of political democracy is a Hegelian Notion,
for the achievement of political democracy is unending and demands
overcoming the undemocratic aspects which are "immanent" in democracy's own development (i.e., the inevitable negation of democracy can

---

[56] Dewey, *Public and Its Problems*, 77, 101, 161.

[57] Ibid., 129.

[58] LW11: 247.

[59] G.W.F. Hegel, *The Phenomenology of Spirit*, translated by A.V. Miller (New York, NY: Oxford University Press, [1807] 1977), 35.

[60] John Dewey, *Individualism Old and New* (New York, NY: Capricorn Books, [1930] 1962), 169.

be a stimulus to the further growth of democracy). Hence, when past forms of political democracy are negated by changing circumstances, the intelligent reconstruction of those forms is a way of further actualizing political democracy by negating that negation.

Hegel's own thinking on the need for development in political institutions is built primarily in response to Rousseau. Although he respects Rousseau, he is troubled by what he sees as an anti-institutional quality in Rousseau's political thought. In *The Social Contract,* Rousseau describes some staggering requirements for experiencing genuine freedom in the midst of the many alienating features of modern society. Because the "natural liberty" of the state of nature has long been lost, he points us toward "moral freedom," which involves "obedience to a law one prescribes to oneself."[61] To experience moral freedom, we must not satisfy ourselves with representative legislative institutions, because freedom demands taking part in making the laws we live by.[62] All citizens must participate in the assembly, because that participation allows us to discover the "general will" – and although the general will does not require complete unanimity, it exists because individuals must share meaningful common ground if they share a polity, and when individuals act as citizens (rather than as private individuals), Rousseau argues they will discover that common ground and make it the basis of law.[63]

Rousseau's ideas here may not seem anti-institutional at all, but it is crucial to recognize how his theory demands a level of unity among citizens – and specifically, a level of unified commitment by all citizens to legislating – that he straightforwardly states cannot likely last for very long. He knowingly conceives of an experience of self-government that is temporary, for a state characterized by such unity will degenerate without "a durability that does not belong to human things."[64] His focus on substantial unity among citizens leads him to decry the existence of all factions, or "sectional associations," to claim that greater harmony and unanimity in the assembly signify moral freedom (whereas long debates and dissensions exhibit the decline of such freedom) and to argue that all institutions that "[destroy] social unity ... are worthless."[65] So, although the legislative body Rousseau describes is a kind of institution,

---

[61] Jean-Jacques Rousseau, *The Social Contract,* translated and introduced by Maurice Cranston (London: Penguin Classics, [1762] 1968), 65.

[62] Ibid., 141–3.

[63] Ibid., 69.

[64] Ibid., 134.

[65] Ibid., 73, 151, 181.

it is defined by a level of unified commitment and shared responsibility among all citizens in a polity that Rousseau absolutely intends to appear unfamiliar to people living in modern conditions – and to be highly difficult to achieve and inevitably temporary even if it is achieved. Further, the factor that Rousseau pinpoints as the primary catalyst for the destruction of a good state is the emergence of institutions that would be more familiar to us, namely, institutions that involve significant division of responsibility among citizens. He presents the establishment of such institutions – which, in his theory, are for executive power – as absolutely necessary, and he does not think it wise to have all citizens involved in executing laws as well as legislating; but he laments that this necessary division of executive power tends to lead the holders of such power to usurp the legislative power of all the citizens. He asserts, "This is the inherent and inescapable defect which, from the birth of the political body, tends relentlessly to destroy it."[66] Ultimately, Rousseau is not willing to moderate what he thinks freedom demands. He recognizes that the undivided unity he requires is very difficult to achieve, that if it is achieved it may not last very long, and that his conditions for achieving that unity are such that it could likely only happen once in an individual's lifetime. This experience would still be worth having, in Rousseau's view, rather than being enslaved our whole lives by representative legislative institutions (and believing mistakenly that we are free). I do not mean to say he is wrong about this, but it should at least be clear that he is presenting us with a temporary, once-in-a-lifetime experience and not a plan for progressively achieving self-government over time.

In *The Phenomenology of Spirit*, Hegel objects to Rousseau's idea that this temporary, largely anti-institutional unity is the pinnacle of modern freedom. Writing after the French Revolution, and after witnessing the Rousseau-inspired methods of the revolutionaries, Hegel presents this moment of "absolute freedom" as a necessary stage in human development – it is the stage where humanity sees the world as "its own will, and this is a general will ... this will is not the empty thought of will which consists in silent assent, or assent by a representative, but a real general will, the will of all *individuals* as such."[67] The "undivided Substance of absolute freedom"[68] conceives the world as its own possession and no longer accepts any institutional structure as handed down by a divinity.

---

[66] Ibid., 131.
[67] Hegel, *Phenomenology of Spirit*, 356–7.
[68] Ibid., 357.

This is a vital stage in humanity's development for Hegel, as people will no longer believe they must uncritically adhere to their current institutions. However, Hegel claims this moment of undivided, unmediated unity by itself "can produce neither a positive work nor a deed; there is left for it only *negative* action; it is merely the *fury* of destruction."[69] His argument is that if a polity is to produce positive legislation, division within the polity over what exactly to do cannot be avoided, due to the irreducible diversity of individuals; positive political action is then generated through the interaction of these opposing sectors of society, an interaction that can create a kind of unity between these individuals within the polity, without eliminating the differences between them.[70] With an unmediated unity like Rousseau's, where there is (as with the French Revolution) an attempt at complete unified upheaval against established institutions, Hegel contends only negation of institutions can take place, without something new being regenerated out of the negation. On Hegel's terms, an overemphasis on unity is bound up with a tendency toward mere destruction of the past, whereas giving positive content to freedom requires that division manifest itself, and that there be interaction among divided sectors of society. In other words, to enact positive legislation, we cannot stay purely in the realm of unified rejection of institutions, but we must work within particular institutions to permit certain "specific wills" or "victorious factions" to legislate one way rather than another.[71] And although Hegel does see it within human power to build uniquely new institutions, he thinks it unreasonable to expect such a development to *wholly* reject the institutions that came before. On Hegel's terms, we can only build on what the prior movement of human development – or, what Hegel calls the prior work of Spirit – has already accomplished, which means we cannot help but draw on past institutions in creating new ones.

Hegel's divergence from Rousseau here illustrates the divide between Dewey's radical democratic theory and that of anti-institutional thinkers like Wolin. Wolin does not specifically advocate for Rousseau's system,[72]

---

[69] Ibid., 359.

[70] Ibid., 358.

[71] Ibid., 360.

[72] Sheldon Wolin, "Democracy, Difference, and Re-Cognition," *Political Theory* 21, no. 3 (1993): 477–8. He does say Rousseau made "the most important modern attempt" at establishing an "integral notion of membership" and putting it "in the service of equality and democratization." But he complains that "[a] Rousseauist conception of incorporation not only refuses to recognize my differences, it suppresses them from my new identity, as though the notion of commonality, which citizenship claims to embody, can exist only if differences do not."

but he exhibits considerable compatibility with the anti-institutional qualities in Rousseau that are highlighted by Hegel. Rousseau's emphasis on a temporary experience of freedom, which rejects the dominant political institutions of our time, coheres well with Wolin's conception of momentary democracy. Wolin describes something akin to Rousseau's general will when he declares that "a free society composed of diversities can nonetheless enjoy moments of commonality when, through public deliberations, collective power is used to promote or protect the well-being of the collectivity."[73] He also gives a rather Rousseauian account of how representative institutions cannot be truly democratized and how democratic action consists solely in temporary transgressions of institutional enslavement:

> Democratic action ... might be defined as collective action that initially gathers its power from outside the system ... The demos becomes political, not simply when it seeks to make a system of governance more responsive to its needs, but when it attempts to shape the political system in order to enable itself to emerge, to make possible a new actor, collective in nature.[74]

Wolin's depiction of democratic action as rare, temporary, and thoroughly anti-institutional is thus consonant with the elements of Rousseau I have described. Wolin is uninterested in trying to make current representative institutions more responsive to the public, and instead associates democracy with momentary transgressions of those established institutions' power.

This anti-institutional approach to democracy continues to be a potent force in democratic theory. It did not end with Wolin's famous formulations in the 1990s, and has persisted into the new century with thinkers like Jacques Ranciere. Ranciere claims democracy "is not a set of institutions" but "a singular disruption" by excluded individuals of "the set of procedures whereby the aggregation and consent of collectivities is achieved, the organization of powers, the distribution of places and roles, and the systems for legitimizing this distribution."[75] In contrast with any kind of stable institutional order, he declares that democracy is "what comes and interrupts the smooth working of this order," and that, although democratic actors "are in no way oblivious to the existence

---

[73] Wolin, "Fugitive Democracy," 31.
[74] Ibid., 34; Wolin, "Transgression, Equality, and Voice," 64.
[75] Jacques Ranciere, *Disagreement: Politics and Philosophy*, translated by Julie Rose (Minneapolis: University of Minnesota Press, 1999), 11, 22, 28, 99.

of elected assemblies, institutional guarantees of freedom of speech and expression, state control mechanisms ... they do not identify with them."[76] Like Wolin, Ranciere conceives democracy as only existing outside of established institutions. Also like Wolin, he does not endorse Rousseau's system specifically,[77] but he demonstrates significant compatibility with Rousseau. His objection to regimes of "consensus" – which give off the appearance of including all parts of society when many are effectively excluded from political power – resembles the Rousseauian charge that representative institutions indubitably make people believe they are free when they are not.[78] Ranciere also claims representation is "an oligarchic form" that allows a small minority to rule to the exclusion of others, and that, therefore, "[d]emocracy can never be identified with a juridico-political form ... the power of the people is always below and beyond these forms."[79] Referencing the social movement activities of "plebeians," "nineteenth-century workers," and "demonstrators and those manning the barricades" – all of whom have been excluded from institutional channels of political power – he contends that "[t]he people through which democracy occurs is a unity that ... superimposes the effectiveness of a part of those who have no part."[80] And like Wolin and Rousseau, he holds that such unified, anti-institutional democratic activity "is rare."[81]

Despite their differences, Rousseau's, Wolin's, and Ranciere's radical conceptions of democracy are each defined by a type of "unity," and that unity is essentially opposed to institutionalization. Wolin and Ranciere each associate democracy with moments of unity or commonality, and Rousseau famously defines freedom by the substantial unity represented in the general will. Institutionalization entails division of responsibility, with certain individuals fulfilling different roles from others, and in some cases possessing greater responsibility or power than others. Wolin and Ranciere both argue that this division reflects the inevitably undemocratic character of institutions. With Rousseau – although his idea of a legislative body in which all citizens equally participate would certainly be a kind of institution – he points to the division of responsibility brought by

---

[76] Ibid., 99–101.

[77] He specifically objects to any notion of a founding "social contract"; see Ibid., 77–8; and "Democracy, Republic, Representation," *Constellations* 13, no. 3 (2006): 297.

[78] Jacques Ranciere, "Ten Theses on Politics," *Theory & Event* 5, no. 3 (2001): para. 32.

[79] Ranciere, "Democracy, Republic, Representation," 298–9.

[80] Ranciere, *Disagreement*, 30, 99.

[81] Ibid., 139.

the establishment of executive institutions as unavoidably disrupting the unity necessary for freedom, and dooming universal participation in legislation to be only temporary. The establishment of executive institutions is absolutely necessary for Rousseau, but he sees the holders of executive power as inevitably usurping the legislative authority of all citizens, and thus they curtail the citizens' experience of freedom.[82]

Hegel's message is that the momentary quality of Rousseau's (and consequently, of Wolin's and Ranciere's) experience of freedom is a symptom of the focus on unmediated unity, that is, a unity that is unblemished by any division within. Such a unity, in Hegel's view, can only destroy and cannot give any positive content to the freedom being sought. Positive content is bound up with what we have seen Hegel call "actuality," and an entity becomes actual for Hegel through an interaction of opposing elements and a preservation of those elements in a higher, mediated unity. As he says, "The actual is therefore *manifestation* ... It just manifests itself, and this means that in its externality, and only in *it*, it is *itself*, that is to say, only as a self-differentiating and self-determining movement."[83] Any entity generates division within itself in the course of becoming actual, and actuality and content indeed come through the manifestation of that division and the interaction of the divided elements. An entity that exists in an unmediated unity can thus have no positive content. If individuals are to experience actual political freedom, then, the manifestation of divisions among those individuals is essential, and also essential is the construction of institutions that allow for division of responsibility and for different groups of individuals to interact, and for the state to legislate one particular way rather than another without firmly excluding anyone along the way. Freedom is not thereby perfectly achieved for Hegel, but it is further actualized from where it was under prior institutions. When we insist on an unmediated unity, unsullied by the division brought by

[82] The fact that Rousseau sees executive institutions as necessary does not work against our suggestion that Rousseau shares similar anti-institutional qualities with Wolin and Ranciere. For Wolin and Ranciere, in fact, established institutions are also "necessary" because it seems large-scale modern politics cannot go on without them. But for Wolin and Ranciere, this necessary quality does not mean that these institutions can be democratic; and Rousseau, in his discussion of executive institutions, specifically argues that these institutions normally cannot have the democratic quality that he requires in the legislative power (see Rousseau, *Social Contract*, 112–14). And the fact that these executive institutions are also the entity that inevitably deprives citizens of democratic freedom only further shows the substantial anti-institutional component in Rousseau's political thinking.

[83] G.W.F. Hegel, *The Science of Logic*, translated and edited by George di Giovanni (Cambridge: Cambridge University Press, [1812] 2010), 478.

institutions, we have a freedom without actuality and are limited to simply negating current institutions.

Dewey's political element of democracy displays these Hegelian qualities. He claims that our familiar institutions may need to be deeply challenged, but actual political self-government still requires institutions, and although those institutions can certainly be different from what they were before, they are unlikely to have *no* connection to their prior forms (as Hegel would again say, our own development must draw on the prior work of Spirit). Dewey's pragmatic principles show how we can preserve qualities of political institutions that have been shown in practice to work democratically, even as we intelligently alter those institutions in the face of new obstacles to political democracy. He explains,

> We are always dependent upon the experience that has accumulated in the past and yet there are always new forces coming in, new needs arising ... We are always possessed by habits and customs, and this fact signifies that we are always influenced by the inertia and the momentum of forces temporally outgrown but nevertheless still present with us ... But change is also with us and demands the constant remaking of old habits and old ways of thinking.[84]

Dewey's position absolutely countenances social movements that directly challenge the undemocratic qualities of current political institutions, which are the movements that are particularly important to Wolin and Ranciere. But such movements for Dewey are democratic not only because they challenge those institutions, but because they can move institutions in a direction that further actualizes political self-government.[85] For example, the wide-ranging protest actions of the 1960s civil rights movement would be absolutely justified in Dewey's eyes, because the established political institutions were evidently exclusionary along racial lines (e.g., voting rights were still effectively denied to many African Americans). John Medearis, in a compelling book that shows the importance of social movements to democracy, has also identified the harmony between Dewey's thinking and these movements that seek to directly overcome the undemocratic aspects of institutions.[86] With Dewey, we can recognize

---

[84] John Dewey, *Liberalism and Social Action* (New York, NY: G. P. Putnam's Sons, 1935), 49.

[85] In Chapter 4, I will provide a fuller discussion of how Dewey's principles and statements display an endorsement of social movements and how these movements are integral to the development of each element of Deweyan democracy – individual, social, and political.

[86] John Medearis, *Why Democracy Is Oppositional* (Cambridge: Harvard University Press, 2015), 47–8, 54, 81, 132, 146.

how American political institutions – even after being altered by the civil rights movement – still display many of the undemocratic qualities that the institutions had before the movement and are still unequally accessible along racial lines. But at the same time, Dewey does not force us to deny any democratic classification to the greater racial inclusion that was achieved through the civil rights movement. The US political institutions still had many of the same qualities as before (e.g., elections for president and for members of Congress), but the institutions had been elevated to the degree that African Americans now had stable access to voting rights. To put this in particularly pragmatist terms, one of our "past most successful achievements" in realizing political democracy (i.e., suffrage) was preserved but also intelligently reconstructed and "put in a form so as best to help sustain and promote" further democratization.[87] Dewey's radical thinking critiques precisely the types of political exclusion that concern Wolin and Ranciere, but Dewey also helps us conceive how these challenges to institutions can bring political democracy progressively, actually into existence.

I am again not claiming here that Dewey is clearly right about political democracy and that Wolin is clearly wrong. But I do think there is good reason to favor Dewey's radical approach to political institutions over Wolin's. Dewey is able to account for the kind of mass uprisings against undemocratic institutions that are valued by Wolin and Ranciere. But his political democracy also requires the negation of the negation, the reconstruction of institutions in a democratic direction so that previously excluded individuals can actually participate in their governance, even if imperfectly. In essence, institutions that have been captured by exclusive interests have already been "negated" by our changing circumstances, and the rejection of such institutions alone does not take us beyond that negation into any positive content of self-government (i.e., we are still stuck in the mere negation of current institutions). On a Deweyan view, an institutional setup that remedies the segregated quality of previous institutions and allows for typically excluded voices to exercise power signifies movement in the direction of political democracy. Dewey's position does not force us to see this change in prior institutions as itself the full, perfect actualization of political democracy, but rather as essential movement in the unending actualization of political democracy. Limiting democracy to only the rejection of institutions, on the other hand, can leave excluded individuals with a freedom that has no actuality or

[87] MW4: 179.

content. Hence, Dewey's position accounts both for how radical upris-ings against political institutions are integral to democracy and for how institutions may become more actually democratic through the work of those uprisings.

If we are to approach Dewey's democratic aim of allowing all indi-viduals to exercise control over their lives, then our political institutions cannot systematically work to benefit certain individuals at the expense of others. Still, Dewey does not lay out exactly what form political democracy must take. He sets up a broad "Notion" of a politics without exclusion, but that Notion itself must evolve as it is filled with content from the ongoing process of bringing it into existence. As Hegel would say, we can set up a desired aim, but proper comprehension of that aim comes through the process of its actualization, the process of negating the negations which that aim endures in the midst of changing circum-stances. Our Notion of political democracy is inevitably negated through the emergence of new forms of exclusive political power. But rather than simply rejecting the current institutions (which again may leave us stuck in the "negative" point that those institutions are indeed undemocratic), Dewey calls on us to negate negation and reconstruct institutions in order to further actualize political democracy. I will now discuss some concrete examples of the kind of radical institutional change that Dewey would lead us to seek.

DEWEYAN INSTITUTIONAL RECONSTRUCTION

Political democracy, as I present it in this book, refers simultaneously to political institutions that can be influenced by individuals throughout a polity and to the types of actions and policies produced by those insti-tutions that help overcome undemocratic aspects of our broader society (e.g., structural social inequalities). The latter quality has been addressed in the first two chapters, and this chapter's discussion of the former qual-ity connects to the fact that government is unlikely to act to overcome social inequality if only socially powerful individuals can truly influence government. Dewey's political element of democracy, as I read it, entails both a continuous process of opening political institutions to more voices (which helps ensure that these institutions will produce policies that do not simply aid the powerful) and continuous action from those institu-tions to help overcome oppressive aspects of society (which helps ensure that more individuals across society can develop political efficacy).

When we ponder how Dewey would try to open political institutions to voices beyond those of a powerful few, we cannot simply give a list of desired institutions. His general unwillingness to advocate for certain specific institutions is frustrating to some readers, but his conception of a continuously developing political democracy ultimately demands that he maintain substantial flexibility in his thinking on institutions.[88] As a pragmatist, Dewey is mainly interested in an intelligent response to pressing problems and a readiness to respond to unforeseen problems in the future. His focus on keeping institutions open for change, in fact, highlights one of the main alterations to US political institutions that he would evidently seek. He laments that "[t]he creation of adequately flexible and responsive political and legal machinery has so far been beyond the wit of man" and that "[t]he belief in political fixity, of the sanctity of some form of state consecrated by the efforts of our fathers and hallowed by tradition, is one of the stumbling-blocks in the way of orderly and directed change."[89] We noted earlier his concern with how clinging uncritically to a constitution can obstruct democracy, and Dewey specifically argues that the US Constitution should be open for more flexible change than is possible under the extremely difficult amendment process (which requires passage by two-thirds of both houses of Congress and three-fourths of the state legislatures). In his commentary on Thomas Jefferson, Dewey praises Jefferson's "belief in the necessity of periodic revisions of the constitution, one to take place every twenty years, and his belief that the process of ordinary amendment had been made too difficult ... and that institutions must change with [a] change of circumstances ... Jefferson saw that periodic overhauling of the fundamental law was the alternative to change effected only by violence."[90] Dewey elsewhere describes how Jefferson "settle[d] upon a period of eighteen years and eight months that fixed the natural span of the life of a generation; thereby indicating the frequency with which it is desirable to overhaul 'laws and institutions' to bring them into accord with 'new discoveries, new truths, change of manners and opinions.'"[91] Thus, opening the US Constitution to potentially significant changes every two decades would, in Dewey's view, allow the American people to alter their institutions so they are not stuck with institutions that are centuries old and poorly suited to the current circumstances. Dewey is not greatly concerned that holding constitutional

---

[88] Dewey, *Public and Its Problems*, 146–7.
[89] Ibid., 31, 34.
[90] LW14: 215–16.
[91] Dewey, *Freedom and Culture*, 157–8.

conventions every twenty years would lead to haphazard and unjustified change to institutions, because people are not inclined toward "abolishing forms to which they are accustomed."[92] These conventions would, though, allow for institutions that are evidently obstructing political democracy to be altered in a timely fashion. As an example, after the controversial *Citizens United v. FEC* decision that allows wealthy corporations to exercise even further disproportionate control over political campaigns, Dewey's process for changing the Constitution would allow opponents of that decision (which polls have shown to be a large majority of American citizens[93]) a genuine opportunity to override it and to alter institutions to keep them from becoming increasingly oligarchic. The current amendment process, by contrast, requires a presently unfeasible level of support from members of Congress and state legislatures to override the Supreme Court's decision.

As we have seen, Dewey wants to keep established institutions open for significant change, but he also renounces ideas of wholesale elimination of those institutions. Within the American context, he provides sharp critiques of institutions such as the presidency and the Senate, though he in no way suggests that those institutions be obliterated, and instead seeks to reconstruct them in a democratic direction. With the presidency, he expresses support for moving presidential elections away from the electoral college,[94] which is a prime example of an institution that today has long outgrown whatever democratic quality it may have had in the past. One purpose of the electoral college when it was established in the late eighteenth century was to protect the autonomy of individual states by giving each state certain numbers of electoral votes, rather than determining the president simply by the nation's popular vote, and at that time the states were more genuinely independent entities than they are now. Today, advances in transportation and communication, as well as historical events such as the Civil War, have led the states toward far greater interdependence, thus making obsolete the idea of determining a president through a number (fifty-one, currently) of individual state elections, rather than taking the nation's vote as one total. The electoral college, of course, does create the possibility of a presidential candidate receiving the highest number of votes from Americans and still losing the office to another candidate, which has indeed happened in both the

[92] LW14: 216.
[93] Dan Eggen, "Poll: Large Majority Opposes Supreme Court's Decision on Campaign Financing," *Washington Post*, February 17, 2010.
[94] LW6: 233.

2000 and 2016 elections. Despite not living to see those two elections, Dewey identifies the electoral college as an undemocratic institution and again seeks a constitutional amendment process that would make it feasible to instead have presidential elections determined by popular vote. With the Senate, Dewey endorses popular election of senators,[95] which was instituted by the Seventeenth Amendment in 1913, and which moved an institution that was in fact originally intended to be undemocratic in a democratic direction. The Senate is still highly suspect as a democratic institution, though, for the principle established in the Constitution that each state would have exactly two senators has left us in a situation today where states with vast differences in population (e.g., California with about 40 million people, Wyoming with about 500,000 people) get the same amount of representation in the Senate. Senators representing a minority of American citizens can therefore often outvote senators representing a majority of citizens. There is good reason, from a Deweyan point of view, to see the Senate as requiring significant further democratic change. The House of Representatives is also deserving of scrutiny, because the existence of "single-member districts" and a "first past the post" electoral system makes it possible for one of the major US political parties to receive the majority of votes for House positions across the nation, while the other party is awarded the majority of House seats. The gerrymandering of House districts of course serves additionally to protect many House members from serious electoral challenge and can perpetuate one party's control of the House.

Much of Dewey's discussion of political institutions is focused on the United States, but he addresses institutions in other nations as well. His analysis of China, for instance, again illustrates his view that institutions should develop in response to novel conditions and that this growth of institutions must still draw on, and preserve certain aspects of, customary institutions. Writing on China in the early twentieth century, Dewey states that "China needs a system of national finance, of national taxation and revenues. But the effort to institute such a system ... has to meet deeply entrenched local customs ... the development must be a transforming growth from within, rather than either an external superimposition or a borrowing from foreign sources."[96] Any nation's institutional development will have its own unique character and will need to build on its own institutional experience in its movement toward political democracy.

---

[95] LW6: 233.
[96] MW11: 213.

Thus, although Dewey would like to see the principles of democratic government extend throughout the world – and he does think democracy can progressively extend itself in that way[97] – he is certainly not looking for any "democratic" nation to impose institutions on another nation that are completely foreign to this latter nation's own customs. This may frustrate some who believe that political democracy must be spread throughout the world as quickly as possible. But for Dewey, the process of actualizing democracy can be long and slow, and it is senseless to expect that this process can be skipped over in order to quickly bring a nation to a purely democratic condition.

I have alluded earlier to Dewey's deep concern over the undemocratic control of political institutions by wealthy interests. His repeated emphasis on the threat posed by wealth to political democracy exhibits how wrong it is to say – as Wolin does – that he is not attuned to fundamental power inequities in modern politics. His focus on wealth also further illuminates the kind of specific changes to current institutions he would call for. When wealthy donors can disproportionately influence election and policy outcomes with their fortunes, Dewey insists we must then "liberate men, women, and children from the enslavement of governmental agencies to selfish and predatory economic interests."[98] The US Constitution does not either condone or forbid the use of wealth to influence institutional procedures and outcomes. But it is hardly possible – in Dewey's time and in ours – to avoid perceiving the oligarchical nature of American political processes, and Dewey thus demands "'radical' perception of the necessity of thoroughgoing changes in the set-up of institutions and corresponding activity to bring the changes to pass."[99] In other words, for Dewey, the institutions of popular elections and universal suffrage have been negated by changing circumstances (i.e., by the increasing influence of wealth on government), and we must negate this negation by reconstructing those institutions so that they account for the effect of wealth. A publicly financed campaign system, for instance, would help bring political democracy further into existence. The oligarchical control of current institutions in fact leads Dewey to one of his few specific suggestions for an institutional design: "[a] coordinating and directive council in which captains of industry and finance would meet with representatives of labor

---

[97] In Chapter 5, I will discuss Dewey's relation to the contemporary model of cosmopolitan democracy, which will help show the possibilities Dewey sees for democracy's extension throughout the globe.

[98] LW6: 152.

[99] Dewey, *Liberalism and Social Action*, 62.

and public officials to plan the regulation of industrial activity."[100] An institution like this would allow workers a typically unavailable opportunity to exercise control over policies that affect their lives, and would thus further achieve political democracy. Dewey hoped his new political party in particular could successfully combat the control of government by wealth, and he made it clear that the party could not address this problem with old solutions alone (e.g., extension of voting rights). The party was intended rather to seek unique institutional changes that would overcome the "enslavement of governmental agencies to selfish and predatory economic interests" (and also to whip up mass support for a more equitable distribution of wealth, which would uproot the foundation of that enslavement[101]).

In recent years, the political science discipline has taken greater notice of the harm to democratic government brought by wealth. For instance, Benjamin Page, Larry Bartels, and Jason Seawright report that a far higher proportion of the wealthy in the United States give money to political campaigns, and have contact with public officials, than do ordinary citizens; the authors also point out that the wealthy tend (more so than the general public) to favor cuts in government spending and reliance on private enterprise to respond to problems like poverty, and the authors suggest that US policy makers' willingness to push for cuts in popular government programs like Social Security and Medicare is related to the fact that the wealthy are not as fond of those programs.[102] Similarly, Martin Gilens[103]; Lawrence Jacobs and Theda Skocpol[104]; and Key Lehman Schlozman, Sidney Verba, and Henry Brady,[105] in each of their own studies, find that government policies are far more strongly associated with the preferences of the affluent than of the poor or the middle class and that the wealthy's large donations of money to campaigns is likely the determining factor here, because middle-income

---

[100] Dewey, *Individualism Old and New*, 118.

[101] LW6: 181. This more equitable distribution of wealth is essential to the social element of Deweyan democracy, which has been discussed at length in the first two chapters.

[102] Benjamin Page, Larry Bartels, and Jason Seawright, "Democracy and the Policy Preferences of Wealthy Americans," *Perspectives on Politics* 11, no. 1 (2013): 51–73.

[103] Martin Gilens, *Affluence and Influence: Economic Inequality and Political Power in America* (Princeton, NJ: Princeton University Press, 2012).

[104] Lawrence Jacobs and Theda Skocpol, *Inequality and American Democracy: What We Know and What We Need to Learn* (New York, NY: Russell Sage Foundation, 2005).

[105] Key Lehman Schlozman, Sidney Verba, and Heny Brady, *The Unheavenly Chorus: Unequal Political Voice and the Broken Promise of American Democracy* (Princeton, NJ: Princeton University Press, 2012).

individuals vote and volunteer at similar rates to the wealthy but donate far less money to campaigns. Dewey's concern with the impact of wealth on politics is undoubtedly as pressing today as it was in the early twentieth century, and political scientists are showing greater awareness of this. I have referred several times in this book to the 2011 fight in Wisconsin over collective bargaining rights and the influence that the Koch brothers were able to exercise in not only bringing Scott Walker to the governor's office, but in driving the legislation that curtails public-sector workers' bargaining rights. This provides a conspicuous example of how political democracy can be obstructed by wealth. Much of this book is focused on how democracy must extend beyond the political realm and how we must see the process of overcoming structural inequality in our broader society as itself integral to democracy. But the political element of democracy is still crucial, particularly because the hope of overcoming social inequality depends significantly on a political system that is not purely controlled by the powerful. As long as wealthy individuals like the Kochs can exercise such excessive influence over political institutions, the political element of democracy, and also the social and individual elements, are severely inhibited.

The Deweyan analysis of political institutions has taken a step forward with a recent book by K. Sabeel Rahman. Rahman focuses in particular on democratizing economic regulatory agencies in order to fight the pernicious effects of wealth, and he draws on Dewey to describe how these institutions can allow citizens to actually be involved in "proposing policies, sharing in implementation, or initiating challenges to existing practices."[106] Rahman emphasizes that he not only seeks to give citizens more control over economic regulatory decisions, but to specifically ensure that marginalized groups have a strong presence within the regulatory institutions.[107] As an example, he explains how the Financial Stability Oversight Council (FSOC) – a major regulatory institution created after the 2008 financial crisis – could be democratized if it gave direct power to workers and to other individuals who represent distinctly nonwealthy sectors of society. He states that "instead of being comprised of the heads of the financial regulatory agencies," the FSOC could give "full membership and a vote" also to "unions, pensioners, consumers, city and state bond managers, and the like."[108] This argument is indeed strikingly

---

[106] K. Sabeel Rahman, *Democracy Against Domination* (New York, NY: Oxford University Press, 2016), 14.

[107] Ibid., 15–16, 22–3.

[108] Ibid., 159.

similar to Dewey's case for giving "representatives of labor" direct power over "the regulation of industrial activity." Dewey also rejects the thinking that such administrative bodies simply should not be created and describes these kinds of agencies as necessary under current economic circumstances, which means that our focus must be on preventing these agencies from becoming firmly undemocratic: "new administrative bodies are so imperatively needed that the real problem is that of building up an intelligent and capable civil-service under conditions that will operate against formation of rigid bureaucracies."[109] With Rahman, we get a more contemporary analysis of how exactly a Deweyan would alter important institutions to further actualize political democracy. And to foreshadow a bit the argument in Chapter 4, it is noteworthy how this Deweyan approach to institutions is not mainly focused on improving the quality of debate that takes place within institutions (e.g., by having participants debate more cordially) or creating ancillary institutions where a more ideal type of debate can materialize. The Deweyan approach focuses on taking existing institutions and directly altering them in order to move political power to the disadvantaged and away from the advantaged who normally control those institutions. The aim is to move political influence from those who have great social power to those who do not,[110] and this does not necessarily relate to creating a more civilized debate between the different viewpoints raised within institutions.

Our analysis here helps us reconcile the "institutional" and "radical" interpretations of Dewey described earlier. On the more radical side, we can see that Dewey does not identify democracy with any particular institution such as representative legislatures or frequent elections. Dewey stresses that "there is no sanctity" in such institutions, which shows how achieving political democracy can require us to develop beyond current legislative bodies and voting processes. In the face of unique obstacles to democratic government (e.g., control of government by wealth), we cannot simply rely on institutions that were created in response to older obstacles. However, on the more institutional side, Dewey's pragmatism requires us to build on advancements in democratic government that

---

[109] Dewey, *Freedom and Culture*, 65–6.
[110] Rahman also references the work of John McCormick, who similarly provides an important examination of how political power can be directly moved from wealthy elites to ordinary citizens, though McCormick's analysis draws on Machiavelli, rather than Dewey. McCormick's work shows how class-specific institutions could be created that specifically prevent elites from having a voice in decision making; see John McCormick, *Machiavellian Democracy* (New York, NY: Cambridge University Press, 2011).

have already been instituted and put into practice. This is necessary to give actual content to the democratization we are seeking and to avoid a simple content-less rejection of the past. There is no positive political action for Dewey that wholly rejects established institutions, and so he holds that although state institutions can (and often need to) be radically altered, the reform of institutions cannot be expected to completely separate from those institutions. Our current legislative bodies, voting processes, administrative agencies, etc., have undemocratic features that require remedy, but this does not mean we should obliterate those institutions but rather reconstruct them in a democratic direction.

Before finishing, I will also comment just briefly on the role of education in Deweyan political democracy.[111] Education was Dewey's favorite topic, and his concern about specifically political education is that "current schooling ... not only does little to make discriminating intelligence a safeguard against surrender to the invasion of bunk, especially in its most dangerous form – social and political bunk – but it does much to favor susceptibility to a welcoming reception to it."[112] He explains further how

there has been a temptation to idealize our institutions ... keeping away from the students' minds, as they mature, a sense of what the problems are that make it difficult to carry on our government successfully. We need methods of teaching that will not merely give pupils a simple paper knowledge of government, but that will give them ... a knowledge of what are the underlying tendencies and problems they must meet in government, local, state, and national.[113]

If individuals are to be prepared to "criticize and re-make [democracy's] political manifestations,"[114] then schools must avoid merely encouraging youth to marvel at how well American political institutions work. Schools must instead cultivate a critical attitude in evaluating whether current institutions are effectively democratic. Students must not simply memorize the content of the US Constitution, for instance, but must critically investigate whether the established institutions are sufficient for overcoming the current threats to political democracy.

Overall, for Dewey it does not appear necessary for individuals to be consistently, directly involved in political decision making, as they must be involved in directing their *social* experience in spheres such as the

---

[111] There will be a thorough analysis of Dewey's educational theory in Chapter 6.
[112] MW13: 332.
[113] MW15: 160–1.
[114] Dewey, *Public and Its Problems*, 144.

workplace. Modern political institutions tend to be more remote than workplaces from individuals' everyday lives, and Dewey recognizes the need for elected representatives to undertake much of the political decision making. Dewey's view on how the political realm pales somewhat in comparison to the social realm in terms of democratic significance – but is still independently important to democracy's overall development – is reflected here:

> Politics is a means, not an end. But thought of it as a means will lead to thought of the ends it should serve. It will induce consideration of the ways in which a worthy and rich life for all may be achieved. In so doing, it will restore directive aims and be a significant step forward in the recovery of a unified individuality.[115]

Political democracy is crucial because it is encompassed by the idea that individuals should be able to exercise control over their lives, and because the policies needed to allow individuals to control their lives in society are unlikely to come if only the powerful have a voice in political institutions. In the political science literature, there are references to how unequal political power emerges alongside severe economic inequality and how that political power is used to exacerbate economic inequality, which then worsens the inequality in political power, and so on. Bartels calls this "a debilitating feedback cycle linking the economic and political realms,"[116] and Gilens describes "a vicious cycle in which growing economic and political inequality are mutually reinforcing"[117]; Jacobs and Skocpol report how "[e]conomic inequality has risen faster in the United States than other advanced industrialized nations in part because American government has failed to enact new social policies ... in the face of market and demographic changes."[118] Dewey's conception of interlocking political and social elements of democracy is thus particularly relevant to the contemporary situation in the United States. The individual element of democracy is also at play here, because the policy makers (who again need to be motivated by our institutions to represent more than just the interests of the wealthy) have to actually make decisions that aim at overcoming social inequality. As we saw in Chapters 1 and 2, it is a major part of democratic individualism to challenge and combat

---

[115] Dewey, *Individualism Old and New*, 118–19.
[116] Larry Bartels, *Unequal Democracy: The Political Economy of the New Gilded Age* (Princeton, NJ: Princeton University Press, 2008), 286.
[117] Gilens, *Affluence and Influence*, 252.
[118] Jacobs and Skocpol, *Inequality and American Democracy*, 224.

forms of inequality. There can certainly be debate within political institutions over the details of policies that genuinely aim to overcome inequality, but on Deweyan terms, policies that we know exacerbate inequality (e.g., tax policies that redistribute wealth from the poor to the rich) must be seen as inconsistent with democracy's development.

In his recent book, Medearis has taken us in a fruitful direction by building a theory of what he calls "oppositional" democracy, in which democracy is seen as "continuous oppositional exertion" against the "alienation" of "the institutions and forces that shape our lives," "without any expectation of transcendent victory."[119] My account of Deweyan political democracy, which is infused with Hegelian insights, is based upon a "Notion" of a government in which no individual or group voice possesses a structurally privileged position over others'. This Notion cannot be completely, eternally achieved in any particular set of institutions, but as Hegel would say, the continuous overcoming of obstacles toward its achievement makes the Notion actual. Such a Notion of political democracy, for Dewey, does give needed direction to the reforms we undertake; Dewey emphasizes that he is not simply advocating "piecemeal policies undertaken *ad hoc*," and that "'reforms' that deal now with this abuse and now with that without having a social goal based upon an inclusive plan, differ entirely from effort at re-forming, in its literal sense, the institutional scheme of things."[120] The actualization of this Notion, then, consists of the intelligent reconstruction – in Hegelian, and pragmatic, fashion – of our governing institutions in response to negation (i.e., the exclusive control of those institutions by powerful interests). The idea of a government that is equally influenced by individuals throughout a polity could then be continuously approximated, if never fully achieved.

DEWEY'S RADICAL POLITICAL DEMOCRACY

This chapter has explored the *political* element of Deweyan democracy. I have shown how for Dewey, political democracy is never perfectly achieved, but can be continuously actualized to the extent the undemocratic qualities of governing institutions are identified and remedied. His Hegelian approach to political democracy emphasizes the continuous reconstruction of democratic governance in response to "negation" – that is, the exclusive control of institutions by powerful actors – in order

[119] Medearis, *Why Democracy Is Oppositional*, 2–4, 9–10, 18, 132.
[120] Dewey, *Liberalism and Social Action*, 62.

to give actual content to political self-government. I have also argued not only that Wolin is wrong to claim that Dewey's democratic theory is blind to power inequities in modern politics, but that there is good reason to favor Dewey's version of radical democratic thought over the anti-institutional version proffered by Wolin. The anti-institutional ideas we find in Wolin, Ranciere, and Rousseau do not take us beyond negation, for by simply rejecting what has already become undemocratic, they do not show how those excluded from institutional power could actually rule themselves. Dewey's version of radical democracy accounts for the kind of temporary uprisings emphasized by thinkers like Wolin, without forcing us to forgo everything that takes place between such uprisings (i.e., within institutions) as inevitably devoid of any democracy. His pragmatic philosophy allows us to negate negation by intelligently reconstructing past institutions in response to new circumstances. This preserves past advancements in democratic governance by stabilizing them within institutions, while avoiding the sanctification of any particular institution.

Dewey's democratic project aims at granting individuals the greatest possible control over their lives, and this project has a distinct political element. He maintains that

[d]emocracy is a word of many meanings. Some of them are of such a broad social and moral import as to be irrelevant to our immediate theme. But one of the meanings is distinctly political, for it denotes a mode of government ... This is not the most inspiring of the different meanings of democracy; it is comparatively special in character. But it contains about all that is relevant to *political* democracy.[121]

The development of political democracy is radical, because it involves potentially significant change to established institutions and justifies the actions of social movements which aim at producing that change. Dewey thereby points the way toward moving political power directly from the socially advantaged to the disadvantaged.

---

[121] Dewey, *Public and Its Problems*, 82.

4

From Deliberative to Participatory Democracy[1]

The first three chapters have explored the interrelated individual, social, and political elements of Dewey's democratic theory. In this chapter, I will argue that Dewey's theory provides a potent challenge to deliberative democracy, which is the preeminent model in contemporary democratic theory. Dewey is actually commonly seen as a forefather of deliberative democracy, but I will dispute that interpretation and will show that Deweyan democracy diverges substantially from the dominant thinking on democracy among political theorists. I will further argue that Dewey's thought can help elevate the model of participatory democracy – an older and currently less prominent model than deliberative democracy – within current democratic thought. Once we have a full picture of Dewey's thinking, we have tools to reverse the current trend in analyses of how to achieve democracy.

As we have seen, democracy for Dewey is fundamentally defined by individuals' exercise of control over their lives. He claims that "[i]f democracy is possible it is because every individual has a degree of power to govern himself."[2] This capacity for self-government is affected at least as much, and perhaps more so, by the quality of individuals' social relations as by their political institutions. Structural social inequality directly interferes with individuals' opportunity to govern their lives, and this inequality also obstructs the achievement of political democracy. I have shown how Dewey links democracy with the overcoming of social

---

[1] Portions of this chapter are modified from an article originally published as "Dividing Deliberative and Participatory Democracy through John Dewey," *Democratic Theory* 2, no. 1 (2015): 63–84.

[2] LW6: 431.

inequality, while also calling for alterations in political institutions that can counteract the excessive control of those institutions by the socially powerful. Deliberative democratic theory, by contrast, defines democracy by a type of ideal political debate. The theory holds that if participants in debate interact in a proper enough way – specifically, if they exchange reasons for their own views that their opponents in the debate can accept – then democracy has been achieved. But if we make this kind of debate the focus of our democratic thinking, we either have to assume that severe social inequality will be effectively neutralized by this debate, or we have to evade the most essential work involved in further achieving democracy, which is the overcoming of that inequality. In other words, we either must assume that a proper exchange of opposing political viewpoints can bracket the impact of social inequality and give all individuals genuine control over their lives – which seems rather implausible – or concede that the kind of debate we are focusing on would only actually be democratic if structural inequality has somehow gone away – which means we are wishing away the most pressing obstacle in the way of democracy. Structural social inequality can surely nullify the democratic value of taking part in an exchange of reasons with political opponents, because individuals who are stuck in poverty, for example, can have little meaningful opportunity to govern their everyday lives. Also, it takes a rather large leap to assume that the political debate itself will not be affected by disparities in social status, in that certain individuals have more time to devote to politics, have greater access to positions of authority throughout society, and speak in ways that are more likely to be seen as eloquent and persuasive than others. As Dewey says, whether differences in social status are determined along older "dynastic" lines or modern "economic" lines, those with advantaged status cannot be prevented from enjoying a privileged position in political institutions unless this social inequality is directly combated.[3]

It is true that Dewey wishes there could be honest, cooperative deliberation over policy. He can agree with deliberative democrats about how political debate would ideally proceed under democratized social conditions. But as a pragmatist, Dewey is particularly concerned that our principles and practices be attuned to the conditions we actually confront. He therefore requires that analysis of democracy focus on combating social inequality, and although concerns over the quality of political debate

[3] John Dewey, *The Public and Its Problems* (Chicago, IL: Swallow Press, [1927] 1954), 77, 107–8, 161.

are not absent from his thinking, he does not make political debate into the centerpiece of his plans for democratization. Furthermore, his work articulates the need for *nondeliberative* practices in order to attack social inequality. This is an often-overlooked aspect of Dewey's thinking, but he demonstrates how practices such as marches, protests, and workers' strikes are integral to democracy under unequal social conditions because they directly combat and potentially help overcome the pressing inequalities. These practices are nondeliberative, in that they hold social inequality to be so pervasive that it cannot be bracketed by certain ideal rules of discourse and debate. Dewey sees these practices as essential for achieving necessary broad-scale social change, as well as for altering our political institutions in order to directly move political power from the advantaged to the disadvantaged.

Interestingly, some deliberative democrats have recently shown greater awareness of their theory's incongruity with our unequal social conditions and have tried to take steps to rectify this issue. Certain deliberative thinkers have in fact added into their theory a requirement that severe social inequality be largely eliminated in order for deliberation to work properly. I will show, though, that these thinkers cannot make this requirement without effectively invalidating their principle that deliberation has intrinsic democratic quality and that the achievement of democracy is indissolubly linked with the practice of deliberation. Relatedly, a few deliberative theorists have attempted to accommodate nondeliberative practices by frankly conceding that nonideal social conditions require us to stray from proper deliberation. I will argue that this further exemplifies how far the theory must diverge from its central commitment to deliberation in order to become relevant to unequal social conditions.

Participatory democracy has become a less prominent model in democratic theory since its heyday in the 1960s and 1970s, and the theory is actually commonly seen today as having been incorporated (and even improved) by deliberative democracy. My argument in this chapter will use Dewey's principles to show not only that participatory democracy is not genuinely captured by deliberative democracy, but that participatory democracy should be elevated above deliberative democracy within contemporary democratic theory. Participatory theory shares Dewey's emphasis on the need to overcome entrenched inequalities in our broader society in order to achieve democracy. Participatory democrats do not focus on instituting a certain kind of political debate, but rather on causing alterations in our unequal society, and also on changing political institutions to work against their effective control by the powerful. Furthermore, participatory democracy stands to benefit from Dewey's *pragmatic* case for nondeliberative practices. A major reason why the participatory theory has been seen as paling in comparison with deliberative theory is that participatory thinkers have not clearly committed to a specific form of participation, whereas deliberative thinkers do commit to deliberation. It is true that participatory theorists primarily look for broad-scale changes in both "governmental" and "nongovernmental" authority structures,[4] without clearly stating whether they think deliberation or any other kind of practice is the path toward achieving those changes. I claim that participatory thinkers can draw on Dewey to show their lack of a specific commitment to deliberation to be a virtue of their theory, because they are not committing wholesale to a practice that has at least very questionable democratic credentials under conditions of structural inequality. They can also use Dewey to justify practices that are nondeliberative and to show that these practices fit very well with their own focus on overcoming social inequality. Although there have been recent attempts to stretch deliberative theory to make room for nondeliberative practices, participatory theory – when infused with Deweyan insights – can straightforwardly say that these practices cohere with participatory theory's fundamental goal of combating social inequality, without having to contradict any basic commitment to deliberation as *the* democratic practice. Neither Dewey nor participatory democrats would forbid deliberation from taking place, but Dewey's pragmatism illuminates why we must be intelligently flexible with the practices we see as further achieving democracy, and participatory theorists' lack of commitment to deliberation – and primary emphasis on fighting social inequality – leave them ready to absorb Dewey's pragmatic insights. With Dewey and participatory democracy, we respond directly to structural social inequality and do not risk abstracting from this most pressing obstacle to democracy with an overemphasis on proper political debate.

DEWEY AS A DELIBERATIVE DEMOCRAT?

Jason Kosnoski reports that "[a] consensus appears to be forming among political theorists that John Dewey's political thought can be subsumed

---

4 The latter refer to authority structures outside the typical institutions of government, such as the workplace.

under the rubric of deliberative democracy."[5] Indeed, over the past dec-
ade and a half there have been an increasing number of democratic
theorists who have linked Dewey with deliberative democracy. James
Bohman claims that Dewey's "pragmatist conception of practical reason
suggests a deliberative form of democracy."[6] Alison Kadlec states that
"a Deweyan view of democracy is, in contemporary parlance, deeply
deliberative,"[7] while Melvin Rogers argues "[i]t is Dewey's appeal to
inquiry as a method for justifying beliefs that feeds directly into and
underwrites democratic deliberation."[8] For Noelle McAfee, Dewey's
emphasis in *The Public and Its Problems* on the notion that the public
"can find itself" is evidently a call for "public deliberation,"[9] and for John
Dryzek, Dewey stands with Edmund Burke and John Stuart Mill as one
of the primary historical "antecedents" to deliberative democracy.[10]

   In his rebuke of Dewey's democratic theory, Richard Posner claims
"deliberative democracy" is "not Dewey's term but a good description
of his approach" and that Dewey's deliberative ideal "is as purely aspira-
tional and unrealistic as rule by Platonic guardians."[11] Jack Knight and
James Johnson, who take a more positive view on Dewey, declare that "the
mechanisms, machinery, devices, or forms provided by political democracy" are the key to understanding Dewey's theory and portray Dewey
as stressing "the role of political argument and ultimately of deliberative
processes in democratic politics."[12] John Shook also emphasizes the *political* element of Dewey's thought, depicting Dewey as providing a theory
of "deliberative polyarchy," in which groups representing different interests "compete for the general public's sympathy and the government's
attention" within political processes defined by "community goodwill

---

[5] Jason Kosnoski, "Artful Discussion: John Dewey's Classroom as a Model of Deliberative
   Association," *Political Theory* 33, no. 5 (2005): 654.
[6] James Bohman, "Democracy as Inquiry, Inquiry as Democratic: Pragmatism, Social
   Science, and the Cognitive Division of Labor," *American Journal of Political Science* 43,
   no. 2 (1999): 590.
[7] Alison Kadlec, *Dewey's Critical Pragmatism* (Lanham, MD: Lexington Books, 2007), 4.
[8] Melvin Rogers, *The Undiscovered Dewey: Religion, Morality, and the Ethos of
   Democracy* (New York, NY: Columbia University Press, 2009), 21.
[9] Noelle McAfee, *Democracy and the Political Unconscious* (New York, NY: Columbia
   University Press, 2008), 115.
[10] John Dryzek, *Deliberative Democracy and Beyond: Liberals, Critics, Contestations*
   (Oxford: Oxford University Press, 2000), 2.
[11] Richard Posner, *Law, Pragmatism, and Democracy* (Cambridge: Harvard University
   Press, 2003), 106–7.
[12] Jack Knight and James Johnson, *The Priority of Democracy: Political Consequences of
   Pragmatism* (Princeton, NJ: Princeton University Press, 2011), 36, 115.

and respect for all participants, even as these processes encourage fierce competition between subgroup aims."[13] Regardless of whether the purpose is explanatory, laudatory, or critical, the classification of Dewey as a deliberative democrat has become predominant among democratic theorists. For my purposes, which will be to show how Dewey's principles can elevate participatory democracy over deliberative democracy, the evolving position of Dewey scholar Robert Westbrook is significant: in his 1991 intellectual biography of Dewey, Westbrook labels Dewey a "most important advocate of participatory democracy"[14]; in 2005, though, he contends that "Dewey was anticipating an ideal that contemporary democratic theorists have dubbed 'deliberative democracy.'"[15] I will show that Westbrook was correct the first time.

DELIBERATIVE DEMOCRATIC THEORY

Dryzek has declared that "[d]eliberative democracy now constitutes the most active area of political theory in its entirety (not just democratic theory)."[16] There is no question that deliberative democracy is the most prominent model in contemporary democratic thought, and Dewey has been deemed one of its primary progenitors. Of course, there is not unanimity among all deliberative thinkers, and the notion of deliberation itself is not the same in all conceptions of the theory. Nonetheless, we can broadly sketch deliberative democracy's central characteristics.

Deliberative democratic theory bears distinct influence from the thought of John Rawls and Jurgen Habermas.[17] Especially important are Rawls's notion of "public reason" and Habermas's description of "opinion-formation in a mobilized public sphere." Rawls explains how

---

[13] John Shook, *Dewey's Social Philosophy: Democracy as Education* (New York, NY: Palgrave Macmillan, 2014), 57, 69.

[14] Robert Westbrook, *John Dewey and American Democracy* (Ithaca, NY: Cornell University Press, 1991), xiv–xv, 164.

[15] Robert Westbrook, *Democratic Hope: Pragmatism and the Politics of Truth* (Ithaca, NY: Cornell University Press, 2005), 187.

[16] John Dryzek, "Theory, Evidence, and the Tasks of Deliberation," in *Deliberation, Participation and Democracy: Can the People Govern?*, ed. Shawn Rosenberg (New York, NY: Palgrave Macmillan, 2007), 237.

[17] Rawls and Habermas do have their differences, but as they both note, those differences are "familial"; see Jurgen Habermas, "Reconciliation Through the Public Use of Reason: Remarks on John Rawls's Political Liberalism," *Journal of Philosophy* 92, no. 3 (1995): 109–31; and John Rawls, "Political Liberalism: Reply to Habermas," *Journal of Philosophy* 92, no. 3 (1995): 132–80.

the "ideal of public reason" requires that citizens "should be ready to explain the basis of their actions to one another in terms each could reasonably expect that others might endorse as consistent with their freedom and equality" and that they show "a willingness to listen to what others have to say and [be] ready to accept reasonable accommodations or alterations in [their] own view"; he also states that "public reason applies ... to citizens when they engage in political advocacy in the public forum, in political campaigns for example ... [and] to public and government officers in official forums, in their debates and votes on the floor of the legislature."[18] Habermas characterizes the formation of public opinion as taking place through a "public sphere [which] can best be described as a network for communicating information and points of view ... the streams of communication are, in the process, filtered and synthesized in such a way that they coalesce into bundles of topically specified *public opinions*"; and ideally, the opinions formed are "motivated solely by the unforced force of the better argument."[19]

As the theory developed in the 1990s, deliberative thinkers primarily insisted that deliberators should argue for their various policy positions in terms of reasons that others can be reasonably expected to endorse and that policy outcomes should be determined simply by the most convincing such arguments within the deliberative forum. Bohman, for instance, remarks that "[d]eliberative democracy is a complex ideal with a variety of forms, but whatever form it takes it must refer to the ideal of public reason, to the requirement that legitimate decisions be ones that 'everyone could accept' or at least 'not reasonably reject'"[20]; and further, "the ensuing collective decision should in some sense be justified by public reasons—that is, reasons that are generally convincing to everyone participating in the process of deliberation."[21] Joshua Cohen provides a similar view, asserting that

[d]eliberation is *reasoned* in that the parties to it are required to state their reasons for advancing proposals, supporting them, or criticizing them. They give reasons with the expectation that those reasons (and not, for example, their power) will settle the fate of their proposal ... the discovery that I can offer no persuasive

---

[18] John Rawls, *Political Liberalism* (New York, NY: Columbia University Press, 1993), 218, 252, 253.

[19] Jurgen Habermas, *Between Facts and Norms* (Cambridge: MIT Press, 1996), 306, 360.

[20] James Bohman, "The Coming of Age of Deliberative Democracy," *Journal of Political Philosophy* 6, no. 4 (1998): 401–2.

[21] James Bohman, *Public Deliberation: Pluralism, Complexity, and Democracy* (Cambridge: MIT Press, 1996), 5.

reasons on behalf of a proposal of mine may transform the preferences that motivate the proposal.[22]

Knight and Johnson focus on the *equality* entailed by the demand for deliberative reason-giving: "all claims and counterclaims are subject to critical public scrutiny and ... when challenged, any participant must defend her proposal or back her objection with reasons."[23] Jon Elster stresses how reason-giving should lead deliberators toward concern with the common good above mere self-interest – because "speakers have to justify their proposals by the public interest ... self-interested or prejudiced speakers have an incentive to argue for a position that differs somewhat from their ideal point."[24] And for Amy Gutmann and Dennis Thompson, reason-giving can ultimately mitigate the intensity of moral disagreement: "In giving reasons for their decisions, citizens and their representatives should try to find justifications that minimize their differences with their opponents."[25] Hence, the practice of reasoned debate, the outcome of which is determined by the strength of arguments based on "reasons that all can accept," is definitive of democracy in the deliberative model.[26]

On the matter of who takes part in this deliberation, it can be unclear whether the theory intends for direct involvement by the citizenry at large or for elected representatives to be the primary deliberators. The phrase "citizens and their representatives" is conspicuous throughout Gutmann and Thompson's work,[27] though they appear to favor deliberation by representatives, stating that "[d]ecision-making by the direct assembly

[22] Joshua Cohen, "Deliberation and Democratic Legitimacy," in *Deliberative Democracy: Essays on Reason and Politics*, eds. James Bohman and William Rehg (Cambridge: MIT Press, 1997), 74, 77.

[23] Jack Knight and James Johnson, "What Sort of Political Equality Does Deliberative Democracy Require?," in *Deliberative Democracy: Essays on Reason and Politics*, eds. James Bohman and William Rehg (Cambridge: MIT Press, 1997), 288.

[24] Jon Elster, "Deliberation and Constitution Making," in *Deliberative Democracy*, ed. Jon Elster (Cambridge: Cambridge University Press, 1998), 104.

[25] Amy Gutmann and Dennis Thompson, *Why Deliberative Democracy?* (Princeton, NJ: Princeton University Press, 2004), 7.

[26] Bohman and Henry Richardson have recently advocated turning away from "reasons that all can accept" and toward "the simpler idea of what people 'do accept'"; their argument for this change in wording would take us too far afield here, but it should be noted that their case does not fundamentally alter the justification or aims of deliberative democracy; see James Bohman and Henry Richardson, "Liberalism, Deliberative Democracy, and 'Reasons that All Can Accept,'" *Journal of Political Philosophy* 17, no. 3 (2009): 264–5.

[27] See also, Bohman, *Public Deliberation*, 4–5.

of all citizens may not yield either the best laws and public policies or the best deliberative justifications for those laws and public policies. Democratically elected and accountable representatives of citizens may be better deliberators, and are likely to be democratically recognized as such."[28] Joseph Bessette even more explicitly prefers deliberation by representatives, calling it "[t]he genius and the peculiar challenge of the American system" that deliberation among representatives be combined with democratic accountability: "Because representatives have the time, information, and institutional environment to reason together on issues facing the nation, the public voice to which they give expression may better promote the public good than the immediate and direct voice of the people."[29] More recently, Stefan Rummens proclaims that "representative politics provides the democratic debate with a kind of *visibility* which allows representative institutions to play an ineliminable role in the connection of political power to public reason as well as in the generation of the epistemic resources and the sources of solidarity required to support ongoing and open-ended democratic deliberation."[30] The idea that representative institutions are well suited to enact deliberative principles is prevalent; although, in the recent empirical literature on deliberative democracy (which I will discuss presently), the focus has generally been on ordinary citizens' involvement in deliberative forums.

Since the turn of the century, the empirical testing of deliberative theory has received considerable attention.[31] This empirical work has largely focused on whether deliberators are, as Gutmann and Thompson put it, "open to the possibility of changing their minds or modifying their positions."[32] For instance, Robert Luskin, James Fishkin, and Roger Jowell study a British example of deliberative polling, in which a national sample of citizens are given briefing materials to inform them on a particular subject and then are gathered together to discuss the subject in small moderated groups, and argue that deliberators do tend to change their initial

---

[28] Gutmann and Thompson, *Why Deliberative Democracy?*, 31.

[29] Joseph Bessette, *The Mild Voice of Reason: Deliberative Democracy and American National Government* (Chicago, IL: University of Chicago Press, 1994), 5, 212.

[30] Stefan Rummens, "Staging Deliberation: The Role of Representative Institutions in the Deliberative Democratic Process," *Journal of Political Philosophy* 20, no. 1 (2012): 25.

[31] Thompson has warned that some of the empirical work on deliberation has not suitably captured the principles of the normative theorists; see Dennis Thompson, "Deliberative Democratic Theory and Empirical Political Science," *Annual Review of Political Science* 11 (2008): 497–520.

[32] Amy Gutmann and Dennis Thompson, *Democracy and Disagreement* (Cambridge: Harvard University Press, 1996), 79.

policy preferences as a result of this process, and that this can help illustrate what public opinion might look like if it were more informed and
reflective.[33] Graham Smith and Corinne Wales focus on citizens' juries,
in which a randomly selected group of citizens is exposed to information
about a particular issue, listen to expert testimony on that issue, and
then provide a report, to again demonstrate how pre-deliberative preferences change through the process of deliberation.[34] Many other studies
have investigated the feasibility of deliberative principles, with their focus
again being on whether individuals are willing to consider the views of
others and potentially revise their own views.[35] The empirical data may
not always match up with deliberative standards (i.e., individuals may at
times show little willingness to listen to others' views and change their
own minds), but some recent works have argued that we should not see
any tension between deliberative theory and empirical study as irresolv-
able, because the theory's validity does not depend on perfect empirical
confirmation in all possible deliberative forums.[36] Overall, this empirical
turn in deliberative democracy seems to show that the theory can be put
into practice and can be used to guide reform of actual political systems.

Even with the increased focus on empirical testing of deliberative
democracy, the theory itself has continued to evolve since the turn of the
century. Specifically, there has been growing recognition of the impact
of unequal social conditions on deliberation and of how requiring all
deliberators to go beyond self-interest and appeal to opponents' views
may leave those conditions basically unchallenged. Some recent accounts
of deliberative democracy have thus sought to move beyond the idea
that debaters must exchange reasons that are strictly oriented toward the

---

[33] Robert Luskin, James Fishkin, and Roger Jowell, "Considered Opinions: Deliberative Polling in Britain," *British Journal of Political Science* 32 (2002): 455–87.

[34] Graham Smith and Corinne Wales, "Citizens' Juries and Deliberative Democracy," *Political Studies* 48 (2000): 51–65.

[35] E.g., John Dryzek and Valerie Braithwaite, "On the Prospects for Democratic Deliberation: Values Analysis Applied to Australian Politics," *Political Psychology* 21, no. 2 (2000): 241–66; Robert Goodin and John Dryzek, "Deliberative Impacts: The Macro-Political Uptake of Mini-Publics," *Politics & Society* 34, no. 2 (2006): 219–44; Damien French and Michael Laver, "Participation Bias, Durable Opinion Shifts and Sabotage through Withdrawal in Citizens' Juries," *Political Studies* 57 (2009): 422–50; Michael Neblo et al., "Who Wants to Deliberate – And Why?," *American Political Science Review* 104, no. 3 (2010): 566–83.

[36] Jurg Steiner, *The Foundations of Deliberative Democracy: Empirical Research and Normative Implications* (Cambridge: Cambridge University Press, 2012); Michael Neblo, *Deliberative Democracy between Theory and Practice* (New York, NY: Cambridge University Press, 2015).

common good. Seyla Benhabib represents the earlier view that policies must be articulated "in discursive language that appeals to commonly shared and accepted public reasons," and she denies the deliberative validity of "greeting, storytelling, and rhetoric."[37] On this view, the kind of reasoned argument which impartially seeks the common good is necessary for deliberative democracy. Dryzek, on the other hand, allows "argument, rhetoric, humour, emotion, testimony or storytelling, and gossip," with the only requirement being "that communication induce reflection upon preferences in non-coercive fashion."[38] This view is supported by Simone Chambers, who argues that rhetoric can be genuinely deliberative,[39] and by Jane Mansbridge et al., who seek to incorporate self-interested policy proposals within deliberative theory.[40] Even more significantly, Archon Fung resolves that under nonideal social conditions, deliberative democrats cannot maintain an unqualified commitment to deliberation. He argues instead that the nonideal extent of social conditions determines the extent to which deliberative democrats may engage in coercive, "nondeliberative" activities.[41] For Fung, the more unequal our conditions are, the more we must engage in nondeliberative practices. Mansbridge et al. make a similar point, stating that the "nondeliberative" act of protesting can be integrated into deliberative theory – although, they consider protesting to be mainly a means to creating a more inclusive deliberation, rather than being a truly democratic practice itself, and they dismiss the validity of protests that are too "partisan and aggressive" (I will return to these points later).[42] These arguments reveal how far deliberative democrats have recently gone to remedy their theory's apparent unsuitability to unequal social conditions and to allow for practices that overstep deliberative norms.

I will return later to this evolution in deliberative democracy. At this point I will just note that although this evolution shows a broadened

[37] Seyla Benhabib, "Toward a Deliberative Model of Democratic Legitimacy," in *Democracy and Difference: Contesting the Boundaries of the Political*, ed. Seyla Benhabib (Princeton, NJ: Princeton University Press, 1996), 83.

[38] Dryzek, *Deliberative Democracy and Beyond*, 1–2.

[39] Simone Chambers, "Rhetoric and the Public Sphere: Has Deliberative Democracy Abandoned Mass Democracy?," *Political Theory* 37, no. 3 (2009): 323–50.

[40] Jane Mansbridge et al., "The Place of Self-Interest and the Role of Power in Deliberative Democracy," *Journal of Political Philosophy* 18, no. 1 (2010): 64–100.

[41] Archon Fung, "Deliberation before the Revolution: Toward an Ethics of Deliberative Democracy in an Unjust World," *Political Theory* 33, no. 3 (2005): 397–419.

[42] Jane Mansbridge et al., "A Systemic Approach to Deliberative Democracy," in *Deliberative Systems: Deliberative Democracy at the Large Scale*, eds. John Parkinson and Jane Mansbridge (Cambridge: Cambridge University Press, 2012), 18–19.

perspective among deliberative theorists, it also signifies how deliberative principles must diminish in importance if we are to build a theory that responds to social inequality. If it is recognized that nondeliberative practices are essential to the further achievement of democracy under unequal conditions, then we must surely wonder why deliberation should be the central feature of democratic thinking. I will argue that Dewey's pragmatism can be employed to illustrate the problems with this foundational commitment to deliberation and to show why participatory democracy (with its lack of commitment to deliberative practices) is better suited to our unequal reality.

A DEWEYAN CRITIQUE OF DELIBERATIVE DEMOCRACY

There are points in Dewey's work which suggest that he could be categorized as a deliberative democrat. For instance, in *The Public and Its Problems* he does attach great importance to "improvement of the methods and conditions of debate, discussion and persuasion."[43] However, Dewey's argument in that book is *not* that the shortcomings of current debate are rooted specifically within the forums established for debate, nor that these shortcomings can be rectified by setting better standards for how to debate. His argument is rather that the power of wealth is such under current conditions that it corrupts our debates over policy and precludes the possibility of honest inquiry into different policy proposals. He asserts,

The forms of associated action characteristic of the present economic order are so massive and extensive that they determine the most significant constituents of the public and the residence of power. Inevitably they reach out to grasp the agencies of government; they are controlling factors in legislation and administration ... the new forms of combined action due to the modern economic regime control present politics, much as dynastic interests controlled those of two centuries ago.[44]

Dewey's point, then, is that powerful social interests are exercising disproportionate influence over political, policy making forums, and are thus standing in the way of honest debate over competing policy options. If we are to improve "the methods and conditions of debate, discussion

---

[43] Dewey, *Public and Its Problems*, 208.
[44] Ibid., 107–8.

and persuasion," we must effectively account for the impact on debate of the inequalities (e.g., those of wealth) prevailing in the broader society.

Elsewhere, Dewey makes it clear that, in the face of such inequalities, the issue of achieving better debate should fade to the background somewhat in our plans for achieving democracy:

> I would not minimize the advance scored in substitution of methods of discussion and conference for the method of arbitrary rule. But the better is too often the enemy of the still better ... discussion and dialectic, however indispensable they are to the elaboration of ideas and policies after ideas are once put forth, are weak reeds to depend upon for systematic origination of comprehensive plans, the plans that are required if the problem of social organization is to be met.[45]

For Dewey, under social conditions rife with structural inequality, we cannot presume democratization will necessarily come with giving political actors "the demand for greater honesty and impartiality"; in fact, within such unequal social conditions, "invention and projection of far-reaching social plans is demanded."[46] In other words, our efforts to achieve democracy must center on enacting broad plans for overcoming iniquitous aspects of current society, such as structural inequality. That inequality inhibits individuals' ability to control their lives and interferes with any attempt to institute a democratic political debate. Improving policy debaters' behavior is thus more of a background feature in democracy's development.

Dewey's own projection of far-reaching social plans is displayed in his efforts (also addressed in Chapter 3) during the 1930s to form a new radical political party in the United States. He describes the attempts of his group, the League for Independent Political Action, toward forming a new party as arising from the "realization that our existing political parties in the conduct of government are more concerned to serve the selfish and financial interests of the few than the human needs of the many."[47] He does not call for violence to solve this problem (more on this later), but he does declare that

> [t]he usurpation of functions of government by an economic group in its own interests gives the opportunity for aggressive attack; and a sense of conflict and battle is a necessary part of any movement which enlists the imagination and the emotions ... The present depression has made clear the incapacity of captains of

[45] John Dewey, *Liberalism and Social Action* (New York, NY: G. P. Putnam's Sons, 1935), 70.
[46] Ibid., 73.
[47] LW6: 149.

industry and finance to lead the social host into anything but chaos, suffering and insecurity.[48]

Bracketing for the moment the recent evolution in deliberative theory toward accommodating coercive, nondeliberative practices, these statements convey Dewey's divergence from the original principles of deliberative democracy. He does not advocate exchanging reasons with the wealthy that can be endorsed by all, but rather inspiring mass support for programs which will reduce the structural advantages possessed by the wealthy, and thus *compelling* concessions from the wealthy. He claims "[o]ur entire history and experience proves that the financial and industrial leaders of the nation will not make these changes voluntarily – they will not, except under compulsion, surrender their most profitable share of a system which has concentrated four-fifths of the nation's wealth in the hands of one twenty-fifth of the people."[49] My endorsement of participatory democracy over deliberative democracy will largely relate to the former's ability to accommodate this kind of direct action aimed at achieving structural social change.

We have seen how Dewey conceives both political and social elements of democracy and how he sees interactions within political forums as greatly affected by the quality of broader social relations. He affirms that

political democracy is not the whole of democracy. On the contrary, experience has proved that it cannot stand in isolation. It can be effectively maintained only where democracy is social ... A social democracy signifies, most obviously, a state of social life where there is a wide and varied distribution of opportunities; where there is social mobility or scope for change of position and station.[50]

When society is ridden with vast economic inequality, though, political forums cannot be isolated from the effects of that inequality: "As long as interests of pecuniary profit are powerful ... those who have this interest will have an unresisted motive for tampering with the springs of political action in all that affects them."[51] For Dewey, political debate itself cannot be democratized in isolation from unequal social conditions, and so the effort to move democracy forward must involve action that directly aims at overcoming the social inequality.

[48] LW6: 176.
[49] LW6: 386.
[50] MW10: 138.
[51] Dewey, *Public and Its Problems*, 182.

From the Deweyan perspective, the early deliberative theorists are isolating the political and social when they indicate that the effects of unequal social status can be neutralized within a deliberative forum, as long as deliberators are equally willing to give reasons that can be accepted by others and are all given an equal opportunity to speak. Cohen establishes that all deliberators are equally bound to "find reasons that are compelling to others,"[52] and he maintains that the conditions of equality are met because everyone "can put issues on the agenda, propose solutions, and offer reasons in support of or in criticism of proposals," and because "the existing distribution of power and resources" does not determine who gets to speak.[53] A Deweyan thinker cannot see this as sufficiently recognizing the possibility that such apparent equality within the political forum will be tarnished by the social inequality experienced by deliberators outside the forum. Rawls attempts to address this issue with his "original position," in which the deliberators' ignorance of their social status ensures that deliberation will "not be affected by the contingencies of the social world," and will "eliminate the bargaining advantages that inevitably arise within the background institutions of any society from cumulative social, historical, and natural tendencies."[54] But although the original position is an interesting abstract thought experiment, it provides little guidance for coping with the unequal social conditions we actually confront and for grasping how these conditions affect political deliberations, which for Dewey must be central to our democratic analysis.

For example, in a debate between business interests and labor unions over collective bargaining rights, each side can likely make its case in terms the other side could "reasonably" be expected to endorse. The business side can appeal to reasons based on freedom, equality, the public good, etc., by claiming that too much money and benefits are guaranteed to workers and that society as a whole will benefit from decreasing unions' bargaining power; the labor side can also appeal to reasons based on freedom, equality, the public good, etc., by arguing that society has a greater interest in protecting economically vulnerable families than in ensuring the unfettered advance of business dealings. We saw precisely these kinds of arguments in the 2011 fight in Wisconsin over public-sector workers' bargaining rights, which I have referenced multiple times

---

[52] Joshua Cohen, "Procedure and Substance in Deliberative Democracy," in *Democracy and Difference: Contesting the Boundaries of the Political*, ed. Seyla Benhabib (Princeton, NJ: Princeton University Press, 1996), 100.

[53] Cohen, "Deliberation and Democratic Legitimacy," 74.

[54] Rawls, *Political Liberalism*, 23.

in earlier chapters. When deliberative theory calls for those on opposing sides of such an issue to exchange reasons and for the outcome of deliberation to be determined by the most convincing argument, it does not effectively account for the structural and discursive privileges (emphasized by Dewey) enjoyed by the business side, privileges which have their root in the broader social context. As I described in the introduction chapter, the Koch brothers' extreme wealth gave them tremendous influence over who became the governor of Wisconsin, over what policies the governor pursued, and over the broader discourse on collective bargaining rights (e.g., through TV ads) once the governor began pursuing the curtailment of those rights. Deliberative democracy has difficulty addressing this kind of structural inequality, because the theory indicates that democracy is achieved when we have a debate in which (in this case) the wealthy and the public-sector workers each exchange reasons that the other side can accept. The Deweyan approach to democracy puts the spotlight on the social inequality itself and takes the overcoming of this inequality as more integral to democracy than the enactment of ideal debate practices. Dewey can indeed be aligned with contemporary critics of early deliberative theory, such as Lynn Sanders, Iris Young, John Medearis, and Tali Mendelberg and John Oleske, who have each argued that deliberation cannot be isolated from the power structures within the broader society.[55] Like these critics, Dewey holds that the greater social resources available to certain individuals rather than others, and the greater impact these advantaged individuals can exercise over the common discourse surrounding pressing policy issues, cannot be prevented from prejudicing policy debate from the outset.[56]

---

[55] Lynn Sanders, "Against Deliberation," *Political Theory* 25, no. 3 (1997): 347–76; Iris Young, "Communication and the Other: Beyond Deliberative Democracy," in *Democracy and Difference: Contesting the Boundaries of the Political,* ed. Seyla Benhabib (Princeton, NJ: Princeton University Press, 1996), 120–35; Iris Young, "Activist Challenges to Deliberative Democracy," *Political Theory* 29, no. 5 (2001): 670–90; John Medearis, "Social Movements and Deliberative Democratic Theory," *British Journal of Political Science* 35 (2005): 53–75; Tali Mendelberg and John Oleske, "Race and Public Deliberation," *Political Communication* 17, no. 2 (2000): 169–91.

[56] An important recent addition to this mode of critiquing deliberative theory has been made by Samuel Bagg, who relies on research in cognitive psychology to argue that deliberation is rather ineffective as a "means" to neutralize power relations, because humans tend to perceive whatever new information they encounter during deliberation in ways that reinforce their current political views and commitments, thus casting further doubt on the capacity of deliberation to challenge power inequities; see Samuel Bagg, "Can Deliberation Neutralise Power?," *European Journal of Political Theory,* forthcoming.

In the last chapter, I discussed the empirical data that certain prominent political scientists have provided regarding the undemocratic features of the American political system. These scholars have helped show how wealthy interests in particular exercise disproportionate influence over political decisions and how it is possible for the policy-making process to disregard the wishes of most US citizens if the wealthy desire a policy that the majority does not. This political science literature has also pointed out, though, that although majority viewpoints in the United States tend to be to the left of those of the wealthy, the majority (in comparison with many European nations) is still very largely unwilling to challenge the justness of the economic system that gives certain individuals extreme wealth and excessive political power, and the majority mostly sees policy matters within terms that are friendly to the ideology that wealth and poverty are reflective of individual merit; this literature further notes that the relative lack of effective social programs in the United States unavoidably obstructs the capacities for political participation among the socially disadvantaged, thus leaving the everyday discourse around political issues to be dominated by those with privileged positions in society.[57] With the general discourse on policy matters being itself so corrupted by structural inequality, we should not at all be operating on the assumption that democracy primarily depends on spaces being carved out where political debate can proceed in an ideally deliberative way. We cannot assume that the ideas individuals bring to this deliberative space, and the way the deliberation proceeds, will be uncorrupted by the inequalities in our broader society. Dewey helps us diagnose this problem, and he takes the necessary and crucial step of defining democracy in a way that transcends the sphere of political debate and that focuses on broad-scale changes to society.

Certain deliberative theorists have tried to avoid an overly political focus by arguing that deliberation should take place in the social realm as well as the political realm. Habermas is one such theorist, arguing that "[a] deliberative practice of self-legislation can develop only in the interplay between, on the one hand, the parliamentary will-formation institutionalized in legal procedures and programmed to reach decisions

---

[57] Larry Bartels, *Unequal Democracy: The Political Economy of the New Gilded Age* (Princeton, NJ: Princeton University Press, 2008), 4, 148–9, 285–6, 294–7; Martin Gilens, *Affluence and Influence: Economic Inequality and Political Power in America* (Princeton, NJ: Princeton University Press, 2012) 251–2; Lawrence Jacobs and Theda Skocpol, *Inequality and American Democracy: What We Know and What We Need to Learn* (New York, NY: Russell Sage Foundation, 2005), 7, 11–12, 217, 219, 224–5, 229.

and, on the other, political opinion-formation along informal channels of political communication."[58] Benhabib[59] and Dryzek[60] offer nearly identical viewpoints. Similarly, Mansbridge et al. offer a "systemic" approach to deliberative theory that looks at how various sites can contribute to the achievement of deliberation on a large scale, including such sites as "informal friendship networks" and "societal decisions ... which have only a very indirect impact on state legislation."[61] By calling for deliberation in these more informal, social settings, these theorists aim to show how their principles can democratize society as well as political decision-making bodies. However, this position still assumes that a proper mode of discourse can neutralize the effects of severe inequality and grant individuals control over their lives. If our main plan for democratizing society is to encourage a more civil interaction of viewpoints, then we are still holding to problematic ideas regarding the capacity of deliberation to ensure that individuals are self-governing, and to not be affected itself by inequalities in social status. Structural inequality can deny individuals any opportunity to determine the direction of their lives and can leave their lives fundamentally at the mercy of more powerful individuals. We could have more deliberation in the social realm, but this does not necessarily do anything to respond to problems of, for example, individuals being unable (due to material insecurity) to determine for themselves what work they will go into and being subject to having their livelihoods taken away by their employers. In fact, as with the call for deliberation in typical political bodies, this deliberation may just give off the appearance of individuals having equal status when they really do not.

It is important to address the workplace here (which we discussed at length in Chapter 2), because these social-minded deliberative theorists might say that their view entails inclusive deliberation within workplaces, and thus democratizes the workplace. On Dewey's terms, though, this is not sufficient. Even if owners and workers are engaged in deliberation, the inequality between the two sides severely inhibits workers from directing the course of their lives. Calling for each side to give reasons that the other side can accept does not help us fundamentally challenge that inequality. To democratize the workplace in a Deweyan sense, workers must not simply be involved in debate over workplace decisions, but we must combat the broader social subordination suffered by workers.

---

[58] Habermas, *Between Facts and Norms*, 275.
[59] Benhabib, "Toward a Deliberative Model of Democratic Legitimacy," 73–4.
[60] Dryzek, *Deliberative Democracy and Beyond*, 162, 171.
[61] Mansbridge et al., "A Systemic Approach to Deliberative Democracy," 8–10.

We must make an effort to overcome the workers' lack of material security and the lack of opportunity many workers have to genuinely determine what work they do with their lives. In the workplace, we must challenge the common hierarchy that places an authority figure above workers who they must ultimately obey and who can deprive them of their jobs. These represent fundamental changes to society and are aimed at directly overcoming poverty and reconstructing the typical organization of the workplace. In other words, democratizing society requires substantial alterations in social conditions that prevent individuals from exercising control over their everyday lives. The deliberative requirement that workers exchange reasons with owners that the latter find acceptable is not necessarily conducive to achieving this change. Certainly, we should not feel as comfortable as thinkers like Habermas do that "fair" discourse will bring genuine social democracy.[62]

Other deliberative theorists have sought to avoid the overly political focus by simply insisting that social inequality be largely overcome in order for deliberation to work properly. Bohman, for instance, disputes the idea that "a theory of deliberative democracy leaves social conditions as they are and adapts to them. Some social conditions will have to be corrected if [deliberative] ideals are to be achieved; large social inequalities are inconsistent with public forms of deliberation in egalitarian institutions."[63] Knight and Johnson endorse "redistribution of income and wealth" because "citizens must possess a certain level of income and resources if they are to develop the basic capacities necessary to be effective participants in democratic deliberation."[64] Dryzek disagrees here, worrying that "if we regard effective distribution as a necessary prerequisite for deliberation we may be in for a long wait," and contending that "deliberative democratization should never wait for material redistribution."[65] Similarly, Gutmann and Thompson assert that critics, who fear that deliberative theory is of little help to structurally disadvantaged individuals, "tend to overlook the fact that disadvantaged groups usually manage to find representatives from within their own ranks who are ... effective at articulating their interests and ideals," and that "suffering

---

[62] Medearis has also noted the silence about structural social disadvantage in Habermas's deliberative-democratic writings; see "Social Movements and Deliberative Democratic Theory," 64, 72–5.

[63] Bohman, *Public Deliberation*, 21.

[64] Knight and Johnson, "What Sort of Political Equality Does Deliberative Democracy Require?," 307.

[65] Dryzek, *Deliberative Democracy and Beyond*, 172.

the effects of discrimination and other forms of injustice often produces leaders who are more committed, more insightful, and more charismatic than leaders of privileged groups in society," thus implying that those disadvantaged by social inequality are usually not at a disadvantage within a proper deliberative forum.[66]

But even if we focus only on Bohman, Knight, and Johnson's position (that the reduction of social inequality is encompassed by deliberative democracy), deliberative theory still cannot take this Deweyan position on social inequality without compromising its commitment to deliberation. Once deliberative theorists agree that such inequality just has to be significantly reduced, they must give up their commitment to equal reason-giving, one way or another. On the one hand, if this reduction in inequality is supposed to result from deliberation, then the principles of deliberation are discredited. The outcome of deliberation is supposed to be indeterminate, and if we insist that deliberation result in reducing social inequality by, for instance, producing policies that significantly redistribute wealth, we would clearly be determining the outcome ahead of time – an outcome that real-life deliberation under present conditions may not likely achieve. Thus, if deliberation itself is to result in the overcoming of social inequality, deliberative theorists must privilege certain reasons (i.e., those advocating redistribution) over others, which negates the democratic validity of an equal exchange of reasons. On the other hand, if the reduction in inequality is simply meant to be a necessary prerequisite to genuine deliberation, then it is recognized that the further achievement of democracy does not really depend on deliberation. Under our current unequal conditions, democratization could not be equated with deliberation, because it must be conceded that deliberation now will be corrupted by the inequality, and so we must instead focus on reducing inequality through other means so that deliberation could afterward become democratic. Deliberative democrats cannot, then, simply require that social inequality be largely eliminated before we start deliberating, for they must admit that deliberation itself cannot solve this democratic problem and that deliberation will be undemocratic so long as this problem still exists. Dewey argues that the effort to achieve democracy should not focus mainly on improving policy debate, but rather on far-reaching social plans for overcoming the social inequality that corrupts debate and prevents individuals from controlling their lives. This shows his divergence from thinkers who must effectively concede that the central feature

---

[66] Gutmann and Thompson, *Why Deliberative Democracy?*, 50–1.

of their theory (deliberation) cannot address the fundamental democratic problem brought by our current social conditions.

In the recent book, *Reflexive Democracy*, Kevin Olson focuses almost entirely on claiming that deliberative theory can rightly insist on significant social welfare provisions for citizens, and that it can thus solve the problem of social inequality. Olson argues that we should use "political equality" rather than economic equality as the grounds to justify welfare, because this will create a more secure and convincing justification for welfare, given that political equality (unlike economic equality) is a widely accepted value and that poverty certainly interferes with individuals' opportunities for political participation.[67] With this "more secure" way of arguing for welfare in hand, Olson states that a deliberative theory can insist on significant "social rights" to welfare as a requirement for getting the democratic project off the ground.[68] He believes deliberative thinkers can make this requirement and still stay committed to the idea that democracy is defined by open deliberation between competing viewpoints, and he believes this for two reasons. One reason is that he again takes this "political" argument for welfare to be particularly convincing, meaning anyone who genuinely believes in political equality should accept it, which in turn means that deliberative theory's commitment to effective reason-giving seems to be upheld. The other reason is that he describes the social right to welfare as a general requirement, and therefore, once the material basis of equal political participation has been generally recognized and addressed, the citizens are then to deliberate about the specific content of that social right. Olson declares that "by inserting a guarantee of enablement" from the start, the citizens can "reflexively" go back and "fine-tune welfare benefits" because "much of the content of social rights [is] open to political deliberation."[69] His argument is thus that a requirement of significant social welfare provision can be made consistent with deliberative principles and that the specific content of this provision can be left open to the process of deliberative reason-giving.

Olson makes a valiant attempt at showing how deliberative democracy can effectively deal with social inequality, but I argue that his case does not really improve on the earlier attempts from Bohman, Knight, and Johnson. By insisting on a requirement of significant social welfare as "a guarantee of enablement" in order to get the project of deliberative

---

[67] Kevin Olson, *Reflexive Democracy: Political Equality and the Welfare State* (Cambridge: MIT Press, 2006), 6, 7, 14, 128, 131.

[68] Ibid., 100, 128, 133.

[69] Ibid., 16, 19, 97–9, 129–30.

democracy going, Olson's argument is responding to structural social inequality – again, the most pressing democratic problem we face – by essentially pretending it does not exist. His argument assumes the existence,
and universal acceptance, of social rights to welfare so that he can move
onto the situation that deliberative democrats are much more interested
in discussing: open deliberation between equal citizens over the specific
content of policy. Olson is not doing the hard work of discussing how,
within a structurally unequal society, and with a political system and
debate that are corrupted by this inequality, we might actually achieve
this monumental democratic task of bringing about an effective social
right to welfare. Thinkers like Olson, Bohman, Knight, and Johnson must
concede that structural social inequality is a more pressing obstacle in the
way of democracy than is improper deliberation, because they state that
proper deliberation is not at all reliably democratic when that inequality exists and that we cannot simply turn to deliberation right now to
help overcome that inequality. By requiring that the inequality not exist
anymore, but still focusing their attention on how deliberation should
then work, these thinkers are essentially wishing away our most pressing
obstacle to democracy in order to focus on an imagined situation where
the process of deliberation can rightly occupy our attention. Surely, a
democratic theory should not just take it as a precondition that the most
important task necessary for the further achievement of democracy has
already been completed. Democratic theorists must theorize the process
of overcoming social inequality and explain why that process is integral to democracy. The challenges involved in achieving an equal society
are immense, and so democratic theory must show how the hard work
involved in meeting those challenges is itself a manifestation of democracy's development. This hard work requires straying from deliberative
principles, which means we must theorize how deliberation and democracy are not identical.

I must also note that Olson's idea that a "political" justification for
welfare can be used to persuade opponents, and can thereby take us to
the point we need to reach for true equality, is just not very convincing.
In the United States, for instance, there is a prominent (and perhaps dominant) ideology which holds that the possession of voting rights is perfectly sufficient for achieving political equality, and that if certain citizens
are too poor to participate effectively, then that is their own fault and
they just need to work harder. The idea that adherents of this ideology
will be convinced by Olson's political justification for welfare requires a
quite massive leap of faith. Dewey's theory, by contrast, stresses the fact

that something like an effective social right to welfare does not currently exist and that there are structurally powerful forces in the way of its achievement. The consequence of this, for Dewey, is that democracy cannot be equated with an attempt to simply convince the powerful that we need more genuine social equality. If we make the overcoming of severe social inequality into a requirement for democracy (as Olson does), then we must see democracy as defined by the efforts and actions that aim at directly overcoming that inequality. We must also recognize how the act of compelling the powerful to concede can be therefore a particularly democratic act, more so than a deliberation that avoids coercion and assumes an equality between the debaters that is not really there.

During its emergence as the predominant model of democratic theory in the 1990s, deliberative democracy was defined by an equal exchange of reasons between individuals with competing viewpoints, and Dewey was and continues to be deemed a forefather of this type of thinking. His emphasis on the omnipresence of social inequality, and his critique of a focus on improved policy debate under unequal social conditions, demonstrate that this portrayal of Dewey is flawed. His efforts to form a radical political party also exhibit his commitment to the idea that inequality must be directly overcome in order to democratize society. Dewey's principles lead us to associate democracy with actions that highlight and directly combat the current social inequality and to see deliberative theory's emphasis on proper political debate as abstracting from this inequality and not necessarily taking us closer to democracy.

PARTICIPATORY DEMOCRATIC THEORY

Participatory democracy, which was a prominent model of democratic thought in the 1960s and 1970s, has been widely regarded as effectively incorporated, and improved, by deliberative theory. Robert Goodin, for instance, declares that "[d]eliberative democrats tend to be participatory democrats, too."[70] Thompson claims "the turn toward deliberative theory has not displaced participatory theory ... Rather than transcending participatory theory, many deliberative democrats see themselves as extending it."[71] Fung sees a similar focus on the public good in the two theories: "participatory democrats have long claimed that deliberative

---

[70] Robert Goodin, *Innovating Democracy: Democratic Theory and Practice After the Deliberative Turn* (Oxford: Oxford University Press, 2008), 266.

[71] Thompson, "Deliberative Democratic Theory and Empirical Political Science," 511–12.

arenas function as schools of democracy where individuals acquire the skills of citizenship and come to consider public interests more highly in their own preferences and dispositions"[72]; Fung and Erik Olin Wright also describe deliberative democracy as "participatory democratic regeneration."[73] And for Denise Vitale, both participatory and deliberative democracy seek "to re-absorb citizens into public debate and political processes by means of participation and public deliberation," but deliberative theory represents progress because "defendants of participatory democracy fail ... to take the next step of guaranteeing these processes through legal institutionalization," whereas "deliberative democracy supports the implementation of forms of direct democracy that are defended by the theorists of participatory democracy."[74]

The theory of participatory democracy has been outlined most fully by Carole Pateman and C. B. Macpherson, and their work does not suggest an intrinsic harmony with deliberative theory. Pateman explains that "[t]he theory of participatory democracy is built round the central assertion that individuals and their institutions cannot be considered in isolation from one another."[75] These institutions are not political institutions alone, because the way in which individuals experience the structures of power in the broader society cannot but influence their capacity for effective political participation: "democracy must take place in other spheres in order that the necessary individual attitudes and psychological qualities can be developed."[76] Pateman thus emphasizes the importance of "a participatory society" and of recognizing that encouraging "the participatory process in non-governmental authority structures requires ...

---

[72] Archon Fung, "Minipublics: Deliberative Designs and Their Consequences," in *Deliberation, Participation and Democracy: Can the People Govern?*, ed. Shawn Rosenberg (New York, NY: Palgrave Macmillan, 2007), 169.

[73] Archon Fung and Erik Olin Wright, "Thinking about Empowered Participatory Governance," in *Deepening Democracy: Institutional Innovations in Empowered Participatory Governance*, eds. Archon Fung and Erik Olin Wright (New York, NY: Verso, 2003), 40.

[74] Denise Vitale, "Between Deliberative and Participatory Democracy: A Contribution on Habermas," *Philosophy & Social Criticism* 32, no. 6 (2006): 753–4. A dissenting view against this prevalent depiction of the deliberative-participatory connection is provided by Emily Hauptmann, who argues that deliberative theory does not aim at the same type of social and political transformation as participatory theory; see Emily Hauptmann, "Can Less Be More? Leftist Deliberative Democrats' Critique of Participatory Democracy," *Polity* 33, no. 3 (2001): 397–421.

[75] Carole Pateman, *Participation and Democratic Theory* (Cambridge: Cambridge University Press, 1970), 42.

[76] Ibid.

that the structures should be democratised."[77] She focuses particularly on the workplace as a nongovernmental authority structure and provides empirical evidence to show that "the development of a sense of political efficacy does appear to depend on whether [an individual's] work situation allows him any scope to participate in decision-making."[78] This workplace democratization requires simultaneous pursuit of "the substantive measure of economic equality required to give the individual the independence and security necessary for (equal) participation."[79] And she stresses that the point here is not to conceive of how democracy can be perfectly achieved, but to take present circumstances into account and "modify ... authority structures in a democratic direction."[80] More recently, Pateman has reaffirmed these tenets, stating that participatory democracy "is about changes that will make our own social and political life more democratic, that will provide opportunities for individuals to participate in decision-making in their everyday lives as well as in the wider political system," and that we must focus on "making substantive steps towards creating a participatory democracy."[81]

Macpherson similarly identifies participatory democracy with the understanding "that the workability of any political system depends largely on how all the other institutions, social and economic, have shaped, or might shape, the people with whom and by whom the political system must operate."[82] He points to social inequality as the root of much of the apathy we see within modern citizenries – because those who are socially disadvantaged know they must exercise far greater effort than the well-off to have an effect on political processes – and, like Pateman, he highlights the democratization of work relations as essential for reducing exclusive control of the political system by powerful interests.[83] Ultimately, he reasons that we cannot have anything approaching a democratic politics without both "a great reduction of the present social and economic inequality" and "a change in people's consciousness" from primarily seeing themselves as isolated consumers in a market and toward recognizing their interdependency with others (I will discuss

---

[77] Ibid., 20, 45.

[78] Ibid., 53.

[79] Ibid., 43.

[80] Ibid., 74–5.

[81] Carole Pateman, "Participatory Democracy Revisited," *Perspectives on Politics* 10, no. 1 (2012): 10, 15.

[82] C. B. Macpherson, *The Life and Times of Liberal Democracy* (Oxford: Oxford University Press, 1977), 4.

[83] Ibid., 88, 103–4.

this issue of "people's consciousness" in more detail later).[84] He also real-
izes, though, that

> it is unlikely that either of these prerequisite changes could be effected without a
> great deal more democratic participation than there is now ... Hence the vicious
> circle: we cannot achieve more democratic participation without a prior change
> in social inequality and in consciousness, but we cannot achieve the changes
> in social inequality and consciousness without a prior increase in democratic
> participation.[85]

For a solution, he describes a process in which a democratic change in
either the social or political dimension of this vicious circle will affect the
other dimension, imagining "an incomplete change in one [dimension]
leading to some change in the other, leading to more change in the first,
and so on ... we needn't expect one of the changes to be complete before
the other can begin"; he further explains how "we may look for loopholes
anywhere in the circle, that is, for changes already visible or in prospect
either in the amount of democratic participation or in social inequality or consumer consciousness."[86] And, again like Pateman, Macpherson
rejects the attempt to "simply try to draw mechanical blue-prints of the
proposed political system" and focuses on the movement in the direction
of democracy by asking "what roadblocks have to be removed, i.e. what
changes in our present society and the now prevailing ideology" are necessary to further democratize both politics and society.[87]

When one sees Pateman's and Macpherson's emphasis on workers
being involved in decision making in their workplaces, one might again
think of deliberative theorists like Habermas who have advocated deliberation in the social realm and assume that this strand of deliberative
theory thus accounts for participatory democracy's concerns. But as
I noted in my discussion of Dewey's divergence from deliberative democracy, a focus on fundamental alterations in hierarchical social relations
and in our broader social conditions does not necessarily cohere with a
call for deliberation. Pateman and Macpherson are demanding, among
other things, that we look to overcome severe economic inequality and
make it possible for workers to have a different social status and different
relationship to their work than they often have when they are forced by

---

[84] Ibid., 99–100.
[85] Ibid., 100.
[86] Ibid., 101.
[87] Ibid., 98–9.

lack of material security into alienating jobs. The participatory theory is not just calling for workers and owners to come together and deliberate, and indeed there is no particular commitment to a type of ideal discourse in the participatory democrats' arguments. Rather, these thinkers look to fundamentally change the working conditions, and broader living conditions, that many individuals experience, and this is not at all defined mainly by an attempt to institute better deliberation. Participatory democracy is defined by a basic concern with how individuals experience the structures of power closest to them and with whether individuals can genuinely make the decisions that determine the course of their lives. The theory seeks to allow individuals to be true participants in the decisions that shape their lives; participation in something like political decision making is important to the theory, but that political participation is seen as depending largely on this more everyday participation.

Although participatory democracy declined in prominence during the 1980s and 1990s, certain thinkers continued to carry the participatory flag. These thinkers have emphasized how democracy must extend beyond the typical political institutions and how it must involve fundamental changes to social phenomena, such as the way many individuals experience their work. Carol Gould, for instance, insists on democracy in social and economic life – and gives particular attention to the workplace – as well as in political life, while also clarifying that she is not providing a "blueprint" but a "guide" for democratization.[88] Peter Bachrach and Aryeh Botwinick focus almost entirely on the workplace, and they similarly explain that we must focus on the "process" of democratizing the workplace, and on how such workplace democratization is itself part of a larger process of democratization that can spread to the political realm and to other spheres of social life.[89] For participatory democrats, democracy is not simply a political concept, and is at least as much a social concept which requires that we combat current social ills in order to develop democracy further.

Participatory democrats are not necessarily opposed to the reason-giving valued by deliberative democrats, but they also have not committed to this reason-giving as though it were equivalent to democratization. Pateman explains that participatory democracy works toward allowing individuals "to exercise the maximum amount of control over their own

---

[88] Carol Gould, *Rethinking Democracy: Freedom and Social Cooperation in Politics, Economy, and Society* (Cambridge: Cambridge University Press, 1988), 25, 29.

[89] Peter Bachrach and Aryeh Botwinick, *Power and Empowerment: A Radical Theory of Participatory Democracy* (Philadelphia, PA: Temple University Press, 1992), 2, 9–10, 12.

lives and environment."[90] This idea of control cannot be grasped simply as engagement in reason-giving on policy matters. Pateman's statement entails the greatest possible control over one's path in life – from one's choice of work and family life to one's capacity to influence political institutions – and it focuses our attention on rectifying the prevalent social threats (e.g., structural inequality) to such individual self-government. When deliberative thinkers like Bohman, Knight, Johnson, and Olson insist on the reduction of social and economic inequality, they hit on an important antideliberative point: under conditions of structural inequality, we move in the direction of democracy by overcoming that inequality, not by instituting a deliberative process with an indeterminate outcome. In its advocacy of this type of social transformation, participatory democracy has given no priority to the practice of deliberation. Participatory theory continuously pursues democracy, rather than continuously pursuing deliberation.[91]

To make this discussion of participatory democracy (and its differences from deliberative democracy) more concrete, it is useful to highlight the theory's endorsement of participatory budgeting institutions. These institutions got their start in Brazil in the late 1980s, and have since expanded to about 250 to 300 cities worldwide.[92] Typically a municipal program, participatory budgeting aims to open up budgetary policy decisions to ordinary citizens, and to allow local communities to select projects and proposals that best suit their needs.[93] Participation in these institutions is incentivized because the level of turnout in the initial neighborhood-level popular assemblies determines the number of elected representatives from each neighborhood at the "regional budget forums," where budget

---

[90] Pateman, *Participation and Democratic Theory*, 43.

[91] Diana Mutz has argued that there is an incompatibility between deliberative and participatory democracy, and provides empirical evidence to show that individuals who confront political views different from their own (as deliberative theory requires) are less likely to passionately participate in political activity, and conversely, that individuals who passionately participate in political activity are less likely to confront views different from their own. The problem with her analysis is that she associates participatory democracy simply with acts such as taking part in political campaigns and attending political speeches, with no attention paid to participatory theory's emphasis on the democratization of social and economic life. See Diana Mutz, *Hearing the Other Side: Deliberative versus Participatory Democracy* (Cambridge: Cambridge University Press, 2006).

[92] Brian Wampler, "A Guide to Participatory Budgeting," in *Participatory Budgeting*, ed. Anwar Shah (Washington, D.C.: The World Bank, 2007), 22; Graham Smith, *Democratic Innovations: Designing Institutions for Citizen Participation* (Cambridge: Cambridge University Press, 2009), 33.

[93] Wampler, "Guide to Participatory Budgeting," 24, 37.

priorities for the region are finalized.[94] Most importantly, participatory budgeting has had the effect of increasing the political participation of historically excluded low-income citizens and of producing policies which benefit those citizens (whereas previous budgetary processes primarily benefited the well-off)[95]; these results have been accomplished because the poor can be free of the normal barriers to their political influence, and because participatory budgeting has made use of a "Quality of Life Index" which ensures that poorer regions receive a greater percentage of budget spending than wealthier regions.[96] Participatory budgeting's successes exhibit participatory theory's commitment to democratizing political institutions by specifically moving political power to the socially disadvantaged. Deliberative theory, though, has difficulty making room for participatory budgeting. Goodin and Dryzek exclude it from their definition of a deliberative institution, because the participation in budgeting is not necessarily statistically representative and is meant to be skewed toward low-income citizens.[97] Fung and Thompson each classify the program as deliberative, but they also claim it does not do enough to lead citizens to put aside their own self-interest and pursue the public good.[98] This again shows the divide between deliberative democrats' emphasis on proper political debate (and their implicit assumption that mutual reason-giving can neutralize the effects of social inequality) and participatory democrats' focus on specifically advancing the interests of the socially disadvantaged.

Participatory budgeting represents an attempt to democratize political institutions by paying specific attention to social class differences, but participatory theory again does not only seek to alter political power

---

[94] Ibid., 23–4, 28, 33, 49–50.

[95] Smith, *Democratic Innovations*, 34, 43–4; Pateman, "Participatory Democracy Revisited," 11–12.

[96] Wampler, "Guide to Participatory Budgeting," 30–1, 36, 40, 51, 52. Not all examples of participatory budgeting are equally successful – in some cases, decision-making power is not genuinely delegated from the government to the citizens, and the poor have not increased their participation or seen more favorable policy outputs; see Brian Wampler, *Participatory Budgeting in Brazil: Contestation, Cooperation, and Accountability* (University Park, PA: Pennsylvania State University Press, 2007), 6, 7–8, 39, 72–3, 143–4, 172, 274–5, 281. Participatory budgeting in Europe, in particular, has largely left citizens as consultants rather than decision makers; see Yves Sintomer, Carsten Herzberg and Anja Rocke, "Participatory Budgeting in Europe: Potentials and Challenges," *International Journal of Urban and Regional Research* 32, no. 1 (2008): 164–78.

[97] Goodin and Dryzek, "Deliberative Impacts," 221–2.

[98] Fung, "Minipublics," 179; Thompson, "Deliberative Democratic Theory and Empirical Political Science," 514–15.

in this way, but to bring significant change to oppressive social conditions themselves. Participatory theorists' endorsement of universal basic income is illustrative of this distinctly social focus. A universal basic income is unconditionally guaranteed to all citizens by the government, and is large enough on its own to ensure the citizens' basic needs are met. Such a policy aims at directly combating oppressive social conditions. This policy can open opportunities to individuals who have been forced by poverty into alienating occupations, while also avoiding, because it is universal, stigmatizing its recipients in the way Medearis[99] observes welfare policies often do.[100] Political democracy is thereby also promoted because the overcoming of social inequality itself reduces the possibilities for exclusive control of political institutions by certain powerful individuals. A policy like universal basic income thus displays the kind of social measures participatory thinkers can take to further achieve democracy. This policy also further illustrates the participatory theory's superior capacity to cope with social inequality, in comparison with deliberative theory. Certain deliberative theorists (specifically, those who have tried to insist on social inequality being largely overcome) would likely endorse a basic income policy, but they again cannot do such a thing without invalidating their primary commitment to deliberation. They must either predetermine the outcome of deliberation by requiring that it produce a basic income policy, or they must concede that the most essential current work of democratization (i.e., the achievement of basic income) depends on practices that are quite different from deliberation.

Before returning to Dewey, let us lastly consider the work of Benjamin Barber, who uses Dewey as support for his arguments. Barber considers himself a participatory theorist[101] (and is often deemed participatory by others[102]) because he wants to move away from representative politics and toward direct citizen involvement in policy discussion. However, he

---

[99] Medearis effectively critiques Gutmann and Thompson's view on welfare, showing how welfare policies can reinforce the stigmatized social status of welfare recipients; see Gutmann and Thompson, *Democracy and Disagreement*, 273–306; and John Medearis, "Deliberative Democracy, Subordination, and the Welfare State," in *Illusion of Consent*, eds. Daniel O'Neill, Mary Shanley, and Iris Young (University Park, PA: Penn State University Press, 2008), 208–30.

[100] See the various selections in *Basic Income Worldwide: Horizons of Reform*, eds. Matthew Murray and Carole Pateman (Houndmills: Palgrave Macmillan, 2012), 12, 13, 38, 39, 41, 46, 74, 75, 78–9, 124, 188–9, 240, 241.

[101] Benjamin Barber, *Strong Democracy: Participatory Politics for a New Age* (Berkeley, CA: University of California Press, 1984), 117.

[102] E.g., Vitale, "Between Deliberative and Participatory Democracy," 750.

largely overlooks issues of social and economic inequality, and mainly calls on all citizens to engage in "public deliberation," or "ongoing talk," and to all be willing to transform – through encountering the interests of others – their initial private interests into concern for the common good of all.[103] The potential for such a "common good," under conditions of structural inequality, to reinforce the privilege of socially advantaged individuals is not addressed. Barber in fact specifically states that his theory "places politics before economics" by giving priority to citizen involvement in political forums over changes in economic relations.[104] As such, he does not capture participatory theory's focus on both overcoming social inequality and moving political power to the disadvantaged. He instead should be classified as a deliberative democrat who is more skeptical of representative politics than many other deliberative theorists.

DEWEY AND PARTICIPATORY DEMOCRACY

The depictions of participatory democracy in the 1960s and 1970s contain little discussion of Dewey. This is perhaps a result of the fact that, after Dewey's death in 1952, his thought had largely faded from view until Richard Rorty's work in the late 1970s and early 1980s. Arnold Kaufman, a participatory democrat from the 1960s, does name Dewey as a proto-participatory democrat, but he also alleges that Dewey does not provide an adequate empirical case for participatory principles.[105] Macpherson provides a more thorough analysis of Dewey, but it is mostly critical. He claims that Dewey "was not interested in any analysis of capitalism," was unaware of the way government had become unresponsive to those who do not belong to the economic elite, and believed "everything would work out to the best advantage of everybody" if citizens would simply make more rational use of current political institutions.[106]

---

[103] Barber, *Strong Democracy*, 119, 132, 133–4, 135, 136–7, 173.

[104] Ibid., 305.

[105] Arnold Kaufman, "Human Nature and Participatory Democracy," in *The Bias of Pluralism*, ed. William Connolly (New York, NY: Atherton Press, 1969), 191.

[106] Macpherson, *Life and Times of Liberal Democracy*, 74–6. Gould, despite writing in the late 1980s (when Dewey's thought had returned to some prominence), oddly associates Dewey with the "elitist" democratic thought of Joseph Schumpeter and Bernard Berelson, in which democracy is defined by political elites' competition for the support of internally homogenous interest groups; see Gould, *Rethinking Democracy*, 97–8. Bachrach and Botwinick, writing in the early 1990s, do link Dewey with participatory democracy by pointing out Dewey's affirmation of the democratic character of "class

To say that Dewey was unconcerned with the undemocratic effects of capitalism is, of course, a great distance from the truth. He in fact argues that "[t]he idea of a pre-established harmony between the existing so-called capitalistic regime and democracy is as absurd a piece of metaphysical speculation as human history has ever evolved"[107]; that the exercise of power by "the political state ... is pale in contrast with that exercised by concentrated and organized property interests"[108]; and that when one calls attention to "how inequitably [capitalism's] economic conditions are distributed," too often it is "considered an aspersion on our rugged individualism and an attempt to stir up class feeling."[109] As we have seen, Dewey is aware of how government is not currently "an instrument in the service of the people," because, "under the system of competition for power and competition for command of power, [government is] the tool and instrument of selfish acquisitive interests."[110] As we have also seen, Dewey does not simply call for more rational use of current political institutions, because the workings of those institutions cannot be isolated from undemocratic qualities in broader social relations.[111]

As with the participatory democrats, Dewey focuses on the current "roadblocks" to the control individuals can exercise over their development and argues that democracy is further achieved to the extent we overcome those obstacles. In essence, Dewey and the participatory democrats are linked by a central concern with maximizing individuals' control over the course of their lives. They also similarly emphasize the multiple, interrelated elements involved in achieving such individual self-government. Dewey seeks for individuals to be able to govern their everyday social experience, as well as their political institutions, and he conceives of how these social and political elements of democracy each affect the other. He thus buttresses the ideas we have just seen proffered by participatory democrats regarding the way direct changes to oppressive social conditions, and direct alterations in political power, are both needed to take us closer to democracy. Dewey declares that "the relations which exist between persons, outside of political institutions ... deeply

---

struggle," though this link is noted only briefly; see Bachrach and Botwinick, *Power and Empowerment*, 155.

[107] John Dewey, *Freedom and Culture* (New York, NY: G. P. Putnam's Sons, 1939), 72.

[108] Dewey, *Liberalism and Social Action*, 64.

[109] John Dewey, *Individualism Old and New* (New York, NY: Capricorn Books, [1930] 1962), 106–7.

[110] LW11: 280.

[111] Dewey, *Public and Its Problems*, 143.

affect the attitudes and habits expressed in government and rules of law. If it is true that the political and legal react to shape the other things, it is even more true that political institutions are an effect, not a cause."[112] He emphasizes the "interaction" between these political and social relations, conceiving policy debate as in-severable from the quality of broader social relations, which are themselves influenced by policy outputs.[113] He describes his planned radical political party as being "opportunistic in application,"[114] taking advantage of available opportunities to achieve progress in both overcoming the exclusive control of political institutions by powerful interests and overcoming social inequality, while holding, like Macpherson, that progress on one task could have a democratic effect on the other (participatory budgeting, in fact, was first achieved through the efforts of an emergent workers' political party[115]). Contra Macpherson, therefore, Dewey should be embraced by participatory theorists, because Dewey's conception of interrelated social and political elements of democracy directly bolsters participatory principles.

Dewey and the participatory democrats both place their attention on the current, pressing social and political obstacles to individuals' self-government. Their focus here is related to their understanding that democracy exists in a process of development, and that it is more fruitful to concentrate effort on moving democracy forward in the present rather than concerning ourselves mainly with a rigid blueprint or remote ideal of what democracy must look like. Further, Dewey's own ideas for bringing democracy further into existence closely resemble those of the participatory democrats. As seen in previous chapters, he considers inequalities along lines of race, gender, and class to represent direct obstacles to democracy; he seeks to democratize currently despotic workplaces (and contra Kaufman, as we saw in Chapter 2, he does provide empirical evidence for the benefits of workplace democratization[116]); he advocates material security for all in a way similar to participatory theorists' arguments for universal basic income; and he aims to directly alter political power by changing institutions such as regulatory agencies to allow typically excluded individuals (e.g., workers) to have significant influence over political decisions. The compatibility between Dewey and

---

[112] Dewey, *Freedom and Culture*, 6.
[113] Ibid., 23.
[114] LW6: 177.
[115] Wampler, "Guide to Participatory Budgeting," 23.
[116] LW5: 239.

participatory theory is, I would say, clearly more substantial than that between Dewey and deliberative theory.

As we notice that both Dewey and participatory theorists base their conceptions of democracy on individuals' self-government, we can also perceive a distinct individual element of democracy in participatory theory that mirrors the individual element emphasized by Dewey. Macpherson states (as noted earlier) that participatory theory requires individuals to move away from seeing themselves as isolated consumers in a market and to recognize their interdependency with others. He calls on individuals to move away "from seeing themselves and acting as essentially consumers to seeing themselves and acting as exerters and enjoyers of the exertion and development of their own capacities."[117] Macpherson is broaching here what Dewey analyzes at length with his idea of a democratic individual way of life.[118] Democratic individuals, for Dewey, continuously develop themselves in interaction with the changing, uncertain, increasingly interconnected world they confront, and they thereby develop, through experience, their capacity to exercise some control over their future experience. They do not seek to somehow avoid the uncertainty and anxiety brought by changing, interconnected circumstances. Dewey indeed anticipates Macpherson's concerns by noting that the "consumer" consciousness "has become the source and justification of inequalities and oppressions,"[119] such as poverty, which (as discussed in Chapter 2) can deny individuals any opportunity for self-directed development. This consciousness leads individuals to believe that poverty and wealth are purely the result of isolated individual effort so that individuals living in poverty are seen as at fault for their situation. The interdependency of individuals, and the ways that economic outcomes are largely determined by social forces outside any individual's independent control, are therefore missed. Moreover, Dewey also identifies (in a way Macpherson should appreciate) how the capacities of all individuals, even the socially advantaged, can be harmed by this consumer mind-set. He warns that "[a]s long as imagination is concerned primarily with obtaining pecuniary success and enjoying its material results," many individuals will look for "some adventitious way of getting the wealth that will make security

---

[117] Macpherson, *Life and Times of Liberal Democracy*, 99.

[118] John Dewey, "Creative Democracy—The Task before Us," in *John Dewey: The Political Writings*, eds. Debra Morris and Ian Shapiro (Indianapolis, IN: Hackett Publishing Company, [1939] 1993), 241.

[119] Dewey, *Individualism Old and New*, 18.

possible."[120] This pursuit of material results is what we have seen Dewey call a "quest for certainty," an attempt to achieve security through the stable attainment of fixed ends (e.g., money). It is an attempt to escape the vicissitudes of experience through the attainment of wealth, and it leads us away from the type of continuous, active, necessarily imperfect exercise of control over our changing circumstances which is possible through democratic individualism.[121] If individuals stick to a consumer consciousness, they will not only defend current inequalities, but will pursue the quickest path to fixed material wealth and to (unrealistic) isolation from the influence of other individuals. This is a more detailed account of what Macpherson is getting at with his statement of how democracy requires changes in individuals' own consciousness.

The first three chapters have shown that Dewey provides a systematic and compelling philosophical basis for precisely what is advocated by the participatory democratic theory. He conceives of individual, social, and political elements of democracy that are each in a process of development and that each affect the development of the other elements. These elements are, in essence (if also less explicitly), all present in the participatory theory, and the idea that democracy exists in an unending process of development is also conveyed in the participatory democrats' arguments. Dewey's principles show a deep harmony with those of participatory thinkers. In the next section, I will further argue that the participatory theory has much to gain from an association with Dewey.

THE PRAGMATIC CASE FOR NONDELIBERATIVE PRACTICES

As noted earlier, Dewey could agree that deliberation is part of the ideal political democracy. But his pragmatic philosophy specifically objects to focusing on an ideal that abstracts from the conditions we currently confront. Pragmatism is associated with intelligent action, or "doing which has intelligent direction, which takes cognizance of conditions, observes relations of sequence, and which plans and executes in the light of this knowledge."[122] Dewey demands that our ideas and practices intelligently evolve in response to current conditions, and although he does uphold

---

[120] Ibid., 55, 136.

[121] I will address this point in greater detail in Chapter 6, within a discussion of Dewey's educational theory.

[122] John Dewey, *The Quest for Certainty* (New York, NY: Minton, Balch & Company, 1929), 36.

the importance of guiding ideals for our action, he warns that "plans of betterment are mere indulgences unless they are based upon taking existing conditions into account,"[123] and that "an aim not framed on the basis of a survey of those present conditions" will lead us to "thrash about in a blind ineffectual way."[124] On Deweyan terms, the deliberative ideal is problematic not only because it has limited applicability to nonideal conditions, but because such a focus on deliberation does not reflect an adequate survey of present conditions and the pressing problems those conditions display. Dewey remarks that "there is at every time a hierarchy of problems, for there are some issues which underlie and condition others."[125] Pragmatism forces us to focus on our truly most pressing problems, and the most pressing problem in the way of democracy is the existence of structural social inequality, rather than improper political debate. This is emphasized by Dewey, and is again effectively conceded by the deliberative theorists who insist that social inequality be largely eliminated. Dewey has a conception of what ideal political debate should look like, but his democratic thought holds that the problem of social inequality "underlies" and "conditions" the inadequacies in current political debate. If we place our primary attention on ideal debate, we are taking ourselves too far away from existing conditions and the most pressing problems those conditions bring.

Dewey's pragmatic suspicion toward principles like those of the deliberative democrats is of great potential value to participatory democrats. Deliberative democracy is defined by commitment to a particular ideal practice (i.e., deliberative reason-giving), and participatory democrats can draw on Dewey to show why our unequal social conditions should lead democratic theory to focus on practices that are distinctly nondeliberative. Jeffrey Hilmer has pointed out how participatory theory does not define itself by a particular "mode of participation" like deliberation, but by the democratization of "sectors of participation," such as the workplace, that Hilmer says are not given sufficient attention by deliberative democrats.[126] Although Hilmer is correct that the democratization of such "sectors of participation" is distinctive of participatory theory, he

---

[123] John Dewey and James Tufts, *Ethics*, rev. ed. (New York, NY: Henry Holt and Company, 1932), 382.

[124] John Dewey, *Human Nature and Conduct* (New York, NY: Henry Holt and Company, 1922), 233.

[125] Dewey, *Individualism Old and New*, 140–1.

[126] Jeffrey Hilmer, "The State of Participatory Democratic Theory," *New Political Science* 32, no. 1 (2010): 43–63.

does not consider whether there are "modes of participation" that are appropriate to participatory theory, but are not comfortably accommodated by deliberative theory. Dewey's pragmatism illuminates the need, under unequal social conditions, for modes of participation that differ greatly from deliberative reason-giving, and I argue that participatory democrats can draw on Dewey here to firmly distinguish their theory from deliberative democracy.

As noted earlier, Dewey refers to "discussion and dialectic" as "weak reeds" to depend upon "if the problem of social organization is to be met." As also described earlier, Dewey sought to create a radical political party during the Great Depression that would be based on a sense of "conflict and battle" with the socially advantaged (the economic elite, in particular) and that would pursue and inspire support for policies that counteract their advantage. In addition, Dewey supported and participated in practices which took to the streets to overcome social inequality. He himself marched in the streets for women's suffrage in the early twentieth century, and during the famous 1894 Pullman workers' strike in Chicago, he displayed strong support for the workers and a belief that such strikes were progressive conflicts.[127] His support for the strike was not expressed publicly and was conveyed instead in private correspondence, but as Westbrook points out, the University of Chicago (where Dewey was employed at the time) had shown a willingness to fire faculty members who publicly supported the striking workers.[128] These types of marches and strikes are practices, or modes of participation, that are much more consistent with participatory democracy than with deliberative democracy. Participatory theory has focused on remedying entrenched inequalities within society, whereas deliberative theory has suggested that social inequality can be neutralized by proper rules of discourse. By drawing on Dewey, participatory theorists can build a case for practices that proceed on the basis that social inequality is insuppressible and must be directly attacked and overcome, as opposed to the deliberative theory's attempt to bracket inequality.

In addition to these practical political activities and arguments, Dewey provides a sustained intellectual defense of practices that stray from deliberative principles. He refers to "direct actionists" who "lead us to inquire whether manifestation of force, threatening and veiled if not overt, is not,

[127] Westbrook, *John Dewey and American Democracy*, 86, 167; Alan Ryan, *John Dewey and the High Tide of American Liberalism* (New York, NY: W. W. Norton & Company, 1995), 111, 161.
[128] Westbrook, *Democratic Hope*, 86.

after all, the only efficacious method of bringing about any social change which is of serious import."[129] On "the question of the justification of force in a strike," Dewey explains that if "the existing legal and economic machinery ... represent an ineffective organization of means" for addressing the power disparities in the relationship of owners to workers, "then recourse to extra-legal means may be indicated."[130] Then, when addressing how we might counteract the iniquities of a capitalist society more generally, he asserts that because the "present methods of capitalistic production" already subject the working class to so much coercive power, we may "require the use of coercive power to abrogate [those methods'] exercise."[131] Dewey's justification of these coercive practices is, once again, fundamentally connected with his pragmatism. The democratic character of these practices, and of what he calls "more refined methods" (which could certainly include deliberative reason-giving), cannot be determined in abstraction from our current social conditions, but can only be appropriately judged in relation to those conditions: "measures condemned as recourse to mere violence may, under the given circumstances, represent an intelligent utilization of energy. In no case, can antecedent or *a priori* principles be appealed to as more than presumptive: the point at issue is concrete utilization of means for ends."[132] I will address Dewey's view on violence more fully later, but his interest in a flexibly intelligent approach to social problems, and to our methods for rectifying those problems, is crucial here. He sees "intelligence" as having a "particular role in bringing about needed social change,"[133] and intelligence here means that we avoid a rigid, universal commitment to one method or practice. Such a method (e.g., deliberative political debate) may be ill suited to the circumstances and problems we currently face. If democracy demands "social change," then methods and practices that can achieve that change within our particular circumstances are themselves integral to democracy. Dewey thus leads us to see why something like a workers' strike can be a more democratic practice than an ideally deliberative political debate, because the former takes direct aim at democracy's current pressing obstacles.

Dewey, of course, has his ideals for guiding his analysis of democracy's development. Most fundamentally, at the individual level, he seeks to

---

[129] MW10: 244–5.
[130] MW10: 247.
[131] MW10: 250–1.
[132] MW10: 248, 251.
[133] LW9: 109.

allow all individuals to control their lives, which is an ideal that is again never fully achieved, but can be progressively approximated. He relatedly pursues the broad goals of a society without rigid, structural inequality and a political system that does not systematically privilege certain individuals' voices over others. Deliberation should be seen as part of Dewey's political ideal (i.e., this is how he would like political decision makers to debate once society and politics have been effectively democratized), but if we overemphasize deliberation at present, we abstract from structural social inequality. Also, as we have seen in the last chapter and this chapter, even with respect to the political element of democracy, Dewey is not primarily calling for more deliberation. He rather calls for changes to current political institutions so as to directly move political power from the socially advantaged to the disadvantaged. On a Deweyan view, the deliberative ideal does not directly respond to even the most pressing *political* obstacles standing in the way of democracy's development. Dewey ultimately warns that if we focus on ideals that are too removed from existing conditions and not attuned to our main problems, "[o]ur sense of the actual is dulled, and we are led to think that in dwelling upon ideal goals we have somehow transcended existing evils. Ideals express possibilities; but they are genuine ideals only in so far as they are possibilities of what is now moving ... save as they are related to actualities, they are pictures in a dream."[134] The deliberative theory would thus be guilty of imagining a time when existing evils have gone away and projecting an ideal that does not tell us how to combat those evils.

Still, this critique of the deliberative ideal should not lead Dewey to be placed at the nonideal pole within the nonideal/ideal theory dichotomy that is often drawn by contemporary political theorists. Dewey clearly has democratic ideals, though they are ideals that speak directly to the current obstacles to individuals' self-government. When he endorses practices like workers' strikes, he looks to bring the ideals of individual, social, and political democracy further into existence, while also dealing effectively and intelligently with the pressing problems brought by our nonideal conditions. Dewey synthesizes nonideal and ideal thinking, and he certainly should not be pigeonholed into one of these two categories.

Dewey's blending of ideal and nonideal generates a justification for social movement action, the type of action that aims at achieving broad-scale changes in society and at altering political institutions to combat forms of exclusive political power. Such action seeks to realize ideals

---

[134] Dewey, *Individualism Old and New*, 147–8.

through a thorough confrontation with our nonideal reality. Medearis has in fact recently identified Dewey as an ally of social movement thinking and used Dewey as inspiration for a version of democracy that is "neither ideal nor nonideal."[135] Medearis aims to "directly theorize what is deeply unsatisfying about contemporary political life without giving up on profound democratic aspirations or consigning democracy to the status of a remote ideal."[136] He draws on Dewey (and also Karl Marx) specifically to argue that "nondeliberative" activity, such as workers' strikes, can be both uniquely suited to nonideal conditions and deeply in touch with the achievement of democratic ideals.[137] In other words, a strike is both an effective practical means for dealing with the reality of structural inequality and itself an expression of democracy in the here and now, because workers are taking self-directed action rather than adhering to the dictates and structural advantage of the owners. With his argument, Medearis highlights Dewey's idea of the interrelationship of means and ends, and shows the value of this idea for democratic thinking. Dewey contends that "the democratic means and the attainment of democratic ends are one and inseparable."[138] If we want to achieve a particular end (e.g., individual self-government), and we recognize that this end cannot be fully, perfectly achieved once and for all, then the essential matter is the *process* of bringing that end further into existence – a process which requires the selection of means that deal directly with the specific imperfections that currently plague the end's achievement: "To *reach* an end we must take our mind off from it and attend to the act which is next to be performed. We must make that the end."[139] Because the end of democracy will not come into full existence, and because we cannot just skip ahead to a point in democracy's development that we would rather be at than the one we are at now, the means for moving democracy forward from the present time are integral to democracy's developing existence. As Dewey puts it, "Until one takes intermediate acts seriously enough to treat them as ends, one wastes one's time in any effort at change of habits. Of the intermediate acts, the most important one is the *next* one. The first or earliest means is the most important *end* to discover."[140] He is thus not

---

[135] John Medearis, *Why Democracy Is Oppositional* (Cambridge: Harvard University Press, 2015), 51.
[136] Ibid.
[137] Ibid., 40–1, 47–8.
[138] LW11: 299.
[139] Dewey, *Human Nature and Conduct*, 34.
[140] Ibid., 35.

eschewing all forms of ideal thinking, but rather seeking a more adequate connection between the ideals represented by democracy and the nonideal reality we confront. He shows how a never fully achieved ideal can be manifested through intelligent responses to nonideal conditions, and this is intimately bound up with his defense of nondeliberative practices such as workers' strikes. These practices can provide both an effective response to our unequal social conditions and an expression of democracy itself.

The Hegelian quality of Deweyan democracy, which was addressed in the previous two chapters, comes through again here. As with Hegel, an end for Dewey is never fully "actual," but exists in a continuous process of actualization that depends on intelligent adaptation to changing circumstances. An end, on Hegel's and Dewey's terms, can already be present to us in imperfect form, and its achievement depends on its further development in response to the current pressing threats to its existence. Dewey uses the term *end-in-view* to explain how the end is present in the efforts to bring it into existence: "an end-in-view is a *means* in present action; present action is not a means to a remote end."[141] Democracy, therefore, is at present neither fully in place nor completely nonexistent; it exists in imperfect form, and its actualization depends on our overcoming the undemocratic qualities we currently face within the individual, social, and political realms. Nondeliberative practices, such as workers' strikes, are uniquely *democratic* practices according to Dewey's pragmatic principles. These practices directly attack structural social inequality – the most pressing undemocratic quality we currently face – and simultaneously represent manifestations of democracy within our nonideal conditions.

Deliberative Responses

I have been arguing that deliberation, on Dewey's terms, is prone toward obstructing democracy's development. I have said that even though deliberation may be contained within Dewey's ideal political democracy, it tends to abstract from social inequality, and it does not even capture Dewey's thinking on how to democratize the political realm – he is more interested in directly moving political power to the socially disadvantaged than in encouraging political actors to debate more properly. He thus endorses nondeliberative practices that combat social inequalities and forms of exclusive political power, rather than calling mainly for policy

---

[141] Ibid., 226.

debaters to improve their behavior. Interestingly, though, some deliberative democrats have suggested that practices like strikes, marches, and protests are actually examples of deliberative reason-giving. Gutmann and Thompson, for instance, claim the actions led by Martin Luther King, Jr. during the civil rights movement exemplified deliberative principles.[142]

To evaluate this claim, let us first look at King's own words. Those words do not show much compatibility with deliberative democracy, and he instead shows a similar distrust in the value of dialogue under unequal conditions as we have seen with Dewey. King speaks of the need for African Americans "to discover how to organize our strength in terms of economic and political power ... Indeed, one of the great problems that the Negro confronts is his lack of power"; because blacks' everyday lives have been and continue to be "subject to the authoritarian and sometimes whimsical decisions of this white power structure," the pursuit of genuine racial equality "is a problem of power – confrontation of the forces of power demanding change and the forces of power dedicated to the preserving of the status quo."[143] For King, the current racial situation is such that power – or more particularly, a deeply iniquitous power relationship – already defines the interactions of whites and blacks in the United States. The pursuit of equality thus cannot escape the confrontation of different forces of power, and must specifically involve the defeat of those forces which seek to preserve the status quo. He cannot simply endorse an interracial dialogue based on equal reason-giving, because there are a multitude of ways the social standing of whites and blacks can make even that dialogue fundamentally unjust. King references as an example how, just in our everyday language, the word "white" is almost universally associated with terms of positive connotation, whereas the word "black" is almost universally associated with terms of negative connotation.[144] He further states that whites' economic power allows them to just ignore blacks' pleas to end discriminatory business practices, unless "direct action" is taken to combat that power; and that "[h]istory is the long and tragic story of the fact that privileged groups seldom give up their privileges voluntarily."[145] King thus denies the democratic

[142] Gutmann and Thompson, *Why Deliberative Democracy?*, 50.
[143] Martin Luther King, Jr., "Where Do We Go from Here?," in *A Testament of Hope: The Essential Writings and Speeches of Martin Luther King, Jr.*, ed. James Melvin Washington (San Francisco, CA: Harper San Francisco, 1991), 246.
[144] Ibid., 245–6.
[145] Martin Luther King, Jr., "Letter from Birmingham City Jail," in *A Testament of Hope: The Essential Writings and Speeches of Martin Luther King, Jr.*, ed. James Melvin Washington (San Francisco, CA: Harper San Francisco, 1991), 290–1, 292, 294–5.

character of an "equal" debate between whites and blacks under current conditions, and instead seeks victory for blacks within an ineradicable power struggle and makes use of direct action to achieve this victory. This view on the shortcomings of pure dialogue, or deliberation, and on the democratic character of direct action under unequal conditions, is the view we have seen Dewey take, and it is a view that participatory democrats *can* take, but deliberative democrats *cannot* take without compromising their basic principles.

Furthermore, just the idea that workers' strikes, or the types of direct actions led by King in pursuit of racial equality, could be classified as "deliberation" causes serious problems for the coherence of deliberative theory. For deliberative democrats like Gutmann and Thompson to uphold this idea, they have to jettison precisely what they hold to be valuable about the reason-giving process they advocate. Reason-giving is meant to mitigate the intensity of moral disagreement, encourage competing interests to make proposals that are acceptable to their opponents, and produce policies that are justified to all involved. Unlike reason-giving, these practices Dewey and King endorse do not require that socially disadvantaged individuals argue only for policies that can be acceptable to the advantaged, and they do not presume that certain rules of discourse can assure equality between the advantaged and the disadvantaged. These practices typically carry the connotation that social inequality is so pervasive that it cannot be merely bracketed – therefore, they aim more at allowing socially disadvantaged individuals to take direct action toward overcoming their unequal conditions, and to do so without having to satisfy the advantaged individuals at each step of the way. A workers' strike, for example, is nondeliberative because it usually emerges from the problem of the discourse between workers and management being intrinsically unfair and imbalanced. The workers withhold their labor in order to disrupt the normal activities of the enterprise, and in order to compel management to concede through this direct disruption – and this cannot be considered "deliberative" behavior on the terms established by deliberative democracy. As Dryzek puts it, deliberative principles require that "any communication that involves coercion or the threat of coercion should be excluded" from political debate.[146] If deliberative thinkers wish to say that coercive practices such as strikes are actually examples of deliberation, then the term "deliberation"

---

[146] Dryzek, *Deliberative Democracy and Beyond*, 68.

becomes so broad that it essentially becomes meaningless. Or, put another way, it becomes just a catch-all term for any practice that we find to have been conducive to democracy. Dewey's pragmatism shows why practices that coerce the advantaged into conceding can be particularly democratic under unequal social conditions, and it is participatory democrats who can incorporate this insight because they have not explicitly equated democracy with noncoercive debate.

It is here that we might turn back to Fung and to Mansbridge et al. to find a seemingly more adequate way for deliberative theory to accommodate coercive practices. Both Fung and Mansbridge et al. grant that such practices are "nondeliberative," and they each argue that these practices can fit into a more expansive deliberative theory, one that recognizes how deliberation will not be suitable for all situations, especially those situations defined by vast inequality among the participants. But with Mansbridge et al. in particular, nondeliberative practices are addressed mainly in order to say that they sometimes can improve deliberation by helping to bring additional voices into a debate. Practices like strikes or protests do not have democratic character on their own, but only serve to improve the practice of deliberation. Relatedly, because deliberation is still the one truly democratic practice, Mansbridge et al. have to deny the democratic legitimacy of social movements that are too "partisan and aggressive" in pursuit of their goals. They state that the protests of the "Radical Left" and the "Tea Party" both have a "tenor" that is unhelpful in promoting good deliberation, and so both groups' protests are similarly lacking in democratic quality.[147] Hence, Mansbridge et al. limit nondeliberative practices to simply bolstering deliberation, and leave deliberation unchallenged as *the* democratic practice. They also problematically link movements like the Radical Left and the Tea Party together based simply on their lack of civility, and do not consider whether either movement serves more to directly attack forms of social inequality, and is thereby more genuinely democratic than the other movement.

Fung's view seems to grant more stand-alone validity to practices that differ greatly from deliberation. He concedes that unequal social conditions can effectively nullify deliberative principles and practices, and he attempts to establish the types of "nondeliberative" action that deliberative democrats may engage in while they are confronted with such unequal conditions. For example, he references a 2001 occupation

---

[147] Mansbridge et al., "A Systemic Approach to Deliberative Democracy," 19.

of Harvard University's administrative offices by students and workers demanding a wage increase for the workers and describes how this nondeliberative mode of participation was necessary to effect the wage increase, given the virtual impossibility of a fair deliberation with administrators who held vastly superior decision-making power and who felt little motivation to take the views of students and workers seriously.[148] I see Fung as having gone the furthest among deliberative theorists toward identifying how deliberation is not necessarily democratic at all under our current conditions. He, more adequately than most, accounts for the threat to democracy represented by social inequality. However, his position ultimately cannot solve deliberative theory's overall inadequacy when it comes to dealing with unequal social conditions. The result of Fung's argument should be that we treat deliberation as not at all the fulcrum in our thinking on democracy, because deliberation does not necessarily bring us closer to democracy and can actually get in the way of democracy under structurally unequal conditions. We should see deliberation mainly as a background consideration in democratic theory – that is, as something we would ultimately like to see more of, but as in no way central to the achievement of democracy – and yet a thinker like Fung, who still maintains that deliberation must be our central democratic category, is not taking this critical next step. As a result, Fung's position must treat actions that combat the most pressing obstacles to democracy as unfortunate filler material before the time when such actions can be rejected. His argument must uncomfortably hold that deliberation is to be both central to our democratic thought and largely disregarded in coping with current conditions. Participatory theory need not go through any contortions to account for the point – emphasized by Dewey's pragmatism, and effectively conceded by this recent deliberative theory – that our modes of participation must be suited to current conditions. If we agree that social inequality is our most fundamental democratic problem, if we agree that the conditions which exclude vulnerable individuals from exercising power (as in Fung's example of the Harvard dispute over wages) are prevalent in current society, then this suggests that the nondeliberative practices necessary to address that inequality should be given a central role in democratic theory. They should not be discussed merely as an accessory to deliberation, which is all we can really do if we insist on being *deliberative* theorists.

---

[148] Fung, "Deliberation before the Revolution," 409–11.

Potential Dangers of Nondeliberative Action

There are a couple of final points that deliberative thinkers may raise here in response to my argument. One point might be that such a strong endorsement of nondeliberative practices is dangerous, because there are individuals and groups who engage in direct action in pursuit of goals that democratic theorists cannot condone.[149] The August 2017 march by the Klu Klux Klan (KKK) and neo-Nazis in Charlottesville, Virginia, would be an obvious example. Relatedly, we might think of the largely racist and xenophobic movement stimulated by Donald Trump's candidacy for US president, and we may wonder if this is not effectively combated if we are not firmly committed to deliberative principles. The question of how we can separate the nondeliberative actions that are consistent with democracy from those that are not is an important one, because it is evident that we cannot just endorse *any* nondeliberative action. Not only are there nondeliberative actions that are clearly problematic, but Dewey's pragmatism would work against a blanket endorsement of nondeliberative practices every bit as much as it would against a blanket endorsement of deliberation. The characteristic "deliberative" resolution to this issue would be to say that everything still ultimately comes down to good reason-giving: nondeliberative practices are justified if the goals they are pursuing can be backed up with good reasons, and they are not justified if their goals cannot be supported by good reasons. This is not, however, a satisfactory solution. If we agree that poverty, despotic workplaces, racism, etc., will corrupt the reason-giving process over normal policy decisions and thus necessitate the use of nondeliberative practices, then the reason-giving process over which nondeliberative practices are justified will be every bit as corrupted. If racism will corrupt a deliberation over affirmative action policy, then surely it will also corrupt a deliberation over whether direct action in support of, or against, affirmative action is more justified and consistent with democratic principles. My argument here would be that we can determine which nondeliberative practices are consistent with democracy by largely relying on deliberative thinkers' own claims about the need for social inequalities to be diminished in order for deliberation to work properly. When these thinkers make these claims, it is clear that they are concerned about issues like poverty, racism, and sexism, and that they see it as beyond debate that these social problems must be overcome.

---

[149] I am grateful to Simone Chambers for an enriching conversation on this point. Not surprisingly, though, Chambers and I are not in agreement on whether this is an effective "deliberative" objection.

Thus, if a protest, march, or strike is aimed at directly combating problems such as these, then we can deem it a democratic action, whereas if it is aimed at upholding these qualities of society (as in a KKK march), then it is not a democratic action. There will, of course, be gray areas when we apply this standard to various concrete examples of direct action, but there is still a useful distinction to be made here between practices that are consistent with the need to reduce social inequality and practices that are not.

Given the way that deliberative democrats have of late taken increasing interest in the overcoming of social inequality, the basic standard for determining if a nondeliberative action is democratic should not be a matter of great dispute. If they grant that policies like basic income, affirmative action, and pay equity for women should not actually be up for open debate and simply need to be in place, then they must grant that the policies themselves are integral to democracy and that the debate over such policies is not necessarily democratic, especially because the absence of those policies would likely corrupt the attempt to have a genuinely fair debate. Actions that step outside the ideal norms of debate and dialogue, and that aim directly at bringing about these policies that help overcome inequality, thus have a uniquely democratic character. Deliberative theorists may say here that debate still has an important role to play, because the details of a policy like basic income still have to be discussed and carefully worked out. I would not dispute that, but as I noted earlier in my discussion of Olson's deliberative theory, the issue of how we should debate the details of such a policy should pale in comparison with the question of how we move toward a world where basic income is in place and only the details of the policy are left to be determined. If we are debating those details, we are in a far different world from the one we have now. To move toward that world, we must rely on the efforts of those who pursue policies like basic income against the powerful forces that seek to preserve an unequal status quo. It follows that democracy should be associated with those efforts, and those who oppose those efforts should be seen as more reflective of something like oligarchy than democracy. In essence, democratic theory must communicate why the pursuits of policies like basic income, affirmative action, pay equity for women, etc., are themselves democratic, and why the opposition to those pursuits is undemocratic, and why simply putting these issues up for debate within current social conditions may likely not be democratic at all. This is the necessary consequence of deliberative democrats' own insistence that these various forms of social inequality be largely eliminated. Hence, the use of nondeliberative, coercive practices to achieve these kinds of policies can be considered distinctly democratic, whereas the use of those practices to uphold structural inequality can be considered undemocratic.

Another question that deliberative thinkers may raise here is whether my position allows for violence in pursuit of overcoming structural inequality. It is well known that Dewey does not endorse violence, and so it might seem that my analysis makes more room for violence than it should. I am not in fact justifying violence, but before I elaborate on that, I would first note that Dewey does not simply condemn violence in an unqualified way – that is, he does not think that, if violence happens, we should just immediately condemn the perpetrators. It could be that those who are seeking legitimate democratic change are firmly blocked from any effective path to bring about that change (because of overly rigid political institutions, for example), and they turn to violence because there seems to be no other method available to resist their oppression. Dewey says that when we rigidly cling to current political institutions despite the forms of exclusive power those institutions permit, we are breeding a situation that may become violent: "The belief in political fixity, of the sanctity of some form of state consecrated by the efforts of our fathers and hallowed by tradition, is one of the stumbling-blocks in the way of orderly and directed change. It is an invitation to revolt and revolution."[150] He also praises Thomas Jefferson's belief that US political institutions should be open for regular fundamental revision, because "Jefferson saw that periodic overhauling of the fundamental law was the alternative to change effected only by violence."[151] Dewey, therefore, might respond to a situation of violence – a race riot, for example – by questioning whether our institutions permit so little possibility for fundamental social and political change that violence is the only way to make some kind of effective resistance to oppression. We get a similar position from King, who is, of course, famously known as an advocate of nonviolence. He remarks that if whites continue to preserve racist oppression and ignore blacks' justified resentment, then that resentment "will come out in ominous expressions of violence."[152] If there are violent riots in response to racism, then, we cannot simply say that the rioters are "wrong" and should have taken another approach, because the blame

---

[150] Dewey, *Public and Its Problems*, 34.
[151] LW14: 215–16.
[152] King, "Letter from Birmingham City Jail," 296–7.

for the violence should lie at least as much with the whites who are per-petuating the racism.

Also, in addition to these points from Dewey and King, it is surely true that there are situations of oppression so deeply rooted in violence that it is nonsensical to tell the oppressed they cannot use violence against their oppressors. This point is famously made by Malcolm X in regard to the situation of African Americans in the United States and by Frantz Fanon in regard to European colonialism. For these thinkers, these situations of oppression are so deeply defined by physical and psychological violence that a violent resistance is the only possible remedy for the injustice.[153] Given that Dewey has a nuanced position on violence, it is unlikely he would respond to Malcolm X and Fanon by simply saying that violence is never okay and that the oppressed are wrong to make use of it. An unqualified condemnation of violence would reflect an insensitivity to the reality of certain situations of oppression.

But all that being said, Dewey does certainly wish to avoid violence, and his principles pull very much against the idea of resorting to violence when more peaceful forms of direct action are possible, and against the idea that violence is even a reliable way to achieve democratic goals. His objection to violence is based simultaneously on practical and moral reasons. In more practical terms, he explains how "[t]he objection to vio-lence is not that it involves the use of force, but that it is a waste of force; that it uses force idly or destructively."[154] When describing the difference between violence and a nonviolent form of coercion (as in a strike or protest), Dewey remarks that

[e]nergy becomes violence when it defeats or frustrates purpose instead of exe-cuting or realizing it. When the dynamite charge blows up human beings instead of rocks, when its outcome is waste instead of production, destruction instead of construction, we call it not energy or power but violence. Coercive force occu-pies, we may fairly say, a middle place between power as energy and power as violence.[155]

There are thus practical shortcomings involved in the use of violence to achieve democracy, because the inherently destructive quality of violence

---

[153] Malcolm X, "The Ballot or the Bullet," in *The Portable Malcolm X Reader*, eds. Manning Marable and Garrett Felber (New York, NY: Grove Press, [1964] 2013), 321–2; Frantz Fanon, *The Wretched of the Earth*, translated by Richard Philcox (New York, NY: Grove Press, [1961] 2004), 1, 2–4, 5–6, 14, 20–4, 42–3, 51–2.

[154] MW10: 212.

[155] MW10: 246.

is not consonant with the task of constructing more democratic social relationships and political institutions. Dewey often references the Soviet Union to illustrate the practical drawbacks of using violence to achieve democracy. He links the "violent Marxist-Leninist class struggle" with a destructiveness that gets in the way of a more stably democratic future, and with "a fanatical and even mystical devotion" that blinds radicals to "alternative philosophies of social change which underlie different strategies and tactics."[156] In other words, violence tends to be purely destructive rather than constructive, and it erases the possibility of employing other potentially effective nonviolent methods once its destructive quality is unleashed. He relatedly objects to ideas of sparking violent communist revolution in the United States, because circumstances in the United States (e.g., the relative strength of the middle class) make it likely that a violent revolt based on the "class struggle" of impoverished workers against wealthy owners would result only in "a blood bath."[157] In his famous exchange of ideas with Leon Trotsky, Dewey states that class struggle can absolutely be one basis upon which democratic progress is pursued, but the assumption that it is the one, universal basis for achieving progress, and that it should be pursued violently, has the result that our "choice of means is not decided upon on the ground of an independent examination of measures and policies with respect to their actual objective consequences."[158] We are not then pragmatically adapting our methods to changing circumstances, but universally committing to one method even when the circumstances might call for very different methods.

Dewey at the same time provides a moral objection to violence. We have seen the importance Dewey places on the harmony of democratic means and ends, and an act of violence which "blows up human beings" is just radically inconsistent with the moral "end" represented by democracy. If our end is defined by an equal society composed of fully developing individuals who are contributing to the development of others, then the assault on others signified by violence is too out of step with that end and cannot be morally defended. Dewey contends that the failures of the Soviet Union may be largely explained by how the means employed for achieving its better future were not "searched for and adopted on the ground of their relation to the moral end of the liberation of mankind."[159]

---

[156] LW13: 347–8, 353.
[157] LW9: 94–5.
[158] LW13: 351–4.
[159] LW13: 354. King can also be brought in here, because his advocacy of nonviolent methods relies on the idea that a nonviolent actor "respect[s] the personhood of his

Marc Stears, who draws on Dewey to help explain the philosophy of the "American radical democratic tradition," similarly argues that radicals can use coercive methods while still opposing violence "on immediate moral grounds," as well as on practical grounds related to how violence can "generate animosity between social groups for decades to come," and may end up "preventing the creation of a peaceful, open, and inclusive democratic order in the realizable future."[160] Alexander Livingston also uses Dewey to build a moral critique of violence, saying that "violence impoverishes experiences" in a way that nonviolent forms of coercion do not,[161] and Medearis associates violence with "action that attacks the needed conditions" of the moral end of democracy where the social world is collectively managed on egalitarian terms.[162] Thus, the concern that my argument, and my interpretation of Dewey, opens the door to great violence can be effectively allayed. Deliberative thinkers need not worry that I am endorsing *any* form of nondeliberative action, for we can declare violent action to be inconsistent with democracy in both moral and practical ways.

Nonviolent, coercive direct action obviously does not always succeed in furthering democracy's development. It does not always produce changes that alleviate social inequality or that combat exclusive control of political power. But this type of action has proven to be capable of producing such changes (e.g., through the protests and marches of the civil rights movement, and various workers' strikes that have won victories for labor over capital), and so it merits particular attention when we are considering what practices are consistent with democracy. Even when a specific instance of direct action does not succeed at bringing concrete gains for structurally disadvantaged individuals, we should not dismiss it as lacking democratic quality. The 1894 Pullman workers' strike did not itself roll back the wage cuts and layoffs by the Pullman Car Company that had instigated the workers' unrest. More recently, the 2011 protests in Wisconsin that I have addressed multiple times did not prevent Scott Walker's Koch brothers–backed effort to significantly

---

opponent" in a way that coheres morally with the type of racially equal society being sought; see Martin Luther King, Jr., "The Ethical Demands for Integration," in *A Testament of Hope: The Essential Writings and Speeches of Martin Luther King, Jr.*, ed. James Melvin Washington (San Francisco, CA: Harper San Francisco, 1991), 125.

[160] Marc Stears, *Demanding Democracy: American Radicals in Search of a New Politics* (Princeton, NJ: Princeton University Press, 2010), 13.

[161] Alexander Livingston, "Between Means and Ends: Reconstructing Coercion in Dewey's Democratic Theory," *American Political Science Review* 111, no. 3 (2017): 528.

[162] Medearis, *Why Democracy Is Oppositional*, 147–8.

restrict public-sector workers' collective bargaining rights. Very recently, protestors have invaded the US Capitol building to try to stop efforts by Donald Trump and Republican Party legislators to end the Affordable Care Act (ACA); the protestors' actions were temporarily successful, but Republicans were still able to write provisions into subsequent tax legislation that would weaken the ACA and may cause millions of Americans to lose their health care. Even if actions like these are not immediately successful, they may still have a crucial role in democracy's development because they can bring greater public awareness to a situation of structural inequality, and can provide an experience that produces lessons for those who subsequently use coercive action to achieve democratic social change. Livingston rightly points out that "[l]abor and social movements need to reconstitute the matter of fact entwining the public together into a reflective matter of concern."[163] Even if a nondeliberative action by itself does not bring discernible democratic progress, it may contribute to the process of taking a fact of structural disadvantage and making it into a broader area of public concern. Also, as we have seen Medearis argue, nondeliberative practices can be considered expressions of democracy on their own because they reflect structurally disadvantaged individuals (e.g., workers) taking self-directed action and making their own decisions. We need not see coercive, nondeliberative practices as always democratic, but we should take them as often being uniquely democratic, and as frequently more democratic than deliberation under conditions of structural inequality.

On Deweyan terms, there can be no universal commitment to one practice as *the* democratic practice. Stears draws from his account of American radicalism that the choice of methods to employ must be "both goal-oriented and context-sensitive" and that "citizen-activists" must "be able to assess both the efficacy of contrasting types of political action in varying contexts and to evaluate the ethical appropriateness of that action in each given instance"; he thus calls for citizen-activists to develop a "practical wisdom" regarding the choice of actions to employ, because "there can be no sweeping rules in democratic theory as to the acceptability of particular political strategies at all times and in all places."[164] If we could identify one specific practice, such as deliberation, as the one uniquely democratic practice, we might be able to feel secure that we know exactly how democracy should look. Dewey's pragmatic principles

[163] Livingston, "Between Means and Ends," 530.
[164] Stears, *Demanding Democracy*, 13, 214, 216.

show how it is likely impossible to have this security without abstracting in highly problematic ways from the unique contexts we confront. As I have noted, deliberation need not be considered wholly undemocratic, because it is fair to say that for Dewey we should make political decisions deliberatively if social conditions were actually equal. We could also say that even under unequal conditions, Dewey would like to see the decisions of groups like labor unions, social movements, etc. – including decisions over what coercive tactics they might employ – be made deliberatively, again as long as members of those groups are genuinely equal. But still, Dewey's pragmatism is alert to problems, and he does not consider the most pressing problem in the way of democracy to be the manner in which groups with actually equal members make decisions. He sees severe social inequality as our most pressing problem, and therefore he focuses the analysis of democracy's development on the overcoming of that inequality. The main lesson that political theorists should take from Dewey's pragmatism is not that political debate needs to proceed more properly. To focus on that issue, we must essentially pretend that the most undemocratic features of our current reality have somehow gone away, or will go away on their own. A pragmatic account of democracy can have no tolerance for this kind of wishing away of our most pressing problem, and it instead forces us to theorize the process of overcoming this problem.

It is for all these reasons that I argue that participatory democracy has significant advantages over deliberative democracy, once we take Dewey and the reality of our structurally unequal social conditions into serious account. Participatory democrats' emphasis on combating social inequality, and their lack of specific commitment to deliberation, allow them to incorporate the Deweyan points that nondeliberative practices are uniquely suited to unequal social conditions and that we are in need of an intelligent, flexible, pragmatic approach to determining which practices are democratic in different contexts. There have been a couple recent attempts to link Dewey with participatory democracy,[165] but these have not identified how a Deweyan case for nondeliberative practices can be incorporated into participatory theory. My analysis shows

---

[165] R. W. Hildreth, "Word and Deed: A Deweyan Integration of Deliberative and Participatory Democracy," *New Political Science* 34, no. 3 (2012): 295–320; Judith Green, *Deep Democracy: Community, Diversity, and Transformation* (Lanham, MD: Rowman & Littlefield, 1999); and Judith Green, *Pragmatism and Social Hope: Deepening Democracy in Global Contexts* (New York, NY: Columbia University Press, 2008).

how Dewey can help elevate participatory over deliberative democracy, because participatory theory can pragmatically accommodate practices that are suited to our current conditions without compromising its own central attributes.

If participatory theory has been unclear on any particular point, it would be the specific practices it endorses for moving democracy forward from our present conditions. This has given room for some thinkers (e.g., Vitale) to argue that deliberative theory's explicit commitment to deliberation shows its superiority to participatory theory. My argument is that this commitment to deliberation should be seen as actually weakening deliberative democracy in comparison with participatory democracy. Participatory democrats would thus be well served by drawing a direct link between their theory and nondeliberative practices that attack social inequality. Certain thinkers in the participatory tradition have alluded to a harmony between their theory and these types of practices – Jack Walker[166] and Meta Mendel-Reyes[167] each link participatory democracy with broadly based social movements, and Bachrach and Botwinick identify "class struggle" as important to participatory theory.[168] With Dewey's pragmatism, participatory theory can convey why exactly a commitment to deliberation is not a virtue and why nondeliberative practices are particularly democratic under unequal social conditions. There is something of an empty spot in participatory democracy regarding the specific practices the theory endorses, and this spot can be filled in with Dewey's pragmatic principle that our practices must be intelligently suited to the unequal conditions we currently confront.

DEMOCRATIC THEORY IN THE MIDST OF SOCIAL INEQUALITY

This chapter has challenged the popular belief that Dewey should be seen as a forefather of deliberative democracy and has argued instead that his theory provides compelling support for participatory democracy. I have shown that, under unequal social conditions, Dewey would see deliberative democracy as displacing our theoretical attention, because this theory associates democracy with a policy debate where individuals are

---

[166] Jack Walker, "A Critique of the Elitist Theory of Democracy," *American Political Science Review* 60, no. 2 (1966): 289, 293, 294.

[167] Meta Mendel-Reyes, *Reclaiming Democracy: The Sixties in Politics and Memory* (New York, NY: Routledge, 1995).

[168] Bachrach and Botwinick, *Power and Empowerment*, 12–13, 31–2, 116, 139, 151–2, 153.

effectively assumed to already have equal status. Dewey's work buttresses participatory theory's emphasis on the threat to democracy represented by social ills such as poverty and hierarchical relationships in nongovernmental authority structures like the workplace. Also, his pragmatism illuminates how deliberation as a practice is not suited to the unequal social conditions we confront and how coercive, nondeliberative practices are frequently more democratic than deliberation in the midst of social inequality. Participatory democrats can incorporate this pragmatic insight, which helps elevate their theory above deliberative democracy in terms of relevance to our current conditions. Democratic theory generally would benefit from this Deweyan analysis, because we should expect that prominent theories of democracy would address the most pressing obstacles in the way of democracy's achievement. If democratic theorists are focusing their work on instituting a proper form of political debate, they are not theorizing how to overcome these most pressing obstacles, and it is certainly not sufficient for these thinkers to just add in a requirement to their theory that structural social inequality be largely eliminated. The task of eliminating this inequality is highly complex, and it is indeed our most important current project for bringing democracy further into existence. Democratic theorists should not simply take it as a precondition of their theory that this most essential work in democracy's development be already completed, just so they can focus their attention on a form of proper political debate. We must instead theorize the process of overcoming structural social inequality and explain why this process itself is manifesting democracy's development.

Dewey's defense of nondeliberative practices for combating social inequality is frequently overlooked, but it is indeed crucial to his multifaceted, continuously developing conception of democracy. For Dewey, democracy is composed of individual, social, and political elements, and these elements are each in a process of development that affects the development of the other elements. Nondeliberative, coercive forms of direct action can bring about the kinds of policies that ameliorate social inequality and can help alter political institutions so as to move political power away from the socially advantaged. This social and political democratization is, of course, directly related to individuals' self-government, because the most basic aim of democratization is the expansion of control that individuals can exercise over their lives. Also, when an individual engages in these practices of direct action, she manifests what Dewey calls the democratic individual way of life. As discussed in Chapters 1 and 2, taking action to combat structural social inequality can be seen as expanding one's own self-government; and as discussed in this chapter, such action can show the disadvantaged taking control of their lives in ways that are typically unavailable to them. This nondeliberative action is essential to each of the individual, social, and political elements of Deweyan democracy.

Dewey holds that we must progressively overcome structural social inequality because the opportunity for individuals to control their lives is affected no less by that inequality than by political institutions. But he stresses that the way individuals themselves develop will simultaneously affect the democratic quality of the social and political realms. The manner in which individuals approach their world, and the way in which they interact with others under increasingly interconnected conditions, cannot be predetermined for them. The social threats to Deweyan democratic individualism – that is, to the continuous, active, necessarily imperfect control that individuals may exercise over their development – may be progressively overcome, but it is still ultimately up to individuals to actualize democratic social relations in their everyday interactions. And, as we noted earlier, individuals' contribution to democracy is intimately bound up with their capacity to transcend a "market" consciousness and ideology. If individuals continue to see themselves primarily as consumers in a market, they will defend present inequalities and will seek the quickest path toward material wealth in order to save themselves from the vicissitudes of experience. Individuals' capacity to overcome market consciousness is certainly influenced by the social and political world they see around them, but they still bear large responsibility for forwarding the democratic movement themselves: "Imagine a society free of pecuniary domination ... If human beings are not strong and steadfast enough to accept the invitation and take advantage of the proffered occasion, let us put the blame where it belongs."[169] The task of helping individuals to overcome market consciousness is, on my reading, a central concern of Dewey's educational theory, and that will be our focus in Chapter 6. In the next chapter, though, I will further explore Dewey's relation to contemporary democratic theory by extending my analysis into other current models of democratic thought.

---

[169] Dewey, *Individualism Old and New*, 158.

5

Agonism, Communitarianism, and Cosmopolitanism

I will now extend the Deweyan principles I have used to elevate participatory democracy over deliberative democracy into an analysis of two
other contemporary models in democratic theory: agonistic democracy
and cosmopolitan democracy. This chapter will also discuss communitarianism, which is a model of political thought that has a complicated
relationship to democracy – and indeed may not be distinctly democratic
at all – but has still been linked to Dewey by several prominent scholars.

I will first address agonistic democracy, which is the most prominent
challenger to deliberative democracy. Agonistic theory has disputed the
idea that power can be eliminated from political debate through the
enactment of deliberative norms. Theorists in this tradition claim that
any decision which results from deliberation will always reflect the victory of one partial perspective over another, and that deliberative democrats are overstating the unity possible between political actors with their
conception of decisions that everyone can legitimately accept. Agonistic
thinkers thus do not seek a debate that will be based on reasons that all
can somehow accept, but rather associate democracy with an open contest between competing political identities, and they insist that democracy
mainly requires political opponents to treat each other as "adversaries"
to debate rather than "enemies" to potentially fight with violence. I will
show, though, that agonistic theory is vulnerable to a similar Deweyan
critique as is deliberative theory, regarding its abstraction from structural social inequality. To maintain consistency, agonistic democrats must
endorse the open contest of political positions and whatever outcome it
produces, regardless of the social statuses of those involved in the contest

(since agonists hold that there are no philosophical foundations that can make one position more universally valid than others). But when these thinkers attempt (as they sometimes do) to simultaneously account for the impact of unequal social status on political debate, and to thus demand significant reduction of social inequality, they must give up their claim that agonistic contest is primary to democracy.[1] As with the deliberative thinkers, agonistic democrats must either predetermine the outcome of agonistic contest by requiring that it produce policies like universal basic income, or they must concede that agonistic contest has little to do with achieving democracy within our unequal social conditions, because the most pressing work of democratization would have to be accomplished before agonistic contest could take place.

Communitarianism will be addressed next, and although communitarianism is not itself a model of democracy, it is still significant for our purposes because there is a substantial literature that places Dewey in the communitarian tradition. Communitarians do not directly critique deliberative democracy, but they do object to the liberal principles underlying much of deliberative theory, particularly the idea that individuals can revise their ends through the process of deliberating with others. The communitarian perspective instead holds that individuals are defined by constitutive ends given to them by their communities – ends from which they cannot stand apart – and that we must preserve and construct forms of community that allow individuals to stay attached to, and flourish within, their traditional roles. Certain communitarians have argued that their principles are in fact democratic, and those thinkers have associated democracy with the protection of traditional communal norms, and with a virtuous participation by citizens who are to put the common good of their community above their own self-interest. However, I will argue that Dewey's democratic individual way of life provides the key to understanding why Dewey should not be seen as a communitarian and to showing why communitarianism is deeply flawed as a model of democracy. I will show that communitarians cannot coherently maintain the standard of individual self-government set by democratic individualism, because they cannot reject oppressive cultural practices and rigid forms of inequality within communities without straying widely from their basic principles. Some communitarians are quite reasonably wary of endorsing communal norms and practices that deny individuals any opportunity to direct their unique growth, and these thinkers do grant that individuals should be

---

[1] My thanks to an anonymous reviewer for leading me to be more precise on this claim.

able to revise their ends. But in so doing, these communitarians must concede that making their theory *democratic* depends on their relinquishing the communitarian idea that our ends are unrevisable. Communitarian and democratic principles lack congruence with one another, and there is not a viable case to be made that Deweyan democracy is fundamentally communitarian.

Cosmopolitan democracy will be discussed last, and as with participatory democracy, I will show that we can make a Deweyan case for this model of democratic thought. Like participatory democracy, cosmopolitan democracy is a model that deliberative democrats see themselves as incorporating, or even improving upon.[2] However, I will show that cosmopolitan democracy, again like participatory democracy, reflects Dewey's insights regarding the multifaceted, continuously developing quality of democracy and has crucial advantages over deliberative democracy. Cosmopolitan theory can be seen as taking the interlocking development of political and social democracy in a necessary global direction. Cosmopolitan democrats emphasize how, under contemporary circumstances, the consequences of governing decisions in one nation certainly stretch into other nations. Under such conditions, democratic theory must account for the diminishing significance of national boundaries, and – because we live in a time where there are already many regional and global political institutions – it must focus on democratizing the undemocratic qualities of already-existing transnational institutions. Further, prominent cosmopolitan thinkers have considered global social inequality (the gulf between rich and poor nations, the enormous gap in resources available to the world's wealthiest as opposed to its poorest individuals, etc.) to directly obstruct the democratic quality of global political institutions and have advocated policies that aim at overcoming this inequality. Because they emphasize the rectification of our unequal global social conditions, and, importantly, because they have not focused their theory on an ideal form of political debate, the cosmopolitan democrats are able to avoid abstracting from vast global inequalities, and to thus provide a theory with significant advantages over deliberative democracy. Cosmopolitan thinkers are not concentrating on a form of debate which assumes the equality of all nations, or of all individuals across the globe. They can treat the reduction of global social inequality as democratically necessary, without contradicting any basic commitment to an ideal debate between competing political positions, because they have

[2] E.g., John Dryzek, *Deliberative Democracy and Beyond: Liberals, Critics, Contestations* (Oxford: Oxford University Press, 2000), 115–39.

not made any such commitment. The cosmopolitan theory, like the participatory theory, is particularly attuned to the reality of structurally unequal social conditions. We can therefore defend the theory on Deweyan terms, and I will further argue that cosmopolitan democrats can benefit in similar ways as participatory democrats from a connection with Dewey, since they can draw on Dewey to show their capacity to flexibly accommodate – in *pragmatic* fashion – the types of coercive, nondeliberative practices that aim at directly overcoming social inequality.

There are indeed a number of important Deweyan qualities within the cosmopolitan theory. We have seen the attention Dewey gives to our increasing interconnectedness, to the way that modern conditions make it increasingly impossible for us to separate ourselves from the impact of decisions and actions taken by others from around the world, and this is a concern that animates the cosmopolitan model of democracy. Also, Dewey frequently argues for the construction of global political institutions, pointing out how the boundaries of the nation-state cannot isolate peoples from one another within the modern world. At the same time, in characteristic fashion, Dewey maintains that such political institutions are inadequate if the vast inequality between individuals, and between nations, across the globe is ignored, and if it is assumed that apparently equal status within global political institutions ensures equal opportunity to influence those institutions, and ensures that individuals across the globe can govern their lives. Cosmopolitan democrats certainly have reason to claim Dewey as one of their own and to draw on him for intellectual support. The cosmopolitan theory would even seem to deserve its own particular Deweyan stamp of approval, since the refusal to take the nation-state for granted reflects Dewey's own insistence on the need for continuous development within democratic thinking itself. We have seen how Dewey conceives of democracy (and its various interrelated elements) as existing in a process of development, and it follows for him that democratic theorizing must similarly develop past fixed ideas and older beliefs when necessary. The cosmopolitan idea that the nation-state may no longer be the most important sphere in which to build democracy is emblematic of the growth Dewey requires of democratic thought.

AGONISTIC DEMOCRACY

The agonistic model of democratic thought developed during the 1990s and early 2000s, largely alongside and in response to the emergence of deliberative democracy. Agonistic democracy challenges deliberative theory's notion that policies can be justified to all who are affected, and claims this notion merely covers over the exclusion that is characteristic of any policy decision. Thinkers in this tradition contend that deliberative thinkers are denying the irreducibility of value pluralism within modern societies, and the irreconcilability of competing political positions, by imagining a policy decision that is accepted by all and is justified with reasons that all can endorse. Agonistic thinkers insist that we must recognize how politics inevitably involves conflicts of power between competing positions and that these positions represent only different sources of power, with no position bringing an inherently more "rational" or "widely acceptable" position than the others. The agonistic model thus holds that deliberative norms cannot succeed at eliminating the effects of power from a political forum, because a political space cannot exist without competing sources of power. Chantal Mouffe describes how "such an 'agonistic' democracy requires accepting that conflict and division are inherent to politics ... We have to accept that every consensus exists as a temporary result of a provisional hegemony, as a stabilization of power, and that it always entails some form of exclusion"; she further argues that deliberative democrats "are unable to recognize that bringing a deliberation to a close always results from a *decision* which excludes other possibilities and for which one should never refuse to bear responsibility by invoking the commands of general rules or principles."[3] Although deliberative theorists could respond that they do not seek consensus in the way agonists claim, the deliberative principle of providing "reasons all can accept" does imply a greater possible unity between political actors than agonists are willing to grant. Agonists see that unity as merely concealing the unavoidable exclusionary quality of political decisions; hence, as Bonnie Honig puts it, we must "secure the perpetuity of political contest" by ensuring "the proliferation of political spaces" where previous decisions are open to challenge.[4] To achieve democracy, we must affirm that any decision represents the victory of one source of power over others, and we must create spaces that ensure that those who are excluded by one particular decision are not prevented from contesting that decision and other decisions in the future.

[3] Chantal Mouffe, *The Democratic Paradox* (London: Verso, 2000), 15–16, 104–5.
[4] Bonnie Honig, *Political Theory and the Displacement of Politics* (Ithaca, NY: Cornell University Press, 1993), 3, 10.

Despite its differences from deliberative theory, agonistic theory does similarly maintain that democracy depends on how political actors debate one another. Agonistic democrats avoid the deliberative requirement of providing reasons that one's opponents can accept, but they still equate democracy mainly with a political contest where participants uphold the right of their opponents to defend ideas that conflict with their own. In other words, political contest is democratic when its participants treat each other as, in Carl Schmitt's sense of these terms, *adversaries* to be argued with rather than *enemies* to be potentially fought with violence.[5] Mouffe writes that "[a]*ntagonism* is struggle between enemies, while *agonism* is struggle between adversaries ... the aim of democratic politics is to transform *antagonism* into *agonism*."[6] For the agonists, democracy is achieved when political contestants uphold their opponents' views as the necessary adversarial element within a debate, rather than seeking to eliminate their opponents from the contest. Agonistic theory, therefore, seeks democracy not through decisions acceptable to all, but through recognizing the exclusionary quality of all political decisions and calling on political actors to uphold their adversaries' right to contest those decisions. As William Connolly sums up, we have agonistic democracy "when the perspective of an identifiable constellation attains predominance in several areas of public debate, resisting factions remain effective in publicly articulating the terms of their opposition and compelling compromises on some of these fronts, and the news media, judiciary, and electoral system function to keep the terms of contestation among coalitions reasonably open."[7]

The overall resemblance between agonism and deliberation comes through clearly in James Tully's agonistic theory. Tully's particular concern is to show how societies can respect cultural diversity, and he focuses on creating an "intercultural dialogue" in which not just policies, but constitutions themselves, are negotiated and agreed to in a way that truly respects the multiplicity of cultures in a modern nation – as opposed to one dominant culture imposing a constitution with the presumption that its particular values are universal.[8] He does critique deliberative theory

[5] Carl Schmitt, *The Concept of the Political*, exp. ed., translated and with an introduction by George Schwab (Chicago, IL: University of Chicago Press, [1932] 2007), 27–8.

[6] Mouffe, *Democratic Paradox*, 102–3.

[7] William Connolly, *Identity\Difference: Democratic Negotiations of Political Paradox* (Ithaca, NY: Cornell University Press, 1991), 213.

[8] James Tully, *Strange Multiplicity: Constitutionalism in an Age of Diversity* (Cambridge: Cambridge University Press, 1995), 24, 25–6, 183–4.

by associating at least certain strands of the theory with a search for "consensus" at the expense of "contestation," and with a commitment to certain norms of discourse and constitutional principles that end up unfairly assimilating peoples of different cultures.[9] At the same time, Tully often identifies "deliberation" as a crucial part of his own theory,[10] and although he sees agonistic theory as holding more issues (e.g., constitutional principles, previous policy decisions) open for contestation than does deliberative democracy, his primary wish is to see "agonistic dialogues and negotiations" between competing viewpoints in order to achieve a "democratic" political debate.[11] Tully's agonistic theory, therefore, is quite straightforwardly an adaptation, rather than a rejection, of deliberative theory. In fact, the phrase that comes up perhaps most frequently in his work is "*audi alteram partem*," or "always listen to the other side,"[12] which conveys a very similar assumption to what we saw among deliberative thinkers: that a proper, respectful dialogue among competing political positions will give us democracy. There is little recognition here of how structural social inequality could make such a dialogue more undemocratic than democratic (more on this in a moment). Tully sounds almost identical to deliberative democrats when he claims that, within the type of dialogue he is advocating, the participants will "gradually come to see that others have reasonable concerns of recognition as well and that their original demands need to be modified to accommodate the others' reciprocal demands."[13] The agonistic democrats do differ in certain ways from deliberative democrats, but they similarly equate democracy with a particular form of political debate and call on participants to be equally willing to see their position lose out for the purpose of sustaining a "fair" dialogue.

There has been little analysis of Dewey's relation to the agonistic model of democracy. Larry Hickman discusses some of the similarities and differences between Dewey and Mouffe, though he focuses more on their underlying philosophical principles than their political theories. For

---

[9] James Tully, "Exclusion and Assimilation: Two Forms of Domination in Relation to Freedom," in *Political Exclusion and Domination*, eds. Melissa Williams and Stephen Macedo (New York, NY: New York University Press, 2005), 208–9, 214–15.

[10] Ibid., 208, 216.

[11] Ibid., 195, 208–9; James Tully, *Public Philosophy in a New Key, Volume I: Democracy and Civic Freedom* (Cambridge: Cambridge University Press, 2008), 145–6, 147, 151–2.

[12] Tully, *Strange Multiplicity*, 183; Tully, "Exclusion and Assimilation," 208; Tully, *Public Philosophy in a New Key*, 151; James Tully, "Struggles over Recognition and Distribution," *Constellations* 7, no. 4 (2000): 475.

[13] Tully, "Struggles over Recognition and Distribution," 480.

instance, he notes that Dewey and Mouffe similarly find a lack of universal truths in the world and view individuals as many-sided, constantly changing entities, but he also points out that Dewey's idea of the progressive attainment of truth through experimental inquiry is lacking in Mouffe.[14] Richard Bernstein sees Dewey as achieving a middle ground between the insights of deliberative and agonistic theories: "Dewey emphasized that without creative conflict there is the danger of complacency and stagnation. But a democracy degenerates into a sheer contest of wills and a naked power struggle if there is not a serious attempt to engage in deliberation and public debate"; in Bernstein's view, a Deweyan cannot quite endorse agonistic democracy because "[a]gonism … can lead to a life-and-death struggle in which one seeks not only to defeat an opponent but to annihilate him."[15] This is not a compelling critique of agonism, though, since agonistic democrats specifically state that their theory requires those engaged in political contest to treat each other as adversaries to debate, not as enemies to annihilate. If the principles of agonism are followed, then it appears we should not be concerned about a potential life-and-death struggle between opponents.

However, agonistic democracy is vulnerable to a similarly Deweyan critique as deliberative democracy regarding its capacity to confront structural social inequality. As with deliberative theory, the agonistic model must abstract from social inequality in order to associate democracy with the particular kind of political debate it advocates, in this case, an open, agonistic contest between adversaries. It is not surprising that agonistic theory would have this quality, given that the theory is particularly influenced by Hannah Arendt,[16] who laments that "[i]n the modern world, the social and the political realms are much less distinct [than in the ancient world] … In the modern world, the two realms indeed constantly flow into each other like waves in the never-resting stream of the life process itself."[17] For Arendt, the "rise of the social" is an especially troubling aspect of the modern world, because she thinks it signifies that politics has become intermingled with private concerns (e.g., individuals'

---

[14] Larry Hickman, "The Genesis of Democratic Norms: Some Insights from Classical Pragmatism," in *Democracy as Culture: Deweyan Pragmatism in a Globalizing World*, eds. Sor-Hoon Tan and John Whalen-Bridge (Albany, NY: State University of New York Press, 2008), 23–7.

[15] Richard Bernstein, *The Pragmatic Turn* (Cambridge: Polity Press, 2010), 84–5.

[16] E.g., Honig, *Political Theory and the Displacement of Politics*, 4, 9, 77, 116, 125.

[17] Hannah Arendt, *The Human Condition* (Chicago, IL: University of Chicago Press, 1958), 33.

material needs) which should be kept hidden in the household, thus turning politics into a realm for satisfying individuals' predetermined needs, rather than the realm for genuinely unpredictable action – separate from mere economic interests – that (she believes) it was in ancient Greece.[18] On an Arendtian view, individual uniqueness and freedom are diminished when the political and social intertwine.[19]

By equating agonistic contest with democracy, agonistic theorists must isolate the political and social by conceiving of a political realm that achieves democracy once political debaters treat each other as valuable adversaries. The underlying idea of agonistic theory is that democracy mainly depends on different political actors putting their views into a proper contest with others – that is, a contest where the participants see the partiality of their own views and affirm the presence of others' views. If this political contest defines democracy, then it follows that the path to democracy lies in creating spaces for this type of contest and in encouraging all individuals to treat opponents as adversaries rather than as enemies. Although different in content, this is similar in form to the deliberative requirement that everyone involved in political debate exchange reasons for their policy positions that their opponents can reasonably endorse. The agonistic theory is similarly focusing on a proper interaction of individuals with different political views. This abstracts from social inequality because such agonistic contest cannot itself account for social factors that deny individuals any effective voice within that contest (and deny them any opportunity to control their everyday lives). Under unequal social conditions, political participants may openly contest one another's positions, while treating each other as adversaries rather than enemies, and yet the social resources enjoyed by certain individuals can give those individuals a structural advantage in determining the outcome of the contest. These resources include, for example, the far greater time that the wealthy have to devote to politics than the poor, and the greater legitimacy that the viewpoints of the wealthy are given over the poor's in everyday social life. Agonistic democrats emphasize that any policy decision will exclude certain perspectives, and they seek to create spaces that allow for the exclusion to be contested, but this does not address the impact of social inequality on the way the contest plays out. As with deliberative democracy, therefore, the principles of agonism must hold

---

[18] Ibid., 38.

[19] Schmitt, another influential thinker for the agonistic tradition, similarly draws a rigid distinction between the political and the nonpolitical; see Schmitt, *Concept of the Political*, 26–7.

that social inequality can be bracketed by the proper interaction of competing political viewpoints. Democratic thinkers who do not consider social inequality to be so containable should not commit to this theory, because the focus on such a contest can create the undemocratic illusion that equal political power has been achieved when it really has not.[20]

Now, also as with the deliberative democrats, there are certain agonistic democrats who insist that social inequality be largely overcome. Connolly maintains that "[a]gonal democracy ... presupposes a reduction in established economic inequalities,"[21] whereas Mouffe actually endorses "the allocation of an unconditional minimum income (basic income),"[22] which is a policy we discussed in Chapter 4. Tully recommends that individuals should have "social and economic rights" that "[have] not been recognized in liberal democracies."[23] But like with deliberative theory, it is difficult to see how these requirements can be compatible with agonistic theory's basic principles. Once it is conceded that social inequality just has to be significantly reduced, the commitment to agonistic contest must be abandoned one way or another. On the one hand, if the reduction in inequality is meant to be the result of agonistic contest, then the theory cannot genuinely commit to an open power contest between different positions, because the correct outcome of the contest has been determined before it has even taken place. To require the contest to produce such an outcome, we have to privilege the views of certain "sources of power" (e.g., those seeking redistribution of wealth) over others, which means we are not genuinely committing to an open contest where no participant is seen as having a necessarily more valid viewpoint than another. On the other hand, if the reduction in inequality is meant simply as a prerequisite to agonistic contest, then it is recognized that agonistic contest under our unequal circumstances has little to do with actually bringing us closer to democracy. To achieve democracy, we must look outside this type of contest, because an agonistic contest would not really be democratic until a lot of monumental work has been done to overcome social inequality. Democracy, then, depends primarily on efforts to specifically reduce social inequality, and not so much on bringing competing political positions into a properly agonistic interaction.

[20] Nancy Fraser has made a similar point, charging that agonistic democracy "tends to bracket political economy"; see *Justice Interruptus: Critical Reflections on the "Postsocialist" Condition* (New York, NY: Routledge, 1997), 181.

[21] Connolly, *Identity\Difference*, 212.

[22] Mouffe, *Democratic Paradox*, 126.

[23] Tully, "Struggles over Recognition and Distribution," 471.

If agonistic democrats thus simply require that social inequality be taken care of before the contest of political perspectives can take place, then they must admit that agonism is not necessarily democratic, and that it would only be democratic once the most pressing current obstacle to democracy – structural social inequality – has already been somehow overcome.

On Deweyan terms, agonistic democracy, like deliberative democracy, mistakenly takes the focus away from the interrelated social and political elements involved in allowing individuals to govern their lives. Agonistic theorists, like deliberative theorists, instead associate democracy with a form of political debate that prescribes how individuals with competing views should interact, regardless of their social statuses. When agonistic and deliberative thinkers realize that the practices they advocate can be corrupted by social inequality, they must contravene the central attribute of their theories to ensure they are actually promoting a *democratic* theory. With agonistic democrats, their inability to account for the impact of social inequality on political interactions is further pronounced, because they insist that there can be no philosophical foundations which give one political viewpoint more intrinsic legitimacy than another. As Mouffe puts it, "[N]o limited social actor can attribute to herself or himself the representation of the totality and claim to have the 'mastery' of the foundation."[24] When agonistic thinkers do throw in the requirement that social inequality be significantly reduced, such as when Mouffe advocates basic income, or when she and Ernesto Laclau endorse leftist principles in general against "the neo-conservative offensive,"[25] they must discard their commitment to seeing democracy as an open contest between competing sources of power. They cannot avoid effectively claiming access to (what they call) "the totality," because they are holding that certain positions in the current agonistic contest simply need to win out over others. By demanding the reduction of social inequality, agonistic theorists must commit to philosophical foundations and to the positions of certain actors (e.g., those seeking a basic income policy) over others in the agonistic struggle, rather than simply maintaining open contestation, as their theory requires. For agonistic theory to remain consistent, it should endorse the victory of any position in the contest, since there are surely sources of power which deny the legitimacy of policies like basic income.

---

[24] Mouffe, *Democratic Paradox*, 100.
[25] Ernesto Laclau and Chantal Mouffe, *Hegemony and Socialist Strategy: Towards a Radical Democratic Politics* (London: Verso, 1985), 186.

But if Mouffe and the agonists want to insist that such policies are necessary to bring us democracy under unequal social conditions, then they should focus their theory on the efforts to pursue those policies, rather than on agonistic contest.

We saw in Chapter 4 how Dewey emphasizes the democratic quality of *nondeliberative* practices when we have unequal social conditions. Agonistic theory would seem to have the virtue of accommodating such practices, because agonistic principles do not demand – as deliberative principles do – that socially disadvantaged individuals find reasons that are acceptable to the advantaged, and agonistic principles instead emphasize the inevitable, unbridgeable divide between such differently situated individuals. Agonistic democracy surely requires there to be a level of respect among political participants for one another, and would not allow participants to try to eliminate others from the contest, but the theory's rejection of the deliberative idea of a policy that is acceptable to all seems to make room for nondeliberative practices like protests, marches, or workers' strikes. Even so, agonistic thinkers still cannot associate democracy specifically with the victory of the socially disadvantaged and remain true to their theory. Rather, they must endorse the contest itself, regardless of who wins, because otherwise they must confess to committing to some form of philosophical foundation. So if we are considering, on the one hand, a march that is advocating the establishment of a basic income and, on the other hand, a march that is advocating the destruction of social welfare and the reduction of tax rates on the wealthy, agonistic democracy has no coherent way to endorse the first of these practices but not the second. With Dewey's theory, we can show that the march in favor of basic income is serving essential democratic purposes by pursuing the type of social conditions that genuinely increase the possibilities for individuals to govern their lives. The march that seeks to destroy such social welfare programs can in turn be seen as undermining essential democratic purposes, because it is standing in the way of the conditions for self-government and is upholding forms of deep inequality. Dewey also helps us make an important distinction between what is permitted to individuals in recognition of their rights (i.e., the negative freedom they must possess) and what is to be affirmed as democratic behavior (i.e., as positive freedom), or as consistent with the democratic individual way of life. In other words, Dewey's principles would not hold that an antiwelfare march should be legally forbidden from taking place; but his principles do indicate that the behavior of antiwelfare marchers is not to be endorsed as democratic. As we discussed in Chapters 1 and 2, ethical standards are involved in Dewey's democratic individualism that call on individuals to combat forms of structural social inequality and to contribute to others' opportunity to govern their lives. We also discussed Dewey's reasoning for why the act of combating inequality expands an individual's own possibilities for self-government. The antiwelfare marchers would not be meeting Dewey's ethical standards, and although their behavior is consistent with negative freedom (which is necessary but not sufficient for democracy), our Deweyan analysis illuminates how individuals' own exhibition of positive freedom is fundamental to democracy. If agonistic theorists wish to say that basic income is necessary to achieve democracy and that a march in favor of basic income is thus more democratic than a march that seeks to destroy welfare, then they must grant these Deweyan points. They must grant that individual conduct that supports policies like basic income is more democratic than conduct that opposes it. They must also accept that democracy is not defined by a contest among competing political positions, but by the victory of particular participants within that contest, and the actions those participants take in pursuit of that victory. We cannot consider a contest itself to be democratic if we are also requiring that only certain sides in that contest can actually win.

In contrast with agonistic theory, Dewey's theory does not hold to the assumption that a particular type of political debate is sufficient to achieve democracy. Dewey's pragmatic philosophy leads us to focus on the forms of structural social inequality that would corrupt even the most properly agonistic debate and that prevent individuals from being able to govern their everyday lives. Dewey leads us to associate democracy with efforts to overcome the inequality experienced by socially disadvantaged individuals, because this inequality is the most pressing democratic problem posed by current social conditions. He thus insists that the practices we endorse must aim at directly overcoming that inequality, or else we miss the mark on how democracy can be brought further into existence.

COMMUNITARIANISM

Contemporary communitarian thought emerged during the 1980s, and it provided a challenge to the liberal tenets of thinkers like John Rawls. Communitarian thinkers are not necessarily presenting a model of democracy, and they do not object to the principles of deliberative democracy per se, although they do seek to separate themselves from deliberative theory's often-liberal underpinnings. Although reason-giving with others is not a problem for communitarians, they do find it problematic when liberals portray individuals as "unencumbered" selves who can freely revise fundamental aspects of their identities (through taking part in a deliberative forum, for example). If we argue for deliberation, then, communitarians would insist that we not assume individuals can freely accept or reject any viewpoint that may be espoused, and that we instead recognize individuals as largely constituted by particular communal identities. Communitarians claim that individuals' identities are chiefly determined through their communal upbringing, which gives individuals aims and purposes that are so essential to them as to be unrevisable. Michael Sandel asserts that

[t]o imagine a person incapable of constitutive attachments such as these is not to conceive an ideally free and rational agent, but to imagine a person wholly without character, without moral depth. For to have character is to know that I move in a history I neither summon nor command, which carries consequences none the less for my choices and conduct.[26]

The communitarian tradition thus holds that we must focus on preserving individuals' attachment to communal norms and traditions, because without such attachment an individual is not a free agent, but is rather without the foundation necessary for any kind of agency at all.

Drawing on Aristotle in particular, Alasdair MacIntyre makes the communitarian point that

we all approach our own circumstances as bearers of a particular social identity. I am someone's son or daughter, someone else's cousin or uncle; I am a citizen of this or that city, a member of this or that guild or profession; I belong to this clan, that tribe, this nation. Hence what is good for me has to be the good for one who inhabits these roles.[27]

Because liberals focus mainly on individuals' capacity to choose and revise their ends, communitarians believe they ask individuals to impossibly separate themselves from the ends which come from the type of communal roles that all individuals inhabit. Sandel thus reasons that "[t]he relevant question is not what ends to choose ... but rather who I am, how

[26] Michael Sandel, *Liberalism and the Limits of Justice* (Cambridge: Cambridge University Press, 1982), 179.
[27] Alasdair MacIntyre, *After Virtue: A Study in Moral Theory* (London: Duckworth, 1981), 204–5.

I am to discern in this clutter of possible ends what is me from what is mine,"[28] and MacIntyre advocates "construction of local forms of community"[29] to allow individuals to flourish within their constitutive roles. For communitarians, we must beware of casting judgment on the traditions and practices of other communities, because we are all products of particular communal norms, and no one community can be said to be inherently more freeing than another. In Michael Walzer's view, communitarianism represents an especially modest philosophical position, for it accepts the diversity of communal practices and avoids imposing the standards and traditions of one community onto any other: "There are an infinite number of possible lives, shaped by an infinite number of possible cultures, religions, political arrangements, geographical conditions, and so on. A given society is just if its substantive life is lived ... in a way faithful to the shared understandings of the members."[30]

Although not as ubiquitous as the depictions of Dewey as a deliberative democrat, there have been several attempts to link Dewey with communitarianism. Sandel sees Dewey as requiring communities to cultivate virtues in individuals which will reinforce those communities,[31] and Daniel Savage suggests that "Dewey's pragmatic philosophy is capable of dissolving many of the problems that occupy contemporary liberals and communitarians," because Dewey makes autonomous self-development into the type of "cultural virtue" that MacIntyre is looking for.[32] Judith Green describes Dewey as a "left-communitarian" who seeks to reinvigorate individuals' attachment to their local communities, rather than just giving individuals the formal right to vote for leaders in large-scale political institutions.[33] Robert Talisse also groups Dewey with communitarianism, though in an extremely unflattering light. He decries Dewey's notion of a democratic way of life, insisting that this concept requires communities to form its individuals in the singular image of a citizen who possesses civic virtue and concern for the greater communal good.

[28] Sandel, *Liberalism and the Limits of Justice*, 59.

[29] MacIntyre, *After Virtue*, 245.

[30] Michael Walzer, *Spheres of Justice: A Defence of Pluralism and Equality* (Oxford: Martin Robertson, 1983), 313.

[31] Michael Sandel, "Dewey Rides Again," *New York Review of Books*, May 9, 1996.

[32] Daniel Savage, *John Dewey's Liberalism: Individual, Community, and Self-Development* (Carbondale, IL: Southern Illinois University Press, 2002), 27, 176.

[33] Judith Green, *Deep Democracy: Community, Diversity, and Transformation* (Lanham, MD: Rowman & Littlefield, 1999), 8; see also Judith Green, *Pragmatism and Social Hope: Deepening Democracy in Global Contexts* (New York, NY: Columbia University Press, 2008).

He equates Dewey in this way with Sandel and argues that Dewey's democratic theory is antipluralist and suppresses individuality "under a common substantive moral image."[34]

I have shown the weakness of Talisse's pluralist objection to Dewey in Chapter 1, but it is further noteworthy how the democratic way of life can actually form the basis of a Deweyan critique of communitarianism. In Chapter 2, I identified the democratic life with a subject-object interaction in which subjects of experience, who are inevitably influenced by the objects of experience they confront, exercise some manner of control over those objects (i.e., exercise control over their growth) rather than being passively molded by objects. This exemplifies the link between Dewey's pragmatism (which I showed in Chapter 2 to have a strong Hegelian influence) and the type of individual self-government that Dewey seeks to achieve. Individual subjects govern themselves by continuously expanding their selves in interaction with unique situations of experience, and not by futilely attempting to isolate themselves from such situations and from the need to revise their ideas and practices. When we follow communitarian thought to its logical conclusion, though, we are left with a static conception of the individual, which is too much "object" and not enough "subject." Sandel explains how he aims to revive "[a] theory of community whose province extended to the subject as well as the object of motivations."[35] On communitarian terms, an individual actualizes her identity by "discovering" who she is within the context of her communal roles, which seems to deny the individual the opportunity to act as a subject exercising a unique effect on her own development. As Sandel puts it, there are "aims and attachments from which [the self] cannot stand apart."[36] The individual is primarily defined by the aims and attachments given to her by her community, and she is meant to achieve freedom by fully discovering how she is so defined, because there is no self, or subject, who can be distinguished from these aims and attachments, and who can be allowed to revise them.

My description of the communitarian conception of individuality as "static" may appear unfair, since communitarians do emphasize that individuals develop within their constitutive roles. As they fully immerse themselves in the activities that characterize their communal roles, individuals develop themselves and can progressively approximate the ideal

34 Robert Talisse, "Can Democracy Be a Way of Life? Deweyan Democracy and the Problem of Pluralism," *Transactions of the Charles S. Peirce Society* 39, no. 1 (2003): 1–21.
35 Sandel, *Liberalism and the Limits of Justice*, 150.
36 Ibid., 182.

standards set by the community for those roles. In Aristotelian fashion, though, the individual development envisioned by communitarians is still in the direction of a given endpoint, which is provided by the community (and, for Aristotle, by nature as well), and which is not revisable by the individual subject. MacIntyre indeed remarks that "[t]o know oneself as such a social person ... is to find oneself placed at a certain point on a journey with set goals; to move through life is to make progress – or to fail to make progress – toward a given end."[37] At the same time, some communitarians are understandably wary of upholding cultural practices that deny individuals any opportunity to step away from their inherited roles. These communitarians include a declaration that they do allow for individuals to step away from inherited roles and revise their identities – as Sandel puts it, "[T]he contours of my identity will in some ways be open and subject to revision."[38] But if traditional practices that suppress individuals' capacity to choose the roles they inhabit are not acceptable, then communitarianism is barely distinct from the liberalism it claims to reject.[39] If communal norms can only be upheld so long as they abide by a universal requirement that individuals be allowed to step away from their inherited roles and revise their identities, then communitarians are advocating a fundamentally liberal position. In order to oppose social customs that oppress, for example, the women within a community, communitarianism must import principles from far outside its chief doctrine of maintaining traditional communal identities.

For Dewey, it is crucial to recognize the inevitable effect of social upbringing on individuals' lives and the way individuals are inextricably connected with, and largely defined by their relations to, other individuals. As we saw in Chapter 2, these are central points in Dewey's critique of liberal theories that treat individuals as isolated beings, unaffected by social circumstances and possessing unproblematically equal opportunity to influence electoral outcomes and to make money on the free market. But unlike the communitarians, Dewey shines a critical light on the quality of social upbringing and social relations, primarily through his critiques of prevalent educational practices[40] and of the iniquitous character of many racial, gender, and economic relations. He does not focus on simply bolstering traditional communal ties, but on the degree to which

---

[37] MacIntyre, *After Virtue*, 32.

[38] Sandel, *Liberalism and the Limits of Justice*, 180.

[39] Will Kymlicka makes a similar point; see "Liberalism and Communitarianism," *Canadian Journal of Philosophy* 18, no. 2 (1988): 192.

[40] Dewey's educational principles will be the focus in Chapter 6.

social practices are upholding the "subject" side of subject-object interaction – that is, whether they allow individuals to exercise their own unique effect on their development. This is actually a major reason why Talisse's connection of Dewey with Sandel is ultimately incoherent. Sandel's theory holds that individuals are defined so deeply by "constitutive ends" given to them by their community that they cannot be expected to stand back and revise them. But Dewey's democratic individual way of life, which Talisse castigates, is characterized by the unending autonomous development of one's unique self in response to changing circumstances, which entails the capacity to revise the ends of one's development. It is not at all clear how Dewey's and Sandel's theories could both be oppressively antipluralist, since Dewey stresses precisely the type of critical distance from one's communal upbringing that Sandel takes as a diminution of one's agency.

This analysis of communitarianism is a bit different from my discussions of deliberative, participatory, agonistic, and (still to come) cosmopolitan democracy. My critiques of deliberative and agonistic democracy, and my defenses of participatory and cosmopolitan democracy, connect explicitly to the central topics of this book: the inadequacy of the currently dominant democratic theories (i.e., those which focus on the quality of political debate) in dealing with structural social inequality, and the value of Dewey's thought in helping to overcome this inadequacy. My discussion of communitarianism makes the more particular point that the communitarians' conception of a self-governing individual is problematic in comparison with Dewey's conception. Indeed, as communitarianism is not distinctly a model of democracy, its discussion necessarily takes on a somewhat different character. This analysis is still called for, though, by the claim of some scholars that Dewey is a communitarian thinker and by the way this analysis further illuminates the individual element of Deweyan democracy.

All the same, certain communitarians have tried to portray their principles as uniquely democratic – and the issue of social inequality does pose significant problems for these thinkers' efforts. I have already pointed out Sandel's attempt to veer away from communal practices that prevent individuals from revising their identities, which indicates some uneasiness on his part over the inequalities that his own principles could permit. However, when Sandel attempts to link communitarian principles to democracy, he ends up resembling Benjamin Barber (discussed in Chapter 4) by calling for individuals to take part in a virtuous republican politics aimed at the common good at local, state, and national levels.

He does not address how this search for a common good may cover over the inequalities contained within communities.[41] As we have seen throughout this book, idealizing a common good can be counterproductive when we have severe social inequality, because democracy will require that the particular interests of certain parts of society (the disadvantaged) win out over others (the advantaged).

Walzer stands out as a communitarian who seeks to directly take on the problem of social inequality. Within his body of work, Walzer does provide insightful analysis of acts of civil disobedience and of how forms of oppression can justify practices in which the oppressed step outside the conventional limits of the law, rather than engaging in dialogue with their oppressors.[42] His arguments there fit nicely with my Deweyan analysis of how nondeliberative practices are uniquely democratic under structurally unequal social conditions. Walzer's distinctly communitarian work, though, defends a problematic conception of "complex equality," which separates large, "differentiated" communities (e.g., the United States) from communities that are sufficiently unified such that we can say they reflect the "shared understandings" of their members (e.g., the Indian caste system). For Walzer, the type of differentiated community we see in large, capitalist nations contains many different "spheres" within itself – political, social, economic, cultural, etc. – and complex equality allows there to be inequality in any one of these spheres, but it does not allow inequality in one sphere to directly translate into inequality in another sphere (e.g., political power cannot directly entitle an individual to economic power, or vice versa). By contrast, a nondifferentiated community is not defined by different spheres, and so any firm inequality that exists in the community is just, as long as the inequality appears to reflect the worldview of all members of the community. Walzer's claim is that there is no justification for allowing the inequality within one of the spheres of a differentiated society to invade another sphere; but a more unified society does not have these different spheres. There is thus no legitimate reason to condemn inequality in this latter society, because the inequality is not spreading beyond its appropriate space.[43]

---

[41] Michael Sandel, *Democracy's Discontent: America in Search of a Public Philosophy* (Cambridge: Harvard University Press, 1996), 5–7, 25, 208, 274, 319–20, 322–3, 345, 348.

[42] Michael Walzer, *Obligations: Essays on Disobedience, War, and Citizenship* (Cambridge: Harvard University Press, 1970), 3–73.

[43] Walzer, *Spheres of Justice*, xiv, 5, 19–20, 78–9, 84–5, 88–90, 121, 312–16, 319–21.

This idea of a firm distinction between communities that are characterized by multiple spheres, and those that have only one sphere, seems right off the bat to be highly tenuous, for we would likely be hard-pressed to find any community that does not actually contain the variety of spheres that Walzer says is unique to highly complex communities like the United States. As a result, there is something just inherently suspect about Walzer's thinking here. Ultimately, though, I do not claim to be able to provide here the perfect way to arbitrate between the substantive social equality required by democracy and the demands of communal groups for the protection of their traditional (even if unequal) ways of life. But I will say that an attempt to describe the maintenance of such communal norms as uniquely democratic (as Walzer does) is unlikely to ever hold up well to scrutiny. We will likely either have to give priority to democracy or to the preservation of those communal norms, rather than convincing ourselves we can do both at the same time. With Dewey, priority is given to democracy. In *The Public and Its Problems*, where he makes some communitarian-type statements such as, "Democracy must begin at home, and its home is the neighborly community," he clarifies that communities must display a "mobility" that will help "the spoils of remote and indirect interaction and interdependence flow back into local life, keeping it flexible, preventing the stagnancy which has attended stability in the past, and furnishing it with the elements of a variegated and many-hued experience"; this will allow "local communal life" to avoid "fettering men and women with chains of conformity" and to "manifest a fullness, variety and freedom of possession and enjoyment of meanings and goods unknown in the contiguous associations of the past."[44] Dewey places great value on local communal attachments, but still challenges communities to bolster, rather than constrict, individuals' capacity to confront a diversity of ways of life and to thereby direct their own unique growth.

Hence, Dewey holds communities to democratic standards, though without committing us to any problematic notion that we must somehow eliminate communities that have traditionally unequal social relations. To connect back to a point I made in Chapter 1 while addressing Talisse's arguments, Dewey's principles do not force anyone to separate from their inherited values and to continuously grow through interaction with diverse worldviews, because individuals who do not want to do this

[44] John Dewey, *The Public and Its Problems* (Chicago, IL: Swallow Press, [1927] 1954), 213, 216.

can be said to be acting within the negative freedom that Dewey sees as necessary (though not sufficient) for democracy. But Dewey does identify why this behavior should not be endorsed as genuinely democratic, because these individuals are not displaying the positive freedom that is characteristic of democratic individualism. Dewey's *social* element of democracy further underscores that communities which are structurally unequal should not be seen as democratic, because they can deny individuals any opportunity to direct their own unique growth. Fundamentally, Dewey wishes to preserve cultural diversity and to see divergent ways of life engaged in an interaction in which each way of life can maintain and expand itself. If certain individuals are kept in a structurally inferior position within a community and are plainly prevented from engaging ways of life beyond their own – and are thus prevented from leading the democratic way of life – then Dewey holds that the community should be subject to critique. Dewey's conception of democracy, with its individual and social (as well as political) elements, requires that we change society in ways that seek to allow all individuals to direct their unique development. Communitarians cannot accommodate democratic individualism, and they must permit social relations that may be firmly unequal. If we commit to democracy, we must be willing to critique certain traditional communal practices.

COSMOPOLITAN DEMOCRACY

The model of cosmopolitan democracy developed in the 1990s and early 2000s, and has emphasized the increasing complexity of the issues confronting modern individuals and the fact that these issues are often not just relevant to one particular nation. Cosmopolitan democrats move the focal point of democratic thinking beyond the sphere of the nation-state and into a more regional and global level. Because we live under such interconnected circumstances, where issues related to the economy, the environment, technological development, etc., can have an impact on the entire globe, the cosmopolitan thinkers argue that we must focus on creating conditions where such issues can be not only addressed, but addressed democratically.

As was the case with participatory democracy, the deliberative democrats have seen their own theory as accounting for the concerns raised by cosmopolitan democracy, and even as addressing those concerns more effectively than cosmopolitan democracy. John Dryzek in particular states that it is more important to focus on global "governance" – which for him refers to a more democratic dialogue among global actors – than on global "government," which he equates with the democratization of institutions of global decision making.[45] He explains how his theory is not so concerned with the global actors who hold formal political power, but with those in "the more informal realm of international public spheres" who are "concerned with public affairs" but are "not seeking to exercise formal policy-making authority."[46] Dryzek's case is that if we focus on how various "civil society" associations and groups, who each possess their own particular discourses, could interact in a properly deliberative fashion within the global public sphere, we will have a "more feasible" project than we find with cosmopolitan democracy; he thinks that by focusing on how such deliberation can influence formal political power, we will have found a plausible way to democratize global political decision making, as opposed to cosmopolitan theory's "utopian" attempt to democratize global institutions themselves.[47]

David Held has been perhaps the most prominent cosmopolitan democrat, and he does show greater concern than Dryzek for global institutions. He points out that "the sovereignty of the nation-state has generally not been questioned" in democratic theory, and he argues that, when we hold to such an assumption, "[p]roblems arise ... because many of the decisions of 'a majority' or, more accurately, its representatives, affect (or potentially affect) not only their communities but citizens in other communities as well."[48] Held identifies a number of contemporary policy issues on which a particular government's decisions and actions will significantly affect other nations – including the building of a nuclear plant; an increase in interest rates; the "harvesting" of rainforests; and decisions regarding security, arms procurement, and AIDS[49] – and he remarks that such complex global issues require "a system of governance which arises from and is adapted to the diverse conditions and interconnections of different peoples

[45] Dryzek, *Deliberative Democracy and Beyond*, 120, 122, 132, 138.

[46] John Dryzek, *Deliberative Global Politics: Discourse and Democracy in a Divided World* (Cambridge: Polity Press, 2006), vii. Recall that in Chapter 4, I discussed how Dryzek, along with other deliberative thinkers such as Jurgen Habermas and Seyla Benhabib, seek to focus on "social" deliberation as well as "political" deliberation, and I argued that this does not solve deliberative theory's inability to properly recognize a *social* element of democracy.

[47] Ibid., 157–61.

[48] David Held, *Models of Democracy*, 3rd ed. (Stanford, CA: Stanford University Press, 2006), 290, 291.

[49] Ibid., 291.

and nations."[50] The cosmopolitan model would thus "seek the creation of regional parliaments (for example, in Latin America and Africa) and the enhancement of the role of such bodies where they already exist (the European Parliament) in order that their decisions become recognized, in principle, as legitimate independent sources of law"; it would also pursue "the formation of an authoritative assembly of all democratic states and agencies ... [that] would become an authoritative international centre for the consideration and examination of pressing global issues."[51] In essence, the cosmopolitan model sees democratic theory's focus on the nation-state as increasingly rendered obsolete by our globally interconnected conditions and calls for political institutions to suitably evolve to account for this fact.

Because we already have many regional and global political institutions, cosmopolitan democrats claim that we must have a primary focus on democratizing these existing institutions. For Daniele Archibugi, "a central role should be given to the United Nations organization in the transition towards a new world order."[52] He argues for the creation of a "second assembly" within the UN's General Assembly that would follow the logic of proportional representation in order to counterbalance the General Assembly's adherence to equal representation, which allows "fewer than 10 percent of the world's population" to "potentially cast the majority of votes in the General Assembly."[53] He also objects to the undemocratic quality of the UN Security Council, which allows "a few members ... [to] invalidate the decisions of the majority" with their veto power, and he suggests that the veto be abolished.[54] Mary Kaldor highlights the International Monetary Fund and recommends that "[n]ational or bloc currencies [be] linked to a genuine form of international money guaranteed by international monetary institutions which are democratically accountable – i.e., a democratized IMF."[55] Carol Gould, whose contribution to participatory democracy was referenced in Chapter 4,

---

[50] David Held, "Democracy and the New International Order," in *Cosmopolitan Democracy: An Agenda for a New World Order*, eds. Daniele Archibugi and David Held (Cambridge: Polity Press, 1995), 106.

[51] Ibid., 108–9.

[52] Daniele Archibugi, "From the United Nations to Cosmopolitan Democracy," in *Cosmopolitan Democracy: An Agenda for a New World Order*, eds. Daniele Archibugi and David Held (Cambridge: Polity Press, 1995), 122.

[53] Ibid., 138–42.

[54] Ibid., 150–2.

[55] Mary Kaldor, "European Institutions, Nation-States and Nationalism," in *Cosmopolitan Democracy: An Agenda for a New World Order*, eds. Daniele Archibugi and David Held (Cambridge: Polity Press, 1995), 88.

contributes to cosmopolitan democracy by focusing on regional institutions such as the EU and encouraging cosmopolitan theorists to avoid moving too quickly to the global realm at the expense of the regional realm, since "one of the main advantages of regionalization would seem to be the retention or enabling of a certain level of cultural diversity around the world."[56] For cosmopolitan democrats, the existence of global and regional institutions such as the UN, IMF, and EU exhibits the transnational quality of important policy issues. These institutions currently display undemocratic features, though, and thus require democratization.

In this book, the ability of contemporary democratic theories to account for the impact of social inequality on democracy is my central topic of investigation. I argue that, like participatory democracy, cosmopolitan democracy can account for social inequality more effectively than a model like deliberative democracy. I maintain this even though certain cosmopolitan thinkers seem to be satisfied with an alteration in global political institutions. Archibugi, for instance, mainly focuses on the more political aims of putting "some constraints on governments' exercise of sovereignty" and giving "the inhabitants of the planet ... a political representation beyond their borders and independently from their national governments."[57] He also claims that "international and regional organizations provide the opportunity for states to come into contact with each other and guide elites of countries in transition to democracy or in unstable democracies," which should help "[reduce] the risk of conflicts associated with misunderstanding and spreading the practice of democracy."[58] His analysis does imply that setting up proper regional and global political institutions is sufficient for achieving a genuine cosmopolitan democracy. Kaldor, similarly, emphasizes how new global political institutions must primarily be "open and accountable to public opinion" through some type of electoral mechanism; she does mention that cosmopolitan democracy should also involve guarantees of "economic and social rights" for individuals, but she does not specify what these rights

---

[56] Carol Gould, "Regional versus Global Democracy: Advantages and Limitations," in *Global Democracy: Normative and Empirical Perspectives*, eds. Daniele Archibugi, Mathias Koenig-Archibugi, and Raffaele Marchetti (Cambridge: Cambridge University Press, 2012), 116.

[57] Archibugi, "From the United Nations to Cosmopolitan Democracy," 134.

[58] Daniele Archibugi, "From Peace between Democracies to Global Democracy," in *Global Democracy: Normative and Empirical Perspectives*, eds. Daniele Archibugi, Mathias Koenig-Archibugi, and Raffaele Marchetti (Cambridge: Cambridge University Press, 2012), 269.

would be.[59] Surely, we should be giving primary attention to how global political representation would be undemocratically affected by the social divide between, for instance, the globally rich and poor.

Richard Falk, however, is a cosmopolitan thinker who tackles head on the importance of reducing global social inequality to the achievement of democracy on a worldwide scale. While he recognizes a "global spread of political democracy," he underscores the importance of global social movements in challenging the power inequities that characterize the current global order and in challenging (for example) the "inter-state complacency about environmental issues" that such power inequities have helped produce.[60] He coins the term "globalization-from-below" to refer to the "transnational democratic forces" that seek to counteract (for the good of the globally disadvantaged) the "globalization-from-above" that has been enacted by powerful economic interests for their own benefit; he further points out that Articles 25 and 28 of the Universal Declaration of Human Rights already guarantee an adequate standard of living for individuals but have been largely ignored, and he urges that such a standard should be actually upheld.[61] Held takes a similar position, by insisting that cosmopolitan democracy entails such social measures as basic income and the democratization of economic enterprises (so that workers may participate in a company's decision making).[62] These are identical to social measures that we showed in Chapter 4 are integral to participatory democracy.

Gould, who again can be placed in both the participatory and cosmopolitan models of democratic thought, particularly emphasizes the role that overcoming global social inequality must play in cosmopolitan democracy. She argues that "to realize democracy and global justice we have to look beyond the strictly political forms and remedies to the underlying social conditions that would enable these norms to be met at local, national, and transnational scales."[63] To address these underlying social conditions, Gould states that we must recognize, at a global level, "an

[59] Kaldor, "European Institutions, Nation-States and Nationalism," 89, 91.

[60] Richard Falk, "The World Order between Inter-State Law and the Law of Humanity: The Role of Civil Society Institutions," in *Cosmopolitan Democracy: An Agenda for a New World Order*, eds. Daniele Archibugi and David Held (Cambridge: Polity Press, 1995), 164–5, 169.

[61] Ibid., 170–1, 172.

[62] David Held, *Democracy and the Global Order: From the Modern State to Cosmopolitan Governance* (Stanford, CA: Stanford University Press, 1995), 252–3.

[63] Carol Gould, *Interactive Democracy: The Social Roots of Global Justice* (Cambridge: Cambridge University Press, 2014), 1.

economic right to the means of subsistence" – like Held, she specifically advocates for basic income policies – and she advises that social and economic rights should be seen as essential on their own for achieving democracy, that is, we need these rights not only "for the sake of political equality" but "for fulfilling basic human needs."[64] Her account of democracy at a transnational level thus identifies what I have called the social element of democracy and draws a similar link between democracy and the overcoming of (global) social inequality. She is not satisfied with the construction of transnational political institutions, even if those institutions appear to meet democratic standards, since those institutions by themselves can likely do little to alter the everyday experiences of those around the globe who suffer from injustices such as severe economic and gender inequality: "global justice requires more than redistribution, whether achieved through foreign aid, resource dividends, or new global taxation schemes, although these are clearly significant. It requires recognition of women's equality and of the particular burdens they shoulder within contemporary political economies."[65] As long as we continue to have extreme global poverty and worldwide oppression of women, cosmopolitan democracy is not fully achieved.

The cosmopolitan thinkers who emphasize a global social democratization, rather than a global political democratization alone, point out how social inequality can prevent global political institutions from displaying the democratic qualities they are meant to have. Held, for instance, stresses how we cannot assume that the formal political equality of nations could bracket the effects of the broader inequalities between nations. Commenting on the idea of bringing all nations into an international free market system, he contends that "while free trade is an admirable objective for progressives in principle, it cannot be pursued without attention to the poorest in the least well-off countries who are extremely vulnerable to the initial phasing in of external market integration (especially of capital market liberalization), and who have few resources, if any, to fall back on during times of economic transformation."[66] He thus advocates that "[a]ll developed countries must adopt legally binding minimum levels of overseas development assistance," and that those countries in particular devote 0.7 percent of their GNP to overseas aid.[67] Gould expresses

---

[64] Ibid., 2, 23, 48.
[65] Ibid., 141.
[66] David Held, *Global Covenant: The Social Democratic Alternative to the Washington Consensus* (Cambridge: Polity Press, 2004), 58.
[67] Ibid., 62.

particular skepticism toward deliberative theory, and toward the idea that transnational democracy depends mainly on proper political deliberation (though her argument is overall less critical of deliberative theory than mine is), by noting that "[t]o the degree that there are inequalities of power or of social condition as the background for discourse, the latter cannot be expected to instantiate the freedom, equality, and reciprocity of all potential participants."[68] As with participatory democracy, these cosmopolitan thinkers focus on actually altering unequal social conditions in order to achieve democracy on (in this case) a global scale. These theorists recognize how even the most proper political institutional setup, and the most proper political debate among nations, can be rendered ineffectual by severe inequalities across the globe.

Although not every cosmopolitan democrat is as attentive as Falk, Held, and Gould to global social inequality, I maintain that the cosmopolitan model is still better suited than the deliberative model for recognizing a social element of democracy, and thus for directly confronting social inequality. This is because, like participatory democracy, cosmopolitan democracy does not define itself by a particular type of ideal debate among competing political viewpoints. I argued in Chapter 4 that participatory democracy's lack of a specific commitment to deliberative practices (which deliberative democrats have taken as a weakness of the participatory model) is a virtue of this theory, in that the theory avoids committing to practices that are unsuited to conditions defined by severe social inequality. As we have seen, there are deliberative thinkers who try to also insist on reducing social inequality, but they cannot make this requirement without conceding that the central feature of their theory – deliberation – is not necessarily democratic at all under the social conditions we confront, and that we have to engage in practices that are very different from deliberation to further achieve democracy from present conditions. Like participatory democracy, the message of cosmopolitan theory is that certain political and social changes are demanded by our current circumstances if we are to bring democracy further into existence. The cosmopolitan theory is not defined by a particular form of debate, deliberative or otherwise, and this allows the theory to conceive of why democracy must be associated with specific outcomes or policies that overcome entrenched social and political power. The theory can relatedly account for how a "fair" debate over those policies will bear the imprint of the inequality that needs to be resolved.

[68] Gould, *Interactive Democracy*, 174–5.

Thus, we can make a Deweyan case for the cosmopolitan theory, as we could with participatory theory. Once we bring Dewey into the discussion, we in fact find similar benefits that cosmopolitan democrats can derive from his thinking as we saw with participatory democrats. To begin with, it is noteworthy how cosmopolitan democracy aligns with Dewey's pragmatic principle that our conception of democracy must evolve to respond to changing circumstances. We have seen Dewey stress that modern conditions are such that an action or decision can produce consequences that spread potentially throughout the world, thus rendering irrelevant any hard-and-fast divisions between peoples: "The career of individuals, their lives and security as well as prosperity is now affected by events on the other side of the world."[69] For Dewey, "Men have to act in view of remote economic and political conditions, and they have to have some notions about the latter upon which to base their actions."[70] Individuals cannot then expect to exercise control over their lives by confining their knowledge of the world only to their particular nation, because aspects of the international world inevitably affect their lives. Consequently, transnational institutions are needed to allow individuals to cognize the global quality of many of the issues they confront, and to potentially exercise some conscious control over those issues: "All of these things mean the discovery of the interdependence of all peoples, and the development of a more highly organized world, a world knit together by more conscious and substantial bonds."[71] Our increasingly interconnected world has effectively negated conceptions of democracy that take the nation-state's centrality for granted, and both Dewey and the cosmopolitan democrats show how our thinking on democracy can develop in order to include global institutions. Dewey warns against allowing our thinking on democracy to become mired in old principles (e.g., that democracy is a matter for individual nation-states), and this lends particular support to the cosmopolitan model of democracy.

For Dewey, the interlocking development of political and social democracy (which we have discussed throughout this book) absolutely applies to the global level. First, with the political element of global democracy, Dewey emphasizes the necessity of constructing global political institutions in the modern world, and – where those institutions already exist – the necessity of counteracting the disproportionate

---

[69] John Dewey, *Freedom and Culture* (New York, NY: G. P. Putnam's Sons, 1939), 165.
[70] MW13: 330.
[71] MW11: 100.

influence that powerful actors have over those institutions. In the years following World War I, he initially supported Woodrow Wilson's attempt to establish the League of Nations, but he pulled his support when, as he puts it, the League was tied "to the iniquities of the Versailles Treaty [and] failed to outlaw war."[72] He protests that "the Constitution of the League of Nations definitely contemplates and even prescribes coercive physical force," and the fact that "the exercise of this force" is effectively given to "the five chief nations among the victorious Allies" from World War I illustrates, in his view, why the League would not effectively prevent war.[73] In Dewey's view, granting that authority to certain powerful nations nullified the legitimacy of this institution. He maintained instead that war must be genuinely outlawed and that all nations must be given equal status in an international court system with effective jurisdiction to rule on disputes between nations:

A judicial substitute for wars as a method of settling disputes [must be] created in the form of a supreme court of the nations of the world, the court sitting and deciding cases under and by an international law that has made war a crime and the instigators or breeders of war as much criminals as any other kind of murderers that now infest the earth.[74]

Such a court would not uphold the privileged position of certain powerful nations in their decisions about war, because "any nation, great or small, can ask to have a hearing in any controversy with any other nation."[75] In addition to powerful nations, Dewey identifies powerful economic interests as a severe threat to global democracy. While noting the disproportionate presence of powerful business interests on the international bodies of the post–World War I period, he suggests as a remedy that "[w]hen international commissions and boards have representatives of big business upon them … they will also have to seat economists and representatives of labor."[76] This is a political democratization that mirrors Dewey's attempts to counteract the disproportionate influence of wealthy interests over national (in particular, American) political institutions. He seeks to intelligently reconstruct institutions (similarly to what we saw in Chapter 3) by pursuing remedies that combat this current pressing

---

[72] MW15: 116.
[73] MW15: 107.
[74] MW15: 89.
[75] MW15: 92–3. The creation of such an international court system has also been emphasized by cosmopolitan democrats; see Held, *Democracy and the Global Order*, 283.
[76] MW11: 134.

obstacle to the political element of democracy – that is, the privileged access to global decision making available to business interests.

The social element of global democracy is, as we would figure, at least as crucial for Dewey as is the political element. He criticizes the attempt to establish international institutions that provide "negative provisions for making war more difficult to enter upon, but which [refrain] from dealing in any positively organized way with those defects in social organization from which wars proceed"; he instead advocates "a league of nations whose object is not the negative one of preventing war but the positive one of looking after economic and social needs which are now at the mercy of chance and the voracity of isolated states."[77] Although Dewey did support the idea of instituting the League of Nations, he should not be derided as a naïve optimist who foolishly believed the League itself would prevent conflicts such as World War II. He in fact stated that "[a] League of Nations whose main purpose is to enforce peace by an extension of legal mechanisms of controversy and litigation ... would break down, in all probability, when confronted with problems of national expansion and a redistribution of the centres of effective power"; by contrast, he argued that "an organization of nations which grew out of common everyday necessities, and which operated to meet the commonplace needs of everyday life with respect to food, labor, securing raw materials for the reparation of a devastated world ... would, once formed, become so indispensable that speedily no one could imagine the world getting on without it."[78] For Dewey, such an international institution cannot hope to eliminate war without ameliorating social and economic ills throughout the world, which exemplifies how global democracy is at least as much a social concept as it is a political concept. Correspondingly, Dewey highlights the problem involved with pursuing political equality alone among nations and overlooking the broader inequalities between nations:

obviously equalization of trade conditions among nations demands something more ... Certain nations have a tremendous superiority in population, natural resources, technical progress in industry, command of credit, and shipping. Nothing better calculated to develop actual inequality of trade relationship among nations could well be found than a system which set up a nominal mathematical equality and then threw matters practically into the hands of the present big nations.[79]

[77] MW11: 125.
[78] MW11: 129.
[79] MW11: 139.

Dewey supports a simultaneous social and political democratization at the global level, with the overcoming of global social inequality being just as critical as any changes to global political institutions.

Thus, in a similar way to participatory democracy, cosmopolitan democracy can find support in Dewey's idea of an interrelated political and social democratization. Furthermore, I argue that cosmopolitan democrats can similarly draw on the Deweyan case for "modes of participation" that are suited to unequal social conditions, in order to elevate their theory above the more prominent deliberative and agonistic theories. We have seen how cosmopolitan democracy principally seeks the types of changes to global social relations and political institutions that are demanded by our present unequal conditions. Like participatory democracy, cosmopolitan democracy is not defined by a proper debate or competition among different political positions, either in the form of deliberative reason-giving or agonistic contest. The cosmopolitan theory has thus not committed to a practice that abstracts from our unequal social conditions. Although, also like the participatory democrats, cosmopolitan theorists have not given much attention to the types of practices that would be consistent with their thinking. As discussed in Chapter 4, Dewey's pragmatism helps build a case for why practices that compel concessions from the socially advantaged are particularly democratic under unequal conditions. The deliberative and agonistic thinkers must contradict their theories' principles when they try to allow for such practices, because they have already each equated democracy with a form of debate that does not privilege any specific viewpoint.[80] Cosmopolitan thinkers have not committed to such a form of debate, and they can draw on Dewey to make a case for practices that proceed on the basis that democracy requires the disadvantaged to actually *win*. These thinkers can thus show why their theory is better suited to conditions of social inequality.

---

[80] In an intelligent account of the current state of agonistic democratic theory, Mark Wenman argues that agonistic theorists could effectively account for the transnational concerns of cosmopolitan thinkers. His argument is that agonistic principles should lead us to focus on how "transnational social movements" can generate "original principles" that are then adopted by "a wide range of spectators" and used to make the changes to our institutions that are necessary for dealing with global policy issues. However, Wenman's argument does not (as mine does) identify how an equation of democracy with agonistic contest prevents agonistic thinkers from being able to say that these types of social movements must win the political contest, as opposed to movements that seek to delegitimize global institutions. See Mark Wenman, *Agonistic Democracy: Constituent Power in the Era of Globalisation* (New York, NY: Cambridge University Press, 2013), 294.

As with the participatory democrats, there have been a few gestures by cosmopolitan democrats toward endorsing these practices that aim directly at overcoming (global) social inequality. Falk references how global social movements have stimulated action to protect the environment and have exposed how market forces allow banks and corporations to shield money from taxation.[81] Held and Anthony McGrew together discuss social movements that have met the summits of major global institutions such as the World Bank, the IMF, and the G8 with mass protests and that have waged successful campaigns for such aims as the cancellation of third world debt.[82] Gould addresses the role of social movements in pursuing political, social, and economic rights for individuals across the globe, and she also describes an ethical requirement that individuals have to challenge systemic forms of oppression around the world that interfere with the conditions of individuals' self-development[83] (and, as we have seen, an ethical requirement of challenging forms of structural inequality is one component of Dewey's democratic individual way of life). The practices alluded to by these theorists are very different from a political debate in which all sides involved are accorded equal legitimacy. They are defined by efforts and actions that specifically aim at benefiting those disadvantaged by global social inequality. We continue to see examples of these efforts and actions, including at the 2017 G20 summit in Hamburg, Germany, where anticapitalist protestors sought to disrupt closed-door meetings in which a small group of powerful world leaders made decisions that affect the entire world's population. Cosmopolitan thinkers have not fleshed out the implications of this point about the practices they can coherently endorse, or explored what this says about their theory in comparison with deliberative and agonistic democracy. Dewey's pragmatism can help cosmopolitan thinkers show why, under unequal conditions, democratic theory must avoid a commitment to an ideal form of political debate and must evolve the practices it endorses to suit the current reality.

---

[81] Falk, "The World Order between Inter-State Law and the Law of Humanity," 169, 176–7. See also, Richard Falk, "The United Nations and Cosmopolitan Democracy: Bad Dream, Utopian Fantasy, Political Project," in *Re-imagining Political Community: Studies in Cosmopolitan Democracy*, eds. Daniele Archibugi, David Held, and Martin Kohler (Stanford, CA: Stanford University Press, 1998), 321–4, 326.

[82] David Held and Anthony McGrew, *Globalization/Anti-Globalization* (Cambridge: Polity Press, 2002), 64, 68–9.

[83] Gould, *Interactive Democracy*, 2, 4, 99–100, 109–10, 116, 122, 126, 131, 136, 141, 201, 223–4, 269.

It is important to clarify the connection I am drawing between cosmopolitan democracy and participatory democracy. We have seen how participatory democracy focuses on moving democracy beyond the typical political institutions and into everyday social spheres, primarily by pointing out how inequitable power relations in the workplace, and social inequality in general, corrupt political debate and are also undemocratic in themselves. Cosmopolitan democracy takes this interlocking political and social democratization in a necessary global direction, emphasizing the interconnectedness of all peoples under contemporary circumstances and calling for both the democratization of global political institutions and the overcoming of global social inequality. Interestingly, Held has not thought an alliance between these two theories is possible. He instead asserts that participatory thinkers such as Carole Pateman and C. B. Macpherson have not been able to go beyond considering "the problem of political accountability as, above all, a national problem," and that participatory thinkers simply hold representative institutions to be "insufficiently responsive to their citizens" and seek to replace those institutions with "various forms of direct democracy."[84] But this is precisely the depiction of participatory democracy that I have shown to be erroneous, because it lackadaisically equates participatory theory with direct citizen involvement in policy making and overlooks the participatory theorists' central focus on the democratization of society. Held's critique of participatory democracy appears even stranger when we consider how he champions, as noted earlier, the enactment of measures like basic income and workplace democratization that are definitive of participatory theory. There is indeed a natural fit between the two theories, once we recognize the way they each focus on the types of changes that are required if we are to further achieve democracy in the face of structural social inequality and exclusive political power.

As a final note, we should point out that neither Dewey nor the cosmopolitan democrats want to somehow eliminate nation-states from the global scene. Rather, they want to preserve nation-states within a new global political framework. Dewey rebukes the belief in the sanctity of the nation-state, objecting that "[n]ationalism starting as an unquestioned emotional loyalty, so supreme as to be religious in quality, has invaded the whole of life," and that "the doctrine of national sovereignty is simply the denial on the part of a political state of either legal or moral

---

[84] Held, *Democracy and the Global Order*, 16.

responsibility."[85] At the same time, he does not seek to erase national divisions and allows for individuals' commitment to their nation to play an updated role within our globalized conditions:

Territorial states and political boundaries will persist; but they will not be barriers which impoverish experience by cutting man off from his fellows; they will not be hard and fast divisions whereby external separation is converted into inner jealousy, fear, suspicion and hostility ... [There] will be less rivalry for acquisition of material goods, and more an emulation of local groups to enrich direct experience with appreciatively enjoyed intellectual and artistic wealth.[86]

Held similarly declares that cosmopolitan democracy "does not entail abandoning the modern state as such ... but rather coming to appreciate it as an element in a wider framework of political conditions, relations and associations."[87] Both Dewey and the cosmopolitan democrats understand national identity and commitment to be persistent forces in modern life, and they seek to essentially "sublate" these forces while taking democratic thinking beyond old beliefs in the sanctity of the nation-state. As described in Chapter 2's discussion of Dewey's debt to Hegel, *sublation* refers to the preservation and elevation of earlier stages of a process, even as that process continues onto higher stages of development. Dewey and cosmopolitan thinkers are thus sublating national divisions by preserving them within a conception of democracy that has evolved to account for the need of global institutions.

Throughout this book, Dewey's conception of democracy has been depicted as deeply Hegelian in nature. I have presented Dewey as positing a foundational "Notion" of what is required to achieve self-government, and this Notion is, in Hegelian fashion, continuously filled with content through its adaptation to changing circumstances, that is, through the reconstruction of democracy in response to the novel threats to self-government that inevitably arise. Dewey's advocacy of global democratization further develops this Notion. He identifies the increasing unsuitability of the nation-state for addressing the complex issues that confront modern individuals and argues for global institutions that "sublate" the nation-state by preserving it within a greater worldwide unity. When individuals have become subject to a globally interconnected world but are without the opportunity to exercise some conscious control

---

[85] LW3: 153, 156.
[86] Dewey, *Public and Its Problems*, 217.
[87] Held, *Democracy and the Global Order*, 22.

over the issues that affect the entire globe – and to do so in a way that will not benefit only a few powerful interests – then democracy has been negated and requires further development in order to negate the negation. For Dewey, we cannot uncritically hold to the idea that national sovereignty is sacrosanct, or we will be clinging to a version of democracy that is progressively irrelevant to our globally interconnected conditions. Cosmopolitan democrats aim to teach us basically this lesson, and they similarly capture the importance of seeing democracy as in a process of continuous development. As Archibugi puts it, "*Democracy is an unfinished journey*. The journey towards democracy has not been completed in any country, including those in which the principles of democracy are most consolidated and developed ... As a journey, the democratic process is not only unfinished but also endless."[88] In Dewey, the cosmopolitan democrats can find philosophical support for their advancement of a democratic theory that overcomes the limits of the nation-state. They can also draw on Dewey to show their lack of commitment to a particular form of political debate to be a virtue for current democratic theory.

OVERCOMING NATIONAL DIVISIONS IN DEMOCRATIC THOUGHT

This chapter has extended the discussion of Dewey into an analysis of agonistic democracy, communitarianism, and cosmopolitan democracy. Although agonistic democracy does challenge many tenets of deliberative democracy, the theory still abstracts from social inequality in a similar fashion to deliberative democracy. Agonistic thinkers associate democracy with an open contest of competing political positions, and are therefore hard-pressed to account for the impact of social inequality on political debate, or for a *social* element in democracy itself, which I have argued must be accounted for in current democratic theory. Meanwhile, the not-infrequent categorization of Dewey as a communitarian thinker is off-target, because if we follow communitarianism through to its own conclusions, it must deny the essentials of individual self-government signified by Dewey's democratic way of life. Communitarians advocate the preservation of traditional communal norms and practices – even if those norms and practices uphold inequality in the community – but when these thinkers attempt to oppose oppressive cultural practices and to

---

[88] Daniele Archibugi, "Principles of Cosmopolitan Democracy," in *Re-imagining Political Community: Studies in Cosmopolitan Democracy*, eds. Daniele Archibugi, David Held, and Martin Kohler (Stanford, CA: Stanford University Press, 1998), 200.

allow individuals meaningful opportunity to revise their identities, they must concede that communal norms may often need to be cast aside if we want individuals to be able to govern their own lives. Cosmopolitan democracy, though, has the Deweyan virtue of emphasizing an inter-related political and social democratization, and has unique value as a theory because of its focus on taking this democratization to the global sphere. This global aspect of democratization is essential to Dewey, and his pragmatism helps cosmopolitan thinkers show the value of their lack of commitment to deliberative or agonistic political debate, and their capacity to accommodate practices that aim to directly overcome global social inequality.

Throughout this book, I have used Dewey's pragmatic principles to conceive of democracy as a continuously developing ideal, and as an ideal that is constituted by multiple, interrelated elements. I have focused throughout on the individual, social, and political elements of democracy that Dewey describes, and on how individuals' self-development, social relations of equality, and governments that are legitimately open to the influence of all individuals who live under them, can each mutually condition and reinforce one another in the never-completed process of giving individuals control over their lives. The inclusion of cosmopolitan democracy in this discussion helps us avoid any assumption that national boundaries can isolate certain political and social realms from others. For Dewey, the political and social realms we experience extend potentially throughout the entire world, because modern conditions have created such an interconnected world that no fixed divisions between peoples can be uncritically upheld. Therefore, our efforts to democratize political institutions and overcome social inequality must take on a more global character.

6

Educating Democratic Individuals

In Chapter 4, I showed that participatory democrats can draw on Dewey to elevate their theory above deliberative democracy. One reason for this, I noted, is that Dewey's democratic individual way of life amplifies the significance of the rather underdeveloped point made by C. B. Macpherson that democracy depends heavily on individuals' everyday behaviors. Macpherson claims that individuals must move away "from seeing themselves and acting as essentially consumers to seeing themselves and acting as exerters and enjoyers of the exertion and development of their own capacities."[1] In Chapter 4, I pointed out how Dewey sees a "consumer" mind-set as leading individuals to seek the quickest path toward stable material wealth in the hopes of escaping from change and uncertainty, and to believe that poverty and wealth result only from isolated individual effort.[2] This mind-set thus works against crucial qualities of Deweyan democratic individualism: continuous, self-directed development in response to inevitably changing circumstances, and critical thought toward current social inequality. I described at the end of Chapter 4 how, even if actions are taken toward overcoming the political and social obstacles to such individual self-government, individuals might still reinforce inequality – and hinder their own development – by continuing to see wealth as a means to avoid change and uncertainty, and by clinging to the idea that money is a reflection of purely personal

---

[1] C. B. Macpherson, *The Life and Times of Liberal Democracy* (Oxford: Oxford University Press, 1977), 99.
[2] John Dewey, *Individualism Old and New* (New York, NY: Capricorn Books, [1930] 1962), 18, 55, 136.

merit. To address this issue, somehow coercing individuals into thinking and acting differently would clearly be neither practical nor desirable. Through changes in our prevalent methods of education, though, it is possible in Dewey's view to appropriately encourage individuals' continuous development and genuine critical thought: "Since a democratic society repudiates the principle of external authority, it must find a substitute in voluntary disposition and interest; these can be created only by education."[3]

Amy Gutmann and Dennis Thompson establish the importance of education to deliberative democracy, stating that "[f]rom a deliberative perspective, the single most important institution outside government is the educational system,"[4] because schools are to cultivate the necessary deliberative skills among young individuals. I will use Dewey's educational thought to show the types of educational principles that participatory democrats (who have given only meager attention to education) should uphold in contrast with deliberative democrats. Macpherson has declared that individuals must cease viewing themselves as isolated consumers in a market and must recognize their interdependency with others; Dewey provides greater elaboration on this point by explaining how individuals' own self-government is threatened by their acceptance of economic inequality and their attempts to isolate themselves from the constantly changing, increasingly interconnected conditions of modern life. This chapter will show how, for Dewey, there are commonly accepted schooling practices that obstruct individuals' capacity for continuous development and for critical thought toward economic inequality. Dewey's insights on education reinforce the principles of participatory democracy and can help build a participatory educational theory that exposes weaknesses in deliberative educational theory. Participatory democrats can thereby identify major problems with current education that extend well beyond students' inadequate capacities for political debate. By drawing on Dewey, participatory democrats will be able to address ways that schooling interferes with individuals' self-government, which deliberative democrats are not equipped to address.

There are a multitude of ways that Dewey's educational theory challenges typical schooling practices by exposing the threats those practices pose to students' possibilities for individual self-government.

---

[3] John Dewey, *Democracy and Education* (New York, NY: The Free Press, [1916] 1966), 87.
[4] Amy Gutmann and Dennis Thompson, *Why Deliberative Democracy?* (Princeton, NJ: Princeton University Press, 2004), 61.

Primary among Dewey's concerns are how students are often taught to expect settled, memorize-able answers to the questions they study; how students typically work at isolated desks and are told that assisting one another is a form of cheating; and how schoolwork tends to be cut off from any practical, real-life significance for students. I will show how Dewey calls for students instead to investigate questions that specifically lack any fixed, ready-made answers, to frequently interact and collaborate with other students, and to work on projects that have distinct practical significance. In each of these ways, Dewey looks to cultivate students' capacities to govern their own lives, by encouraging them to develop their own intelligent responses to practical problems, and to do so while interacting with diverse others and avoiding any reliance on ideas of fixed truth.

Furthermore, I see another major concern with typical schooling that animates Dewey's educational theory, and this is his concern with the effects of "external aims" – specifically, grades and standardized test scores[5] – on students' educational experience. In Dewey's view, these external aims produce a belief among students that the process of learning is naturally an intrinsically insignificant chore done primarily for a reward and that individuals' worth can be determined by the possession of that reward. External aims thus interfere with the main qualities of democratic individualism, in that they can lead students to focus on finding an endpoint to their growth and can inhibit students' critical thought toward relations of inequality that are based on the attainment of such an external aim (e.g., on the attainment of money). Dewey's case against external aims has often been overlooked in analyses of his educational theory, and so I will give particular attention to his reasoning for why external aims inhibit individuals' self-government.

Dewey argues that we must pay attention to

all of the school machinery that hinges around the giving of marks – the eternal presence of the record book, the never-absent consciousness on the part of the child that he is to be marked for the poorness or goodness of his lesson, the sending home of graded reports upon purely conventional, mathematical or alphabetical schemes, the comparing by the children of their respective grades and all the scheming (sometimes cheating) thereby called forth.[6]

---

[5] For a valuable account of the use of external aims (particularly standardized testing) during Dewey's time, see Mark Garrison, *A Measure of Failure: The Political Origins of Standardized Testing* (Albany, NY: State University of New York Press, 2009).

[6] MW3: 241.

Dewey believes this "marking" encourages students to try to finish their learning as quickly and easily as possible. With their "never-absent consciousness" of being graded for their work, students gravitate toward seeking strict instructions from their teachers on what exactly is required to receive the desired grade. Dewey thus sees grades as obstructing students' capacity for continuous, self-directed growth. Also, he points to grades as helping to develop an ideology among students that justifies current economic relations. Students grow familiar with the idea that work is primarily about meeting an authority figure's standards (which are often opaque and mysterious to those doing the work) in order to receive a socially established reward at the end of the work – that is, a grade at the end of a semester, and then money at the end of a work period for adults. In this way, grades harm students' capacities to critically challenge the economic world they see around them (and the inequalities that world creates), because students are familiarized with a work environment where an authority figure needs to be satisfied in order to receive a "wage," and where individuals' efforts are supposedly reflected by that wage (the grade). If schools would instead allow students to learn without the "eternal presence of the record book," and without being led to judge both themselves and others by their status within that record book, then schools would resist the consumer consciousness and would allow greater space for the continuous development and critical thought entailed by democratic individualism.

My analysis in this chapter will not only explore how education can promote continuous development and critical thought, but will further illustrate how deliberative democracy is inadequate for dealing with social inequality. I will show that the deliberative educational theory does not address how certain school practices (e.g., grading, standardized testing) already reflect the structural advantage of certain social interests over others, or how a "fair" debate over educational policy may simply reinforce those advantaged social interests. Further, this chapter will show the importance that should be placed on education within any democratic theory that identifies a social element to democracy, as participatory theory does. If we are to see democracy as a social concept, and not only as a political mechanism for allowing various interests to compete with each other (or to reason with each other), then we must examine how individuals can manifest democracy in their everyday social relations. We must therefore give due attention to the attitudes and behaviors encouraged in young individuals during school. We must also ask how schooling can be altered to allow individuals a greater opportunity to live democratically and contribute to a democratic society. Education should be seen as an essential pillar in participatory democratic theory, and Dewey helps us effectively construct that pillar.

COOPERATIVE, PRACTICAL INQUIRY IN DEWEYAN EDUCATION

For Dewey, the cultivation of students' capacities for *inquiry* is central to a democratic education. Rather than encouraging habits of memorization of ready-made answers, Dewey calls for students to be assigned projects that do not have a predetermined result, that reflect the complexity and uncertainty of the students' natural and social surroundings, and that allow students to inquire themselves into a variety of possible answers to challenging questions. If school subject matter is open-ended and provides opportunities for inquiry, then Dewey believes students can develop their abilities to direct their own unique, open-ended growth.[7]

Dewey remarks that "[j]ust because a second-handed material has been supplied wholesale and retail, but anyway ready-made, the tendency is to reduce the activity of mind to a docile or passive taking in of the material presented – in short, to memorizing, with simply incidental use of judgment and of active research. As is frequently stated, acquiring takes the place of inquiring."[8] This problem of students being led to "acquire" information, rather than to "inquire" into unsettled problems, arises when (for example) "science is still taught very largely as a separate and isolated subject" with a set of biological, chemical, and physical facts which students are to memorize in order to exhibit scientific knowledge.[9] This does not mean that Dewey thinks the previous work and past

---

[7] A number of scholars have discussed Dewey's interest in assigning projects that lack any fixed, ready-made answers; see James Johnston, *Deweyan Inquiry: From Education Theory to Practice* (Albany, NY: State University of New York Press, 2009), 11, 35; James Johnston, *Inquiry and Education: John Dewey and the Quest for Democracy* (Albany, NY: State University of New York Press, 2006), 193; Gert Biesta, "The Communicative Turn in Dewey's *Democracy and Education*," in *John Dewey and Our Educational Prospect: A Critical Engagement with Dewey's Democracy and Education*, ed. David Hansen (Albany, NY: State University of New York Press, 2006), 32; Sharon Feiman-Nemser, "A Teacher Educator Looks at *Democracy and Education*," in *John Dewey and Our Educational Prospect: A Critical Engagement with Dewey's Democracy and Education*, ed. David Hansen (Albany, NY: State University of New York Press, 2006), 134; and Elizabeth Minnich, "Dewey's Philosophy of Life," in *John Dewey and Our Educational Prospect: A Critical Engagement with Dewey's Democracy and Education*, ed. David Hansen (Albany, NY: State University of New York Press, 2006), 156.

[8] MW3: 236.

[9] LW11: 187.

accomplishments of a field like science should be treated as irrelevant to students' education; he in fact states that schools should "[put] the net product of past experience in the form which makes it most available for the future."[10] But he stresses that students should not accept this past experience uncritically. When studying previously established scientific facts, students should get the sense that scientific subject matter is a continuously developing entity – they should be exposed to the conflicts and debates among scientists which gave rise to currently accepted facts, and should be given opportunities to use these past facts to inquire into new biological, chemical, and physical problems:

Learning [in traditional education] means acquisition of what already is incorporated in books and in the heads of the elders. Moreover, that which is taught is thought of as essentially static. It is taught as a finished product, with little regard either to the ways in which it was originally built up or to changes that will surely occur in the future.[11]

Dewey highlights a political significance to the presence, or lack, of inquiry within education. He contends that "current schooling ... not only does little to make discriminating intelligence a safeguard against surrender to the invasion of bunk, especially in its most dangerous form – social and political bunk – but it does much to favor susceptibility to a welcoming reception to it."[12] One of the main reasons schooling has had this effect, he argues, is that there has been

a systematic, almost deliberate, avoidance of the spirit of criticism in dealing with history, politics, and economics. There is an implicit belief that this avoidance is the only way by which to produce good citizens. The more undiscriminatingly the history and institutions of one's own nation are idealized, the greater is the likelihood, so it is assumed, that the school product will be a loyal patriot, a well equipped good citizen.[13]

American schools, therefore, should confront students with the undesirable aspects of America's current political and economic reality (e.g., governmental gridlock, income inequality) and of America's history (e.g., genocide of Native Americans). The students should be exposed to

---

[10] John Dewey, *The Child and the Curriculum* (Chicago, IL: University of Chicago Press, 1902), 27.
[11] John Dewey, *Experience and Education* (New York, NY: Macmillan Company, 1938), 5.
[12] MW13: 332.
[13] Ibid.

various positions on the meanings and lessons of these defects in American life and encouraged to critically inquire into each position. Any attempts to conceal the undesirable aspects of American politics, economics, and history, and to orient the social studies curriculum toward simply portraying the United States as the greatest nation in the world,[14] are antithetical to students' self-government. As Dewey puts it, "[O]ur instruction in history and geography and our social studies in general should be intellectually more honest, they should bring students into gradual contact with the actual realities of contemporary life."[15] With political education specifically, he insists that "[w]e need methods of teaching that will not merely give pupils a simple paper knowledge of government, but that will give them ... a knowledge of what are the underlying tendencies and problems they must meet in government, local, state, and national."[16]

It is also crucial for Dewey that schools allow students greater opportunity to work with, and learn from, other students, rather than passively listening to the teacher alone.[17] Dewey describes how, in typical educational settings, "for one child to help another in his task has become a school crime. Where the school work consists in simply learning lessons, mutual assistance, instead of being the most natural form of cooperation and association, becomes a clandestine effort to relieve one's neighbor of his proper duties."[18] When students are not given sufficient opportunity to work with other students and to learn from the experiences of other students, they are cut off from potential sources of learning and come to think they should only listen to their teacher. Furthermore, as Dewey explains, individuals have capacities that are not expressed when working in isolation, but are expressed "when the individual is working with others, where there is a common project,

---

[14] This issue has emerged in particular within debates over the content of school textbooks; e.g., see Michael Brick, "Texas School Board Set to Vote Textbook Revisions," *New York Times*, May 20, 2010.

[15] MW15: 156.

[16] MW15: 161.

[17] This aspect of Dewey's thought has been emphasized in Leonard Waks, "John Dewey on Listening and Friendship in School and Society," *Educational Theory* 61, no. 2 (2011): 202–3; Leonard Waks, "Dewey's Theory of the Democratic Public and the Public Character of Charter Schools," *Educational Theory* 60, no. 6 (2010): 677; Jason Kosnoski, *John Dewey and the Habits of Ethical Life: The Aesthetics of Political Organizing in a Liquid World* (Lanham, MD: Lexington Books, 2010), 205, 206, 207; and Eric Weber, *Rawls, Dewey, and Constructivism: On the Epistemology of Justice* (London: Continuum International, 2010), 136.

[18] John Dewey, *The School and Society* (Chicago, IL: University of Chicago Press, 1900), 29.

something of interest to them all, but where each has his own part."[19] A student may have a particular capacity to synthesize others' views – on a social studies question or a scientific experiment, for instance – and to thereby expand both her own understanding and that of others regarding a problem that is being investigated in the classroom. But that capacity can remain undeveloped if she and her classmates are mainly relegated to working alone at isolated desks. Encouraging cooperative work relations with others is indeed critical for Dewey if students are to learn to engage with, and grow from, the differing views of peers, rather than seeing their peers merely as hindrances to their own isolated activity: "the best and deepest moral training is precisely that which one gets through having to enter into proper relations with others in a unity of work and thought. The present educational systems, so far as they destroy or neglect this unity, render it difficult or impossible to get any genuine, regular moral training."[20]

Perhaps the most frequently underlined theme in Dewey's educational theory is that students must see the concrete, practical value of subject matter so that they can connect with the subject matter and use it to illuminate their experiences outside the school.[21] Dewey declares that "the great waste in the school comes from [the child's] inability to utilize the experiences he gets outside the school in any complete and free way within the school itself; while, on the other hand, he is unable to apply in daily life what he is learning at school."[22] In his view, too much of the information tossed at students during school is completely foreign to the students' everyday lives. The students are asked to accumulate mathematical techniques, scientific facts, historical events, etc., in their minds for the sake of the subject matter itself, while their ordinary experiences are left at the schoolhouse door. They have difficulty,

---

[19] MW15: 176.

[20] EW5: 88.

[21] This theme is emphasized in Stephen Fishman and Lucille McCarthy, *John Dewey and the Philosophy and Practice of Hope* (Urbana: University of Illinois Press, 2007), 110; Herbert Kliebard, "Dewey's Reconstruction of the Curriculum: From Occupation to Disciplined Knowledge," in *John Dewey and Our Educational Prospect: A Critical Engagement with Dewey's Democracy and Education*, ed. David Hansen (Albany, NY: State University of New York Press, 2006), 120; Reba Page, "Curriculum Matters," in *John Dewey and Our Educational Prospect: A Critical Engagement with Dewey's Democracy and Education*, ed. David Hansen (Albany, NY: State University of New York Press, 2006), 53; and Jim Garrison, *Dewey and Eros: Wisdom and Desire in the Art of Teaching* (New York, NY: Teachers College Press, 1997), 121, 144–5.

[22] Dewey, *School and Society*, 89.

then, seeing how math, science, or history might illuminate situations they experience outside of school. Being unable to form an authentic connection with the subject matter, they will likely expel the subject matter from their minds once it is not necessary for their school work. When describing how school subject matter could be made more practical, Dewey argues that mathematical subject matter "arises in connection with the measuring of things for purposes of constructive activity; and hence arithmetic should be so taught," meaning that students could connect more deeply with mathematical concepts by (for example) seeing their value for construction projects.[23] He also suggests cooking and sewing as activities which can allow students to perceive the practical, real-life value of the chemical and physical aspects of scientific study.[24] With this focus on practical activities, Dewey assures us that schools would not then fail to provide students with necessary facts and information: "a child cannot garden intelligently without learning about soils, seeds, measures, plants and their growth, the facts of rain, sunshine, etc."; by applying these facts to concrete experience, though, the students will less likely accept these facts simply on hearing them, but will treat them as "working hypotheses" to be altered if they do not have the concrete effects that the students expect.[25] Most importantly, this *pragmatic* focus on the real-life significance of subject matter would, for Dewey, allow students to expand their everyday experience through their school experience. Students would less likely see subject matter as an alien entity with no relevance to their normal lives, and may instead use each encounter with subject matter to shed further light on the situations they experience outside of school.

If students are to become Deweyan democratic individuals and exercise control over their lives – that is, if they are to intelligently direct their lives in interaction with a changing, increasingly interconnected world – then it is essential that students find opportunity for open-ended inquiry, and that this inquiry involve cooperation with fellow students and have distinct practical significance. A school environment that focuses on such cooperative, practical inquiry would be treating students as continuously developing beings and would convey to students that their paths of development are largely determined by their own unique decisions and activities.

[23] EW5: 205.
[24] MW3: 238.
[25] MW4: 187–8.

EXTERNAL AIMS AND CONTINUOUS
INDIVIDUAL DEVELOPMENT

Although the topics addressed in the previous section have received considerable attention in commentaries on Dewey's educational theory, the critique Dewey builds of "external aims" (i.e., grades and standardized test scores) in education has largely been overlooked. In his discussions of external aims, the point Dewey immediately impresses upon us is that these aims are detrimental to students' growth. In *Democracy and Education*, his central work on educational philosophy, Dewey writes that

[i]n contrast with fulfilling some process in order that activity may go on, stands the static character of an end which is imposed from without the activity ... When one has such a notion, activity is a mere unavoidable means to something else; it is not significant or important on its own account. As compared with the end it is but a necessary evil; something which must be gone through before one can reach the object which is alone worth while.[26]

In other words, when students see their grade at the end of a semester, or their score on a state-mandated standardized test, as *the* mark of evaluation that will legitimize their learning, the learning process itself comes to lack intrinsic value to the students. Their encounters with school subject matter tend to be seen as meaningless chores, which must be endured mainly because the students have been told this subject matter is necessary to receive the grades and test scores that will make schoolwork worthwhile: "the external idea of the aim leads to a separation of means from end ... Every divorce of end from means diminishes by that much the significance of the activity and tends to reduce it to a drudgery from which one would escape if he could."[27] For Dewey, the value attached to these external aims inhibits students from growing through each encounter with subject matter, because students are likely to view learning itself as insignificant, and to focus their attention on just finishing the learning process so that this process can be validated through attainment of the desired reward.

Elsewhere, Dewey warns that grading leads students to expect that growth has a predetermined path and to try to follow that path with as little deviation as possible. Students get the sense that there is one way to

---

[26] Dewey, *Democracy and Education*, 105–6.
[27] Ibid., 106.

do their work and expect to be measured well if they also work in that one way:

> I have seen a powerful indictment against the marking and examination system, as ordinarily conducted, to the effect that it sets up a false and demoralizing standard by which the students come to judge their own work. Instead of each one considering himself responsible for the highest excellency to which he can possibly attain, the tendency is to suppose that one is doing well enough if he comes up to the average expectation.[28]

This, Dewey contends, should nullify those "arguments which imply that there is something particularly strenuous in the disciplinary ideals of rigid tests and marks, and that their surrender means the substitution of a less severe and exacting standard."[29] Grading and testing do not reliably lead students toward fully engaging with school activities and subject matter, because students are led to seek a clearly delineated path that will lead them directly to the external aim: "It points out to students certain particular things which are to be done and certain particular things which are to be avoided. And it not only permits but encourages them to believe that the whole duty of man is done when just these special things have been performed, and just these special things avoided."[30] Students' growth is thus hindered by external aims, because students end up searching for the quickest, easiest path toward a fixed end where learning can stop. As Dewey remarks, "In education, the currency of these externally imposed aims is responsible for ... rendering the work of both teacher and pupil mechanical and slavish."[31]

We have seen that Deweyan democratic individualism largely relates to the way an individual responds to *uncertainty*. For Dewey, the fact that we live in a changing world lacking any fixed truths means that individuals must see themselves as changing beings who inevitably confront uncertainty as they develop in unforeseen directions. Democratic individuals exercise control over their lives by actively engaging with their changing world – and the substantial uncertainty it brings – and thereby developing provisional (not certain) ideas and principles for guiding future interaction with the world. Fundamentally, we can say that Dewey's complaint against grading and standardized testing comes

---

[28] MW3: 243.
[29] MW3: 243–4.
[30] MW3: 244.
[31] Dewey, *Democracy and Education*, 110.

down to the way these practices affect students' approach to uncertainty. Dewey attests that

[t]o say that thinking occurs with reference to situations which are still going on, and incomplete, is to say that thinking occurs when things are uncertain or doubtful or problematic ... It also follows that all thinking involves a risk. Certainty cannot be guaranteed in advance. The invasion of the unknown is of the nature of an adventure; we cannot be sure in advance.[32]

If we are to exercise any control over the direction these adventures take, we must accept this uncertainty, as well as the sheer difficulty involved in trying to direct the course of experiences that proceed in unforeseen ways: "Every vital activity of any depth and range inevitably meets obstacles in the course of its effort to realize itself."[33] However, when students cannot escape the feeling that their grades and test scores are the sole validating measures of their school activities, then uncertainty and difficulty become, not necessary and invigorating aspects of the process of development, but treacherous signs that the all-important grade or test score may not be received. It becomes increasingly burdensome for students to actively seek out new paths of development in school and to accept and value the missteps they make within such uncertain paths. It will likely appear senseless to students to risk their academic record by making themselves vulnerable to missteps. Instead, the quick, easy path toward the external aim, with the least possibility of error, will seem desirable:

Insistence upon avoiding error instead of attaining power tends ... to interruption of continuous discourse and thought. Children who begin with something to say and with intellectual eagerness to say it are sometimes made so conscious of minor errors in substance and form that the energy that should go into constructive thinking is diverted into anxiety not to make mistakes, and even, in extreme cases, into passive quiescence as the best method of minimizing error.[34]

In Chapter 2, where I analyzed Hegel's influence on Dewey's democratic individual way of life, I associated democratic individualism with individuals exercising a unique effect on the novel "objects of experience" they inevitably confront, and thus, exercising control over their lives. Within grade-based schooling, Dewey finds students seeking a clear, unambiguous path of learning, provided by others, which they can follow

---

[32] Ibid., 148.
[33] John Dewey, *How We Think* (Boston, MA: D. C. Heath & Co., 1910), 64.
[34] Ibid., 186.

in order to reach the fixed endpoint of the grade.[35] Such schooling does not promote students' capacity to actively interact with novel objects of experience, because the students seek to be told by the teacher precisely what to do in response to all possible objects of experience. Dewey maintains that "[t]here is ... no point in the philosophy of progressive education which is sounder than its emphasis upon the importance of the participation of the learner in the formation of the purposes which direct his activities in the learning process."[36] When schools lead students toward fearing the difficulty inherent in uncertain development, and toward seeking a clearly delineated path that can be followed to a given endpoint, the students are hindered from becoming subjects exercising a unique effect on the objects of experience they confront. In other words, they are hindered from exercising control over their lives.

Dewey's argument is, of course, highly relevant to contemporary circumstances, given the emphasis on practices like high-stakes testing in both the "No Child Left Behind" and "Race to the Top" policies of the Bush and Obama administrations, respectively. For Dewey, the kind of obsession with test scores that we see in recent educational policy represents "the substitution of a conventional average standard of expectation and requirement for a standard which concerns the specific powers of the individual under instruction."[37] He says specifically about standardized testing that

[t]he practical educational use to which testers propose that the results of testing should be put strengthens the proposition that even cultivated minds are dominated by the concept of quantitative classes – so much so that the quality of individuality escapes them ... An individual is not conceived as an individual with his own distinctive perplexities, methods and rates of operation. The classificatory submergence of individuals in averaged aggregates is perpetuated.[38]

We can thus see recent educational policy as threatening students' unique individuality, because a single, universal test is given to massive numbers of students, and the students are placed in predetermined educational strata according to their ability to find predetermined answers to test

---

[35] Elsewhere, I have thoroughly drawn out the Hegelian qualities of Dewey's case for how external aims lead students away from continuous individual growth; see Jeff Jackson, "Reconstructing Dewey: Dialectics and Democratic Education," *Education and Culture* 28, no. 1 (2012): 62–77.

[36] Dewey, *Experience and Education*, 77.

[37] Dewey, *Democracy and Education*, 55.

[38] MW13: 292.

questions. Dewey similarly rebukes grading practices, proclaiming that "given two schools of otherwise equal conditions, in one of which the marking system prevailed, and in the other did not," in the latter school "the individual has to be known and judged in terms of his own unique self, unrepeatable in any other self," whereas the former school "permits and encourages the teacher to escape with the feeling that he has done his whole duty when he has impartially graded the external and dead product of such a personality."[39] With students being largely seen as entities to fit into predetermined categories, rather than as unique beings each proceeding through unique processes of development, experiences of uncertainty are only further devalued, because students sense that they are to repeat what others have done before them, and any attempt to take up an unusual path carries the risk of falling outside of the educational reward system. Consequently, external aims breed a "failure to develop initiative in coping with novel situations,"[40] and "the result is a random groping after what is wanted, and the formation of habits of dependence upon the cues furnished by others,"[41] as students come to feel anxiety over diverging from established standards of academic achievement: "Originality is gradually destroyed, confidence in one's own quality of mental operation is undermined, and a docile subjection to the opinion of others is inculcated."[42]

In previous chapters, we have seen Dewey associate pragmatism with a rejection of the "quest for certainty" – that is, the search for a perfectly stable existence which is safe from the vicissitudes of constantly changing experience. Dewey challenges individuals to instead continuously generate greater (though inevitably imperfect) certainty for themselves through active engagement with their changing, unstable world. The use of external aims in schools, however, "sets up as an ideal and standard a static end. The fulfillment of growing is taken to mean an *accomplished* growth: that is to say, an Ungrowth, something which is no longer growing."[43] The uncertain process of learning is devalued, and the stable attainment of sufficiently high grades and test scores is set up as the foundational purpose of students' education. Dewey alleges that those who defend external aims "[pay] the tribute of speaking much of development, process, progress. But all of these operations are conceived

[39] MW3: 243.
[40] Dewey, *Democracy and Education*, 50.
[41] Ibid., 57.
[42] Ibid., 303.
[43] Ibid., 42.

to be merely transitional; they lack meaning on their own account. They possess significance only as movements *toward* something away from what is now going on."[44] When "progress" is measured by improvement in standardized test scores, for instance, whatever genuine growth the students make is meaningless on its own and only attains value by being affixed with a static, quantitative measure. As a result, students are more likely to see "endeavor as proof not of power but of incompletion," and to conceive of "a completed activity, a static perfection" as their educational ideal.[45] Dewey argues that, more properly, "[t]he criterion of the value of school education is the extent in which it creates a desire for continued growth and supplies means for making the desire effective in fact."[46] When schools are evaluated by measures such as standardized test scores, students are led to devalue opportunities for growth within school and to focus primarily on finding the point where uncertain growth can finally stop.

EXTERNAL AIMS AND MARKET IDEOLOGY

There is more to be said about Dewey's argument against external aims, particularly about the way he sees these aims cultivating a "market" ideology that is detrimental to democracy. We have seen Macpherson declare that participatory democracy requires individuals to stop viewing themselves as isolated consumers in a market. With Dewey, we get fuller elaboration on this point through his account of how a market culture inhibits democratic individualism. In Chapter 2, I pointed out Dewey's concern that the tendency to "[identify] the power and liberty of the individual with ... ability to make money"[47] serves to justify economic inequality which hinders individuals from leading democratic lives, that is, from exercising a self-directed impact on the objects of experience they confront. Dewey explains that there has been "a perversion of the whole ideal of individualism to conform to the practices of a pecuniary culture. It has become the source and justification of inequalities and oppressions."[48] And he stresses that this pecuniary culture cannot help but affect the education provided to young individuals: "That which prevents

---

[44] Ibid., 57.
[45] John Dewey, *Human Nature and Conduct* (New York, NY: Henry Holt and Company, 1922), 174.
[46] Dewey, *Democracy and Education*, 53.
[47] LW11: 366.
[48] Dewey, *Individualism Old and New*, 18.

the schools from doing their educational work freely is precisely the pressure – for the most part indirect, to be sure – of domination by the money-motif of our economic regime."[49] Dewey is especially troubled here by the cultivation of the type of individualism (described in Chapter 1) that is not democratic, but coheres with the capitalistic conception of individuals as isolated beings who have a worth that is legitimately measured by their possession of money. This kind of individualistic ideology leads students to believe that fixed measures of achievement (e.g., grades, test scores) are indicative of individual quality. He charges that "almost the only measure for success is a competitive one, in the bad sense of that term – a comparison of results in the recitation or in the examination to see which child has succeeded in getting ahead of others in storing up, in accumulating the maximum of information."[50] As a result, students become accustomed to the idea that individual worth is to be judged by the possession of certain static markers of achievement and that a hierarchy based on such possession is legitimate: "Just because all are doing the same work, and are judged (both in recitation and in examination, with reference to grading and to promotion) ... the feeling of superiority is unduly appealed to."[51] Dewey's point here, then, is that schools familiarize students with an environment in which ostensibly isolated effort will determine one's status within a hierarchy, and that schools thereby cultivate a market ideology:

Our economic and political environment leads us to think in terms of classes, aggregates and submerged membership in them ... Instead of mixing up together a lot of pupils of different abilities we can divide them into a superior, a middle and an inferior section, so that each can go its own gait without being kept back or unduly forced by others.[52]

Dewey does not mean to suggest that schools alone are responsible for legitimizing the class boundaries generated by capitalism. But he does maintain that schools contribute to a worldview that conceives of poverty and wealth as the results of purely isolated individual effort, and thus as the fair outcomes of a legitimate competition. He explains, "I refer to the schools in connection with this problem of American culture because they are the formal agencies for producing those mental attitudes, those

---

[49] Ibid., 127.
[50] Dewey, *School and Society*, 29.
[51] EW5: 65.
[52] MW13: 291–2.

modes of feeling and thinking, which are the essence of a distinctive culture"; he professes further that, within typical schooling, "[t]here is little preparation to induce either hardy resistance, discriminating criticism, or the vision and desire to direct economic forces in new channels."[53] Hence, schools help to validate economic inequality because the students' mental attitudes are formed in the context of an individualistic pursuit of grades, and are therefore well suited to a wider economic environment defined by an apparently fair, individualistic pursuit of money. Dewey further traces this lack of critical thought toward current economic relations to the fact that school performance (i.e., attainment of grades, high test scores) is commonly assumed to directly indicate how a student will perform in the capitalist economy as an adult:

We accept standards of judging individuals which are based on the qualities of mind and character which win under existing social conditions conspicuous success. The 'inferior' is the one who isn't calculated to 'get on' in a society such as now exists. 'Equals' are those who belong to a class formed by like chances of attaining recognition, position and wealth in present society.[54]

The students, therefore, are not only placed in an environment that mirrors the image of the broader capitalist economy, but are led to believe that their performance in that environment will directly bear on their economic success as adults. There is little room within such schooling, Dewey reasons, for students to develop genuine critical thought toward the economic relations generated by capitalism.

We saw in Chapter 2 how democratic individuals participate in decision making in their work and exercise a self-generated impact on the methods and aims involved in their work. They are not forced to simply obey an authority figure in order to receive a money reward at the end of their activities. I described in Chapter 2 how Dewey sees market ideology interfering with democracy in the workplace, and Dewey specifically points to external aims in schools as blocking critical thought toward the typical work relations of capitalism. He laments that our schooling tacitly

assumes that in the future, as in the past, getting a livelihood, 'making a living,' must signify for most men and women doing things which are not significant, freely chosen, and ennobling to those who do them; doing things which serve

---

[53] Dewey, *Individualism Old and New*, 128–9.
[54] MW15: 295.

ends unrecognized by those engaged in them, carried on under the direction of others for the sake of a pecuniary reward.[55]

Of course, changes in prevalent educational practices could not alone alter the undemocratic quality of many workplaces; but Dewey's point here is that schoolwork which is done primarily for a grade can lead students to accept that work must be an intrinsically insignificant chore done primarily for an external reward. He does not suggest that all students will then invariably spend their entire lives in undemocratic workplaces, but rather that students – having had little opportunity to exercise a unique effect on the objects of experience they confront – will more likely deem undemocratic work relations in general to be natural and just. Schools should instead diminish the importance attached to external aims if "pupils are to ... [become] active instead of passive economic units."[56]

I noted in the previous section that when the uncertainty and difficulty of development lack intrinsic value for students, Dewey sees students looking for an impossible realm of certainty, wherein sufficient external rewards will let them escape from the vicissitudes of growth: "A goal of finished accomplishment has been set up which if it were attained would mean only mindless action ... The practical impossibility of reaching, in an all around way and all at once such a 'perfection' has been recognized. But such a goal has nevertheless been conceived as the ideal, and progress has been defined as approximation to it."[57] For Dewey, the manner in which this "quest for certainty" feeds into market ideology heightens its consequences for democratic individualism. As he construes it, the desire for escape from uncertain activity corresponds with the capitalistic goal of sufficient monetary gain so that one can stop working: "the accumulation of investments such that a man can live upon their return without labor."[58] This is again not to say that Dewey sees schools as universally producing the same effect on all students, in terms of educating them to approach work only for the money reward it brings and to stop working as soon as it is financially possible. But he does determine that schools help contribute to powerful ideological messages in support of capitalism. Schools acquaint students with the idea that work is done to reach a static realm of certainty where work is no longer necessary, and with the

---

[55] Dewey, *Democracy and Education*, 192.
[56] MW15: 169.
[57] Dewey, *Human Nature and Conduct*, 173–4.
[58] Ibid., 124.

idea that those individuals who possess enough resources to stop working (e.g., the wealthy) are deserving of their social status.

Typical schooling, for Dewey, thus places students on an anxious,
acquisitive quest for certainty, a pursuit that feeds into the capitalistic
goal of attaining sufficient individual wealth in order to isolate oneself
from uncertain development. When discussing why schools could potentially work against the cultivation of such behavior, Dewey advises that
"the absence of economic pressure in schools supplies an opportunity for
reproducing industrial situations of mature life under conditions where
the occupation can be carried on for its own sake."[59] Because students
do not yet face the economic pressure endured by adults in capitalist
society, schools might provide a space of resistance against the dominant
capitalistic image of work, particularly if they allow students opportunity to work without concern for external aims. Of course, if students
are to attach greater value to the intrinsic character of their schoolwork
than to a reward received at the end of work, this type of education
will have to begin early on. Although he was a college professor, Dewey
would not suggest that colleges take students as they are typically educated in the earlier years of school and remove the motivation of grades,
because "college reaches their minds too late"[60] to fundamentally alter
the students' mind-set. In the elementary school that Dewey established
during his time at the University of Chicago, he specifically aimed to provide an education that would "make unnecessary a servile dependence
upon the ordinary machinery of petty rules, constant markings, reports,
etc."[61] This was crucial in his view for allowing students to exercise critical thought toward the broader economic world, for otherwise "children
are ... prematurely launched into the region of individualistic competition."[62] When they are brought up in this latter environment, students are
led to adopt the market ideology that in a variety of ways works against
their own self-government.

Dewey does not expect the undemocratic, capitalistic nature of schooling to be completely changed without concurrent change in the undemocratic, capitalistic nature of social and political life. He also does not
expect changes in schooling alone to lead to all the social and political change he would like to see. At the same time, though, he holds
that schools need not simply mirror the present society, and can in fact

[59] Dewey, *Democracy and Education*, 204.
[60] LW3: 279.
[61] MW3: 283.
[62] EW5: 65.

contribute to the broader aims of social and political democratization: "The school cannot immediately escape from the ideals set by prior social conditions. But it should contribute through the type of intellectual and emotional disposition which it forms to the improvement of those conditions."[63] In line with his idea of democracy as in a continuous process of development, and as constituted by various interrelated elements, Dewey sees education having a crucial role in democratization, particularly with respect to the individual element of democracy which is interconnected with – and can promote the realization of – the social and political elements of democracy:

This does not mean that we can change character and mind by direct instruction and exhortation, apart from a change in industrial and political conditions ... But it does mean that we may produce in schools a projection in type of the society we should like to realize, and by forming minds in accord with it generally modify the larger and more recalcitrant features of adult society.[64]

By bringing up students in environments where they are not all measured by the same quantitative, external standard, schools could form students' minds in accord with a society in which firm inequalities on the basis of such a standard are absent. Undemocratic work environments, and the influence wielded by wealthy people like the Koch brothers over political institutions and over the everyday lives of other individuals, would then appear strange to students. On Dewey's terms, students' critical thought toward these forms of inequality expands their own capacity to govern their lives, and simultaneously promotes the possibilities for combating social inequality and exclusive political power. The development of each of the individual, social, and political elements of Deweyan democracy, therefore, could be aided by schools that counteract the dominance of external aims over students' educational experience.

A DEWEYAN CRITIQUE OF DELIBERATIVE EDUCATIONAL THEORY

In Chapter 4, I showed that Dewey should not be seen as a forefather of deliberative democracy and that his democratic theory instead helps refute the idea that deliberative democracy has subsumed participatory

---

[63] Dewey, *Democracy and Education*, 136.
[64] Ibid., 316–17.

democracy. My analysis of Dewey's educational theory, and of its role in the development of Deweyan democracy, adds more layers to the separation of participatory theory from deliberative theory. Once we compare deliberative educational principles with those of a participatory theory infused with Deweyan insights, we have further reason to see deliberative theory as inadequate for coping with social inequality.

As noted earlier, Gutmann and Thompson have named the education system as the most important institution outside of government for enacting deliberative democracy, because "[s]chools should aim to develop their students' capacities to understand different perspectives, communicate their understandings to other people, and engage in the give-and-take of moral argument with a view to making mutually acceptable decisions."[65] Deliberative theory again holds that when political debaters exchange reasons that could reasonably be endorsed by their opponents, democracy is achieved because everyone involved in the debate has been treated respectfully, has had their views considered, and has had the policy decisions justified to them in terms they can accept. I separated Dewey from deliberative democracy in Chapter 4 by focusing on Dewey's central point that political democracy cannot be achieved without concurrently overcoming social inequality. I showed that deliberative democrats isolate the political and social realms when they indicate that the effects of unequal social status can be neutralized as long as deliberation in political forums is proceeding properly. And when these thinkers do try to insist on the reduction of social inequality, I argued they must compromise the principles of deliberation: either they must predetermine the outcome of deliberation by requiring the debate to only produce policies that reduce social inequality; or they must concede that, under unequal social conditions, deliberation itself is not democratic, and that deliberation would only be democratic after the most pressing work of democratization (i.e., overcoming social inequality) is achieved through nondeliberative means.

With respect to deliberative educational principles, Gutmann in particular proclaims that "the content of education should be reoriented toward teaching students the skills of democratic deliberation."[66] If schools were to teach deliberative skills, she argues, the students could "develop capacities for criticism, rational argument, and decisionmaking by being taught how to think logically, to argue coherently and

[65] Amy Gutmann and Dennis Thompson, *Democracy and Disagreement* (Cambridge: Harvard University Press, 1996), 359.
[66] Amy Gutmann, *Democratic Education* (Princeton, NJ: Princeton University Press, 1987), 171.

fairly, and to consider the relevant alternatives before coming to conclusions."[67] Gutmann displays here that quality of deliberative democracy which presumes that greater deliberation is equivalent to democratization: "Deliberation is connected, both by definition and practice, with the development of democracy."[68] This shows the tendency of isolating political and social – that is, of maintaining that, even under unequal social conditions, the key to democracy is getting all individuals to deliberate together on political matters. Gutmann contends that "[h]owever students have been socialized outside of school, there should be room within school for them to develop the capacity to discuss and defend their political commitments with people who do not share them"; she further suggests that we "[redirect] concern away from the question of whether high-school graduates can get good jobs and toward the question of whether they have the capacity to deliberate about the political issues that affect their lives."[69] This deliberative educational theory, like deliberative theory in general, abstracts from social inequality by associating democracy with a debate in which all individuals involved, regardless of social status, put their political views up for challenge and are equally willing to modify their views in order to reach "mutually acceptable decisions." The theory does not directly address social inequality, and instead implies that a fair and equal political debate can be created against an unequal social background.

Gutmann also focuses attention on the way educational policy gets made, and here again she does not attend closely to the problem of certain (e.g., wealthy) interests and perspectives already being reflected in existing policies. She instead concentrates on "improving the quality of American education not directly by changing school policy, but indirectly by improving the quality of our public deliberations over education."[70] She calls on deliberators to be willing to reconcile their differences, without addressing how these differences can reflect broader social inequities in which certain elements of society already enjoy a privileged position in the educational debate: "We can do better to try ... to find the fairest ways of reconciling our disagreements, and for enriching our collective life by democratically debating them. We may even find ourselves modifying our moral ideals of education in the process of participating in

---

[67] Ibid., 50.
[68] Ibid., 52.
[69] Ibid., 107, 147–8.
[70] Ibid., 5.

democratic debates and of publicly reconciling our differences."[71] There is little room, then, within Gutmann's theory for establishing that grading and standardized testing practices already exhibit the dominance of one set of ideas of how students should be educated over others. Her theory does not recognize how a "fair" debate over such practices – a debate in which all must be equally willing to modify their positions to reach mutually acceptable decisions – may simply reinforce the privileged position of that dominant set of ideas. Gutmann does in fact discuss grading and standardized testing, but the point she makes is simply that universities should consider additional factors in their criteria for admissions, rather than relying solely on grades and test scores – she does not challenge these external aims themselves in terms of how they affect students' capacity for continuous development or students' view of the legitimacy of current economic relations.[72]

Dewey's educational theory, by contrast, shines a light on how prevalent educational practices reflect undemocratic social interests. He illustrates why democratizing education requires that we change these practices, rather than simply create a debate over education where all interests are assumed to be already equal. His theory also demonstrates how students may pick up undemocratic attitudes from these practices, even if students are not explicitly taught to have those attitudes. Dewey pronounces that "[p]erhaps the greatest of all pedagogical fallacies is the notion that a person learns only the particular thing he is studying at the time. Collateral learning in the way of formation of enduring attitudes, of likes and dislikes, may be and often is much more important."[73] In this chapter, I have examined Dewey's point that external aims (grades, standardized test scores) can diminish students' desire to seek the greatest possible growth within their schooling and can help legitimize current economic relations in students' eyes. Dewey would not object specifically to Gutmann's idea that students be taught skills of cooperative, respectful debate, but he would not presume that those skills will even be what students primarily pick up from their classroom experience. He instead

---

[71] Ibid., 12.

[72] Ibid., 197–203. Gutmann even endorses the practice of "merit pay" – the use of external standards (e.g., students' test scores) to determine teachers' effectiveness, and thus teachers' pay – by asserting that "[t]he institution of merit pay is another way of mitigating the ossification of office among the best teachers"; she also criticizes the efforts of teachers' unions to oppose merit pay by calling such efforts "an attempt to shield teachers from legitimate external evaluation" (Ibid., 81).

[73] Dewey, *Experience and Education*, 49.

questions what "collateral" learning students may do as a result of grading and testing practices which are uncritically accepted as necessary for schooling. Students may then see those lessons on debate as simply something to get through on the way to an external aim, and they may primarily learn (from their search for external aims) to pick up qualities that interfere with their own continuous development and their ability to critically challenge their existing society.

Even with this analysis of Dewey's divergence from Gutmann, we should not align Dewey with educational theories that present the school as *only* capable of inculcating the dominant capitalist values existing in society. This kind of theory is famously put forward by Samuel Bowles and Herbert Gintis, who do provide compelling analysis of how grades and test scores help justify the presence of economic inequality and the idea that work is a naturally insignificant chore done primarily for a reward, but they go in an extreme direction by implying that market ideology is not only a powerful influence on education, but the *sole* influence on education.[74] They depict the impact of capitalist relations of production on education as essentially all-encompassing, and so they give little space for schools to resist market ideology and to contribute to the process of democratization. On Dewey's terms, although education cannot rectify the undemocratic qualities of society on its own, the classroom is also not assumed to be so thoroughly colonized by capitalistic norms that there is no room for resistance within the school whatsoever. We noted earlier Dewey's point that the "absence of economic pressure in schools" creates such an opportunity for resistance against undemocratic social norms, if schools could diminish their reliance on external aims. Because they are not yet fully ensnared by the pressure of the capitalist pursuit of money, young individuals have space to become accustomed to "conditions where the realization of the activity rather than merely the external product is the aim," and to perhaps learn to demand such work conditions in the future.[75] Dewey thus makes us aware of the many

---

[74] Samuel Bowles and Herbert Gintis, *Schooling in Capitalist America: Educational Reform and the Contradictions of Economic Life* (London: Routledge & Kegan Paul, 1976), 9, 11, 12, 39, 103, 125, 131, 266.

[75] Dewey, *Democracy and Education*, 309. Whereas neither Gutmann nor Bowles and Gintis capture Dewey's principles, there have been some more recent educational theorists who have identified the powerful influence of market ideology over schools, while also accounting for the factors of resistance that are available within schools – e.g., see Paulo Freire, *Pedagogy of the Oppressed* (New York, NY: Continuum International, 1970); Michael Apple, *Ideology and Curriculum* (London: Routledge & Kegan Paul, 1979); Henry Giroux, *Ideology, Culture, and the Process of Schooling* (Philadelphia, PA: Temple

ways that schooling is often infected by capitalist norms – which may not be effectively combated by improving students' debating skills – while avoiding the assumption that schools can provide no effective challenge at all to dominant social ideas.

Indeed, if we see schools as heavily affected by other spheres of social and political life, but also as having their own independent significance and as capable of affecting other spheres of social and political life, then schools should surely be a primary topic of interest for participatory democrats. Participatory theory emphasizes that the individual behaviors cultivated in one institution can substantially affect the democratic quality of other institutions, and thus there is no institution (e.g., a forum for political debate) that can be isolated and made democratic while it is surrounded by other institutions in society that are plainly undemocratic. The participatory democrats have focused on critiquing entrenched inequalities in social as well as in political institutions, and their underlying goal is to increase the control that individuals can exercise over their lives by combating these aspects of institutions which obstruct that control. But despite this very Deweyan approach to democracy, participatory theorists have not paid significant attention to how schools can either inhibit or promote individuals' self-government. This is surprising, because the school is obviously a crucial social institution that affects young individuals' behaviors and worldviews in lasting ways. Participatory democracy, from a Deweyan perspective, is right to depict democracy as more of a social (rather than simply political) concept, but an emphasis on the social element of democracy requires particular attention to the individual attitudes developed during school, for these attitudes heavily affect individuals' ability to govern their lives and to actualize democratic social relations.

Participatory democracy is certainly ready to accommodate Dewey's insights on education. Macpherson's statement that individuals must stop seeing themselves as isolated consumers in a market, and must focus instead on the exertion and development of their capacities, seems to call for a thorough investigation into how young individuals should be educated (though Macpherson does not provide this investigation). Dewey's analysis of education fleshes out how young individuals can be led to

---

University Press, 1981); Stanley Aronowitz and Henry Giroux, *Education under Siege: The Conservative, Liberal, and Radical Debate over Schooling* (South Hadley, MA: Bergin & Garvey Publishers, 1985); Ira Shor, *Empowering Education: Critical Teaching for Social Change* (Chicago, IL: University of Chicago Press, 1992); bell hooks, *Teaching to Transgress: Education as the Practice of Freedom* (New York, NY: Routledge, 1994).

live democratically, by learning to value the process of uncertain, never-finished growth and to critically challenge current social relations and the inequalities within those relations. In this way, Dewey can help to buttress participatory democracy and to elevate the participatory theory above deliberative democracy. I already showed in Chapter 4 how Dewey's democratic theory should lead us to favor participatory democracy over deliberative democracy when we are confronting a structurally unequal society. Dewey's educational principles further reveal the problems deliberative democracy has dealing with social inequality, and they are principles that participatory thinkers can readily integrate. Dewey exposes how commonly accepted schooling practices both reflect, and reinforce, social inequality, and thus he highlights how students' self-government can be obstructed in ways that are not remedied by preparing students to engage in a properly deliberative political debate. Participatory theory's main virtue lies in the way it emphasizes the manifold threats to individuals' self-government that extend beyond the political realm and into everyday society. By identifying how schooling practices are bound up with the existence of social inequality, and how they cultivate individual qualities that interfere with self-government (whether or not students are taught skills of political debate), participatory thinkers can further show the strength of their theory in comparison with deliberative democracy.

THE DEMOCRATIC POTENTIAL OF EDUCATION

In this chapter, we have seen how education can contribute to the individual element – and by extension, the social and political elements – of Deweyan democracy. For Dewey, an education that gives students opportunities to engage in inquiry into open-ended problems; to cooperate meaningfully with fellow students; and to investigate questions with real-life, practical significance would promote students' capacity to intelligently direct their own development in the midst of constantly changing circumstances. But also, schools must diminish their use of grades and standardized test scores, because these external aims can lead students to see the process of growth as an insignificant chore that they are to simply finish as quickly as possible and to see unequal social relations that are based on the attainment of an external aim (e.g., money) as legitimate and just. External aims obstruct the self-government signified by democratic individualism, as students wind up searching (futilely) for a static realm of certainty where they can be comfortably isolated from the challenges of growth and accepting the existence of structural inequality that hinders both their own self-government and that of others. Deliberative educational theory has focused on teaching students to debate properly and on encouraging good deliberation over educational policy, but this does not get to the heart of how commonly accepted schooling practices inhibit students' self-government. If students see the uncertainty and difficulty of experience as something to escape from and accept a social hierarchy that is based on the resources one has to try to make this escape, then their capacity to direct their development is obstructed in ways that cannot be rectified by cultivating skills of debate: "Until the democratic criterion of the intrinsic significance of every growing experience is recognized, we shall be intellectually confused by the demand for adaptation to external aims."[76]

Dewey's case against external aims has in fact been supported by significant empirical research, which has found that when students are able to engage in tasks – particularly difficult tasks – without grades and receive ungraded, *individualized* feedback specifically related to their performance on the tasks, the students have greater interest in continuing on with those tasks than when they receive the typical grades.[77] It is also noteworthy that some current schools operate without grading their students.[78] These schools are not numerous enough for us to be able to draw firm conclusions regarding the social effects we would see if American

---

[76] Dewey, *Democracy and Education*, 109.

[77] Farideh Salili et al., "A Further Consideration of the Effects of Evaluation on Motivation," *American Educational Research Journal* 13, no. 2 (1976): 96; Ruth Butler and Mordecai Nisan, "Effects of No Feedback, Task-Related Comments, and Grades on Intrinsic Motivation and Performance," *Journal of Educational Psychology* 78, no. 3 (1986): 213; Billie Hughes, Howard Sullivan, and Mary Lou Mosley, "External Evaluation, Task Difficulty, and Continuing Motivation," *The Journal of Educational Research* 78, no. 4 (1985): 212–13; Susan Harter, "Pleasure Derived from Challenge and the Effects of Receiving Grades on Children's Difficulty Level Choices," *Child Development* 49, no. 3 (1978): 794–6; Eric Anderman, Tripp Griesinger, and Gloria Westerfield, "Motivation and Cheating During Early Adolescence," *Journal of Educational Psychology* 90, no. 1 (1998): 87–9. For studies that show standardized testing to have similarly detrimental effects on students' growth, see David Hursh, "The Growth of High-Stakes Testing in the USA: Accountability, Markets, and the Decline in Educational Equality," *British Educational Research Journal* 31, no. 5 (2005): 613–14; Eric Grodsky, John Robert Warren, and Erika Felts, "Testing and Social Stratification in American Education," *Annual Review of Sociology* 34 (2008): 397–8.

[78] Examples include Carolina Friends School in Durham, North Carolina (www.cfnsc.org); Eagle Rock School in Estes Park, Colorado (www.eaglerockschool.org); Poughkeepsie Day School in Poughkeepsie, New York (www.poughkeepsieday.org); Waring School in Beverly, Massachusetts (www.waringschool.org).

education were not dominated so heavily by grades. But the fact that such schools exist, and that we have empirical work showing the kind of positive impact Dewey expects from allowing students to work more without grades, should show that Dewey's critique of external aims is not based on any impractical flight from the reality of how schools must work.

In his most famous account of the democratic individual way of life, Dewey proclaims that, as opposed to democracy,

> [e]very other form of moral and social faith rests upon the idea that experience must be subjected at some point or other to some form of external control; to some 'authority' alleged to exist outside the processes of experience. Democracy is the faith that the process of experience is more important than any special result attained ... Since the process of experience is capable of being educative, faith in democracy is all one with faith in experience and education.[79]

With his educational theory, Dewey identifies how schools can devalue the process of experience in favor of the attainment of a particular special result. Grading and standardizing testing diminish the importance of the process of experience by setting up the stable attainment of fixed markers – rather than the fullest open-ended development that each individual can actualize – as the essential aim in schooling. Deweyan democracy is fundamentally defined by individuals, as subjects of experience, exercising a unique, self-generated impact on the objects of experience they confront (i.e., exercising control over their lives). External aims in education subject the process of experience to the attainment of a special result and help justify a society in which those who have attained much of that type of result (i.e., money) exercise substantial power over the lives of others. The project of achieving a democracy that actualizes individual self-government is deeply jeopardized if we do not build an education that genuinely promotes that self-government.

[79] John Dewey, "Creative Democracy – The Task before Us," in *John Dewey: The Political Writings*, eds. Debra Morris and Ian Shapiro (Indianapolis, IN: Hackett Publishing Company, [1939] 1993), 244.

Conclusion

This book has aimed to overturn current democratic theory's focus on the quality of political debate. Rather than concentrating on a proper debate among competing political positions, my argument pushes the overcoming of structural social inequality into the spotlight in democratic thinking. The current dispute between deliberative democracy and agonistic democracy, on my reading, takes us away from what should be the truly pressing concerns in democratic theory, because this dispute takes place between two conceptions of how political debate should work. The question of whether political debaters should give reasons for their views so that they can identify some common ground with their opponents, or should forgo the idea of common ground and should mainly uphold opponents' views as the necessary adversarial element within a debate, does little to tell us about how we can deal with the structural inequality that still pervades our society. The deliberative and agonistic thinkers who seem to hold that their preferred forms of political debate will not be corrupted by social inequality are making a rather radical assumption. They have to assume that the greater material resources available to structurally advantaged individuals, and the greater impact that those individuals can exercise over the common discourse on policy issues, will be effectively bracketed so long as political debate proceeds properly. By contrast, the deliberative and agonistic thinkers who wish to require significant reduction of social inequality are somewhat on the right track, but I have argued that this requirement itself dissolves the idea that democracy should be defined by a type of political debate. John Dewey's democratic thought, I have shown, allows us to move political debate out of its central spot in democratic theory and to deal straightforwardly with the implications of recognizing that democracy requires the overcoming of social inequality. Dewey does not eliminate all ideas of fair and equal debate from his theory of democracy, but he is able to identify the fight against social inequality as the more central task for democracy.

When we say that society is characterized by structural inequality, we mean that there is an entrenched gap between the opportunities available to certain individuals as opposed to others for affecting the world around them, and that those who lack these opportunities are particularly subject to the dictates of those who do have these opportunities. The existence of poverty, as well as systemic racism and sexism, exemplify this structural inequality. As long as society displays these highly problematic qualities, something should feel askew when the dominant concern in democratic thinking is that political debate is not proceeding properly enough. The idea of a debate in which political actors respect one another and show equal willingness to not see their particular position win out is, of course, admirable, but it assumes an equality between the different viewpoints that cannot be credibly accepted if we take seriously the inequalities that pervade present society. The focus on proper debate shortcuts away from the most pressing obstacle – structural inequality – that stands in the way of individuals' exercise of control over their lives (i.e., the essence of democracy) and winds up giving us forms of debate that could likely only be democratic once that obstacle has somehow gone away. The deliberative and agonistic thinkers who insist on a reduction of social inequality are in a way conceding this, but they have not realized what this does to their equation of democracy with deliberation or agonism. I have shown that whichever way they might intend to fulfill this requirement of significantly reducing inequality, they must acknowledge that their preferred forms of political debate would not be democratic at present and could have little to do with actually bringing democracy further into existence. These thinkers must either predetermine the outcome of debate by only allowing the debate to produce policies that significantly reduce inequality (e.g., a basic income policy), or grant that such debate simply cannot address the most pressing obstacle to democracy, and that the debate will likely be undemocratic as long as that obstacle still exists.

I have used Dewey in this book to show how the process of overcoming social inequality can be placed at the forefront of democratic thinking. Dewey provides a multifaceted, continuously developing conception of democracy, one that is constituted by individual, social, and political elements that are each developing interrelatedly with the other elements. This conception highlights the interlocking nature of the democratic (or undemocratic) qualities of the political and social realms and shows why the attempt to create an equal political debate in abstraction from social inequality is misguided. Instead, this conception leads us toward seeing practices that take direct aim at overcoming social inequality – even if those practices compel concessions from the socially advantaged in a way that ideal forms of debate would not allow – as more democratic than practices that simply give equal validity to different political viewpoints. Dewey's version of democracy is *pragmatic*, in that it takes democracy as never fully achieved and as enduring a process of unending development, and it calls for identifying and overcoming the novel obstacles to democracy's development that emerge from changing circumstances. New problems inevitably emerge that obstruct individuals' control over their lives – for instance, formal political equality may be achieved, while many individuals fall into poverty that prevents them from exercising any control over their everyday lives, much less over political decisions. Identifying structural social inequality as the most pressing current obstacle to democracy, and endorsing actions that might compel concessions from the advantaged in order to fight inequality, reflect pragmatic insights. Importantly, Dewey does not focus much attention on any kind of finishing point for democracy beyond the broad goal of having individuals exercise control over their lives, as well as the related goals of a substantively equal society and a political system that does not systematically privilege the views of certain individuals. He does not tell us how far we must ultimately go in fighting forms of inequality, or if there are inequalities that we know we can accept as consistent with democracy. What he focuses on, and what I have focused on in this book, are the structural inequalities that we can see as clearly antithetical to democracy. The inequalities reflected by poverty and by structural racism and sexism undoubtedly obstruct any meaningful existence of democracy, and this is exemplified by the fact that the deliberative and agonistic thinkers who do insist on reducing inequality have said that these specific inequalities must be done away with. There is actually broad consensus among democratic theorists that certain existent inequalities must simply go away, but Dewey's pragmatism helps us avoid an unhelpful emphasis on ideal norms of political debate and points us toward seeing democracy as existing in a process of development which demands that we directly combat these inequalities.

To be clear, I am not suggesting that we need only and can only turn to Dewey to solve what is wrong with democratic theory. We could draw, for instance, on John Stuart Mill for an emphasis on more *social*, rather than exclusively *political*, threats to self-government (though Mill appears to be more placid than Dewey about the effects of laissez-faire capitalism and of economic inequalities[1]), and on Karl Marx for an emphasis on how individuals' alienating experience of work can render any apparent "political emancipation" essentially meaningless (though Marx appears to diminish the significance of any social inequalities that are not distinctly "economic"[2]). Still, I do argue that Dewey is particularly valuable for helping democratic theory figure out how to link democracy with the overcoming of social inequality. The way Dewey conceives of multiple elements in democracy, and of the unending, interrelated development of these elements, speaks directly to the problems with current democratic theory's simple equation of democracy with a type of political debate. Dewey's approach exposes how democratic theory is unjustifiably isolating the political realm from the broader social realm, and how the pursuit of democracy must instead be sensitive to the unpredictable emergence of a wide variety of interrelated social and political threats to individuals' self-government.

My argument also does not suggest that participatory democrats and cosmopolitan democrats can only turn to Dewey to show how their theories differ from deliberative democracy. These thinkers could point out their greater focus on social inequality, and could make the idea of "nondeliberative" practices into a more central aspect of their theories, without necessarily having to draw on Dewey's particular justifications for these principles.[3] Dewey is nonetheless an especially valuable thinker for participatory and cosmopolitan thinkers to draw upon, even if he is not the only resource available to them. His pragmatic reasoning for why the overcoming of social inequality is essential to democracy, and for why

---

[1] John Stuart Mill, *On Liberty*, in *J. S. Mill: On Liberty and Other Writings*, ed. Stefan Collini (Cambridge: Cambridge University Press, [1859] 1989), 95; John Stuart Mill, *Chapters on Socialism*, in *J. S. Mill: On Liberty and Other Writings*, ed. Stefan Collini (Cambridge: Cambridge University Press, [1879] 1989), 249–53; John Stuart Mill, *Considerations on Representative Government*, edited with an introduction by Currin V. Shields (Indianapolis, IN: Bobbs-Merrill Educational Publishing, [1861] 1958), 24, 44–7, 54–5, 82–3, 94, 95, 99–101, 114, 116, 128, 133, 134, 177, 184–5, 187–8.

[2] Karl Marx, "On the Jewish Question," in *Karl Marx: Selected Writings*, ed. David McLellan (Oxford: Oxford University Press, [1843] 1977), 42–5, 47–8, 51, 53, 55–6, 58–62. Karl Marx and Friedrich Engels, "Manifesto of the Communist Party," in *The Marx-Engels Reader*, 2nd ed., ed. Robert Tucker (New York, NY: W. W. Norton & Company, [1848] 1978), 482–3, 487–91.

[3] William Caspary, in response to my previous writings, has argued that the New Left thought of the 1960s may be a more fruitful resource than Dewey for participatory democracy; see William Caspary, "John Dewey between Participatory Democracy and Direct Action: A Commentary on Jeff Jackson," *Democratic Theory* 4, no. 1 (2017): 109–20. For my full response to Caspary, see Jeff Jackson, "Dethroning Deliberation: A Response to Caspary," *Democratic Theory* 4, no. 2 (2017): 102–10.

nondeliberative practices can be particularly democratic under unequal conditions, provides compelling intellectual support for participatory and cosmopolitan democracy over deliberative democracy. Also, showing that someone who is widely believed to be a forefather of deliberative democracy actually provides backing for participatory and cosmopolitan democracy is an effective way for these latter two theories to challenge the preeminence of the deliberative model. Democratic theorists commonly draw on canonical thinkers within the history of political thought to buttress their ideas, and so it is worthwhile to understand how Dewey provides valuable support for participatory and cosmopolitan democrats, rather than for (as commonly believed) deliberative democrats.

Overall, this book not only challenges the focus on political debate in democratic theory, but also the basic idea of linking democracy with a search for the "common good." The thought of pursuing the common good of course comes naturally to advocates of democracy, but this is problematic when we are thereby distracted from the undeniably conflicting interests that are contained within a polity and the structural inequalities between those who hold these interests. Ian Shapiro has recently taken aim at the idea of a common good and has argued that democracy should instead be seen as the best available way to minimize the domination of some individuals by others. Shapiro indeed names deliberative democracy as a theory that pursues a common good without accounting for factors that still leave individuals vulnerable to domination. I agree with Shapiro's critical approach to the idea of the common good, but at the same time, his own argument still suffers from an exclusive association of democracy with the political realm. His call for minimizing domination leads to an endorsement of the type of "competitive" democracy offered by Joseph Schumpeter,[4] which equates democracy with competition among political elites for votes (rather than with any deliberation toward the common good). When Shapiro recognizes that such competition does not necessarily mitigate the social qualities that leave individuals vulnerable to domination, he can only say that democracy is better than any alternative political system for potentially reducing domination and that a democracy can permit domination.[5] Shapiro's critique of the common good is valuable, but I have shown why democratic theorists must link democracy with

---

[4] Joseph Schumpeter, *Capitalism, Socialism, and Democracy*, 2nd ed. (New York, NY: Harper & Brothers, 1947).

[5] Ian Shapiro, *The State of Democratic Theory* (Princeton, NJ: Princeton University Press, 2003), 3, 10–11, 35, 58–9, 100, 104–5, 144–5, 146, 147, 148, 150–1.

the actual overcoming of *social* forms of domination, and thus conceive democracy as having a social element as well as a political element. We can then recognize the problems with assuming the existence of a common good, while also perceiving the democratic need for those disadvantaged by social inequality to actually win out over those who are advantaged.

Relatedly, this book helps exhibit the pitfalls involved with treating the citizenry in a polity as one homogenous body with no class distinctions. As with the common good, this idea of erasing class distinctions has natural appeal to democratic thinkers, because it reflects the principle of giving equal status to all citizens without any entrenched privilege or exclusion. This becomes a big problem, though, when this idea of equal status takes (as it often does) the form of applying a legal and political equality to all, while ignoring the continuing relevant differences between individuals. We can certainly insist, as a matter of principle, that citizens, whether rich or poor, white or black, male or female, should all have equal status and that a citizenry is thus one homogenous body, but when these differences – though they are, of course, socially constructed and not "natural" differences – are still creating social inequalities and are affecting individuals' capacity to govern their lives, we cannot simply act as though the differences are irrelevant. The attempt to treat citizens as composing one uniform body without internal distinctions ends up maintaining (by way of ignoring) the very real forms of inequality that still exist. My argument holds that we must give primary attention to class distinctions, because individuals do undoubtedly occupy different classes in present society, and it is only by taking these distinctions seriously that we can establish the need for plans and policies that specifically benefit those who suffer from these distinctions. The presumed political equality of all citizens cannot even be said to exist under our current conditions, because the class inequalities largely determine who wields effective political power.[6]

My analysis of Dewey's democratic individual way of life carries additional broad implications for how we think about democracy. Leading

---

[6] A very similar point about class distinctions has been made by John McCormick, who argues this by way of Niccolo Machiavelli's democratic principles. McCormick's work indeed provides a valuable parallel to mine, because he both challenges the dominant interpretations of Machiavelli and shows what his own interpretation of Machiavelli has to offer to contemporary democratic theory – which is precisely what I have done here with Dewey. See John McCormick, *Machiavellian Democracy* (New York, NY: Cambridge University Press, 2011).

a democratic life means that an individual is exercising control over her development, as well as meeting ethical requirements to challenge forms of structural inequality and interact with others without seeking their subordination. It may appear problematic to uphold this kind of ethical standard, though, since in a world defined by pluralism and a diversity of worldviews, we must be careful of imposing a paradigm of conduct on individuals from different walks of life. This is the kind of point Robert Talisse is making in his objection to Dewey's ethical program. But if we recognize democracy as more than a purely political mechanism for allowing current interests to compete with each other (or to reason with each other), then we cannot avoid considering individuals' own responsibility to contribute to democracy's realization in their everyday social relations. Deweyan democratic individualism does not rigidly restrict individuals' paths in life, but conveys the need for critical thought toward past habits and beliefs, and for self-directed growth in response to inevitably changing circumstances, in order for genuine self-government by individuals to be possible at all. Democratic individualism also conveys how individual views and actions that uphold the subordination of other individuals – views and actions that are racist or sexist, for instance – are obstructing the social and political elements of democracy, and can simultaneously limit the self-government of the racist or sexist individuals themselves when we have increasingly interconnected circumstances. Ethical responsibilities are involved in democratic individualism, but they are responsibilities that are justified if we take seriously the idea that social inequality inhibits democracy. And we must recall that the basic goal of Dewey's discussion is for all individuals to govern their own lives to the greatest degree possible, without having to rely on structural barriers to others' self-government, or on somehow achieving an isolation from others. I maintain that we can uphold Dewey's standards and be confident that we are doing well at spreading the possibilities for self-governed development as widely as possible, and that we are certainly not rigidly restricting individuals.

Dewey was not likely to have seen himself as any kind of ideal individual, but it could be said that he lived by the standards that the democratic individual way of life promotes. James Good remarks that "Dewey lived the life of a philosopher of *Bildung*,"[7] and indeed, the qualities that were addressed in Chapter 1's discussion of *Bildung* and the

---

[7] James Good, *A Search for Unity in Diversity: The "Permanent Hegelian Deposit" in the Philosophy of John Dewey* (Lanham, MD: Lexington Books, 2006), 246.

democratic way of life are qualities that Dewey exhibited. He enjoyed, and made use of, the opportunity to exercise significant control over his work; he interacted with diverse others and traveled widely across the world, including significant time spent in Japan, China, Turkey, Mexico, and Russia for teaching and for advising on educational practices; he was known as a considerate colleague and engaged in respectful "deliberation" with others when there was a genuine, substantive equality among the individuals involved, but he also took part in "nondeliberative" efforts to directly overcome the control of political institutions by wealth, to gain access to workplace governance for all workers, and to achieve policies that would alleviate social inequality. Friedrich Nietzsche famously says that every philosophy is an "unconscious and involuntary memoir" by its author,[8] which would suggest that the idea of democratic individualism simply expresses Dewey's unconscious desire to give his own way of living a supposedly objective justification. It is beyond my purposes here to try to prove someone like Nietzsche wrong, but we can at least see that Dewey was not preaching one thing and practicing another. Through his academic career in particular, he exemplified the kind of self-government that is defined by continuous development and interaction with diverse others; and concurrently, it appears he saw his own self-government as depending largely on others' opportunities for self-government, and he made precisely the type of effort that a democratic individual should make toward challenging and overcoming forms of structural inequality.

It may still seem though that Dewey's is an overly optimistic philosophy. The idea of democratic individualism may come across as overselling the possibilities for individuals to control their lives and make their lives go in the direction they want. But as I have indicated throughout, the implication of democratic individualism is not that individuals will be able to completely control their lives, achieve everything they want to achieve, and avoid anything terrible or unfair happening to them. We can consider Dewey to have approximated democratic individualism, even though he certainly had at times to endure significant professional disappointment (e.g., the bitter end of his time at the University of Chicago) and severe tragedy (e.g., the deaths of two of his children). The main purpose of democratic individualism, and of Dewey's democratic thought as a whole, is not to make everyone's lives perfect, but to identify and overcome the

---

[8] Friedrich Nietzsche, *Beyond Good and Evil*, translated by R. J. Hollingdale (London: Penguin Classics, [1886] 1973), 37.

structural obstacles that continue to get in the way of any possibility of self-government for many individuals. These are obstacles that democratic theorists of seemingly all stripes – including a good number of deliberative and agonistic democrats – agree are pressing and directly interfere with democracy. Overcoming those obstacles does not then guarantee that individuals' lives will go perfectly, but it does help ensure that many individuals are not excluded from self-government from the outset.

Before we finish, let us come back to the issue of how we can challenge democratic theory's focus on political debate, while not also acting as if political debate should have no importance in our analysis of democracy. It may seem that an attempt to devalue political debate under structurally unequal social conditions cannot work, because determining what the pressing inequalities are, and what to do about them, would require some kind of debate among divergent viewpoints. But, for one, my analysis to a great extent simply forms the logical conclusion of what has been said by the deliberative and agonistic thinkers who insist that social inequalities need to be largely overcome. This conclusion is that our society is characterized by unjust economic, racial, and gender inequalities; that it is not up for discussion (as far as democracy goes) whether these inequalities need to be overcome; and that a debate between competing views over whether to address these inequalities is problematic because those who argue for directly combating the inequalities are likely arguing from a disadvantaged social position. These debate-focused thinkers are themselves conceding that topics like the elimination of poverty and the fight against systemic racism and sexism need mainly to be held outside of debate. My willingness to say that political debate should not be the focus of democratic thought under unequal social conditions logically follows from what these thinkers have said.

Second, I would grant the point that debate is necessary, if we are talking about debate among the structurally disadvantaged over what exactly it is they need to change about society and how exactly they are to accomplish that change. My discussion of the political institutions that Dewey would seek reflects this, as I established that these would be institutions that directly move political power to the disadvantaged and away from the advantaged. Dewey's theory certainly sees value in debate among the structurally disadvantaged, but the fact that we are talking about a debate that aims to exclude those who oppose overcoming structural inequality (i.e., those who see this inequality as unimportant or nonexistent) shows that we have traveled some distance from the deliberative and agonistic theories. These theories primarily pride themselves on their ability to be inclusive and to allow a healthy debate between just about all current viewpoints. Excluding the views from debate that are predominant among the wealthy, for instance, would certainly appear to go much further in the direction of exclusion than deliberative and agonistic thinkers would be willing to endorse. But if the only justification we have left for a focus on political debate in democratic theory is that debate is needed for identifying and figuring out how to combat structural inequality, then we have to recognize that only a specific (and rather limited) kind of debate can actually be considered democratic under our current conditions. Dewey's theory recognizes this, whereas deliberative and agonistic theory can only do so by admitting that deliberation and agonism are, at best, contingently democratic.

Thus, a democratic theory that is attuned to social inequality would not have to forbid forums of debate that include a variety of political positions. But we do need to find a way for democratic theory to account more effectively than it presently does for how social inequality directly obstructs democracy, and for all the implications of insisting that social inequality be reduced in order to achieve democracy. At the very least, this requires the issue of political debate to be removed from its central spot in democratic theorizing, and that we limit the types of situations where we consider an open, "fair" debate between competing positions to signify democracy. In essence, we need to find a way to conceive why the pursuits of basic income, affirmative action, pay equity for women, etc., are themselves democratic; why the opposition to these pursuits is undemocratic; and why simply putting such matters up for debate under conditions of social inequality may not be democratic at all. We must be able to conceive why workers taking collective action to combat the power of owners, and to improve their wages and working conditions, is more democratic than a deliberative exchange of reasons where workers and owners seek mutually acceptable decisions, or an agonistic contest where the sides treat each other as adversaries rather than enemies. These are the issues democratic theory is inescapably driven toward when it seeks to take social inequality more seriously, and so democratic theorists must place these issues at the forefront of their thinking. I do not claim to have resolved all the specific questions that could be raised by this way of theorizing about democracy; I cannot say that I have delineated all the specific situations where a policy issue could be put up for an open political debate, versus the situations where we must consider the particular issue to be beyond debate (due to the impact of structural inequality) and to require resolution in a particular direction only. Dewey's theory does not answer all these questions for us, but he does provide an extremely important way of thinking about democracy, given the difficulty which current democratic theory has coping with social inequality. I hope to have turned democratic thought in a more productive direction and that further research can fill in the more specific content of this Deweyan theory.

Bibliography

Alexander, T. (1987). *John Dewey's Theory of Art, Experience, and Nature: The Horizons of Feeling*. Albany, NY: State University of New York Press.

Ames, R. (2008). Tang Junyi and the Very "Idea" of Confucian Democracy. In Sor-Hoon Tan & John Whalen-Bridge (Eds.), *Democracy as Culture: Deweyan Pragmatism in a Globalizing World* (pp. 177–99). Albany, NY: State University of New York Press.

Anderman, E., Griesinger, T., & Westerfield, G. (1998). Motivation and Cheating During Early Adolescence. *Journal of Educational Psychology* 90 (1), 84–93.

Anderson, E. (2010). *The Imperative of Integration*. Princeton, NJ: Princeton University Press.

(2017). *Private Government: How Employers Rule Our Lives (and Why We Don't Talk about It)*. Princeton, NJ: Princeton University Press.

Apple, M. (1979). *Ideology and Curriculum*. London: Routledge & Kegan Paul.

Archibugi, D. (1995). From the United Nations to Cosmopolitan Democracy. In Daniele Archibugi & David Held (Eds.), *Cosmopolitan Democracy: An Agenda for a New World Order* (pp. 121–62). Cambridge: Polity Press.

(1998). Principles of Cosmopolitan Democracy. In Daniele Archibugi, David Held, & Martin Kohler (Eds.), *Re-imagining Political Community: Studies in Cosmopolitan Democracy* (pp. 198–228). Stanford, CA: Stanford University Press.

(2012). From Peace between Democracies to Global Democracy. In Daniele Archibugi, Mathias Koenig-Archibugi, & Raffaele Marchetti (Eds.), *Global Democracy: Normative and Empirical Perspectives* (pp. 254–73). Cambridge: Cambridge University Press.

Arendt, H. (1958). *The Human Condition*. Chicago, IL: University of Chicago Press.

Aronowitz, S., & Giroux, H. (1985). *Education under Siege: The Conservative, Liberal, and Radical Debate over Schooling*. South Hadley, MA: Bergin & Garvey Publishers.

Bachrach, P., & Botwinick, A. (1992). *Power and Empowerment: A Radical Theory of Participatory Democracy*. Philadelphia, PA: Temple University Press.

Bagg, S. (forthcoming). Can Deliberation Neutralise Power? *European Journal of Political Theory*.

Barber, B. (1984). *Strong Democracy: Participatory Politics for a New Age*. Berkeley, CA: University of California Press.

Bartels, L. (2008). *Unequal Democracy: The Political Economy of the New Gilded Age*. Princeton, NJ: Princeton University Press.

Benhabib, S. (1996). Toward a Deliberative Model of Democratic Legitimacy. In Seyla Benhabib (Ed.), *Democracy and Difference: Contesting the Boundaries of the Political* (pp. 67–94). Princeton, NJ: Princeton University Press.

Bernstein, R. (1987). One Step Forward, Two Steps Backward: Richard Rorty on Liberal Democracy and Philosophy. *Political Theory* 15 (4), 538–63.

(2010). *The Pragmatic Turn*. Cambridge: Polity Press.

Bessette, J. (1994). *The Mild Voice of Reason: Deliberative Democracy and American National Government*. Chicago, IL: University of Chicago Press.

Biesta, G. (2006). The Communicative Turn in Dewey's Democracy and Education. In David Hansen (Ed.), *John Dewey and Our Educational Prospect: A Critical Engagement with Dewey's Democracy and Education* (pp. 23–37). Albany, NY: State University of New York Press.

Bohman, J. (1996). *Public Deliberation: Pluralism, Complexity, and Democracy*. Cambridge: MIT Press.

(1998). The Coming of Age of Deliberative Democracy. *Journal of Political Philosophy* 6 (4), 400–25.

(1999). Democracy as Inquiry, Inquiry as Democratic: Pragmatism, Social Science, and the Cognitive Division of Labor. *American Journal of Political Science* 43 (2), 590–607.

Bohman, J., & Richardson, H. (2009). Liberalism, Deliberative Democracy, and "Reasons that All Can Accept." *Journal of Political Philosophy* 17 (3), 253–74.

Bowles, S., & Gintis, H. (1976). *Schooling in Capitalist America: Educational Reform and the Contradictions of Economic Life*. London: Routledge & Kegan Paul.

Brick, M. (2010). Texas School Board Set to Vote Textbook Revisions. *New York Times*, 20 May.

Bruford, W. H. (1975). *The German Tradition of Self-Cultivation: 'Bildung' from Humboldt to Thomas Mann*. Cambridge: Cambridge University Press.

Butler, R., & Nisan, M. (1986). Effects of No Feedback, Task-Related Comments, and Grades on Intrinsic Motivation and Performance. *Journal of Educational Psychology* 78 (3), 210–16.

Campbell, J. (1995). *Understanding John Dewey: Nature and Cooperative Intelligence*. Chicago, IL: Open Court.

Caspary, W. (2000). *Dewey on Democracy*. Ithaca, NY: Cornell University Press.

(2017). John Dewey between Participatory Democracy and Direct Action: A Commentary on Jeff Jackson. *Democratic Theory* 4 (1), 109–20.

Chambers, S. (2009). Rhetoric and the Public Sphere: Has Deliberative Democracy Abandoned Mass Democracy? *Political Theory* 37 (3), 323–50.

Church, J. (2012). G. W. F. Hegel on Self-Determination and Democratic Theory. *American Journal of Political Science* 56 (4), 1021–39.

Cohen, J. (1996). Procedure and Substance in Deliberative Democracy. In Seyla Benhabib (Ed.), *Democracy and Difference: Contesting the Boundaries of the Political* (pp. 95–119). Princeton, NJ: Princeton University Press.

    (1997). Deliberation and Democratic Legitimacy. In James Bohman & William Rehg (Eds.), *Deliberative Democracy: Essays on Reason and Politics* (pp. 67–91). Cambridge: MIT Press.

Connolly, W. (1991). *Identity\Difference: Democratic Negotiations of Political Paradox*. Ithaca, NY: Cornell University Press.

Curtis, W. (2015). *Defending Rorty: Pragmatism and Liberal Virtue*. New York, NY: Cambridge University Press.

Davey, M., & Greenhouse, S. (2011). Angry Demonstrations in Wisconsin as Cuts Loom. *New York Times*, February 16.

Dewey, J. (1900). *The School and Society*. Chicago, IL: University of Chicago Press.

    (1902). *The Child and the Curriculum*. Chicago, IL: University of Chicago Press.

    (1910). *How We Think*. Boston, MA: D. C. Heath & Co.

    ([1916] 1966). *Democracy and Education*. New York, NY: The Free Press.

    (1922). *Human Nature and Conduct*. New York, NY: Henry Holt and Company.

    ([1925] 1958). *Experience and Nature*. New York, NY: Dover Publications, Inc.

    ([1927] 1954). *The Public and Its Problems*. Chicago, IL: Swallow Press.

    (1929). *The Quest for Certainty*. New York, NY: Minton, Balch & Company.

    (1930). From Absolutism to Experimentalism. In George Adams & Wm. Pepperell Montague (Eds.), *Contemporary American Philosophy*, Vol. II (pp. 13–27): New York, NY: Macmillan Company.

    ([1930] 1962). *Individualism Old and New*. New York, NY: Capricorn Books.

    ([1934] 1980). *Art as Experience*. New York, NY: Perigee Books.

    (1935). *Liberalism and Social Action*. New York, NY: G. P. Putnam's Sons.

    (1938). *Experience and Education*. New York, NY: Macmillan Company.

    (1938). *Logic: The Theory of Inquiry*. New York, NY: Henry Holt and Company.

    (1939). *Freedom and Culture*. New York, NY: G. P. Putnam's Sons.

    ([1939] 1993). Creative Democracy – The Task before Us. In Debra Morris & Ian Shapiro (Eds.), *John Dewey: The Political Writings* (pp. 240–5). Indianapolis, IN: Hackett Publishing Company.

    ([1948] 1957). *Reconstruction in Philosophy*, enl. ed. Boston, MA: Beacon Press.

    (1969–1972). *The Early Works of John Dewey, 1882–1898*. 5 vols. Ed. Jo Ann Boydston. Carbondale, IL: Southern University Press.

    (1976–1988). *The Middle Works of John Dewey, 1899–1924*. 15 vols. Ed. Jo Ann Boydston. Carbondale, IL: Southern Illinois University Press.

    (1981–1991). *The Later Works of John Dewey, 1925–1953*. 17 vols. Ed. Jo Ann Boydston. Carbondale, IL: Southern Illinois University Press.

Dewey, J., & Tufts, J. (1932). *Ethics*, rev. ed. New York, NY: Henry Holt and Company.

Dow, G. (2003). *Governing the Firm: Workers' Control in Theory and Practice.* Cambridge: Cambridge University Press.

Dryzek, J. (2000). *Deliberative Democracy and Beyond: Liberals, Critics, Contestations.* Oxford: Oxford University Press.

(2006). *Deliberative Global Politics: Discourse and Democracy in a Divided World.* Cambridge: Polity Press.

(2007). Theory, Evidence, and the Tasks of Deliberation. In Shawn Rosenberg (Ed.), *Deliberation, Participation and Democracy: Can the People Govern?* (pp. 237–50). New York, NY: Palgrave Macmillan.

Dryzek, J., & Braithwaite, V. (2000). On the Prospects for Democratic Deliberation: Values Analysis Applied to Australian Politics. *Political Psychology* 21 (2), 241–66.

Dykhuizen, G. (1973). *The Life and Mind of John Dewey.* Carbondale, IL: Southern Illinois University Press.

Eggen, D. (2010). Poll: Large Majority Opposes Supreme Court's Decision on Campaign Financing. *Washington Post*, February 17.

Eldridge, M. (1998). *Transforming Experience: John Dewey's Cultural Instrumentalism.* Nashville, TN: Vanderbilt University Press.

Elster, J. (1998). Deliberation and Constitution Making. In Jon Elster (Ed.), *Deliberative Democracy* (pp. 97–122). Cambridge: Cambridge University Press.

Emerson, B. (2015). The Democratic Reconstruction of the Hegelian State in American Progressive Political Thought. *The Review of Politics* 77 (4), 545–74.

Falk, R. (1995). The World Order between Inter-State Law and the Law of Humanity: The Role of Civil Society Institutions. In Daniele Archibugi & David Held (Eds.), *Cosmopolitan Democracy: An Agenda for a New World Order* (pp. 163–79). Cambridge: Polity Press.

(1998). The United Nations and Cosmopolitan Democracy: Bad Dream, Utopian Fantasy, Political Project. In Daniele Archibugi, David Held, & Martin Kohler (Eds.), *Re-imagining Political Community: Studies in Cosmopolitan Democracy* (pp. 309–31). Stanford, CA: Stanford University Press.

Fanon, F. ([1961] 2004). *The Wretched of the Earth*, translated by Richard Philcox. New York, NY: Grove Press.

Feiman-Nemser, S. (2006). A Teacher Educator Looks at Democracy and Education. In David Hansen (Ed.), *John Dewey and Our Educational Prospect: A Critical Engagement with Dewey's Democracy and Education* (pp. 129–45). Albany, NY: State University of New York Press.

Festenstein, M. (1997). *Pragmatism and Political Theory: From Dewey to Rorty.* Chicago, IL: University of Chicago Press.

Fishman, S., & McCarthy, L. (2007). *John Dewey and the Philosophy and Practice of Hope.* Urbana, IL: University of Illinois Press.

Fott, D. (1998). *John Dewey: America's Philosopher of Democracy.* Lanham, MD: Rowman & Littlefield.

Fraser, N. (1997). *Justice Interruptus: Critical Reflections on the "Postsocialist" Condition.* New York, NY: Routledge.

Freire, P. (1970). *Pedagogy of the Oppressed.* New York, NY: Continuum International.

French, D., & Laver, M. (2009). Participation Bias, Durable Opinion Shifts and Sabotage through Withdrawal in Citizens' Juries. *Political Studies* 57, 422–50.

Fung, A. (2005). Deliberation before the Revolution: Toward an Ethics of Deliberative Democracy in an Unjust World. *Political Theory* 33 (3), 397–419.

   (2007). Minipublics: Deliberative Designs and Their Consequences. In Shawn Rosenberg (Ed.), *Deliberation, Participation and Democracy: Can the People Govern?* (pp. 159–83). New York, NY: Palgrave Macmillan.

Fung, A., & Wright, E. O. (2003). Thinking about Empowered Participatory Governance. In Archon Fung & Erik Olin Wright (Eds.), *Deepening Democracy: Institutional Innovations in Empowered Participatory Governance* (pp. 3–42). New York, NY: Verso.

Garrison, J. (1997). *Dewey and Eros: Wisdom and Desire in the Art of Teaching.* New York, NY: Teachers College Press.

   (2006). The "Permanent Deposit" of Hegelian Thought in Dewey's Theory of Inquiry. *Educational Theory* 56 (1), 1–37.

Garrison, M. (2009). *A Measure of Failure: The Political Origins of Standardized Testing.* Albany, NY: State University of New York Press.

Gilbert, C. (2011). Budget Fight TV Ads Top $3 Million. *Milwaukee Journal Sentinel*, 15 March.

Gilens, M. (2012). *Affluence and Influence: Economic Inequality and Political Power in America.* Princeton, NJ: Princeton University Press.

Giroux, H. (1981). *Ideology, Culture, and the Process of Schooling.* Philadelphia, PA: Temple University Press.

Good, J. (2006). *A Search for Unity in Diversity: The "Permanent Hegelian Deposit" in the Philosophy of John Dewey.* Lanham, MD: Lexington Books.

   (2006). John Dewey's "Permanent Hegelian Deposit" and the Exigencies of War. *Journal of the History of Philosophy* 44 (2), 293–313.

   (2008). Dewey's "Permanent Hegelian Deposit": A Reply to Hickman and Alexander. *Transactions of the Charles S. Peirce Society* 44 (4), 577–602.

Good, J., & Garrison, J. (2010). Traces of Hegelian Bildung in Dewey's Philosophy. In Paul Fairfield (Ed.), *John Dewey and Continental Philosophy* (pp. 44–68). Carbondale, IL: Southern Illinois University Press.

Goodin, R. (2008). *Innovating Democracy: Democratic Theory and Practice after the Deliberative Turn.* Oxford: Oxford University Press.

Goodin, R., & Dryzek, J. (2006). Deliberative Impacts: The Macro-Political Uptake of Mini-Publics. *Politics & Society* 34 (2), 219–44.

Gould, C. (1988). *Rethinking Democracy: Freedom and Social Cooperation in Politics, Economy and Society.* Cambridge: Cambridge University Press.

   (2012). Regional versus Global Democracy: Advantages and Disadvantages. In Daniele Archibugi, Mathias Koenig-Archibugi, & Raffaele Marchetti (Eds.), *Global Democracy: Normative and Empirical Perspectives* (pp. 115–31). Cambridge: Cambridge University Press.

   (2014). *Interactive Democracy: The Social Roots of Global Justice.* Cambridge: Cambridge University Press.

Green, J. (1999). *Deep Democracy: Community, Diversity, and Transformation.* Lanham, MD: Rowman & Littlefield.

(2008). *Pragmatism and Social Hope: Deepening Democracy in Global Contexts.* New York, NY: Columbia University Press.

Grodsky, E., Warren, J. R., & Felts, E. (2008). Testing and Social Stratification in American Education. *Annual Review of Sociology* 34, 385–404.

Gutmann, A. (1987). *Democratic Education.* Princeton, NJ: Princeton University Press.

Gutmann, A., & Thompson, D. (1996). *Democracy and Disagreement.* Cambridge: Harvard University Press.

(2004). *Why Deliberative Democracy?.* Princeton, NJ: Princeton University Press.

Haack, S. (1993). *Evidence and Inquiry: Towards Reconstruction in Epistemology.* Oxford: Blackwell Publishers.

Habermas, J. (1995). Reconciliation through the Public use of Reason: Remarks on John Rawls's Political Liberalism. *Journal of Philosophy* 92 (3), 109–31.

(1996). *Between Facts and Norms.* Cambridge: MIT Press.

Harter, S. (1978). Pleasure Derived from Challenge and the Effects of Receiving Grades on Children's Difficulty Level Choices. *Child Development* 49 (3), 788–99.

Hauptmann, E. (2001). Can Less Be More? Leftist Deliberative Democrats' Critique of Participatory Democracy. *Polity* 33 (3), 397–421.

Hegel, G. W. F. ([1807] 1977). *The Phenomenology of Spirit,* translated by A. V. Miller. New York, NY: Oxford University Press.

([1812] 2010). *The Science of Logic,* translated and edited by George di Giovanni. Cambridge: Cambridge University Press.

([1821] 1945). *The Philosophy of Right,* translated with notes by T. M. Knox. Oxford: Clarendon Press.

([1830] 2010). *Encyclopedia of the Philosophical Sciences in Basic Outline, Part I: Science of Logic,* translated and edited by Klaus Brinkmann and Daniel Dahlstrom. Cambridge: Cambridge University Press.

([1830] 2004). *Philosophy of Nature: Part Two of the Encyclopedia of the Philosophical Sciences,* translated by A. V. Miller. Oxford: Oxford University Press.

([1830] 1971). *Philosophy of Mind: Part Three of the Encyclopedia of the Philosophical Sciences,* translated by A. V. Miller. Oxford: Oxford University Press.

([1837] 2004). *The Philosophy of History,* translated by J. Sibree. Mineola, NY: Dover Publications.

Held, D. (1995). *Democracy and the Global Order: From the Modern State to Cosmopolitan Governance.* Stanford, CA: Stanford University Press.

(1995). Democracy and the New International Order. In Daniele Archibugi & David Held (Eds.), *Cosmopolitan Democracy: An Agenda for a New World Order* (pp. 96–120). Cambridge: Polity Press.

(2004). *Global Covenant: The Social Democratic Alternative to the Washington Consensus.* Cambridge: Polity Press.

(2006). *Models of Democracy,* 3rd ed. Stanford, CA: Stanford University Press.

Held, D., & McGrew, A. (2002). *Globalization/Anti-Globalization*. Cambridge: Polity Press.

Hickman, L. (2007). *Pragmatism as Post-Postmodernism: Lessons from John Dewey*. New York, NY: Fordham University Press.

(2008). Dewey's Hegel: A Search for Unity in Diversity, or Diversity as the Growth of Unity? *Transactions of the Charles S. Peirce Society* 44 (4), 569–76.

(2008). The Genesis of Democratic Norms: Some Insights from Classical Pragmatism. In Sor-Hoon Tan & John Whalen-Bridge (Eds.), *Democracy as Culture: Deweyan Pragmatism in a Globalizing World* (pp. 21–30). Albany, NY: State University of New York Press.

Hildebrand, D. (2003). *Beyond Realism and Antirealism: John Dewey and the Neopragmatists*. Nashville, TN: Vanderbilt University Press.

Hildreth, R. W. (2012). Word and Deed: A Deweyan Integration of Deliberative and Participatory Democracy. *New Political Science* 34 (3), 295–320.

Hilmer, J. (2010). The State of Participatory Democratic Theory. *New Political Science* 32 (1), 43–63.

Honig, B. (1993). *Political Theory and the Displacement of Politics*. Ithaca, NY: Cornell University Press.

Honneth, A. (1998). Democracy as Reflexive Cooperation: John Dewey and the Theory of Democracy Today. *Political Theory* 26 (6), 763–83.

hooks, b. (1994). *Teaching to Transgress: Education as the Practice of Freedom*. New York, NY: Routledge.

Hughes, B., Sullivan, H., & Mosley, M. L. (1985). External Evaluation, Task Difficulty, and Continuing Motivation. *The Journal of Educational Research* 78 (4), 210–15.

Hursh, D. (2005). The Growth of High-Stakes Testing in the USA: Accountability, Markets and the Decline in Educational Equality. *British Educational Research Journal* 31 (5), 605–22.

Jackson, J. (2012). Reconstructing Dewey: Dialectics and Democratic Education. *Education and Culture* 28 (1), 62–77.

(2014). The Democratic Individual: Dewey's Back to Plato Movement. *The Pluralist* 9 (1), 14–38.

(2014). The Resolution of Poverty in Hegel's "Actual" State. *Polity* 46 (3), 331–53.

(2015). Dividing Deliberative and Participatory Democracy through John Dewey. *Democratic Theory* 2 (1), 63–84.

(2017). Dethroning Deliberation: A Response to Caspary. *Democratic Theory* 4 (2), 102–10.

Jacobs, L., & Skocpol, T. (2005). *Inequality and American Democracy: What We Know and What We Need to Learn*. New York, NY: Russell Sage Foundation.

James, W. (1907). *Pragmatism: A New Name for Some Old Ways of Thinking*. New York, NY: Longmans, Green, and Co.

Johnston, J. (2006). *Inquiry and Education: John Dewey and the Quest for Democracy*. Albany, NY: State University of New York Press.

(2009). *Deweyan Inquiry: From Education Theory to Practice*. Albany, NY: State University of New York Press.

Kadlec, A. (2007). *Dewey's Critical Pragmatism*. Lanham, MD: Lexington Books.

Kaldor, M. (1995). European Institutions, Nation-States and Nationalism. In Daniele Archibugi & David Held (Eds.), *Cosmopolitan Democracy: An Agenda for a New World Order* (pp. 68–95). Cambridge: Polity Press.

Kaufman, A. (1969). Participatory Democracy and Human Nature. In William Connolly (Ed.), *The Bias of Pluralism* (pp. 178–200). New York, NY: Atherton Press.

King, M. L. (1991). The Ethical Demands for Integration. In James Melvin Washington (Ed.), *A Testament of Hope: The Essential Writings and Speeches of Martin Luther King, Jr.* (pp. 117–25). San Francisco, CA: Harper San Francisco.

(1991). Letter from Birmingham City Jail. In James Melvin Washington (Ed.), *A Testament of Hope: The Essential Writings and Speeches of Martin Luther King, Jr.* (pp. 289–302). San Francisco, CA: Harper San Francisco.

(1991). Where Do We Go from Here? In James Melvin Washington (Ed.), *A Testament of Hope: The Essential Writings and Speeches of Martin Luther King, Jr.* (pp. 245–52). San Francisco, CA: Harper San Francisco.

Kliebard, H. (2006). Dewey's Reconstruction of the Curriculum: From Occupation to Disciplined Knowledge. In David Hansen (Ed.), *John Dewey and Our Educational Prospect: A Critical Engagement with Dewey's Democracy and Education* (pp. 113–27). Albany, NY: State University of New York Press.

Knight, J., & Johnson, J. (1997). What Sort of Equality Does Deliberative Democracy Require? In James Bohman & William Rehg (Eds.), *Deliberative Democracy: Essays on Reason and Politics* (pp. 279–319). Cambridge: MIT Press.

(2011). *The Priority of Democracy: Political Consequences of Pragmatism*. Princeton, NJ: Princeton University Press.

Koopman, C. (2009). *Pragmatism as Transition: Historicity and Hope in James, Dewey, and Rorty*. New York, NY: Columbia University Press.

Kosnoski, J. (2005). Artful Discussion: John Dewey's Classroom as a Model of Deliberative Association. *Political Theory* 33 (5), 654–77.

(2010). *John Dewey and the Habits of Ethical Life: The Aesthetics of Political Organizing in a Liquid World*. Lanham, MD: Lexington Books.

Kymlicka, W. (1988). Liberalism and Communitarianism. *Canadian Journal of Philosophy* 18 (2), 181–203.

Laclau, E., & Mouffe, C. (1985). *Hegemony and Socialist Strategy: Towards a Radical Democratic Politics*. London: Verso.

Lippmann, W. (1925). *The Phantom Public*. New York, NY: Harcourt, Brace and Company.

Lipton, E. (2011). Billionaire Brothers' Money Plays Role in Wisconsin Dispute. *New York Times*, February 21.

Livingston, A. (2017). Between Means and Ends: Reconstructing Coercion in Dewey's Democratic Theory. *American Political Science Review* 111 (3), 522–34.

Luskin, R., Fishkin, J., & Jowell, R. (2002). Considered Opinions: Deliberative Polling in Britain. *British Journal of Political Science* 32, 455–87.

MacIntyre, A. (1981). *After Virtue: A Study in Moral Theory*. London: Duckworth.

Macpherson, C. B. (1977). *The Life and Times of Liberal Democracy*. Oxford: Oxford University Press.

Malcolm X. ([1964] 2013). The Ballot or the Bullet. In Manning Marable & Garrett Felber (Eds.), *The Portable Malcolm X Reader*. New York, NY: Grove Press.

Malleson, T. (2013). Making the Case for Workplace Democracy: Exit and Voice as Mechanisms of Freedom in Social Life. *Polity* 45 (4), 604–29.

Manicas, P. (2008). *Rescuing Dewey: Essays in Pragmatic Naturalism*. Lanham, MD: Lexington Books.

Mansbridge, J., Bohman, J., Chambers, S., et al. (2010). The Place of Self-Interest and the Role of Power in Deliberative Democracy. *Journal of Political Philosophy* 18 (1), 64–100.

(2012). A Systemic Approach to Deliberative Democracy. In John Parkinson & Jane Mansbridge (Eds.), *Deliberative Systems: Deliberative Democracy at the Large Scale* (pp. 1–26). Cambridge: Cambridge University Press.

Margolis, J. (2002). *Reinventing Pragmatism: American Philosophy at the End of the Twentieth Century*. Ithaca, NY: Cornell University Press.

(2007). *Pragmatism without Foundations: Reconciling Realism and Relativism*, 2nd ed. London: Continuum International.

Marx, K. ([1843] 1977). On the Jewish Question. In David McLellan (Ed.), *Karl Marx: Selected Writings* (pp. 39–62). Oxford: Oxford University Press.

Marx, K., & Engels, F. ([1848] 1978). Manifesto of the Communist Party. In Robert Tucker (Ed.), *The Marx-Engels Reader*, 2nd ed. (pp. 469–500). New York, NY: W. W. Norton & Company.

McAfee, N. (2008). *Democracy and the Political Unconscious*. New York, NY: Columbia University Press.

McCormick, J. (2011). *Machiavellian Democracy*. New York, NY: Cambridge University Press.

Medearis, J. (2005). Social Movements and Deliberative Democratic Theory. *British Journal of Political Science* 35, 53–75.

(2008). Deliberative Democracy, Subordination, and the Welfare State. In Daniel O'Neill, Mary Shanley, & Iris Young (Eds.), *Illusion of Consent* (pp. 208–30). University Park, PA: Pennsylvania State University Press.

(2015). *Why Democracy Is Oppositional*. Cambridge: Harvard University Press.

Mendel-Reyes, M. (1995). *Reclaiming Democracy: The Sixties in Politics and Memory*. New York, NY: Routledge.

Mendelberg, T. & Oleske, J. (2000). Race and Public Deliberation. *Political Communication* 17 (2), 169–91.

Midtgarden, T. (2011). The Hegelian Legacy in Dewey's Social and Political Philosophy, 1915–1920. *Transactions of the Charles S. Peirce Society* 47 (4), 361–388.

Mill, J. S. ([1859] 1989). On Liberty. In Stefan Collini (Ed.), *On Liberty and Other Writings* (pp. 5–115). Cambridge: Cambridge University Press.

([1861] 1958). *Considerations on Representative Government*, edited with an introduction by Currin V. Shields. Indianapolis, IN: Bobbs-Merrill Educational Publishing.

([1879] 1989). *Chapters on Socialism*. In Stefan Collini (Ed.), *On Liberty and Other Writings* (pp. 221–79). Cambridge: Cambridge University Press.

Minnich, E. (2006). Dewey's Philosophy of Life. In David Hansen (Ed.), *John Dewey and Our Educational Prospect: A Critical Engagement with Dewey's Democracy and Education* (pp. 147–64). Albany, NY: State University of New York Press.

Monoson, S. S. (2000). *Plato's Democratic Entanglements: Athenian Politics and the Practice of Philosophy*. Princeton, NJ: Princeton University Press.

Mouffe, C. (2000). *The Democratic Paradox*. London: Verso.

Murray, M., & Pateman, C., eds. (2012). *Basic Income Worldwide: Horizons of Reform*. Houndmills: Palgrave Macmillan.

Mutz, D. (2006). *Hearing the Other Side: Deliberative versus Participatory Democracy*. Cambridge: Cambridge University Press.

Neblo. M. (2015). *Deliberative Democracy between Theory and Practice*. New York, NY: Cambridge University Press.

Neblo, M., Esterling, K., Kennedy, R., Lazer, D., & Sokhey, A. (2010). Who Wants to Deliberate – And Why? *American Political Science Review* 104 (3), 566–83.

Nietzsche, F. ([1886] 1973). *Beyond Good and Evil*, translated by R. J. Hollingdale. London: Penguin Classics.

Olson, K. (2006). *Reflexive Democracy: Political Equality and the Welfare State*. Cambridge: MIT Press.

Page, B., Bartels, L., & Seawright, J. (2013). Democracy and the Policy Preferences of Wealthy Americans. *Perspectives on Politics* 11 (1), 51–73.

Page, R. (2006). Curriculum Matters. In David Hansen (Ed.), *John Dewey and Our Educational Prospect: A Critical Engagement with Dewey's Democracy and Education* (pp. 39–65). Albany, NY: State University of New York Press.

Pappas, G. (2008). *John Dewey's Ethics: Democracy as Experience*. Bloomington, IN: Indiana University Press.

Pateman, C. (1970). *Participation and Democratic Theory*. Cambridge: Cambridge University Press.

(2012). Participatory Democracy Revisited. *Perspectives on Politics* 10 (1), 7–19.

Peirce, C. S. (1878). How to Make Our Ideas Clear. *Popular Science Monthly* 12, 286–302.

Phillips, D. C. (1971). James, Dewey, and the Reflex Arc. *Journal of the History of Ideas* 32 (4), 555–68.

Plato. (1924). Apology. In *The Dialogues of Plato*, 3rd ed., Vol. II (pp. 95–135), translated into English, with analyses and introductions, by B. Jowett. London: Oxford University Press.

(1924). Crito. In *The Dialogues of Plato*, 3rd ed., Vol. II (pp. 137–56), translated into English, with analyses and introductions, by B. Jowett. London: Oxford University Press.

(1924). Euthyphro. In *The Dialogues of Plato*, 3rd ed., Vol. II (pp. 65–93), translated into English, with analyses and introductions, by B. Jowett. London: Oxford University Press.

(1924). Protagoras. In *The Dialogues of Plato*, 3rd ed., Vol. I (pp. 113–87), translated into English, with analyses and introductions, by B. Jowett. London: Oxford University Press.

(1941). *The Republic of Plato*, translated with introduction and notes by Francis Cornford. London: Oxford University Press.

(2004). *Gorgias*, rev. ed., translated by Walter Hamilton and Chris Emlyn-Jones. London: Penguin Classics.

Polanyi, K. ([1944] 2001). *The Great Transformation: The Political and Economic Origins of Our Time*. Boston, MA: Beacon Press.

Posner, R. (2003). *Law, Pragmatism, and Democracy*. Cambridge: Harvard University Press.

Putnam, H. (1992). *Renewing Philosophy*. Cambridge: Harvard University Press.

Rahman, K. S. (2016). *Democracy against Domination*. New York, NY: Oxford University Press.

Ralston, S. (2008). In Defense of Democracy as a Way of Life: A Reply to Talisse's Pluralist Objection. *Transactions of the Charles S. Peirce Society* 44 (4), 629–60.

(2010). Can Pragmatists be Institutionalists? John Dewey Joins the Non-ideal/Ideal Theory Debate. *Human Studies* 33 (1), 65–84.

Ranciere, J. (1999). *Disagreement: Politics and Philosophy*, translated by Julie Rose. Minneapolis, MN: University of Minnesota Press.

(2001). Ten Theses on Politics. *Theory & Event* 5 (3).

(2006). Democracy, Republic, Representation. *Constellations* 13 (3), 297–307.

Rasmussen, S. (2011). What You Can Learn about Wisconsin Dispute from Differences in Poll Questions. *Rasmussen Reports*, 7 March.

Rawls, J. (1993). *Political Liberalism*. New York, NY: Columbia University Press.

(1995). Political Liberalism: Reply to Habermas. *Journal of Philosophy* 92 (3), 132–80.

Reck, A. (1984). The Influence of William James on John Dewey in Psychology. *Transactions of the Charles S. Peirce Society* 20 (2), 87–117.

Rockefeller, S. (1991). *John Dewey: Religious Faith and Democratic Humanism*. New York, NY: Columbia University Press.

Rockmore, T. (2010). Dewey, Hegel, and Knowledge after Kant. In Paul Fairfield (Ed.), *John Dewey and Continental Philosophy* (pp. 26–43). Carbondale, IL: Southern Illinois University Press.

Rogers, M. (2009). *The Undiscovered Dewey: Religion, Morality, and the Ethos of Democracy*. New York, NY: Columbia University Press.

Rorty, R. (1979). *Philosophy and the Mirror of Nature*. Princeton, NJ: Princeton University Press.

(1982). *Consequences of Pragmatism (Essays: 1972–1980)*. Minneapolis, MN: University of Minnesota Press.

(1988). The Priority of Democracy to Philosophy. In Merrill D. Peterson & Robert C. Vaughan (Eds.), *The Virginia Statute for Religious Freedom: Its Evolution and Consequences in American History* (pp. 257–82). Cambridge: Cambridge University Press.

(1989). *Contingency, Irony, and Solidarity*. Cambridge: Cambridge University Press.

(1991). *Objectivity, Relativism, and Truth: Philosophical Papers,* Vol. I. Cambridge: Cambridge University Press.

(1998). *Achieving Our Country: Leftist Thought in Twentieth-Century America.* Cambridge: Harvard University Press.

(1998). Pragmatism as Romantic Polytheism. In Morris Dickstein (Ed.), *The Revival of Pragmatism: New Essays on Social Thought, Law, and Culture* (pp. 21–36). Durham, NC: Duke University Press.

Rousseau, J. J. ([1762] 1968). The Social Contract, translated and introduced by Maurice Cranston. London: Penguin Classics.

Rummens, S. (2012). Staging Deliberation: The Role of Representative Institutions in the Deliberative Democratic Process. *Journal of Political Philosophy* 20 (1), 23–44.

Ryan, A. (1995). *John Dewey and the High Tide of American Liberalism.* New York, NY: W. W. Norton.

Salili, F., Maehr, M., Sorensen, R., & Fyans, L. (1976). A Further Consideration of the Effects of Evaluation on Motivation. *American Educational Research Journal* 13 (2), 85–102.

Sandel, M. (1982). *Liberalism and the Limits of Justice.* Cambridge: Cambridge University Press.

(1996). *Democracy's Discontent: America in Search of a Public Philosophy.* Cambridge: Harvard University Press.

(1996). Dewey Rides Again. *New York Review of Books,* 9 May.

Sanders, L. (1997). Against Deliberation. *Political Theory* 25 (3), 347–76.

Sargent, G. (2011). Americans for Prosperity to Run Ads in Wisconsin. *Washington Post,* February 22.

Savage, D. (2002). *John Dewey's Liberalism: Individual, Community, and Self-Development.* Carbondale, IL: Southern Illinois University.

Schlozman, K. L., Verba, S., & Brady, H. (2012). *The Unheavenly Chorus: Unequal Political Voice and the Broken Promise of American Democracy.* Princeton, NJ: Princeton University Press.

Schmitt, C. ([1932] 2007). *The Concept of the Political,* exp. ed., translated and with an introduction by George Schwab. Chicago, IL: University of Chicago Press.

Schumpeter, J. (1947). *Capitalism, Socialism, and Democracy,* 2nd ed. New York, NY: Harper & Brothers.

Shapiro, I. (2003). *The State of Democratic Theory.* Princeton, NJ: Princeton University Press.

Shook, J. (2000). *Dewey's Empirical Theory of Knowledge and Reality.* Nashville, TN: Vanderbilt University Press.

(2014). *Dewey's Social Philosophy: Democracy as Education.* New York, NY: Palgrave Macmillan.

Shook, J., & Good, J. (2010). *John Dewey's Philosophy of Spirit, with the 1897 Lecture on Hegel.* New York, NY: Fordham University Press.

Shor, I. (1992). *Empowering Education: Critical Teaching for Social Change.* Chicago, IL: University of Chicago Press.

Shusterman, R. (1994). Pragmatism and Liberalism between Dewey and Rorty. *Political Theory* 22 (3), 391–413.

Sintomer, Y., Herzberg, C., & Rocke, A. (2008). Participatory Budgeting in Europe: Potentials and Challenges. *International Journal of Urban and Regional Research* 32 (1), 164–78.

Smith, G. (2009). *Democratic Innovations: Designing Institutions for Citizen Participation*. Cambridge: Cambridge University Press.

Smith, G., & Wales, C. (2000). Citizens' Juries and Deliberative Democracy. *Political Studies* 48, 51–65.

Snider, K. (2000). Response to Stever and Garrison. *Administration & Society* 32 (4), 487–9.

Stears, M. (2010). *Demanding Democracy: American Radicals in Search of a New Politics*. Princeton, NJ: Princeton University Press.

Steiner, J. (2012). *The Foundations of Deliberative Democracy: Empirical Research and Normative Implications*. Cambridge: Cambridge University Press.

Stever, J. (2000). The Parallel Universes: Pragmatism and Public Administration. *Administration & Society* 32 (4), 453–7.

Stuhr, J. (2003). *Pragmatism, Postmodernism, and the Future of Philosophy*. New York, NY: Routledge.

Talisse, R. (2003). Can Democracy Be a Way of Life? Deweyan Democracy and the Problem of Pluralism. *Transactions of the Charles S. Peirce Society* 39 (1), 1–21.

(2007). *A Pragmatist Philosophy of Democracy*. New York, NY: Routledge.

Thayer, H. S. (1981). *Meaning and Action: A Critical History of Pragmatism*, 2nd ed. Indianapolis, IN: Hackett Publishing Company.

Thompson, D. (2008). Deliberative Democratic Theory and Empirical Political Science. *Annual Review of Political Science* 11, 497–520.

Tully, J. (1995). *Strange Multiplicity: Constitutionalism in an Age of Diversity*. Cambridge: Cambridge University Press.

(2000). Struggles over Recognition and Distribution. *Constellations* 7 (4), 469–82.

(2005). Exclusion and Assimilation: Two Forms of Domination in Relation to Freedom. In Melissa Williams & Stephen Macedo (Eds.), *Political Exclusion and Domination* (pp. 191–229). New York, NY: New York University Press.

(2008). *Public Philosophy in a New Key, Volume I: Democracy and Civic Freedom*. Cambridge: Cambridge University Press.

Vitale, D. (2006). Between Deliberative and Participatory Democracy: A Contribution on Habermas. *Philosophy & Social Criticism* 32 (6), 739–66.

Vlastos, G. (1991). *Socrates, Ironist and Moral Philosopher*. Ithaca, NY: Cornell University Press.

Waks, L. (2010). Dewey's Theory of the Democratic Public and the Public Character of Charter Schools. *Educational Theory* 60 (6), 665–81.

(2011). John Dewey on Listening and Friendship in School and Society. *Educational Theory* 61 (2), 191–205.

Walker, J. (1966). A Critique of the Elitist Theory of Democracy. *American Political Science Review* 60 (2), 285–95.

Walzer, M. (1970). *Obligations: Essays on Disobedience, War, and Citizenship*. Cambridge: Harvard University Press.

(1983). *Spheres of Justice: A Defence of Pluralism and Equality*. Oxford: Martin Robertson.

Wampler, B. (2007). A Guide to Participatory Budgeting. In Anwar Shah (Ed.), *Participatory Budgeting* (pp. 21–54). Washington, DC: The World Bank.

(2007). *Participatory Budgeting in Brazil: Contestation, Cooperation, and Accountability*. University Park, PA: Pennsylvania State University Press.

Weber, E. (2010). *Rawls, Dewey, and Constructivism: On the Epistemology of Justice*. London: Continuum International.

Wenman, M. (2013). *Agonistic Democracy: Constituent Power in the Era of Globalisation*. New York, NY: Cambridge University Press.

Westbrook, R. (1991). *John Dewey and American Democracy*. Ithaca, NY: Cornell University Press.

(2005). *Democratic Hope: Pragmatism and the Politics of Truth*. Ithaca, NY: Cornell University Press.

White, M. (1943). *The Origin of Dewey's Instrumentalism*. New York, NY: Columbia University Press.

Wolin, S. (1993). Democracy, Difference, and Re-Cognition. *Political Theory* 21 (3), 464–83.

(1993). Democracy: Electoral and Athenian. *PS: Political Science and Politics* 26 (3), 475–7.

(1994). Norm and Form: The Constitutionalizing of Democracy. In J. Peter Euben, John Wallach, & Josiah Ober (Eds.), *Athenian Political Thought and the Reconstruction of American Democracy* (pp. 29–58). Ithaca, NY: Cornell University Press.

(1996). Fugitive Democracy. In Seyla Benhabib (Ed.), *Democracy and Difference: Contesting the Boundaries of the Political* (pp. 31–45). Princeton, NJ: Princeton University Press.

(1996). Transgression, Equality, and Voice. In Josiah Ober & Charles Hedrick (Eds.), *Demokratia: A Conversation on Democracies, Ancient and Modern* (pp. 63–90). Princeton, NJ: Princeton University Press.

(2004). *Politics and Vision*, exp. ed. Princeton, NJ: Princeton University Press.

Young, I. (1996). Communication and the Other: Beyond Deliberative Democracy. In Seyla Benhabib (Ed.), *Democracy and Difference: Contesting the Boundaries of the Political* (pp. 120–35). Princeton, NJ: Princeton University Press.

(2001). Activist Challenges to Deliberative Democracy. *Political Theory* 29 (5), 670–90.

Index